Alice in Kyoto Forest

1

Art by Haruki Niwa
Story by Mai Mochizuki

Contents

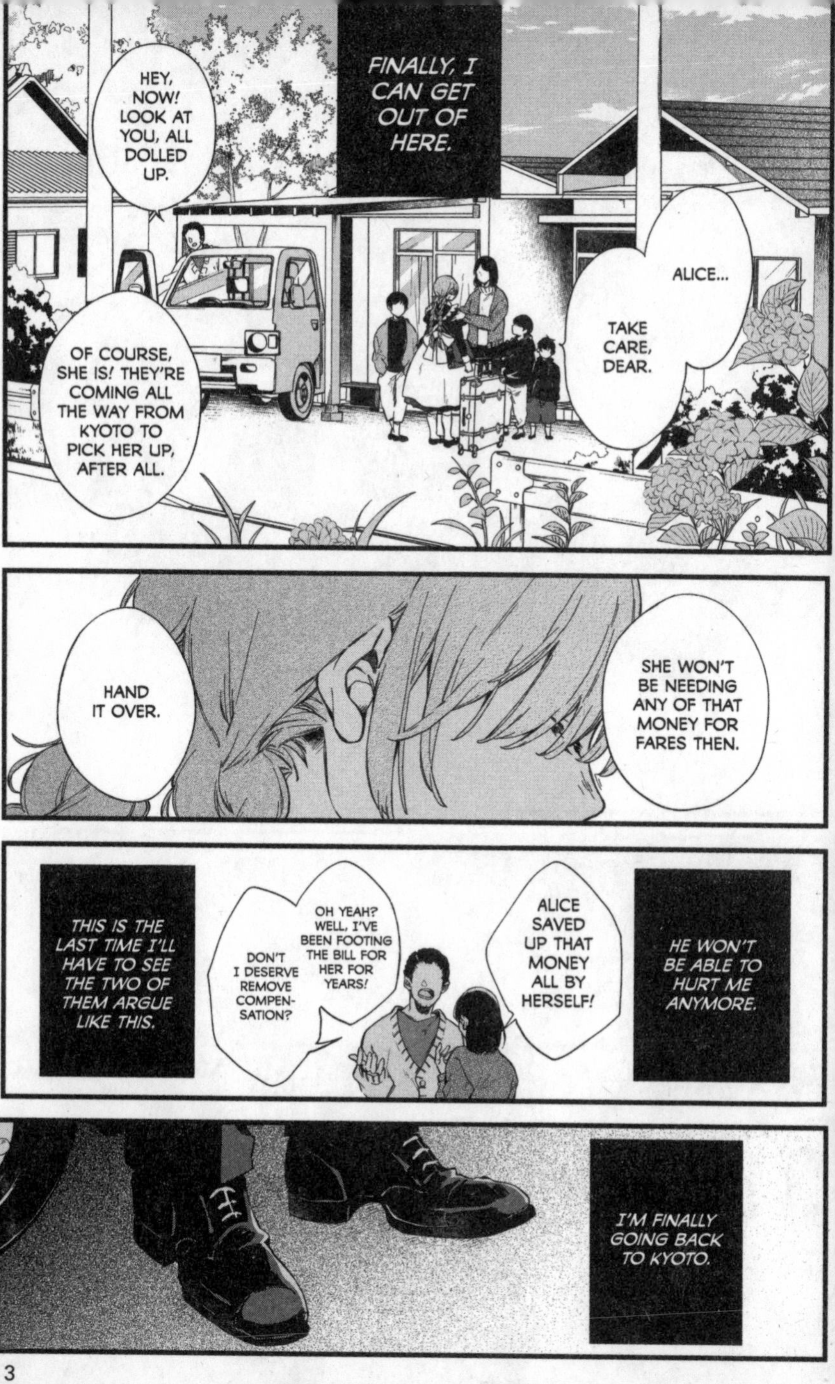
FINALLY, I CAN GET OUT OF HERE.
ALICE...
TAKE CARE, DEAR.
HEY, NOW! LOOK AT YOU, ALL DOLLED UP.
OF COURSE, SHE IS! THEY'RE COMING ALL THE WAY FROM KYOTO TO PICK HER UP, AFTER ALL.
SHE WON'T BE NEEDING ANY OF THAT MONEY FOR FARES THEN.
HAND IT OVER.
HE WON'T BE ABLE TO HURT ME ANYMORE.
ALICE SAVED UP THAT MONEY ALL BY HERSELF!
OH YEAH? WELL, I'VE BEEN FOOTING THE BILL FOR HER FOR YEARS!
DON'T I DESERVE REMOVE COMPEN-SATION?
THIS IS THE LAST TIME I'LL HAVE TO SEE THE TWO OF THEM ARGUE LIKE THIS.
I'M FINALLY GOING BACK TO KYOTO.

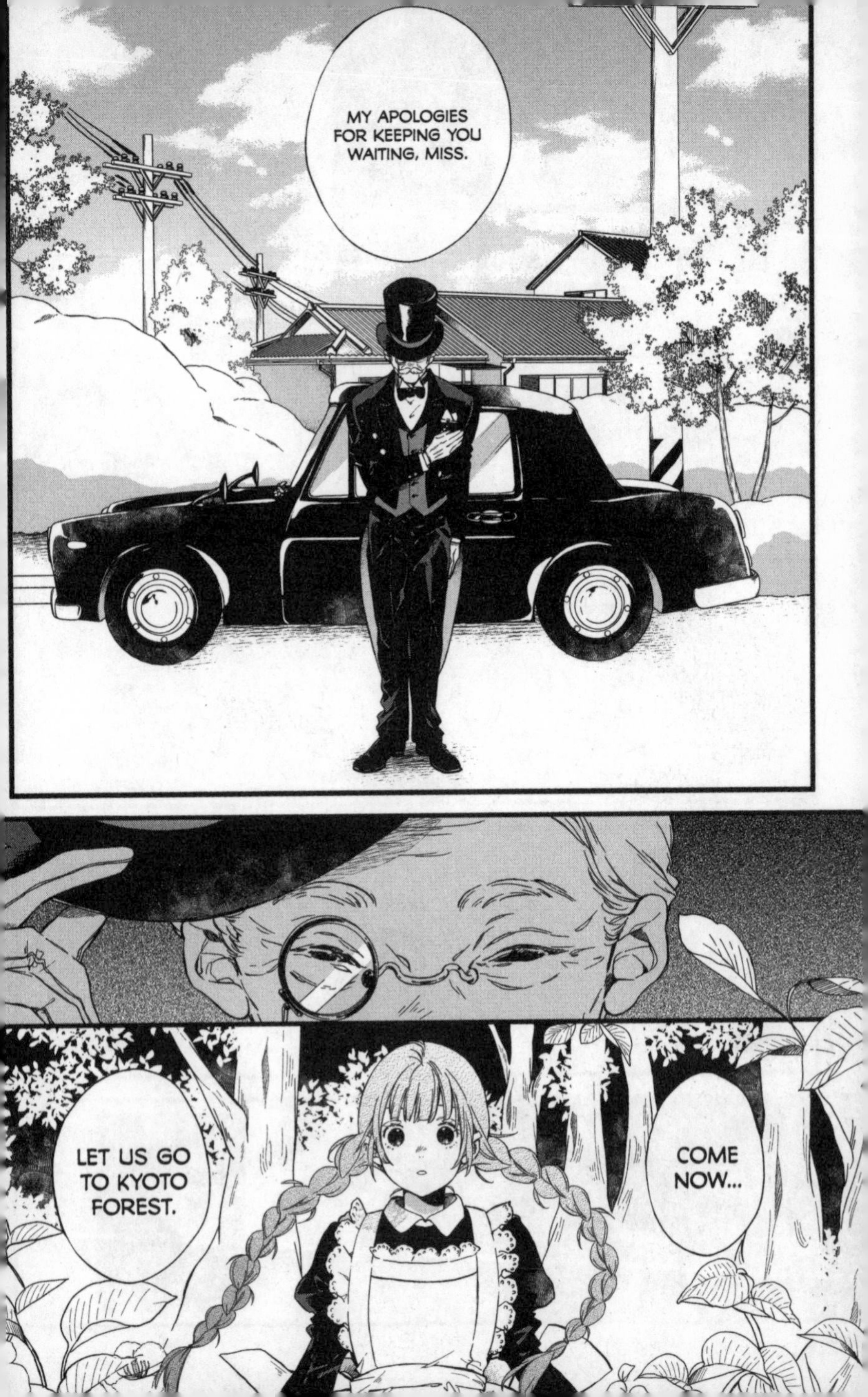
MY APOLOGIES FOR KEEPING YOU WAITING, MISS.
COME NOW...
LET US GO TO KYOTO FOREST.

Chapter 1

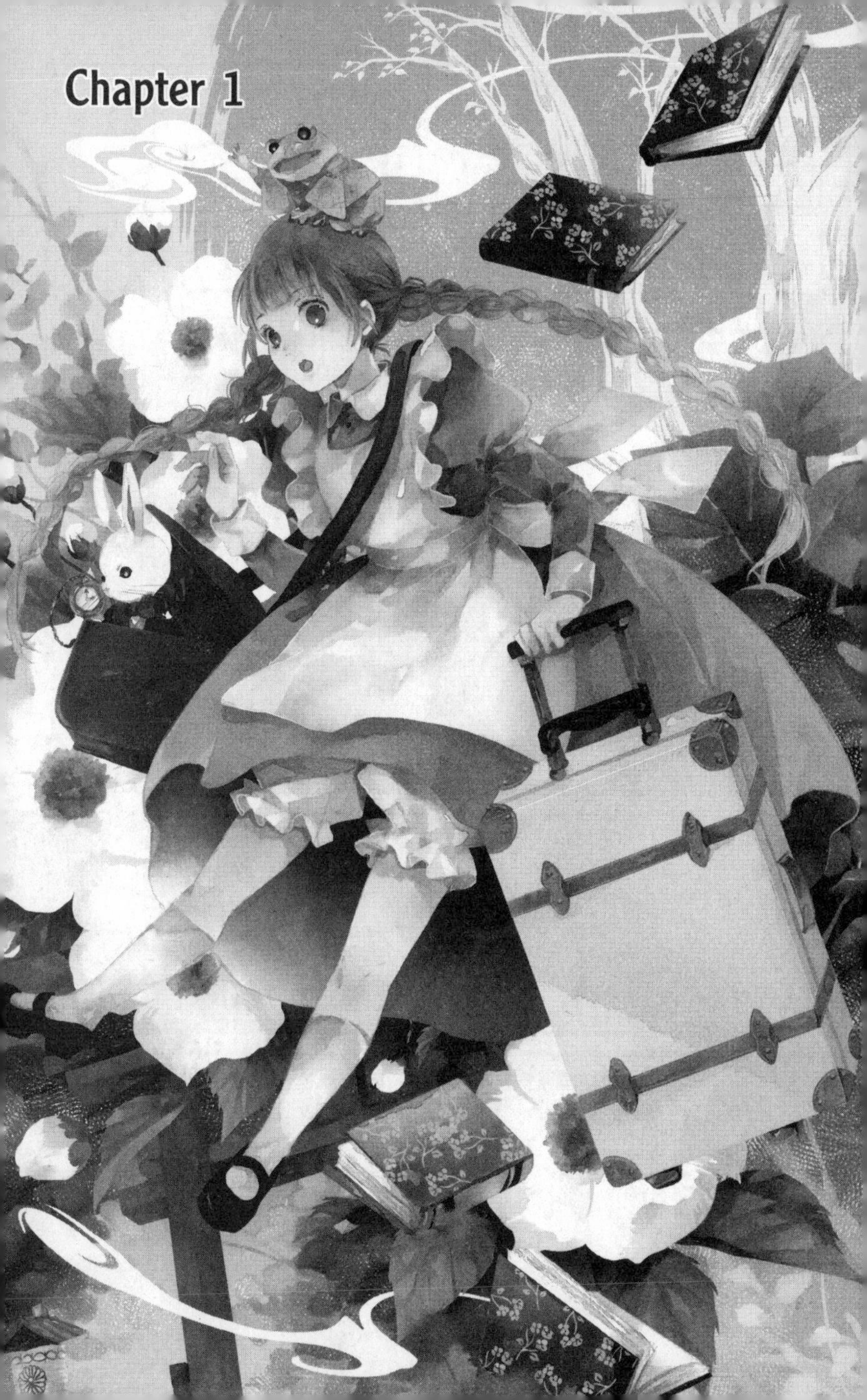

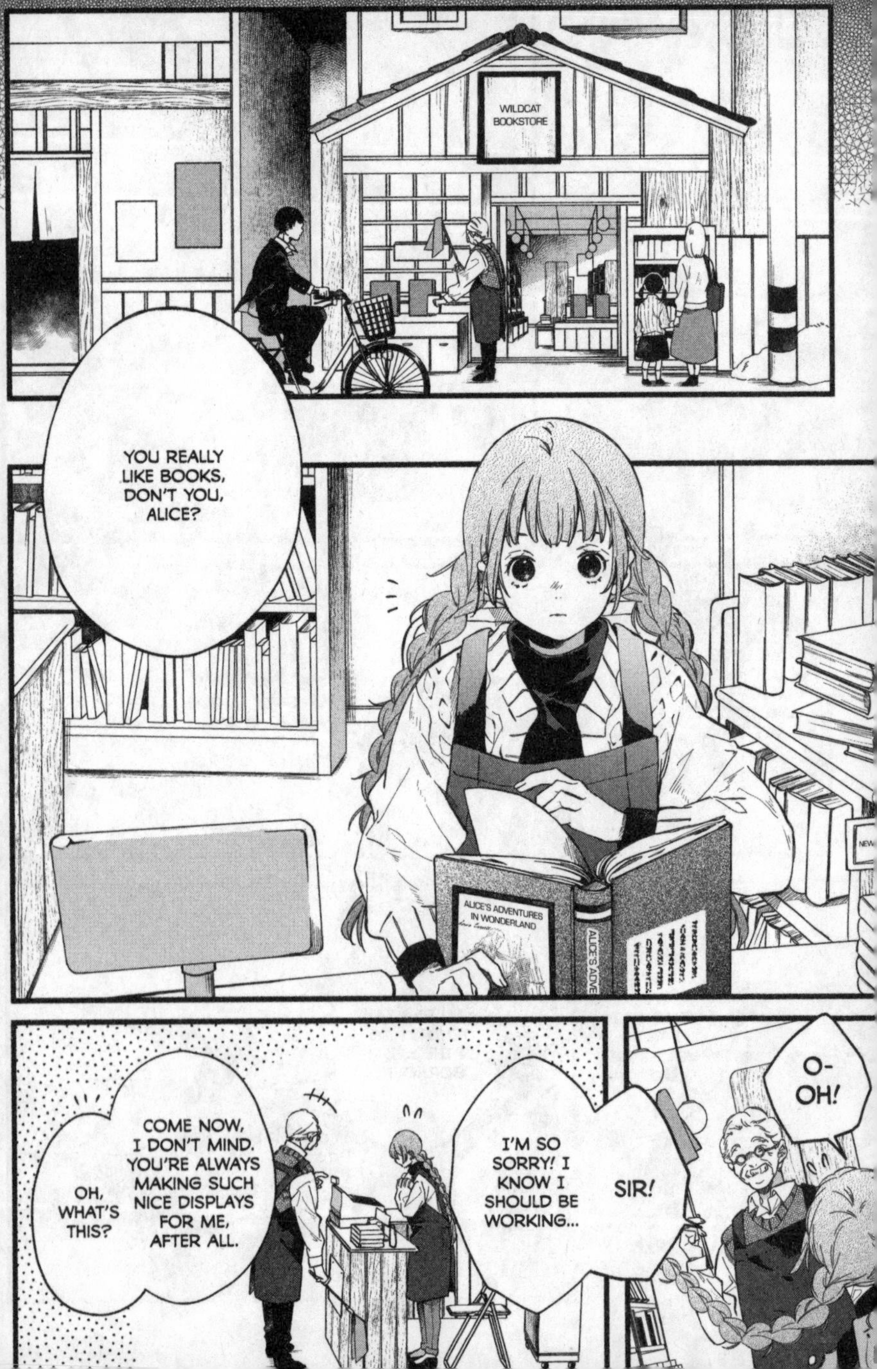
WILDCAT BOOKSTORE
YOU REALLY LIKE BOOKS, DON'T YOU, ALICE?
ALICE'S ADVENTURES IN WONDERLAND
O-OH!
SIR!
I'M SO SORRY! I KNOW I SHOULD BE WORKING...
COME NOW, I DON'T MIND. YOU'RE ALWAYS MAKING SUCH NICE DISPLAYS FOR ME, AFTER ALL.
OH, WHAT'S THIS?

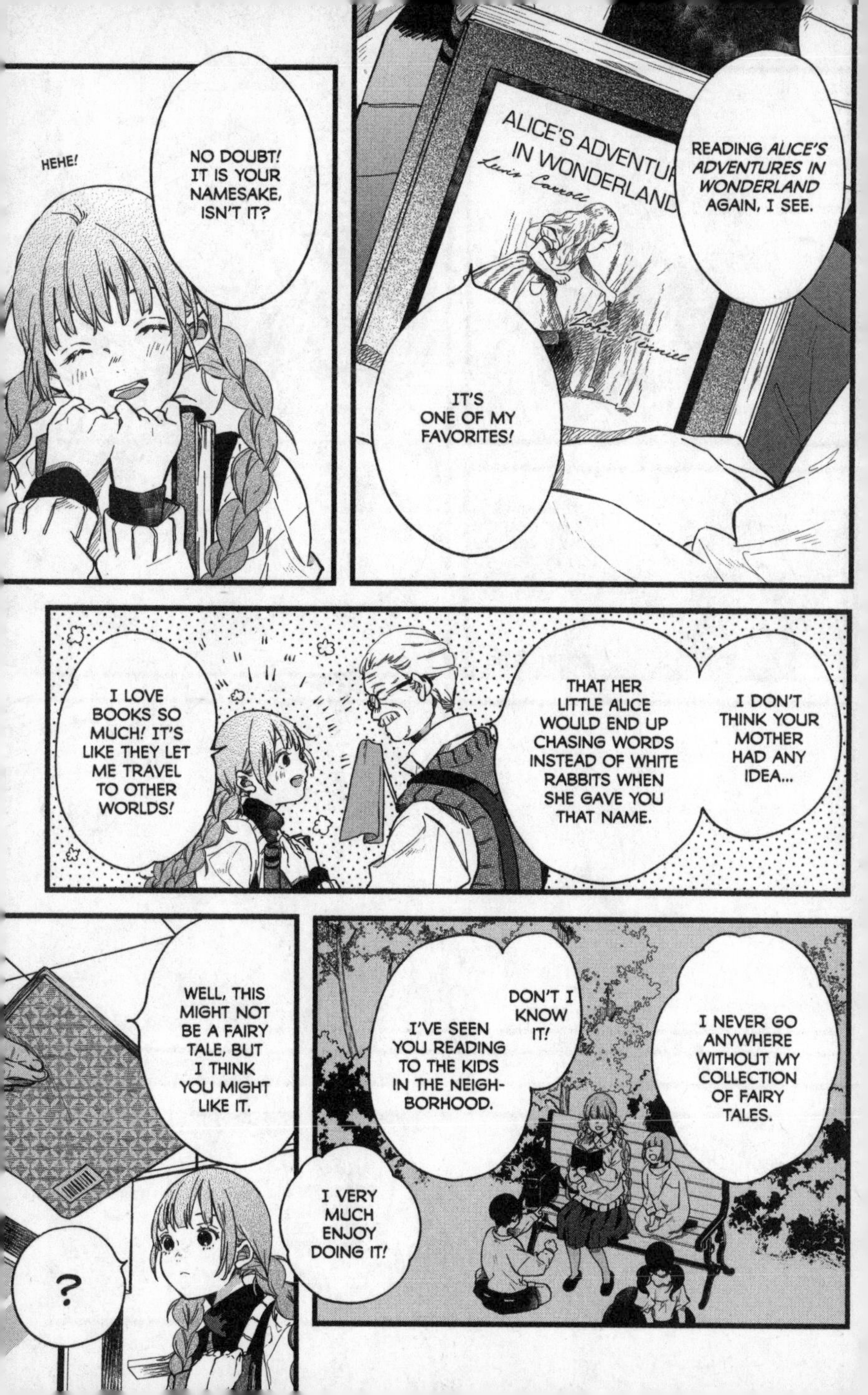
READING *ALICE'S ADVENTURES IN WONDERLAND* AGAIN, I SEE.
IT'S ONE OF MY FAVORITES!
NO DOUBT! IT IS YOUR NAMESAKE, ISN'T IT?
HEHE!
I DON'T THINK YOUR MOTHER HAD ANY IDEA...
THAT HER LITTLE ALICE WOULD END UP CHASING WORDS INSTEAD OF WHITE RABBITS WHEN SHE GAVE YOU THAT NAME.
I LOVE BOOKS SO MUCH! IT'S LIKE THEY LET ME TRAVEL TO OTHER WORLDS!
I NEVER GO ANYWHERE WITHOUT MY COLLECTION OF FAIRY TALES.
DON'T I KNOW IT!
I'VE SEEN YOU READING TO THE KIDS IN THE NEIGH-BORHOOD.
I VERY MUCH ENJOY DOING IT!
WELL, THIS MIGHT NOT BE A FAIRY TALE, BUT I THINK YOU MIGHT LIKE IT.
?

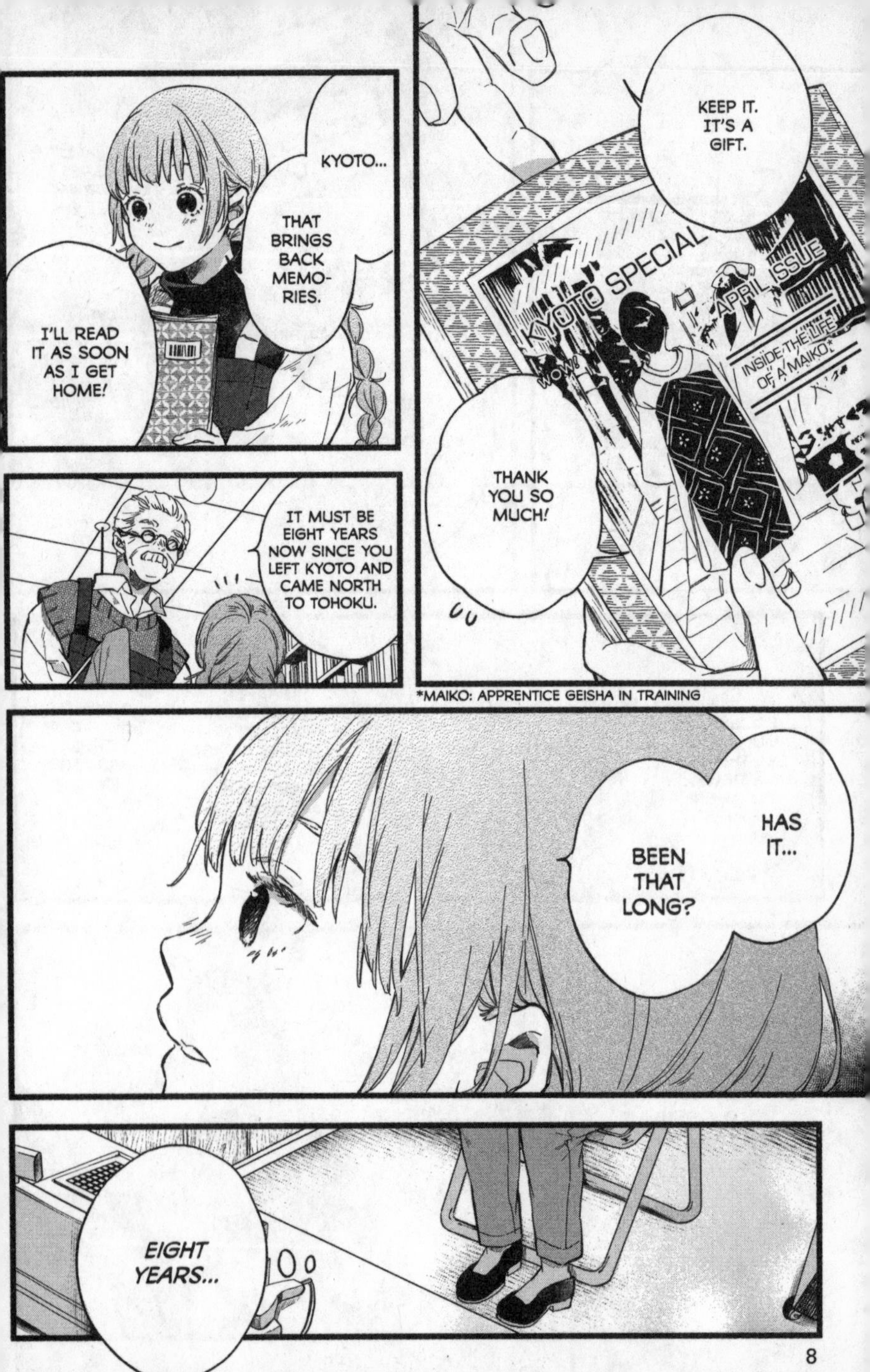
KEEP IT. IT'S A GIFT.
APRIL ISSUE
KYOTO SPECIAL
INSIDE THE LIFE OF A MAIKO*
WOW
THANK YOU SO MUCH!
KYOTO...
THAT BRINGS BACK MEMORIES.
I'LL READ IT AS SOON AS I GET HOME!
IT MUST BE EIGHT YEARS NOW SINCE YOU LEFT KYOTO AND CAME NORTH TO TOHOKU.
HAS IT...
BEEN THAT LONG?
EIGHT YEARS...

*MAIKO: APPRENTICE GEISHA IN TRAINING

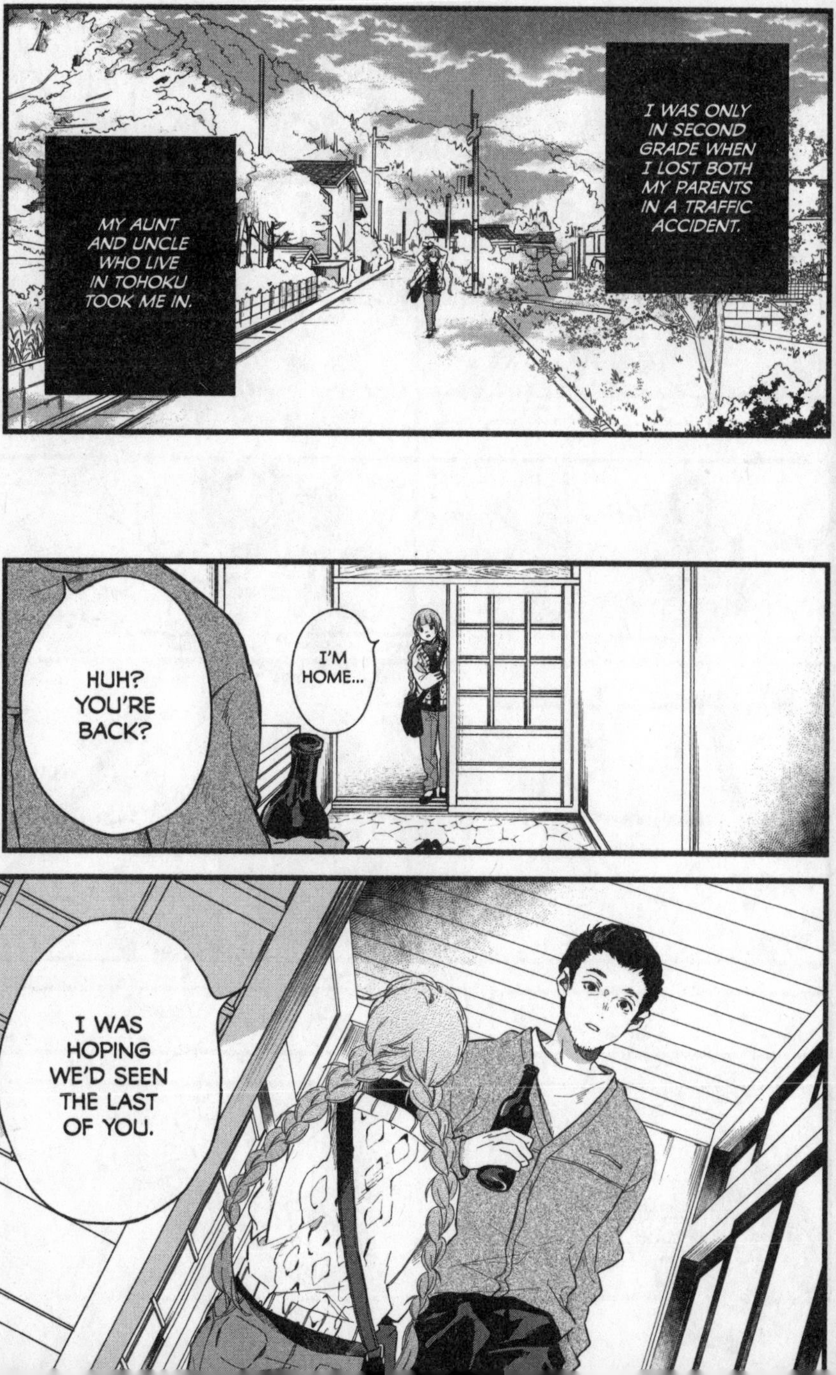
I WAS ONLY IN SECOND GRADE WHEN I LOST BOTH MY PARENTS IN A TRAFFIC ACCIDENT.
MY AUNT AND UNCLE WHO LIVE IN TOHOKU TOOK ME IN.
I'M HOME...
HUH? YOU'RE BACK?
I WAS HOPING WE'D SEEN THE LAST OF YOU.

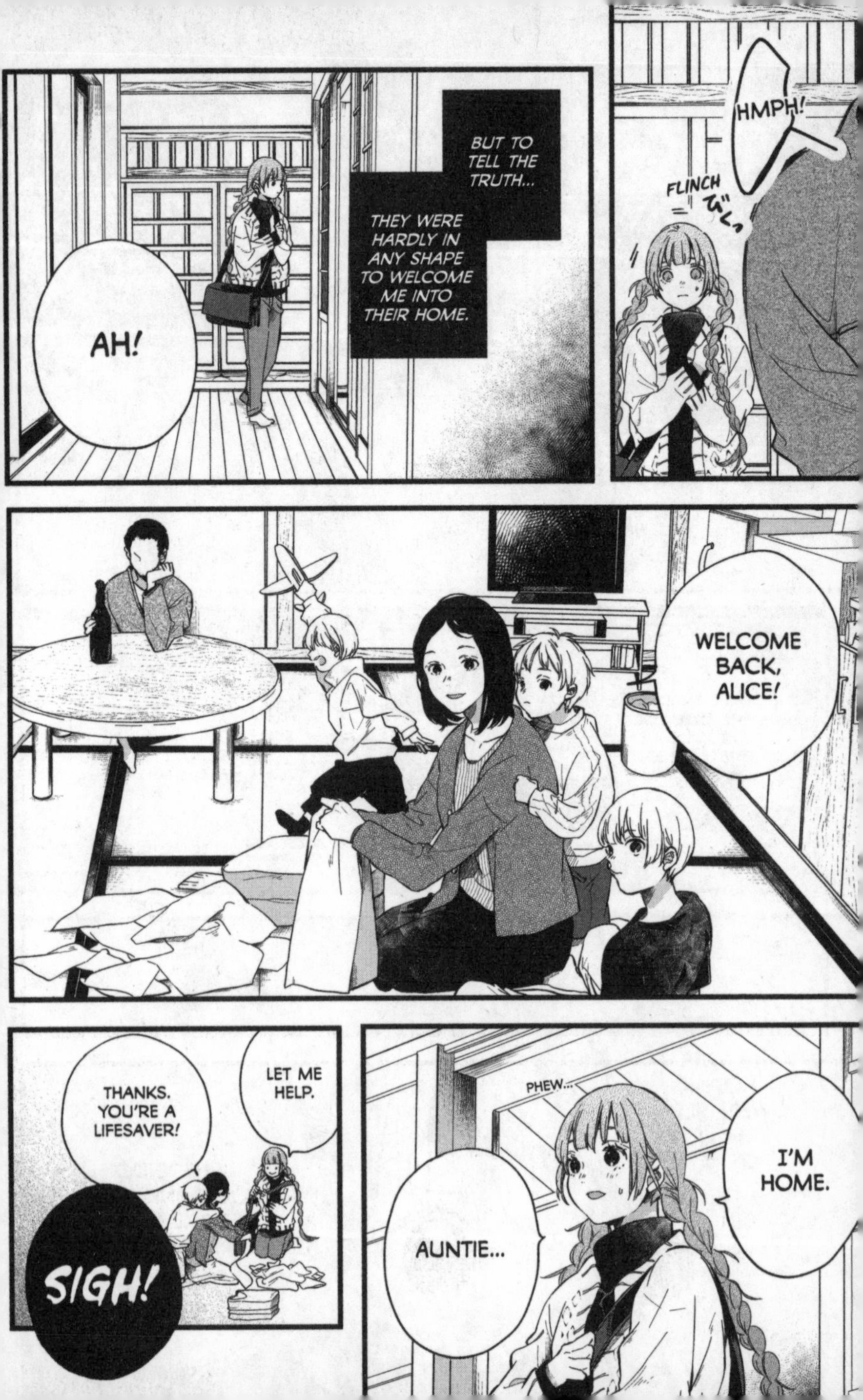
HMPH!
FLINCH
びくっ
BUT TO TELL THE TRUTH...
THEY WERE HARDLY IN ANY SHAPE TO WELCOME ME INTO THEIR HOME.
AH!
WELCOME BACK, ALICE!
PHEW...
I'M HOME.
AUNTIE...
LET ME HELP.
THANKS. YOU'RE A LIFESAVER!
SIGH!

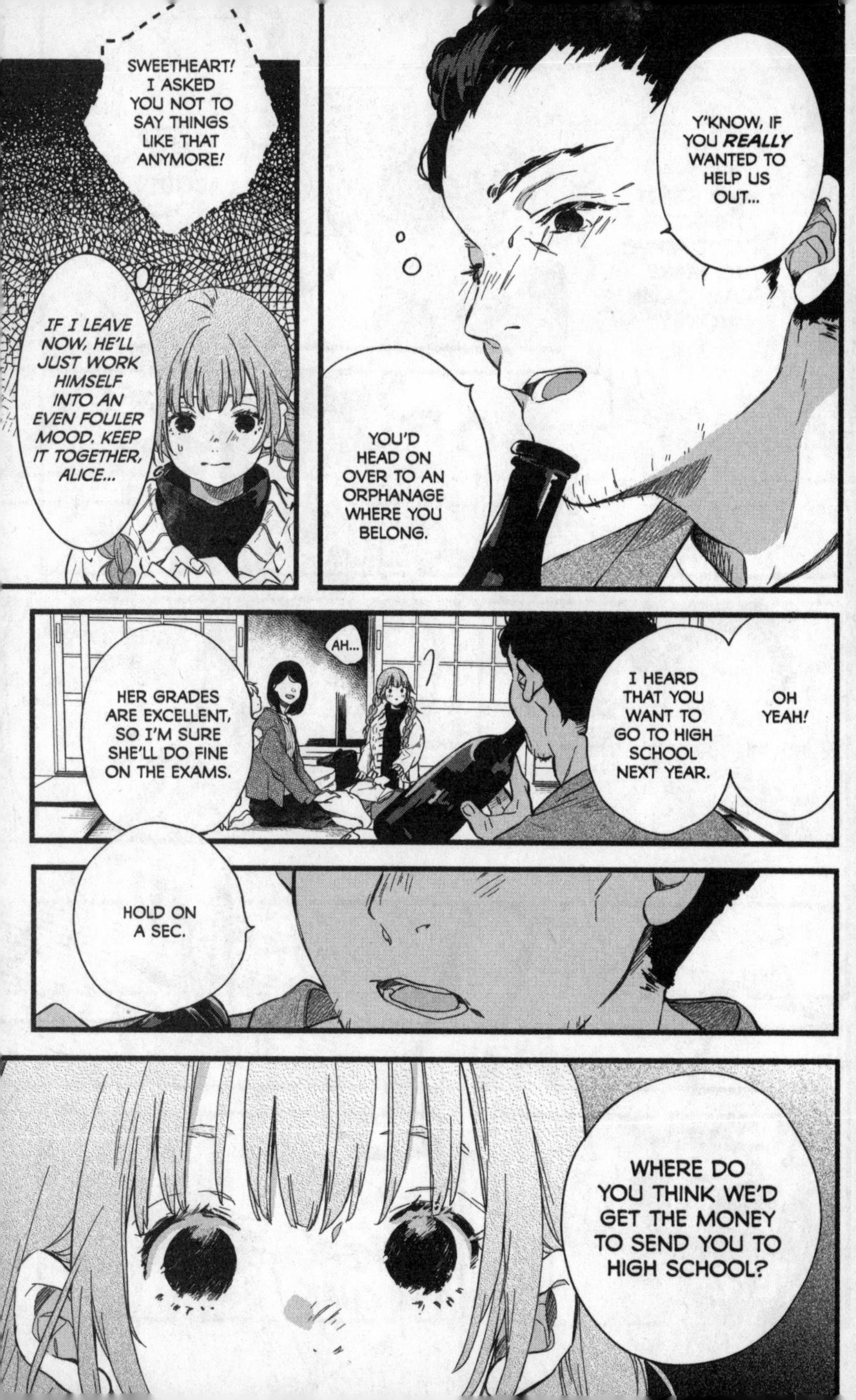
Y'KNOW, IF YOU *REALLY* WANTED TO HELP US OUT...
YOU'D HEAD ON OVER TO AN ORPHANAGE WHERE YOU BELONG.
SWEETHEART! I ASKED YOU NOT TO SAY THINGS LIKE THAT ANYMORE!
IF I LEAVE NOW, HE'LL JUST WORK HIMSELF INTO AN EVEN FOULER MOOD. KEEP IT TOGETHER, ALICE...
OH YEAH!
I HEARD THAT YOU WANT TO GO TO HIGH SCHOOL NEXT YEAR.
AH...
HER GRADES ARE EXCELLENT, SO I'M SURE SHE'LL DO FINE ON THE EXAMS.
HOLD ON A SEC.
WHERE DO YOU THINK WE'D GET THE MONEY TO SEND YOU TO HIGH SCHOOL?

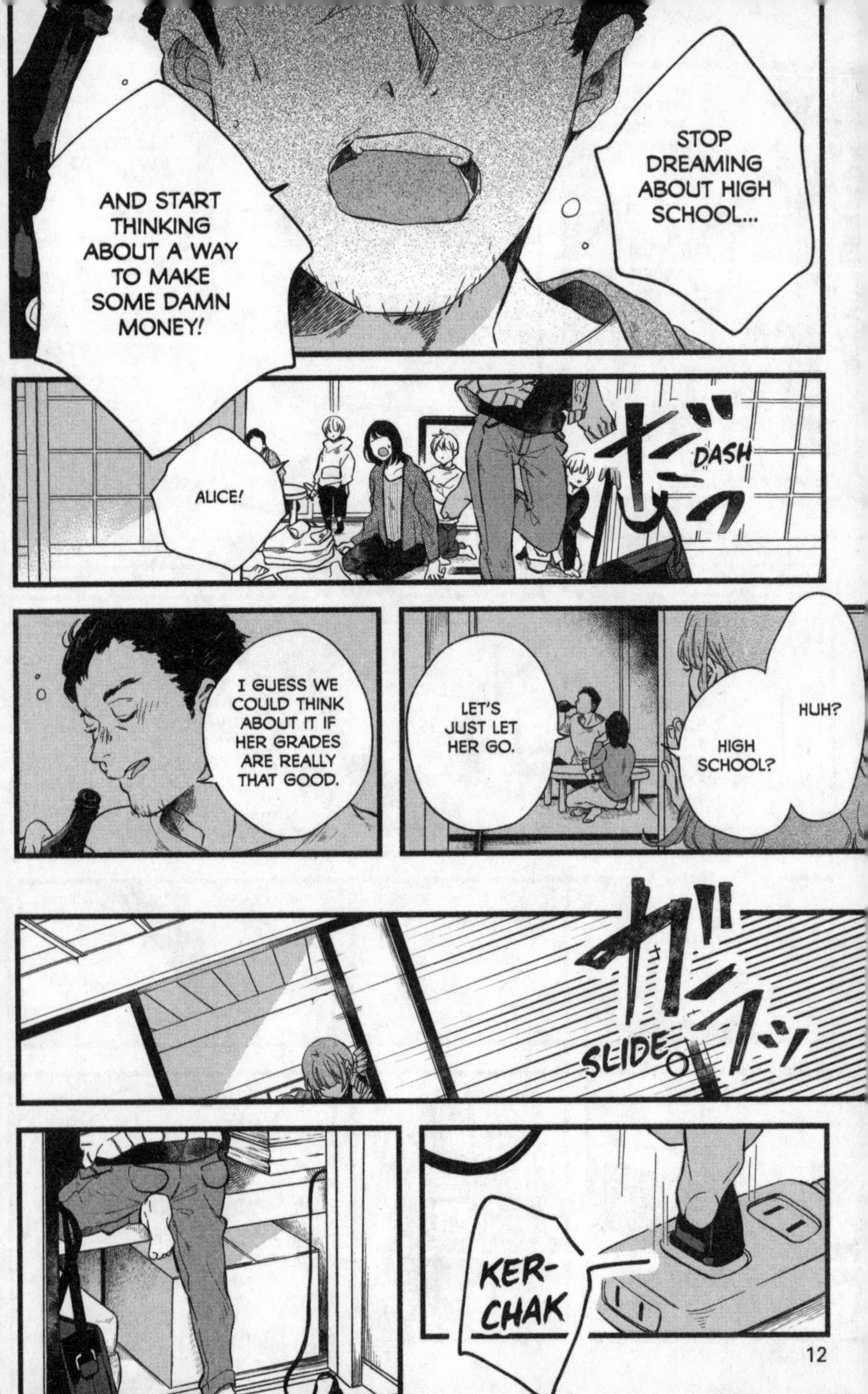
STOP DREAMING ABOUT HIGH SCHOOL...
AND START THINKING ABOUT A WAY TO MAKE SOME DAMN MONEY!
DASH
ALICE!
HUH?
HIGH SCHOOL?
LET'S JUST LET HER GO.
I GUESS WE COULD THINK ABOUT IT IF HER GRADES ARE REALLY THAT GOOD.
SLIDE
KER-CHAK

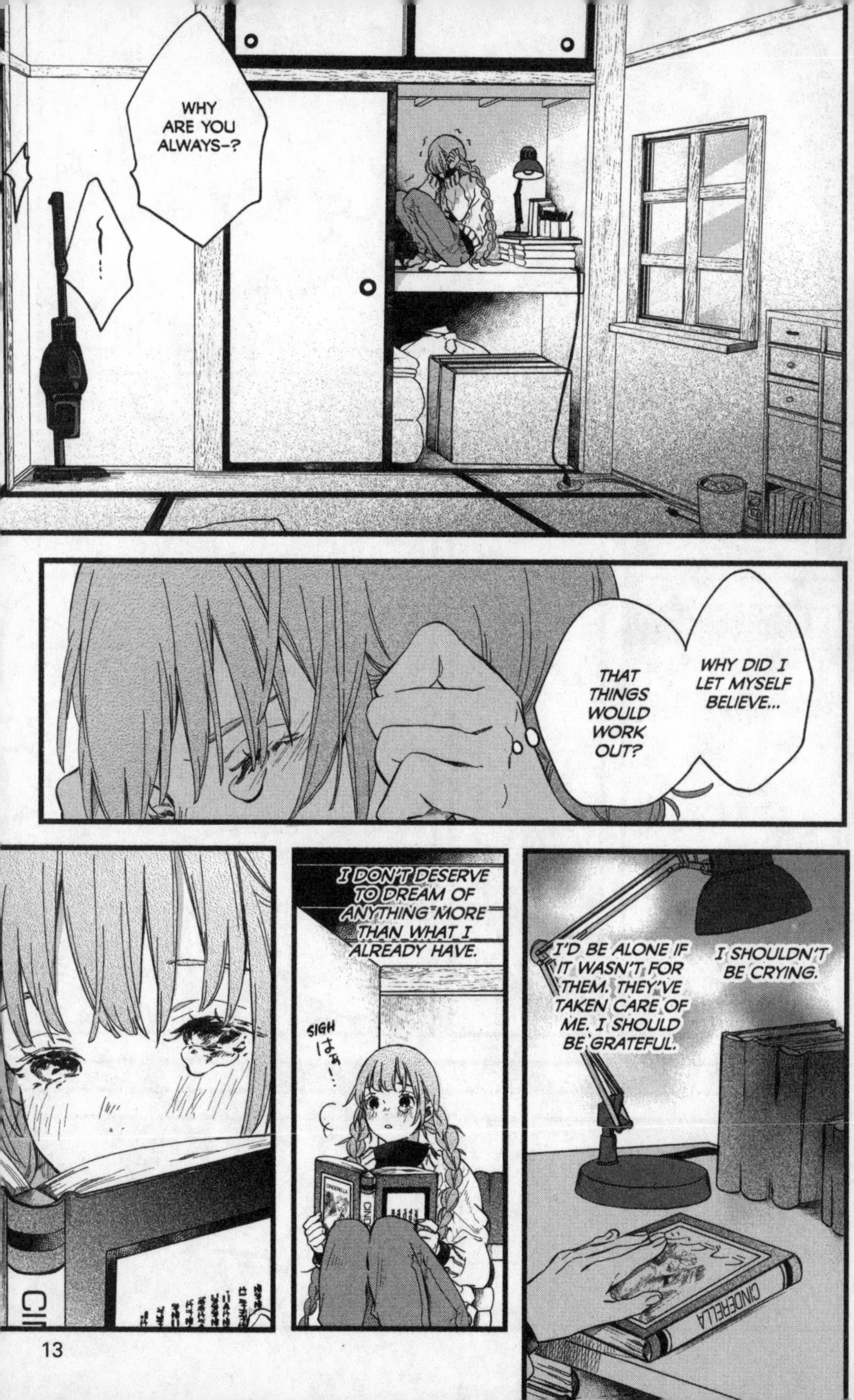
WHY ARE YOU ALWAYS-?
WHY DID I LET MYSELF BELIEVE...
THAT THINGS WOULD WORK OUT?
I SHOULDN'T BE CRYING.
I'D BE ALONE IF IT WASN'T FOR THEM. THEY'VE TAKEN CARE OF ME. I SHOULD BE GRATEFUL.
CINDERELLA
I DON'T DESERVE TO DREAM OF ANYTHING MORE THAN WHAT I ALREADY HAVE.
SIGH はぁ…
CINDERELLA
CIN

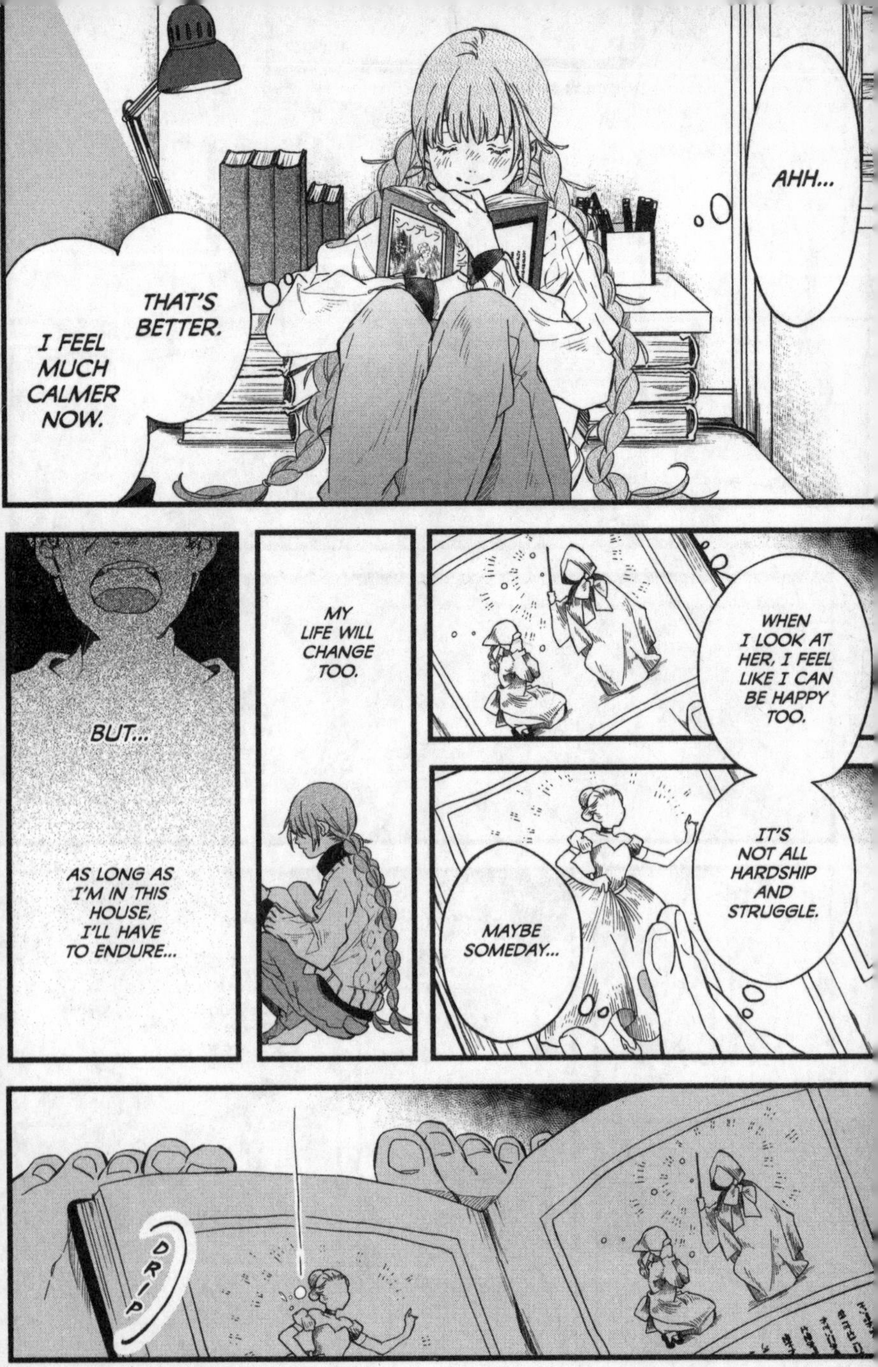
AHH...
THAT'S BETTER.
I FEEL MUCH CALMER NOW.
WHEN I LOOK AT HER, I FEEL LIKE I CAN BE HAPPY TOO.
IT'S NOT ALL HARDSHIP AND STRUGGLE.
MAYBE SOMEDAY...
MY LIFE WILL CHANGE TOO.
BUT...
AS LONG AS I'M IN THIS HOUSE, I'LL HAVE TO ENDURE...
DRIP

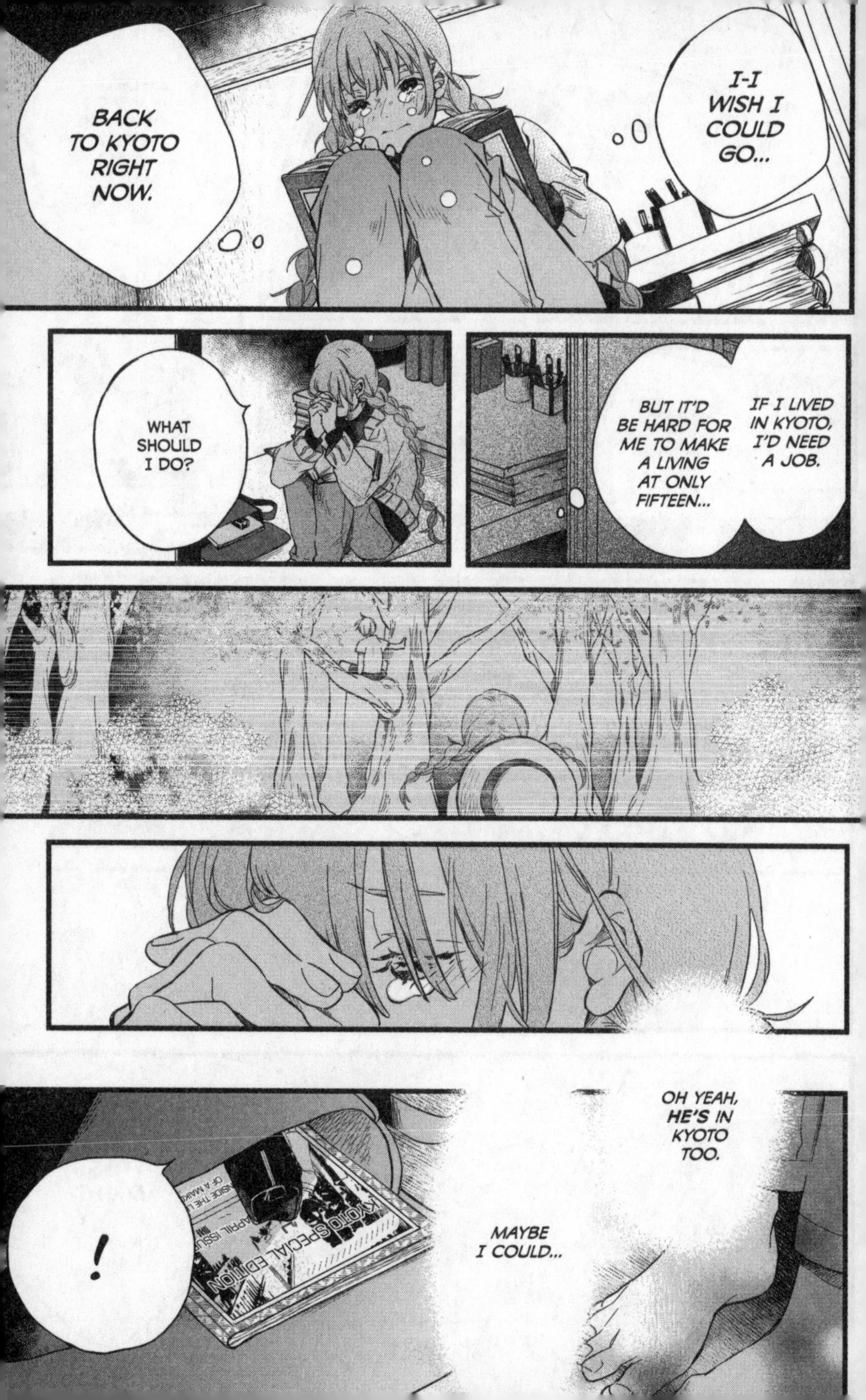
I-I WISH I COULD GO...
BACK TO KYOTO RIGHT NOW.
IF I LIVED IN KYOTO, I'D NEED A JOB.
BUT IT'D BE HARD FOR ME TO MAKE A LIVING AT ONLY FIFTEEN...
WHAT SHOULD I DO?
OH YEAH, HE'S IN KYOTO TOO.
KYOTO SPECIAL EDITION
MAYBE I COULD...
!

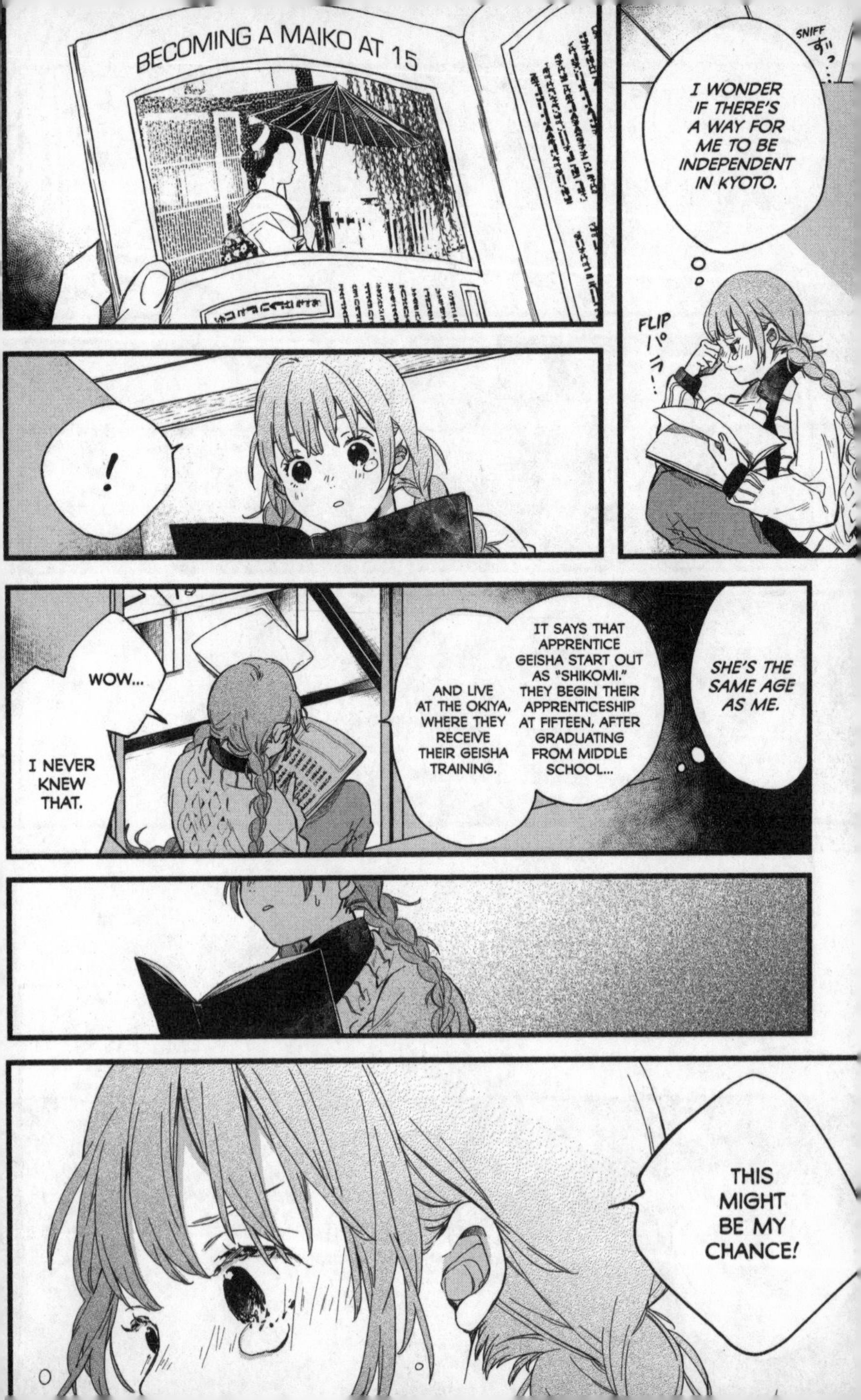
SNIFF
ずっ…
I WONDER IF THERE'S A WAY FOR ME TO BE INDEPENDENT IN KYOTO.
FLIP
パラ…
BECOMING A MAIKO AT 15
!
SHE'S THE SAME AGE AS ME.
IT SAYS THAT APPRENTICE GEISHA START OUT AS "SHIKOMI." THEY BEGIN THEIR APPRENTICESHIP AT FIFTEEN, AFTER GRADUATING FROM MIDDLE SCHOOL...
AND LIVE AT THE OKIYA, WHERE THEY RECEIVE THEIR GEISHA TRAINING.
WOW...
I NEVER KNEW THAT.
THIS MIGHT BE MY CHANCE!

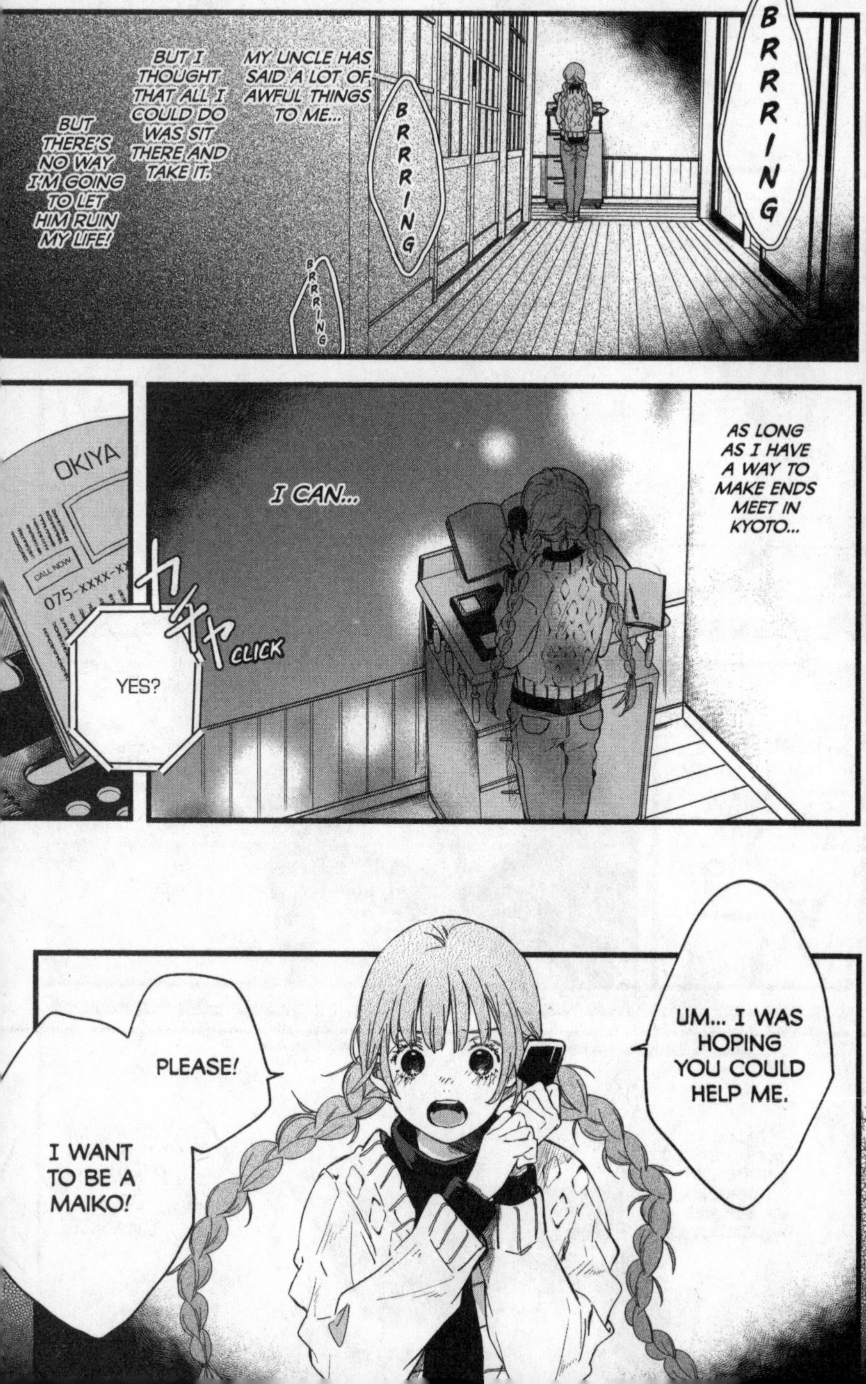
BRRRING
BRRRING
BRRRING
MY UNCLE HAS SAID A LOT OF AWFUL THINGS TO ME...
BUT I THOUGHT THAT ALL I COULD DO WAS SIT THERE AND TAKE IT.
BUT THERE'S NO WAY I'M GOING TO LET HIM RUIN MY LIFE!
AS LONG AS I HAVE A WAY TO MAKE ENDS MEET IN KYOTO...
I CAN...
OKIYA
CALL NOW
075-xxxx-xx
カチャ CLICK
YES?
UM... I WAS HOPING YOU COULD HELP ME.
PLEASE!
I WANT TO BE A MAIKO!

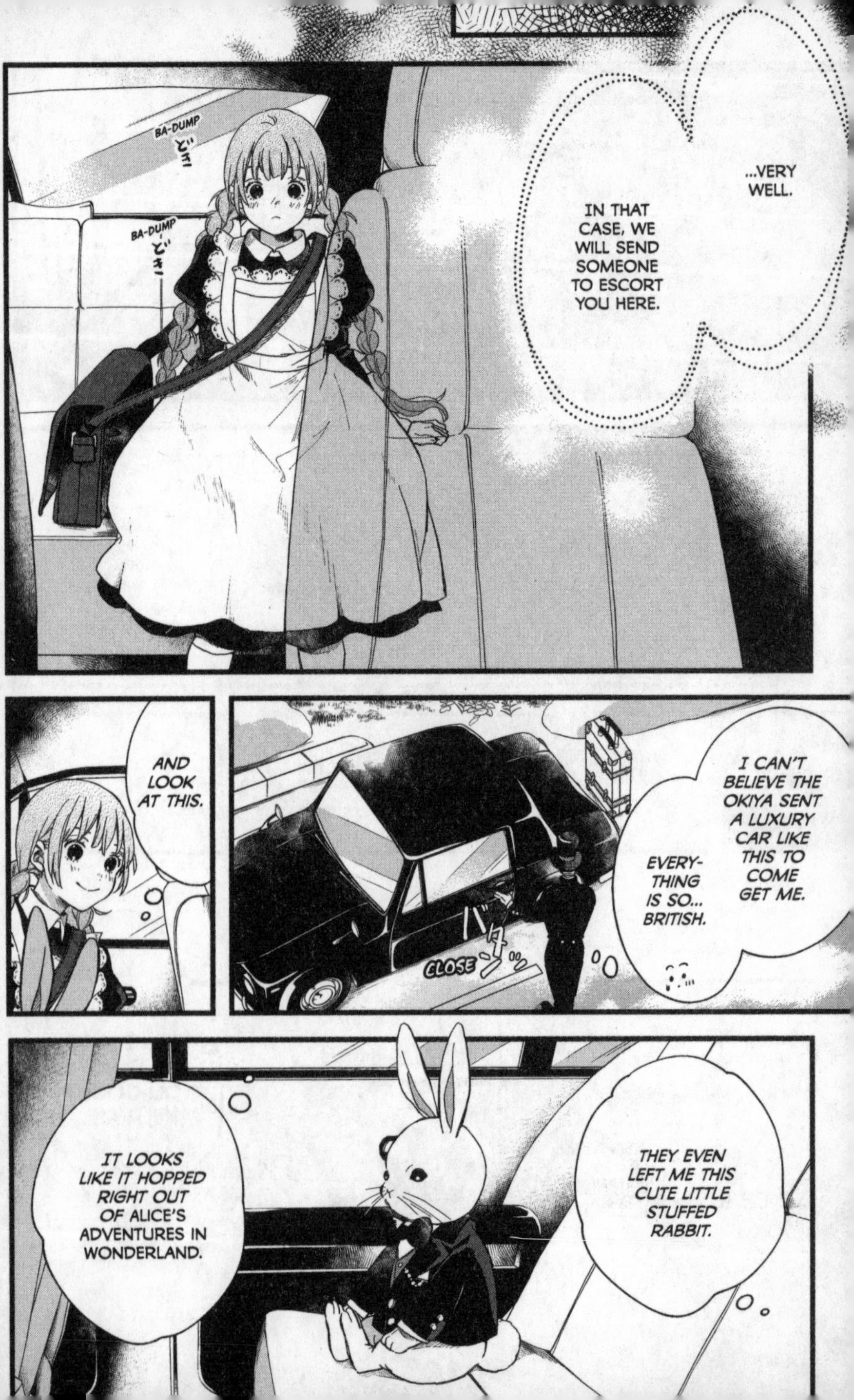
...VERY WELL.
IN THAT CASE, WE WILL SEND SOMEONE TO ESCORT YOU HERE.
BA-DUMP
BA-DUMP
I CAN'T BELIEVE THE OKIYA SENT A LUXURY CAR LIKE THIS TO COME GET ME.
EVERY-THING IS SO... BRITISH.
CLOSE
AND LOOK AT THIS.
THEY EVEN LEFT ME THIS CUTE LITTLE STUFFED RABBIT.
IT LOOKS LIKE IT HOPPED RIGHT OUT OF ALICE'S ADVENTURES IN WONDERLAND.

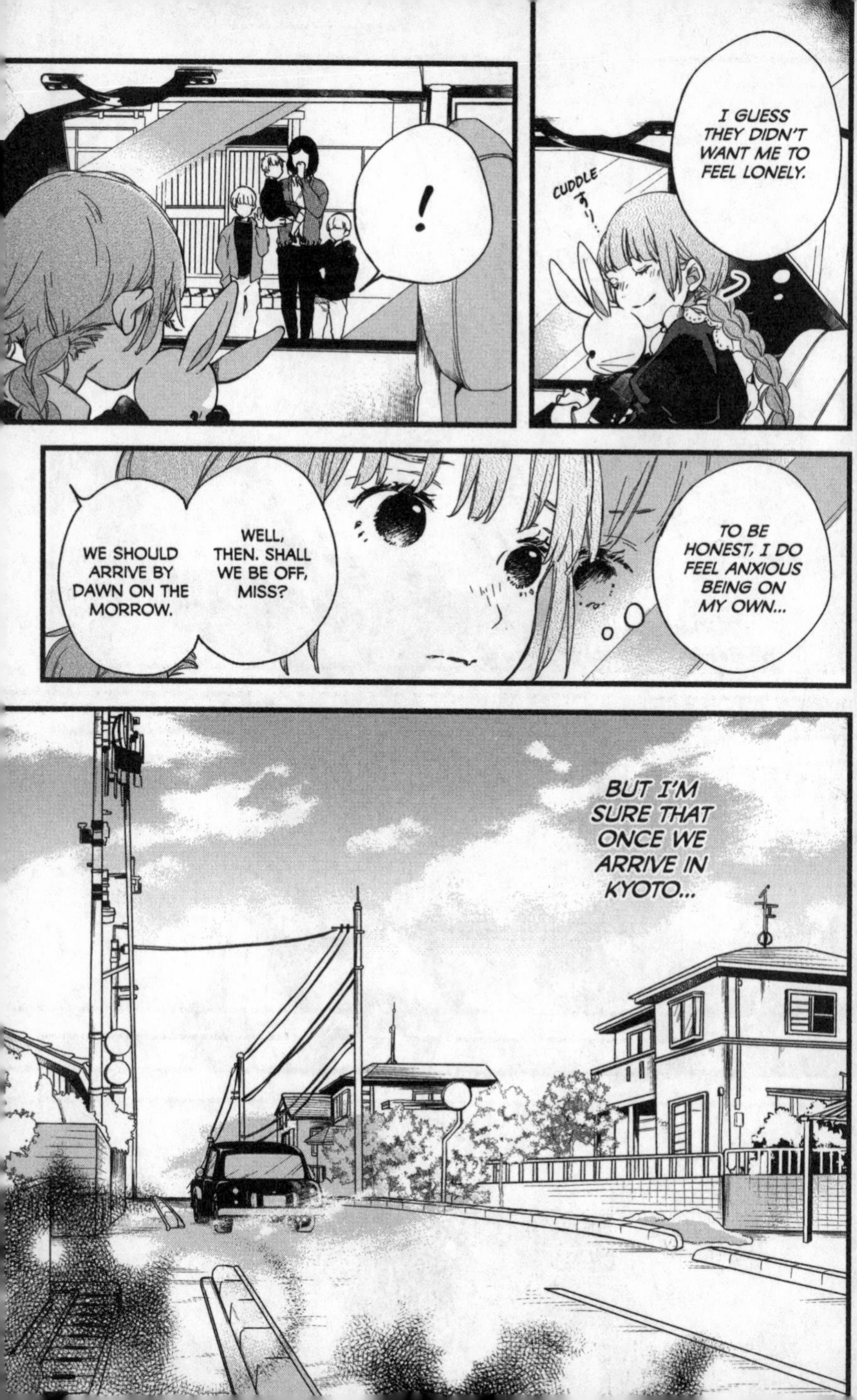

I GUESS THEY DIDN'T WANT ME TO FEEL LONELY.
CUDDLE
すり…
!
TO BE HONEST, I DO FEEL ANXIOUS BEING ON MY OWN...
WELL, THEN. SHALL WE BE OFF, MISS?
WE SHOULD ARRIVE BY DAWN ON THE MORROW.
BUT I'M SURE THAT ONCE WE ARRIVE IN KYOTO...

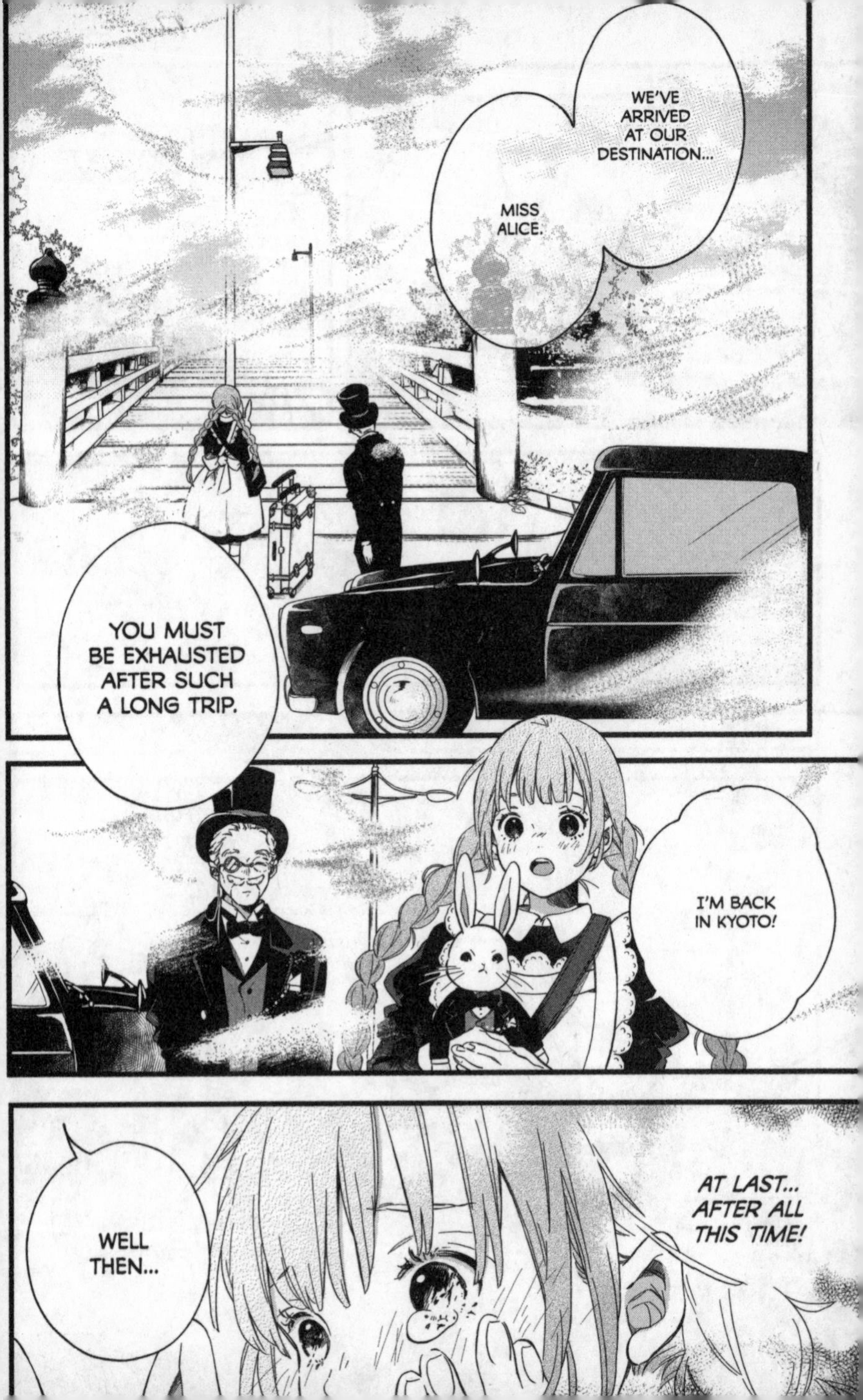
WE'VE ARRIVED AT OUR DESTINATION...
MISS ALICE.
YOU MUST BE EXHAUSTED AFTER SUCH A LONG TRIP.
I'M BACK IN KYOTO!
AT LAST... AFTER ALL THIS TIME!
WELL THEN...

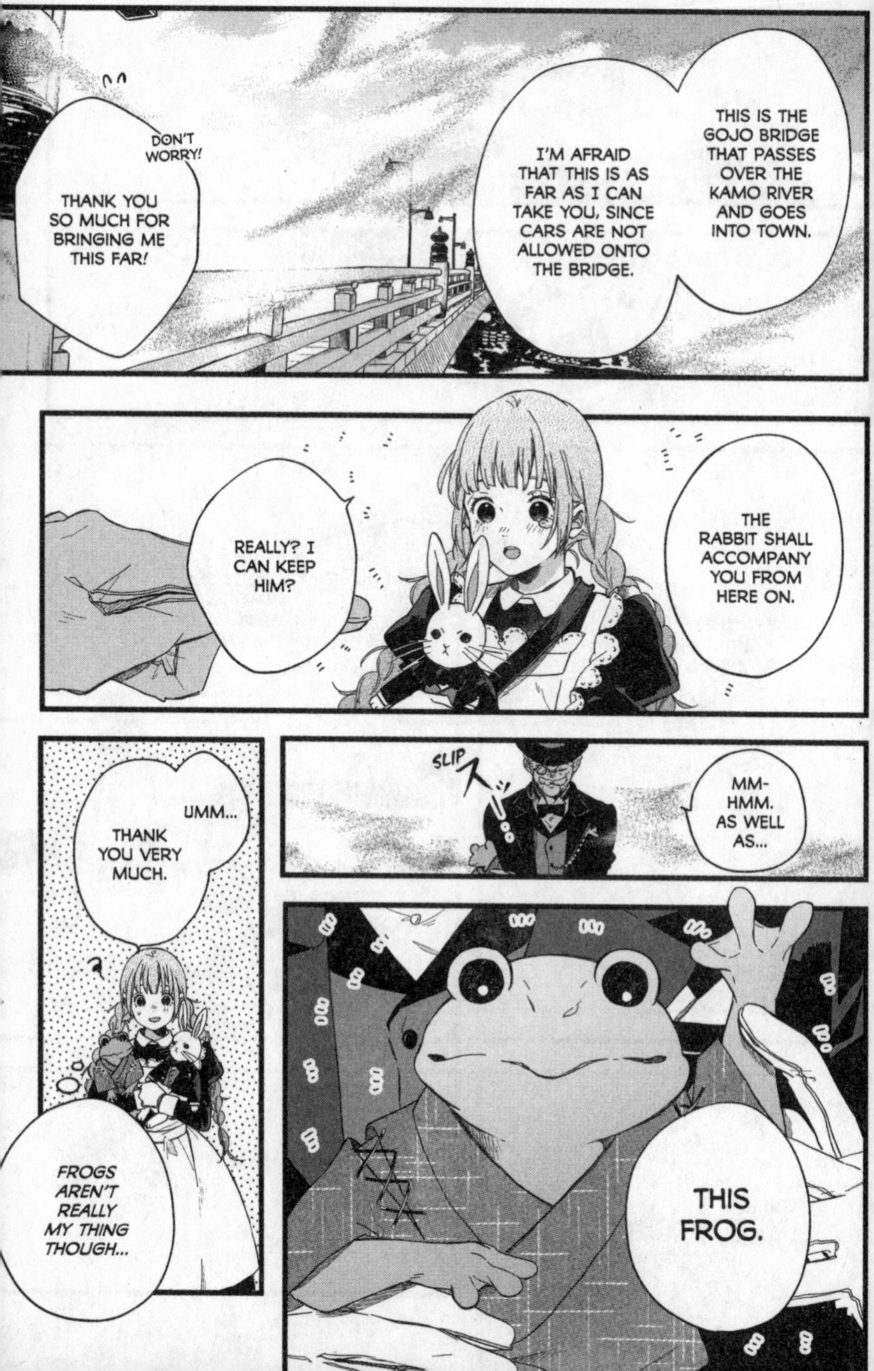
THIS IS THE GOJO BRIDGE THAT PASSES OVER THE KAMO RIVER AND GOES INTO TOWN.
I'M AFRAID THAT THIS IS AS FAR AS I CAN TAKE YOU, SINCE CARS ARE NOT ALLOWED ONTO THE BRIDGE.
DON'T WORRY!
THANK YOU SO MUCH FOR BRINGING ME THIS FAR!
THE RABBIT SHALL ACCOMPANY YOU FROM HERE ON.
REALLY? I CAN KEEP HIM?
MM-HMM. AS WELL AS...
SLIP
THIS FROG.
UMM...
THANK YOU VERY MUCH.
FROGS AREN'T REALLY MY THING THOUGH...

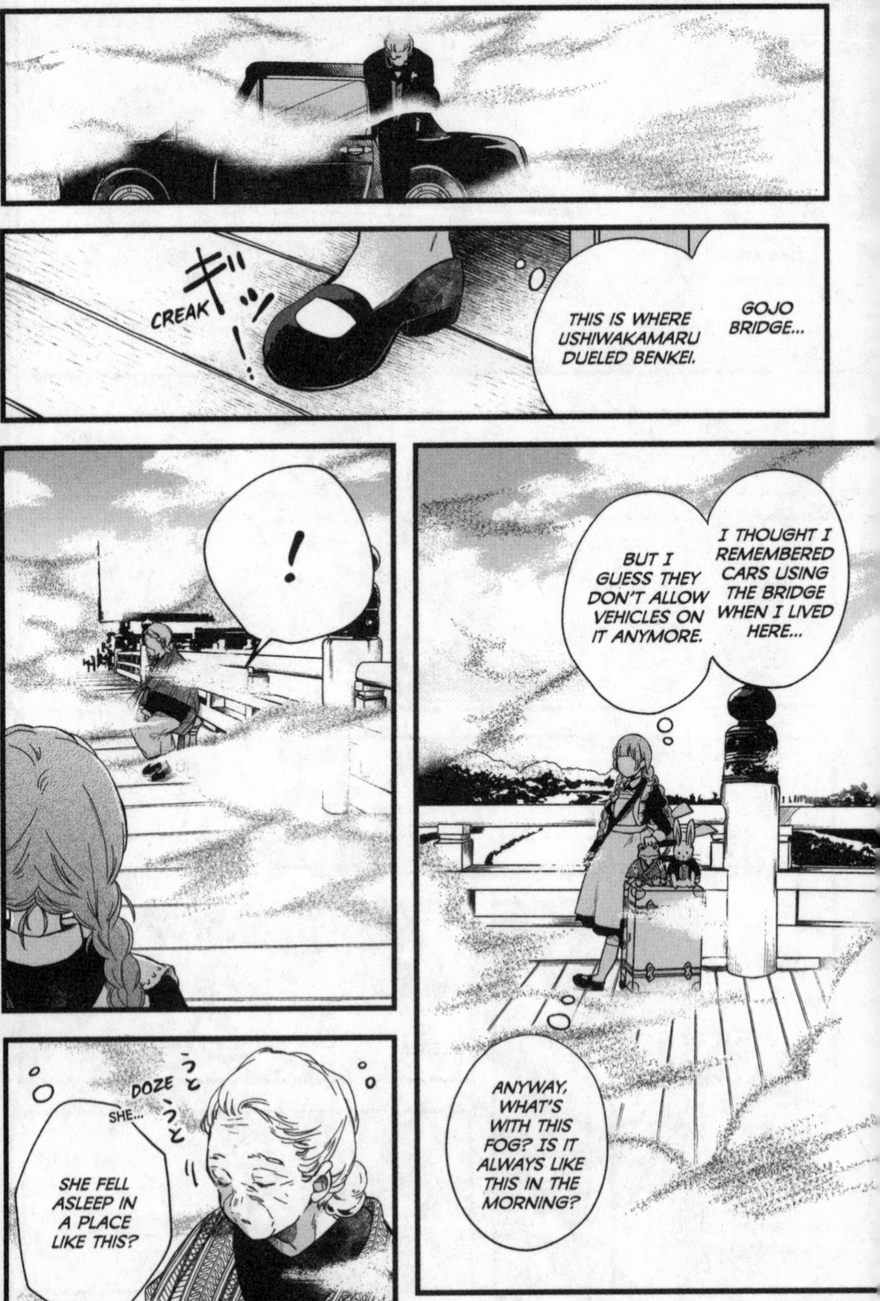
GOJO BRIDGE...
THIS IS WHERE USHIWAKAMARU DUELED BENKEI.
ギッ
CREAK
I THOUGHT I REMEMBERED CARS USING THE BRIDGE WHEN I LIVED HERE...
BUT I GUESS THEY DON'T ALLOW VEHICLES ON IT ANYMORE.
ANYWAY, WHAT'S WITH THIS FOG? IS IT ALWAYS LIKE THIS IN THE MORNING?
!
うとうと
DOZE
SHE...
SHE FELL ASLEEP IN A PLACE LIKE THIS?

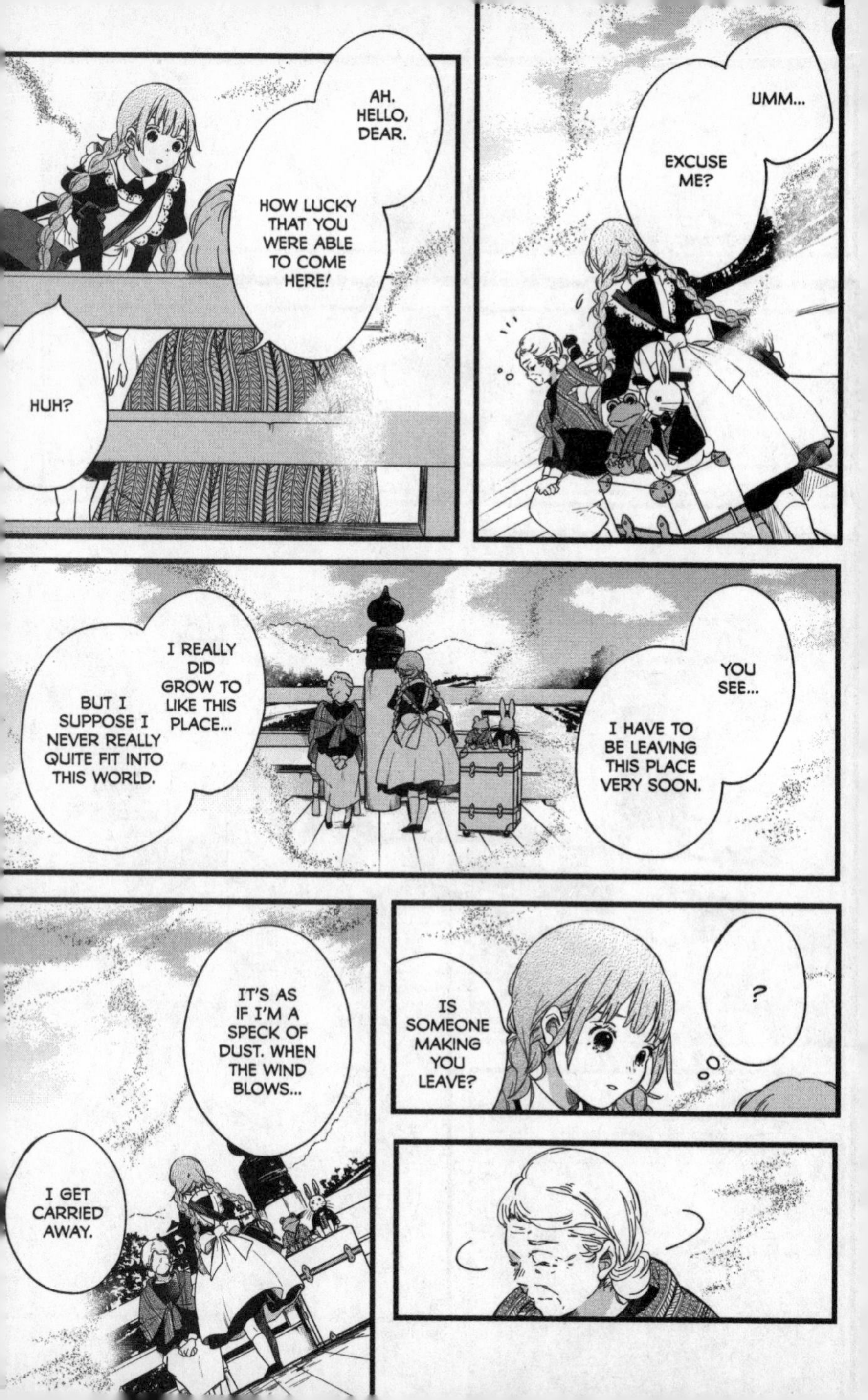
UMM...
EXCUSE ME?
AH. HELLO, DEAR.
HOW LUCKY THAT YOU WERE ABLE TO COME HERE!
HUH?
YOU SEE...
I HAVE TO BE LEAVING THIS PLACE VERY SOON.
I REALLY DID GROW TO LIKE THIS PLACE...
BUT I SUPPOSE I NEVER REALLY QUITE FIT INTO THIS WORLD.
?
IS SOMEONE MAKING YOU LEAVE?
IT'S AS IF I'M A SPECK OF DUST. WHEN THE WIND BLOWS...
I GET CARRIED AWAY.

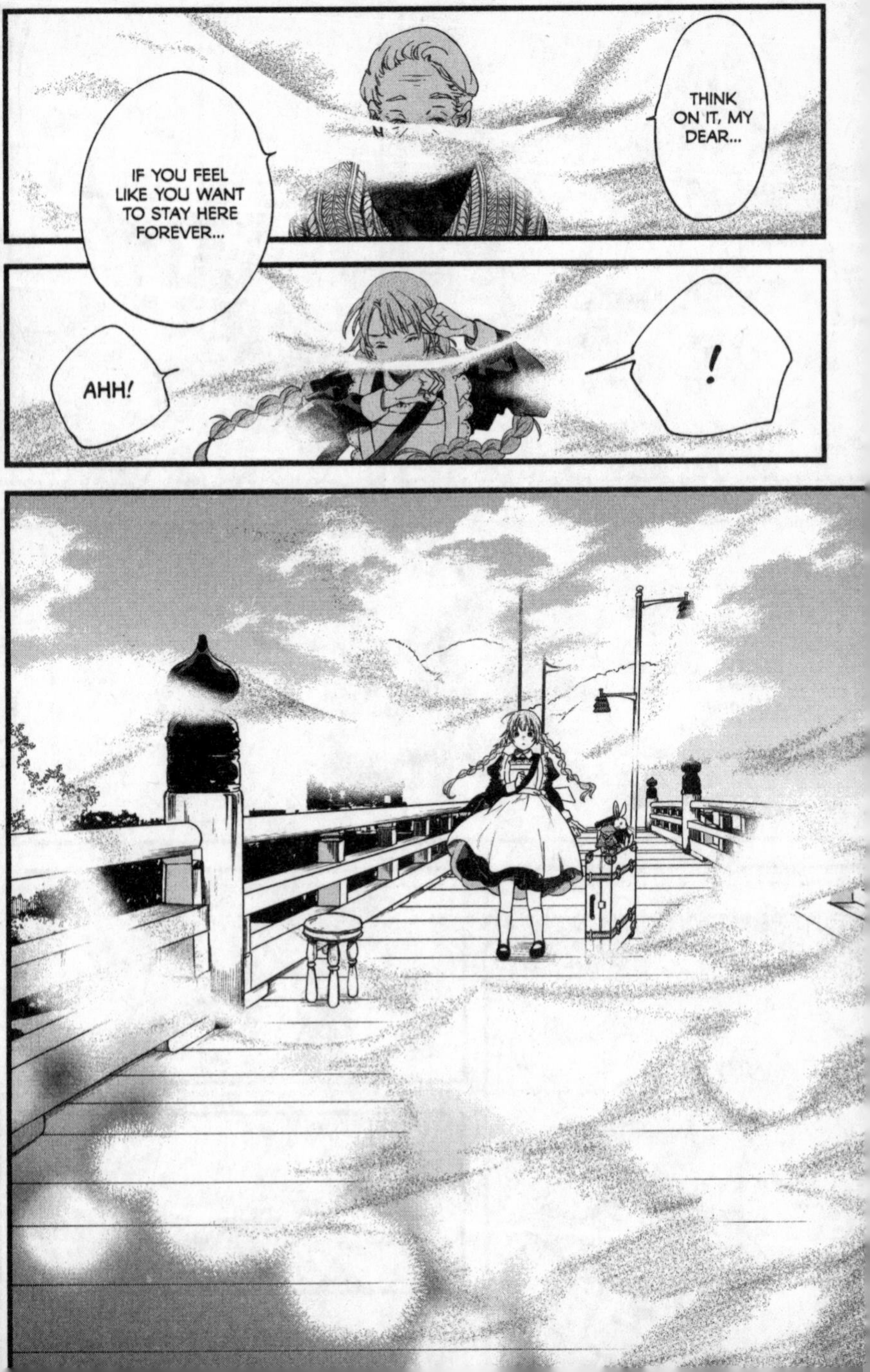
THINK ON IT, MY DEAR...
IF YOU FEEL LIKE YOU WANT TO STAY HERE FOREVER...
!
AHH!

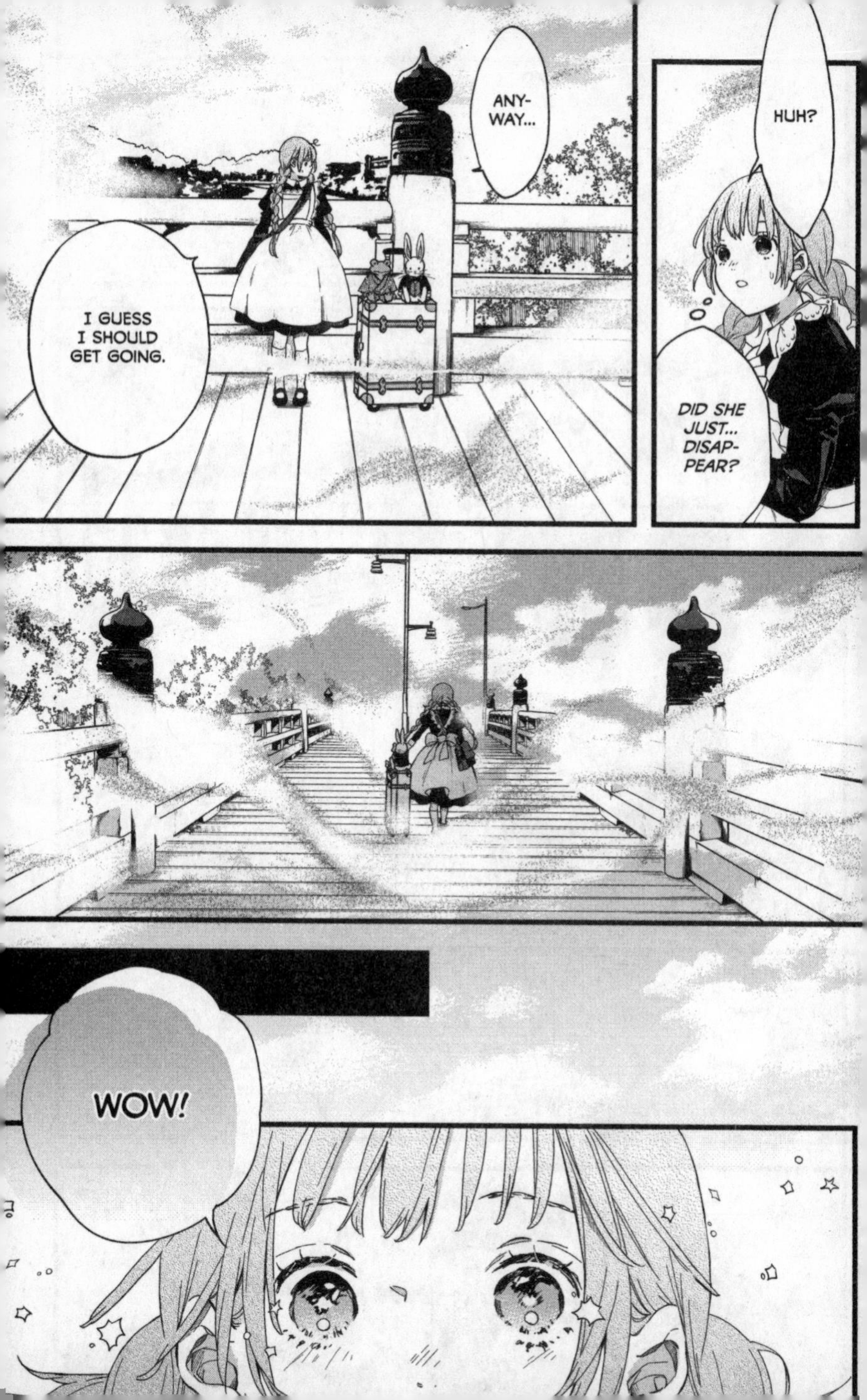
HUH?
DID SHE JUST... DISAPPEAR?
ANY-WAY...
I GUESS I SHOULD GET GOING.
WOW!

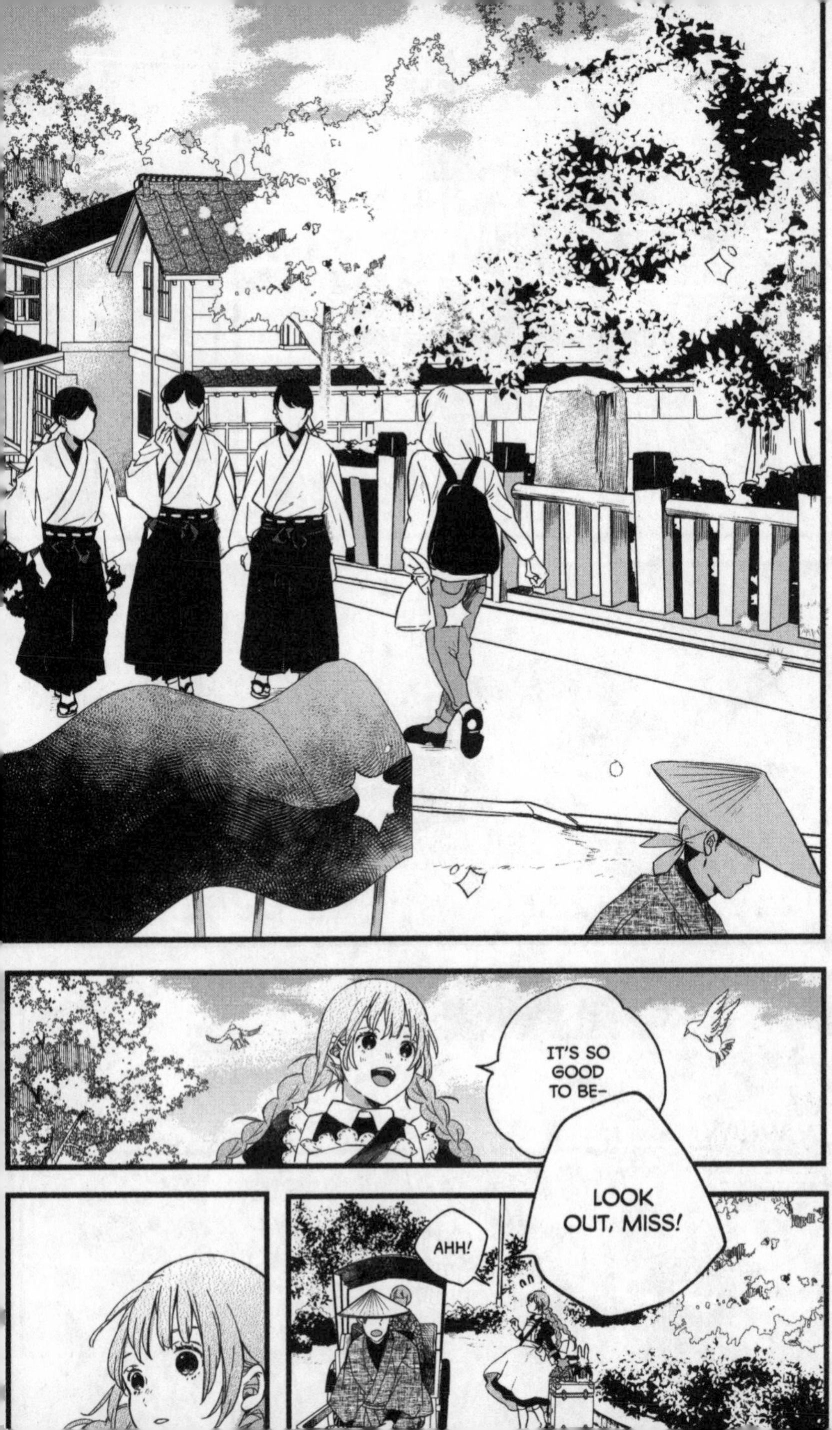
IT'S SO GOOD TO BE-
LOOK OUT, MISS!
AHH!

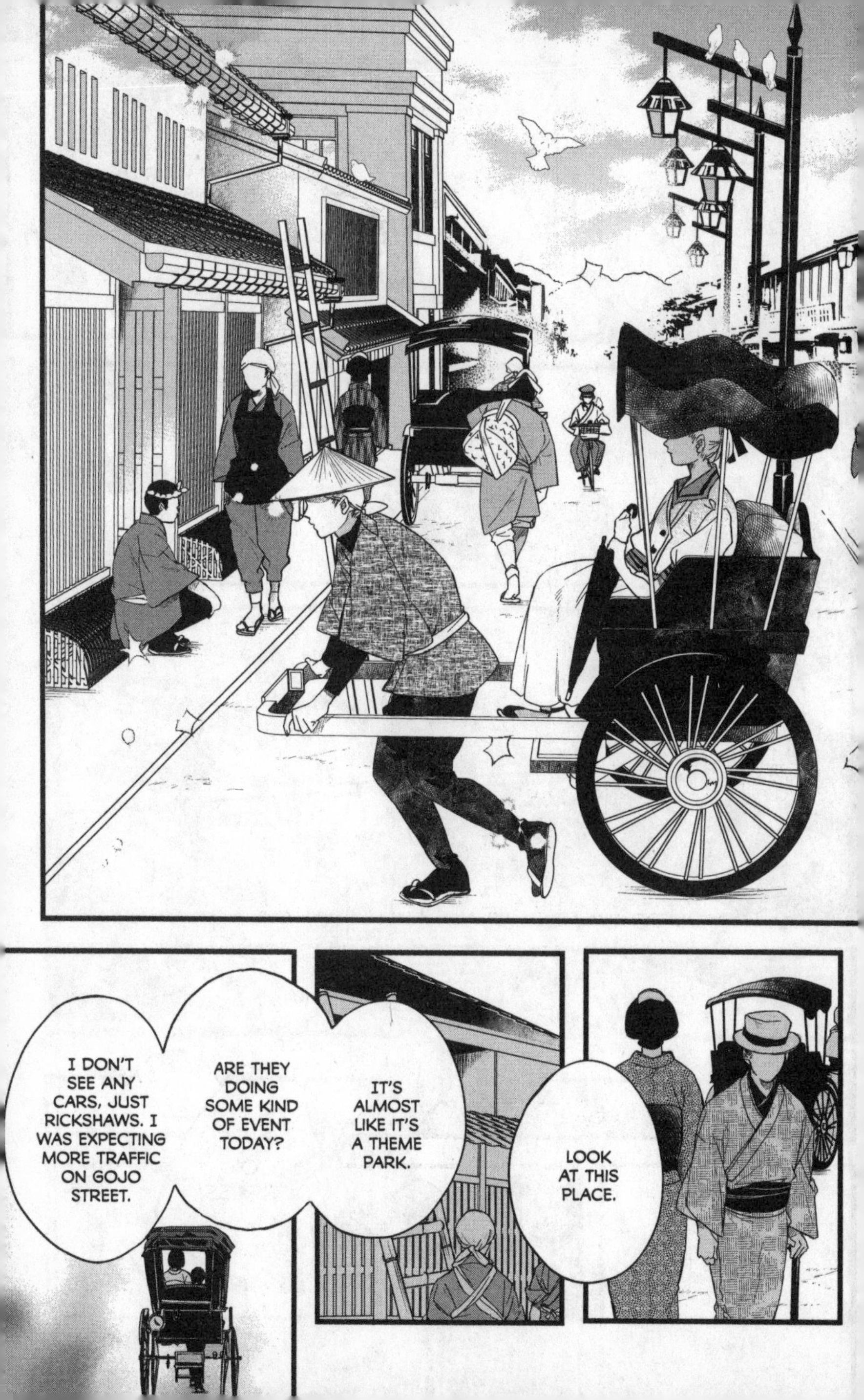
LOOK AT THIS PLACE.
IT'S ALMOST LIKE IT'S A THEME PARK.
ARE THEY DOING SOME KIND OF EVENT TODAY?
I DON'T SEE ANY CARS, JUST RICKSHAWS. I WAS EXPECTING MORE TRAFFIC ON GOJO STREET.

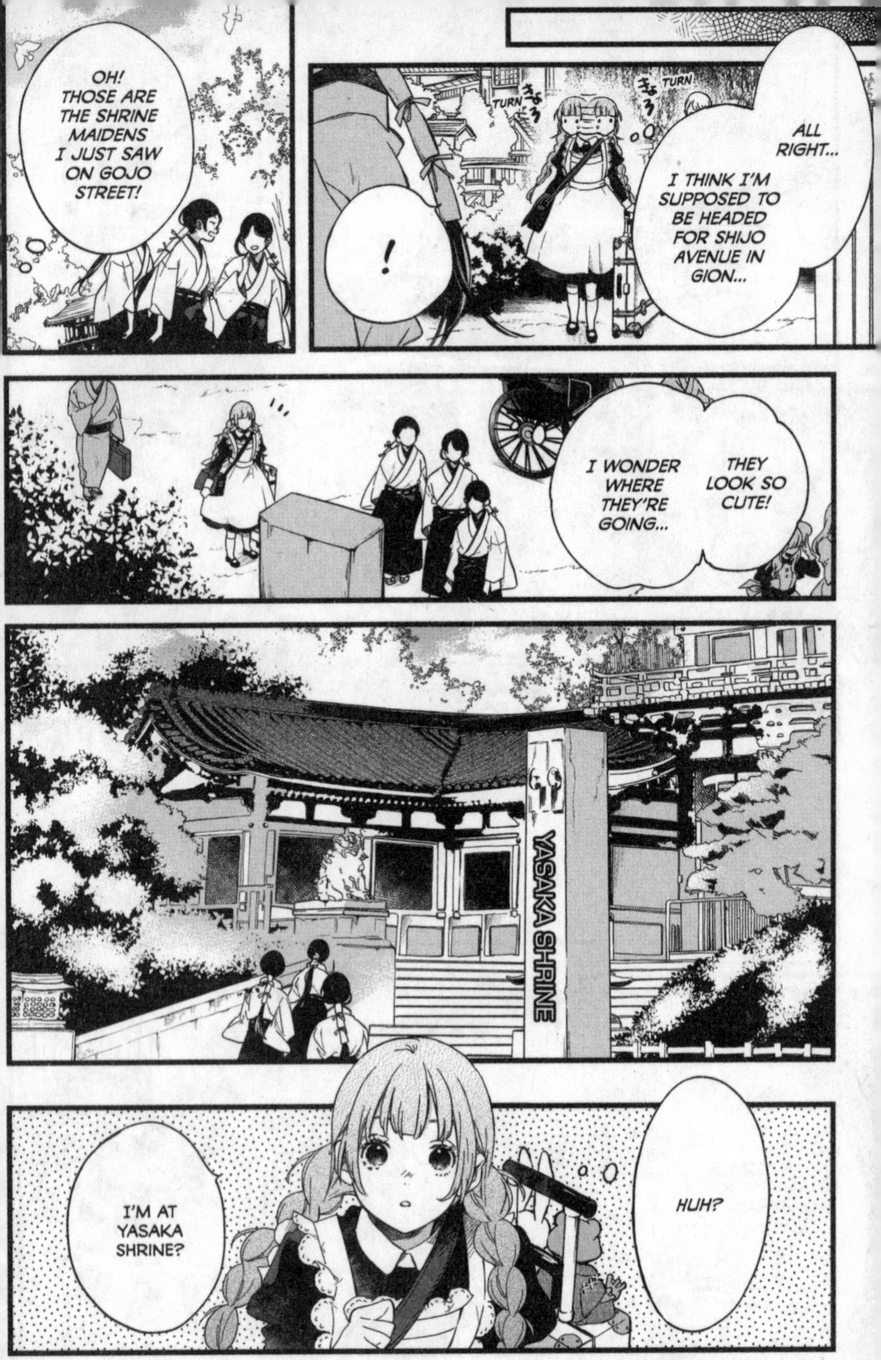

ALL RIGHT...
I THINK I'M SUPPOSED TO BE HEADED FOR SHIJO AVENUE IN GION...
TURN きょろ
TURN きょろ
!
OH! THOSE ARE THE SHRINE MAIDENS I JUST SAW ON GOJO STREET!
THEY LOOK SO CUTE!
I WONDER WHERE THEY'RE GOING...
YASAKA SHRINE
HUH?
I'M AT YASAKA SHRINE?

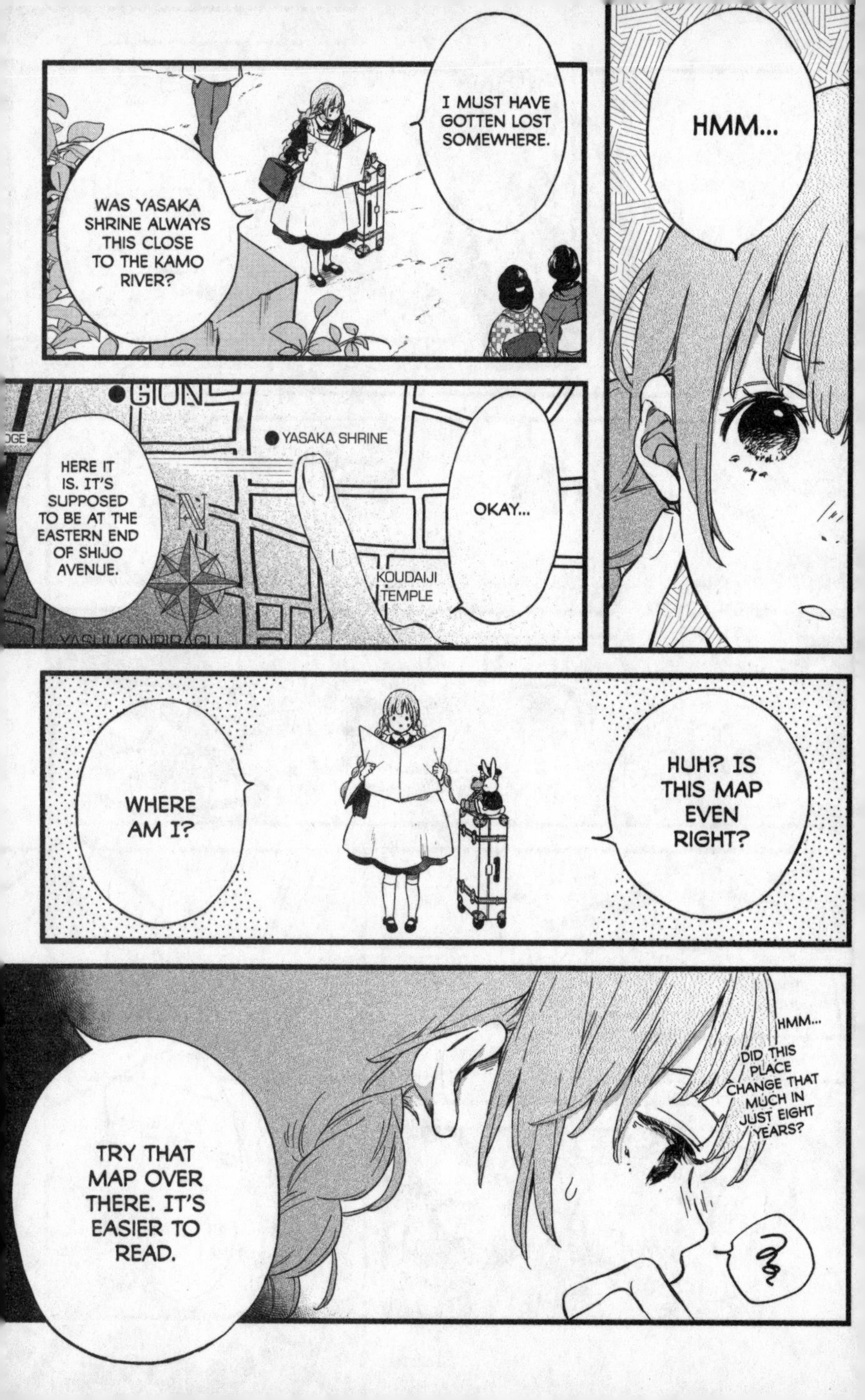
HMM...
I MUST HAVE GOTTEN LOST SOMEWHERE.
WAS YASAKA SHRINE ALWAYS THIS CLOSE TO THE KAMO RIVER?
OKAY...
GION
YASAKA SHRINE
KOUDAIJI TEMPLE
HERE IT IS. IT'S SUPPOSED TO BE AT THE EASTERN END OF SHIJO AVENUE.
HUH? IS THIS MAP EVEN RIGHT?
WHERE AM I?
HMM...
DID THIS PLACE CHANGE THAT MUCH IN JUST EIGHT YEARS?
TRY THAT MAP OVER THERE. IT'S EASIER TO READ.

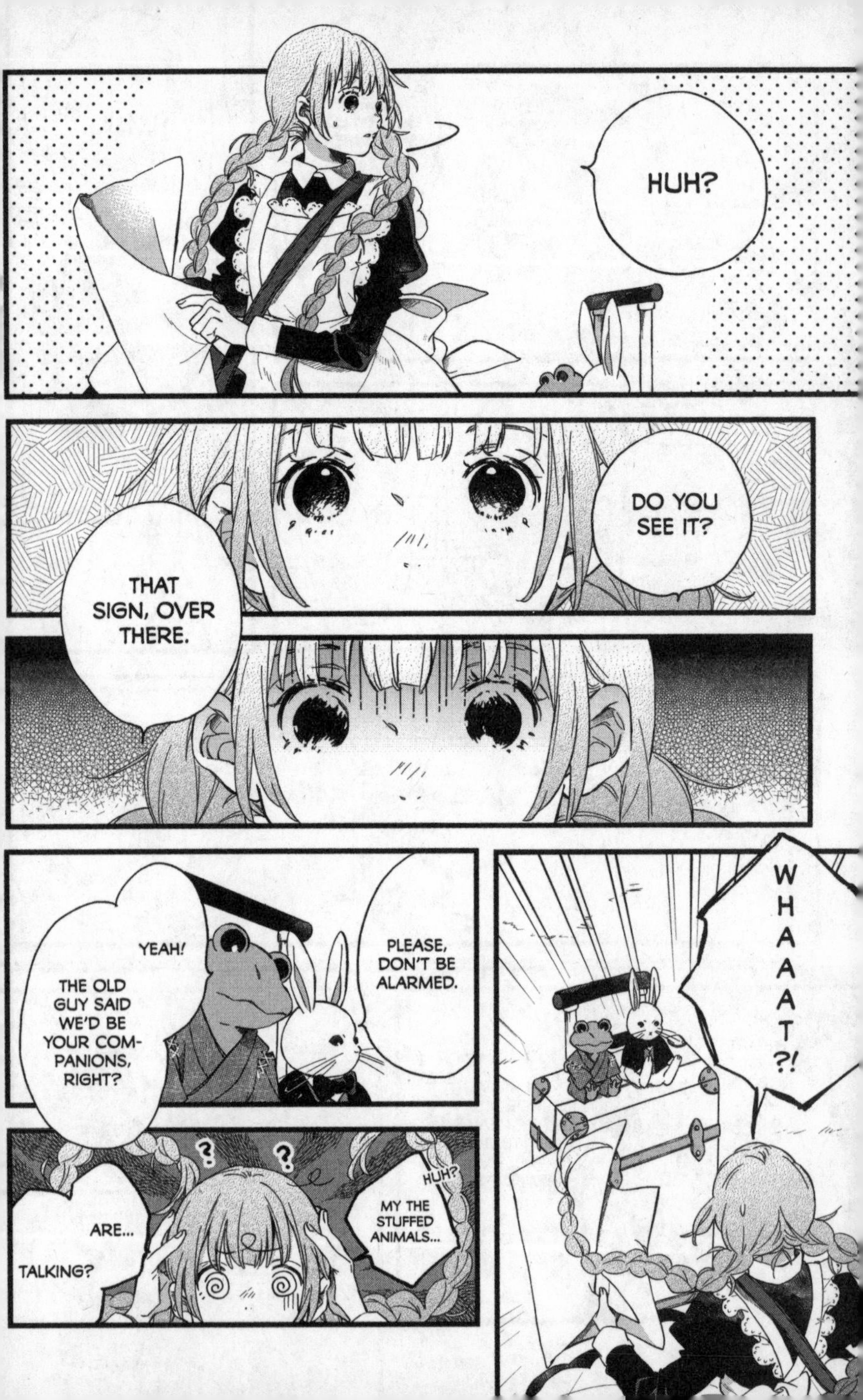
HUH?
DO YOU SEE IT?
THAT SIGN, OVER THERE.
WHAAAT?!
PLEASE, DON'T BE ALARMED.
YEAH!
THE OLD GUY SAID WE'D BE YOUR COMPANIONS, RIGHT?
HUH?
MY THE STUFFED ANIMALS...
ARE...
TALKING?

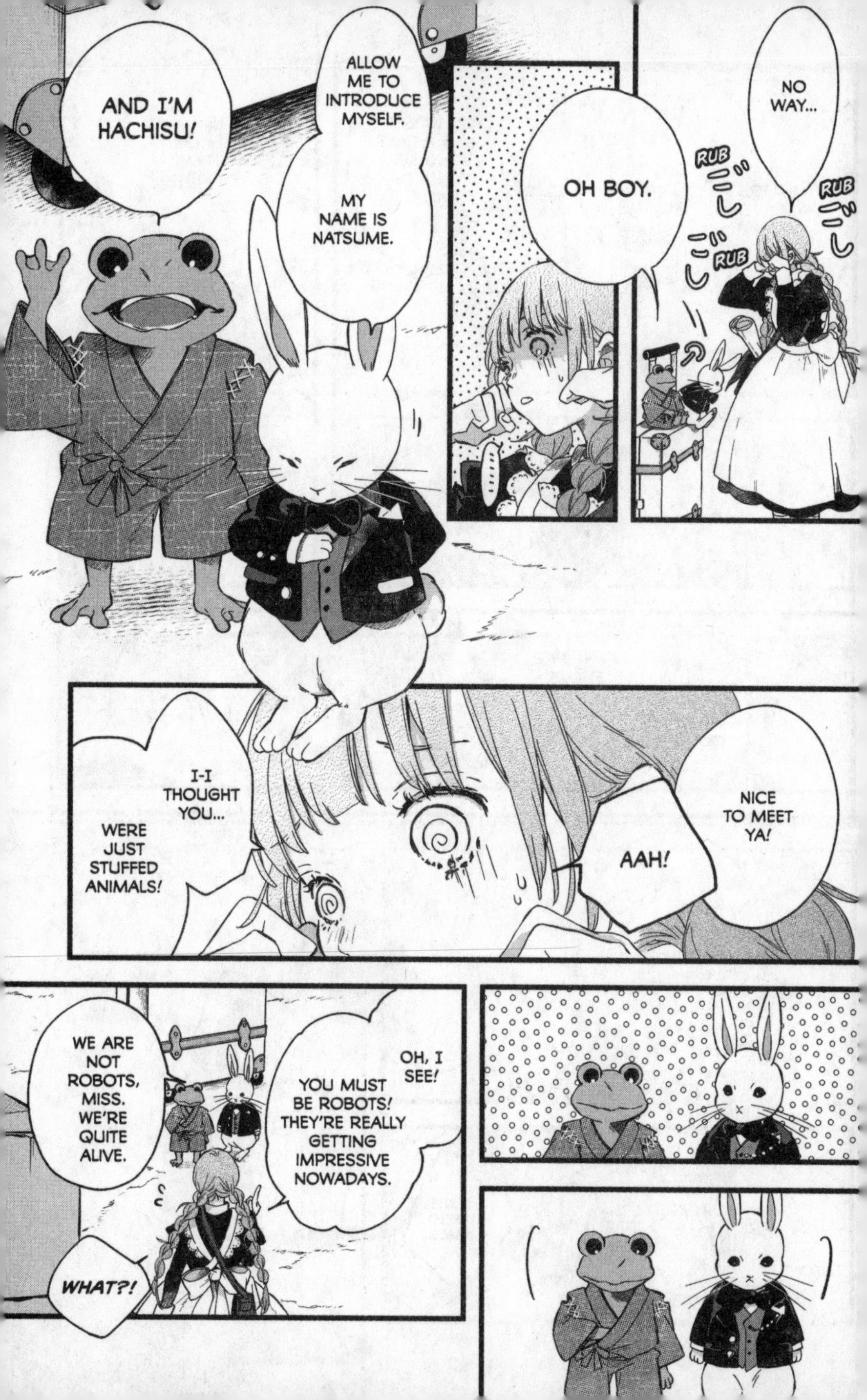
NO WAY...
RUB
RUB
RUB
OH BOY.
ALLOW ME TO INTRODUCE MYSELF.
MY NAME IS NATSUME.
AND I'M HACHISU!
NICE TO MEET YA!
AAH!
I-I THOUGHT YOU...
WERE JUST STUFFED ANIMALS!
OH, I SEE!
YOU MUST BE ROBOTS! THEY'RE REALLY GETTING IMPRESSIVE NOWADAYS.
WE ARE NOT ROBOTS, MISS. WE'RE QUITE ALIVE.
WHAT?!

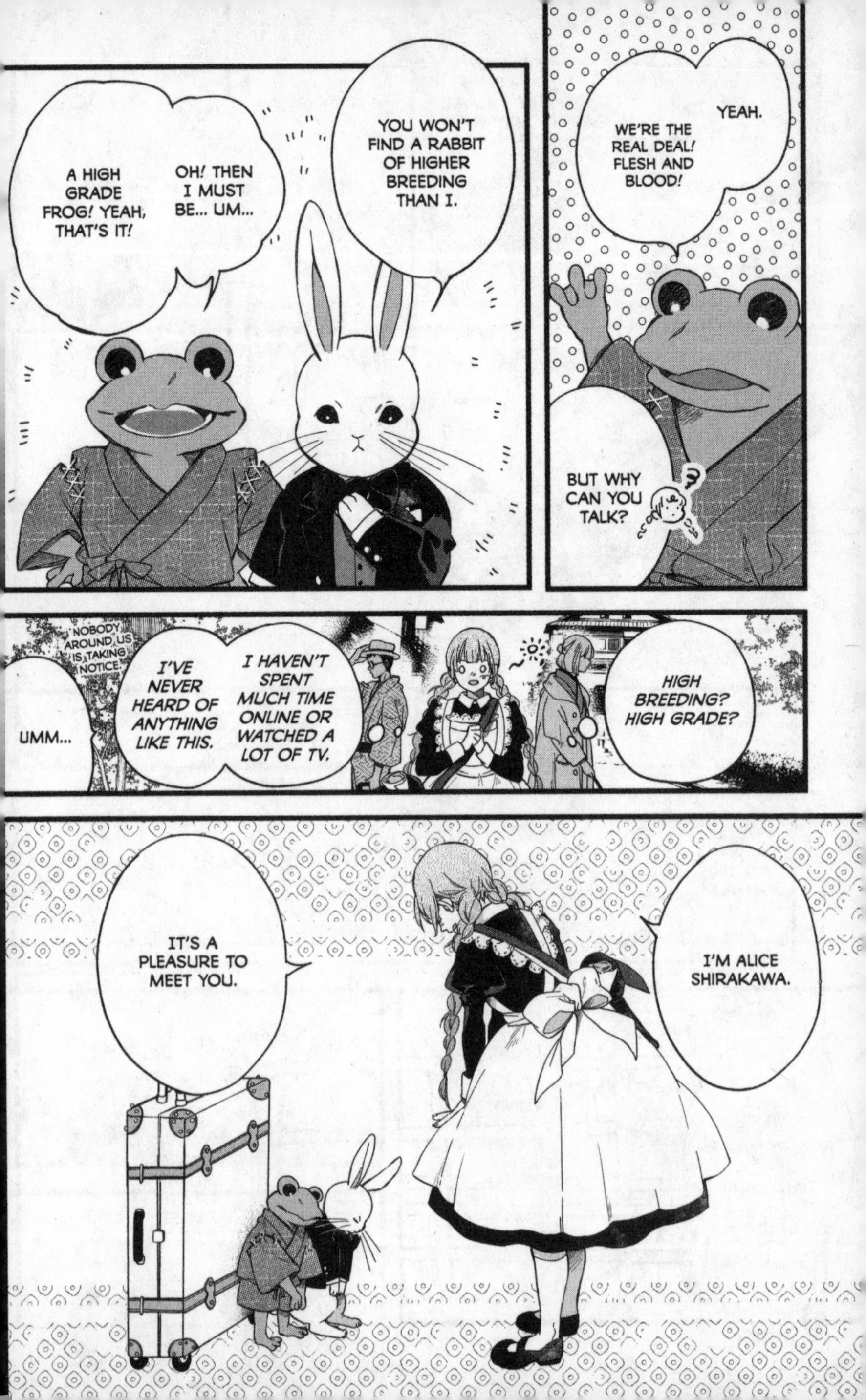
YEAH.
WE'RE THE REAL DEAL! FLESH AND BLOOD!
BUT WHY CAN YOU TALK?
YOU WON'T FIND A RABBIT OF HIGHER BREEDING THAN I.
OH! THEN I MUST BE... UM...
A HIGH GRADE FROG! YEAH, THAT'S IT!
HIGH BREEDING? HIGH GRADE?
I HAVEN'T SPENT MUCH TIME ONLINE OR WATCHED A LOT OF TV.
I'VE NEVER HEARD OF ANYTHING LIKE THIS.
NOBODY AROUND US IS TAKING NOTICE.
UMM...
I'M ALICE SHIRAKAWA.
IT'S A PLEASURE TO MEET YOU.

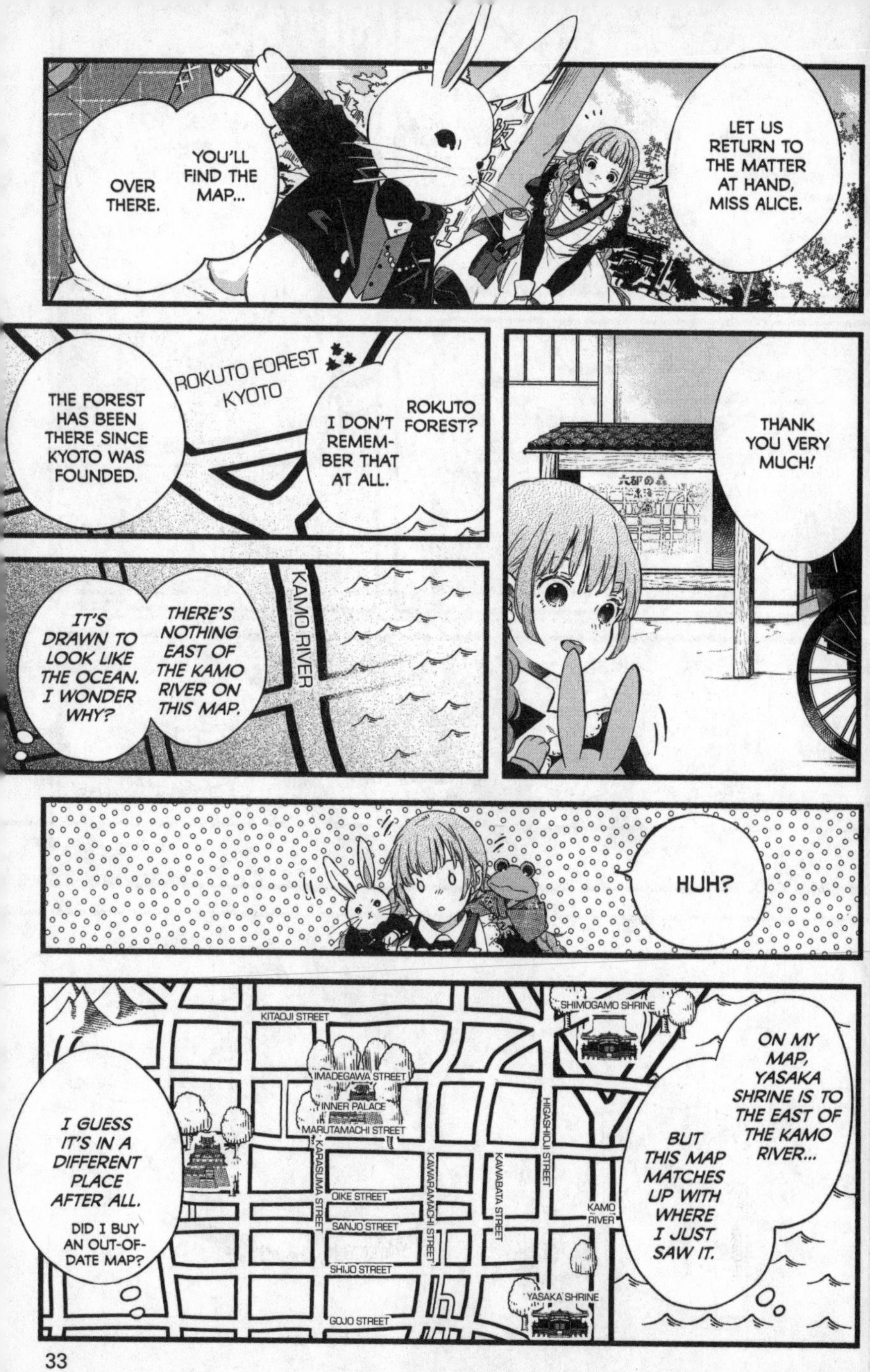
LET US RETURN TO THE MATTER AT HAND, MISS ALICE.
YOU'LL FIND THE MAP...
OVER THERE.
THANK YOU VERY MUCH!
ROKUTO FOREST?
I DON'T REMEMBER THAT AT ALL.
ROKUTO FOREST KYOTO
THE FOREST HAS BEEN THERE SINCE KYOTO WAS FOUNDED.
KAMO RIVER
THERE'S NOTHING EAST OF THE KAMO RIVER ON THIS MAP.
IT'S DRAWN TO LOOK LIKE THE OCEAN. I WONDER WHY?
HUH?
ON MY MAP, YASAKA SHRINE IS TO THE EAST OF THE KAMO RIVER...
BUT THIS MAP MATCHES UP WITH WHERE I JUST SAW IT.
SHIMOGAMO SHRINE
KITAOJI STREET
IMADEGAWA STREET
INNER PALACE
MARUTAMACHI STREET
HIGASHIOJI STREET
KAWABATA STREET
KAWARAMACHI STREET
KARASUMA STREET
OIKE STREET
SANJO STREET
SHIJO STREET
GOJO STREET
KAMO RIVER
YASAKA SHRINE
I GUESS IT'S IN A DIFFERENT PLACE AFTER ALL.
DID I BUY AN OUT-OF-DATE MAP?

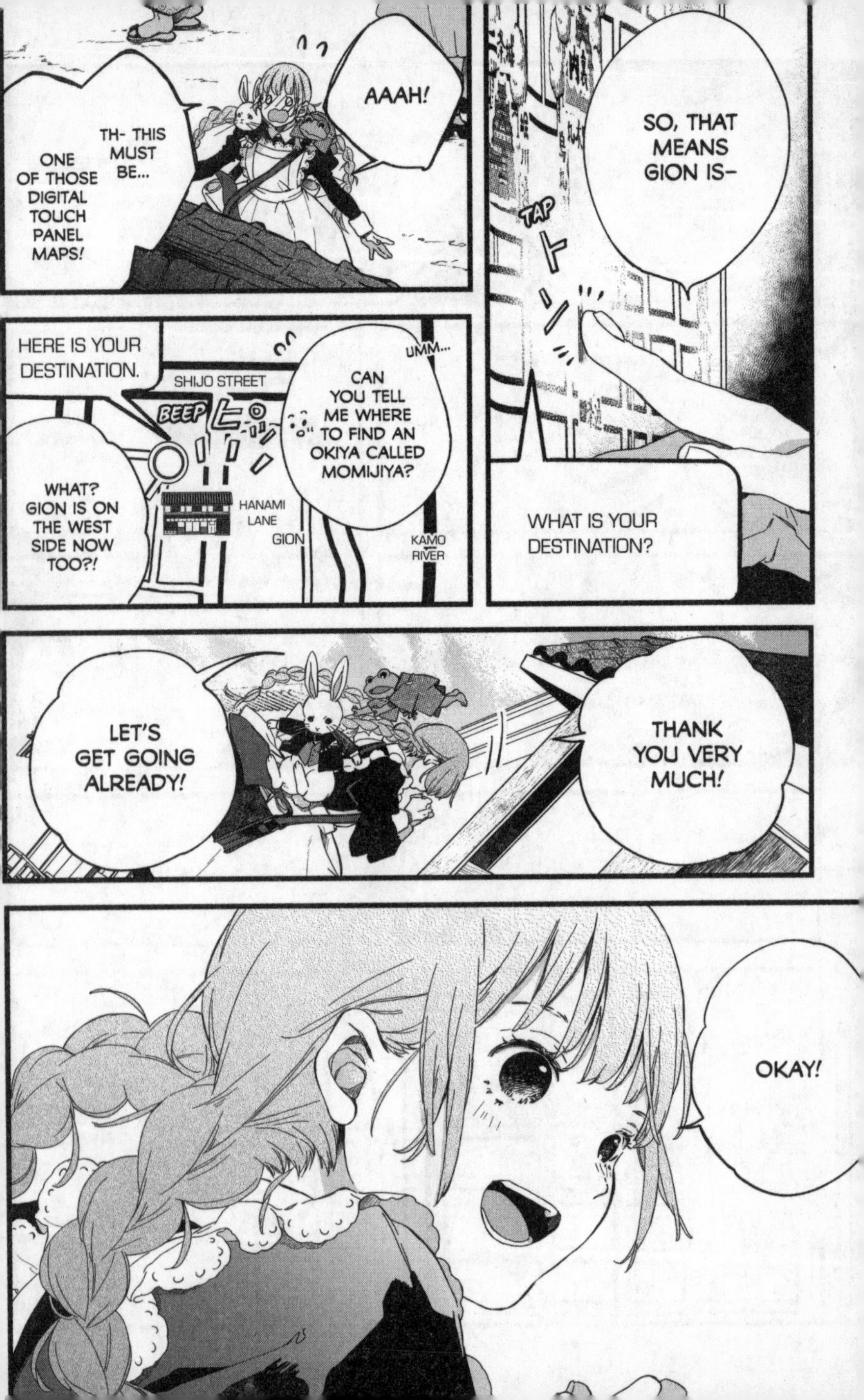
SO, THAT MEANS GION IS–
TAP
WHAT IS YOUR DESTINATION?
AAAH!
TH- THIS MUST BE...
ONE OF THOSE DIGITAL TOUCH PANEL MAPS!
UMM...
CAN YOU TELL ME WHERE TO FIND AN OKIYA CALLED MOMIJIYA?
BEEP
HERE IS YOUR DESTINATION.
SHIJO STREET
HANAMI LANE
GION
KAMO RIVER
WHAT? GION IS ON THE WEST SIDE NOW TOO?!
THANK YOU VERY MUCH!
LET'S GET GOING ALREADY!
OKAY!

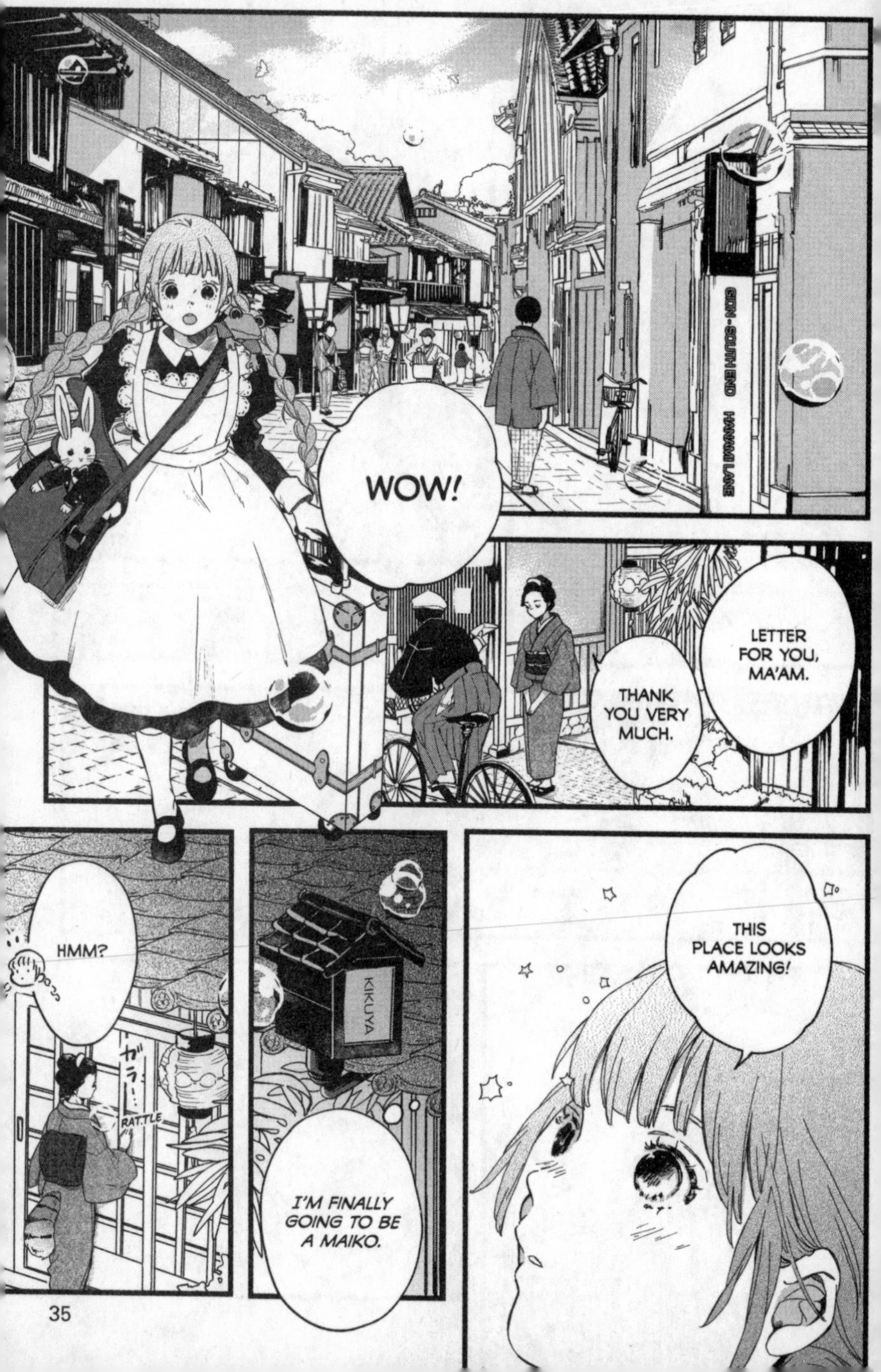
GION-SOUTH END HANAMI LANE
WOW!
LETTER FOR YOU, MA'AM.
THANK YOU VERY MUCH.
THIS PLACE LOOKS AMAZING!
KIKUYA
I'M FINALLY GOING TO BE A MAIKO.
HMM?
ガラ…
RATTLE

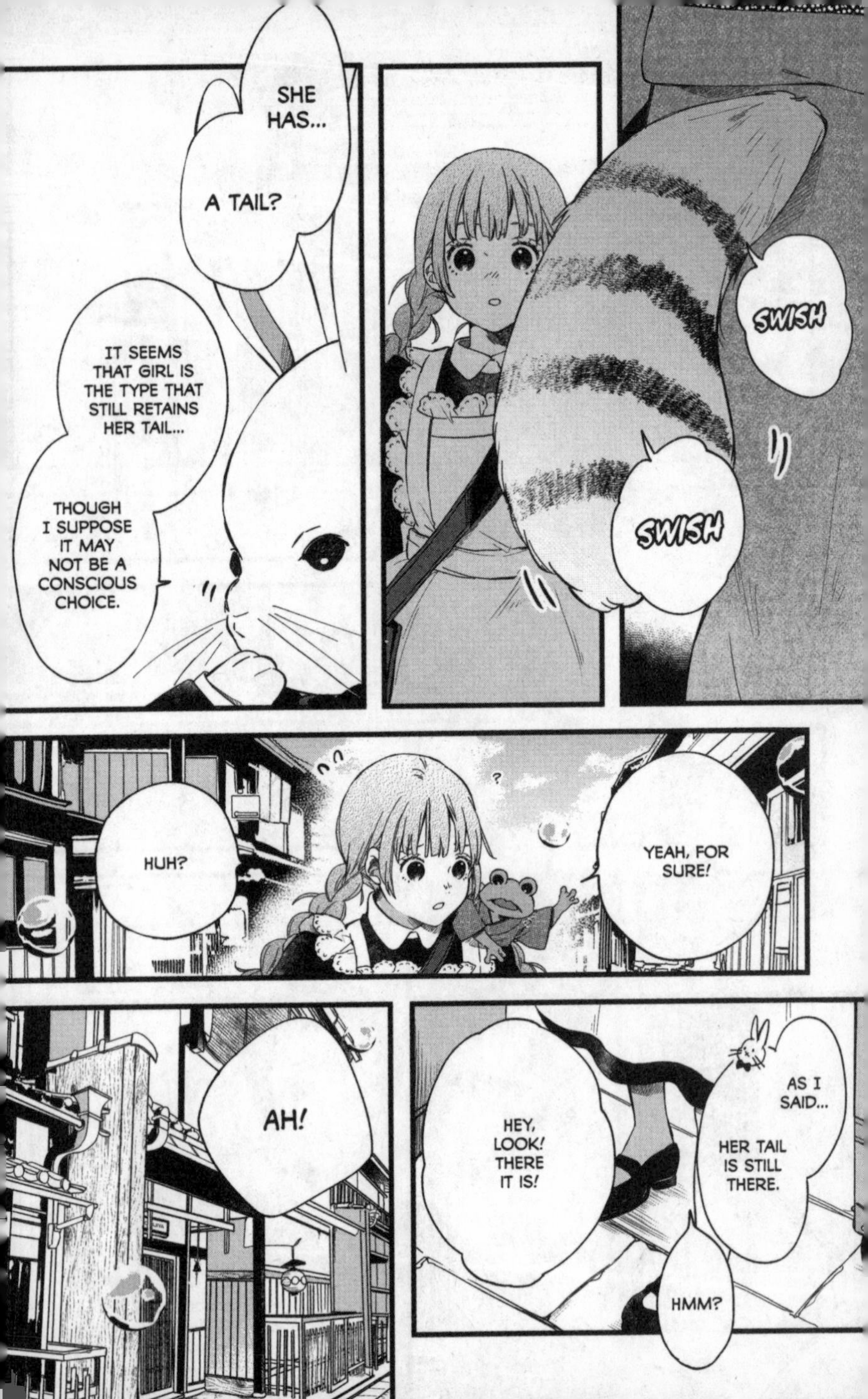
SWISH
SWISH
SHE HAS... A TAIL?
IT SEEMS THAT GIRL IS THE TYPE THAT STILL RETAINS HER TAIL...
THOUGH I SUPPOSE IT MAY NOT BE A CONSCIOUS CHOICE.
YEAH, FOR SURE!
HUH?
AS I SAID... HER TAIL IS STILL THERE.
HEY, LOOK! THERE IT IS!
HMM?
AH!

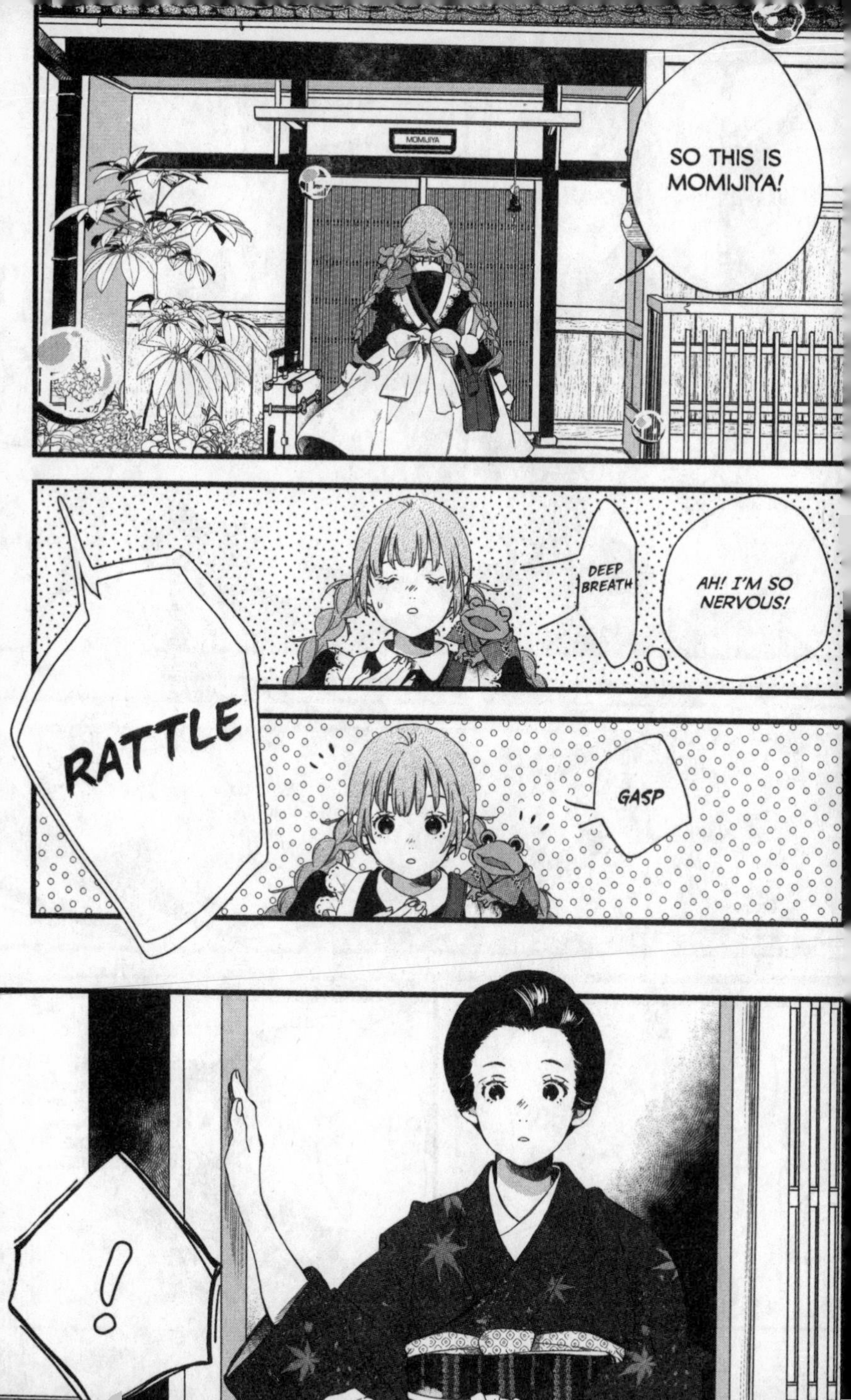
MOMIJIYA
SO THIS IS MOMIJIYA!
AH! I'M SO NERVOUS!
DEEP BREATH
GASP
RATTLE
!

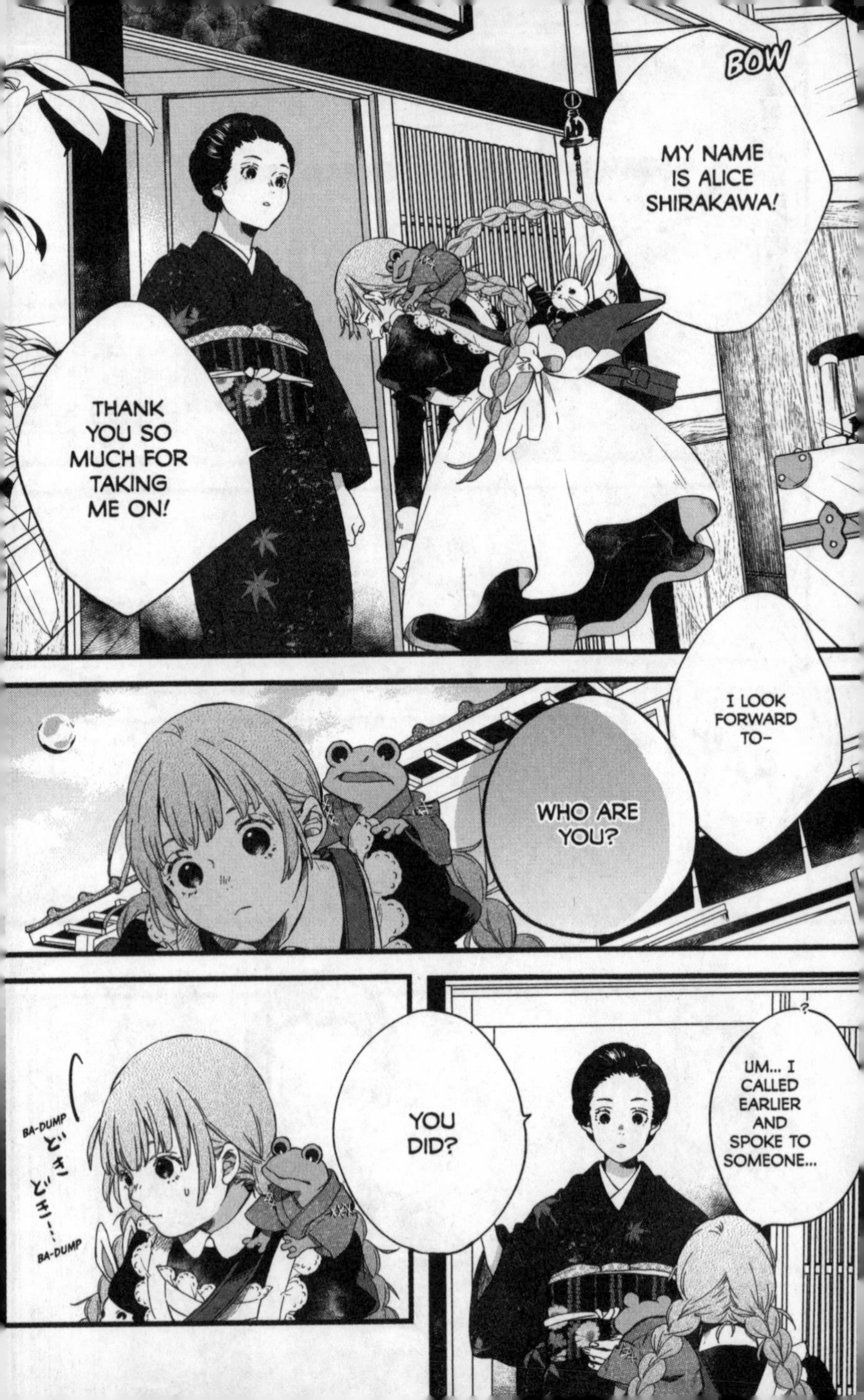
BOW
MY NAME IS ALICE SHIRAKAWA!
THANK YOU SO MUCH FOR TAKING ME ON!
I LOOK FORWARD TO–
WHO ARE YOU?
?
UM... I CALLED EARLIER AND SPOKE TO SOMEONE...
YOU DID?
BA-DUMP
BA-DUMP

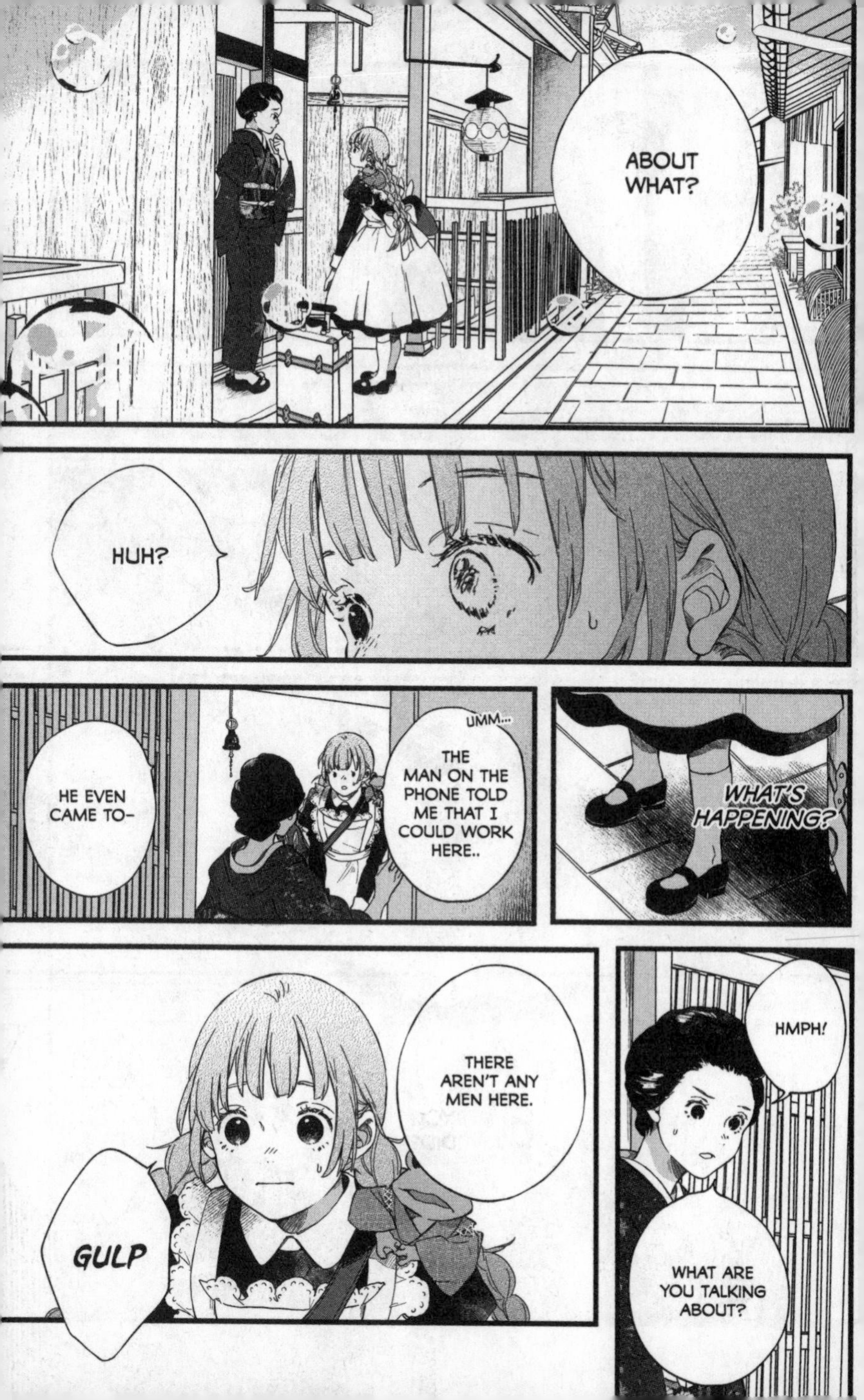
ABOUT WHAT?
HUH?
WHAT'S HAPPENING?
UMM...
THE MAN ON THE PHONE TOLD ME THAT I COULD WORK HERE..
HE EVEN CAME TO-
HMPH!
WHAT ARE YOU TALKING ABOUT?
THERE AREN'T ANY MEN HERE.
GULP

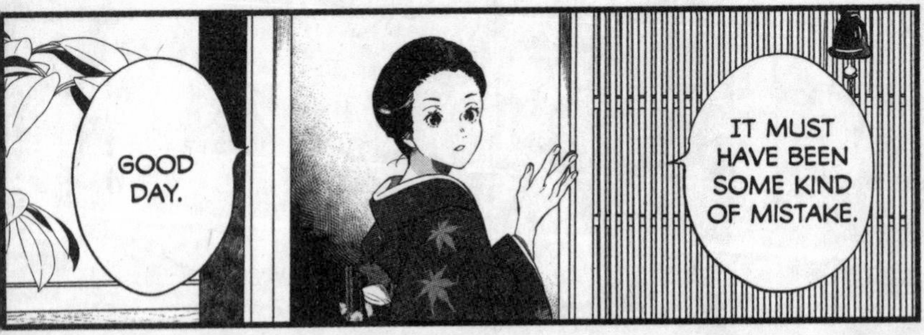
IT MUST HAVE BEEN SOME KIND OF MISTAKE.
GOOD DAY.
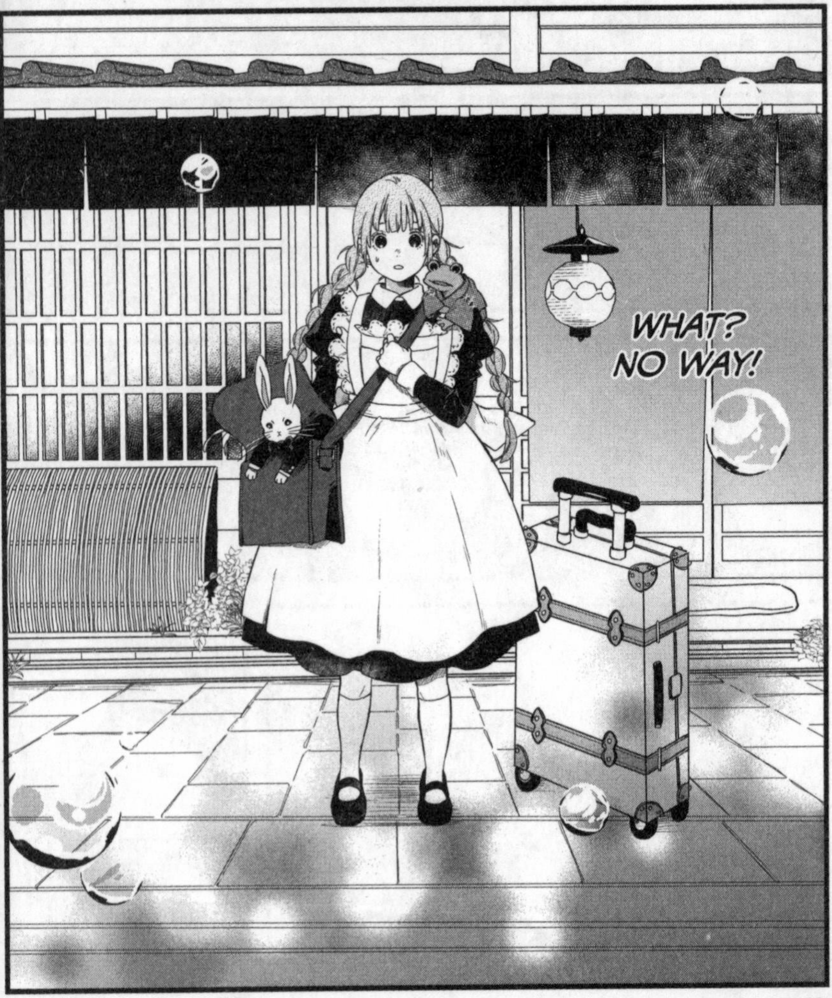
WHAT? NO WAY!

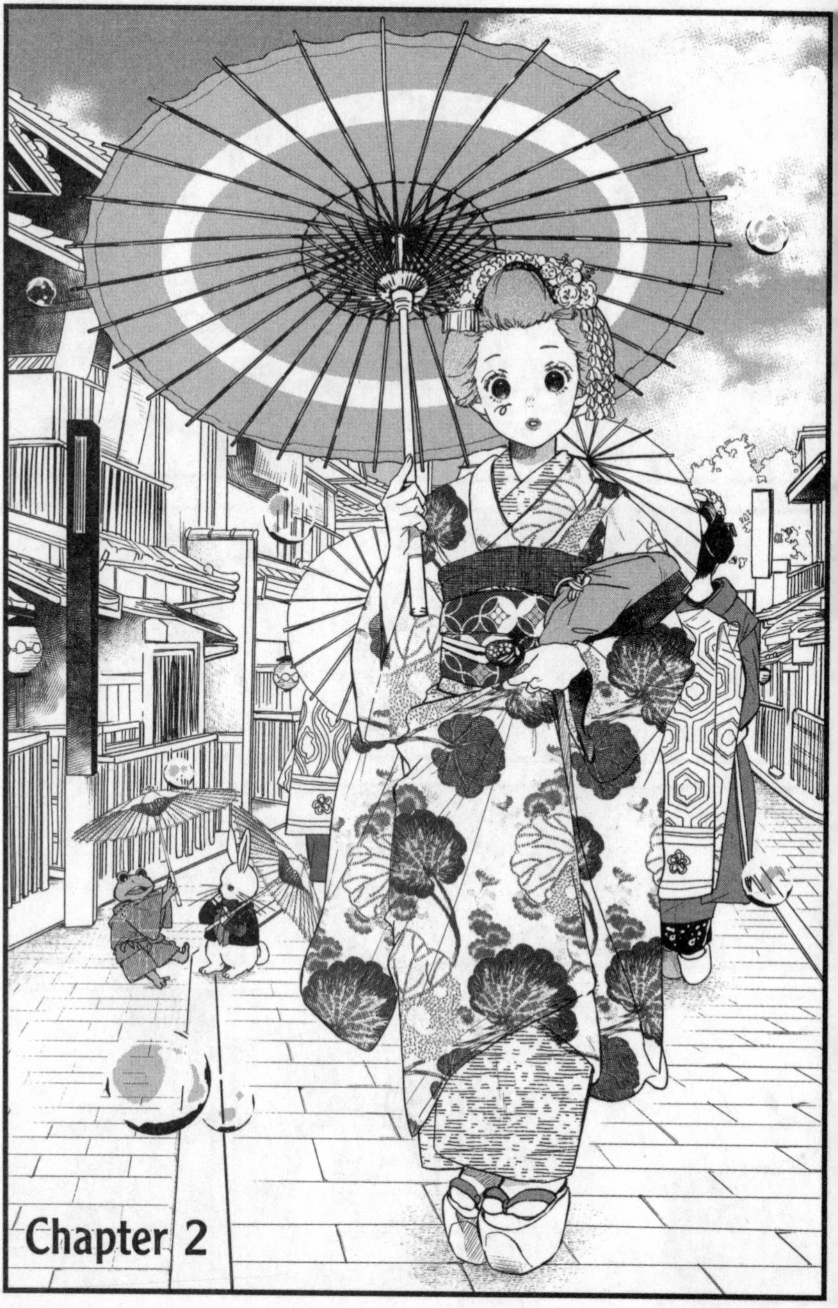
Chapter 2

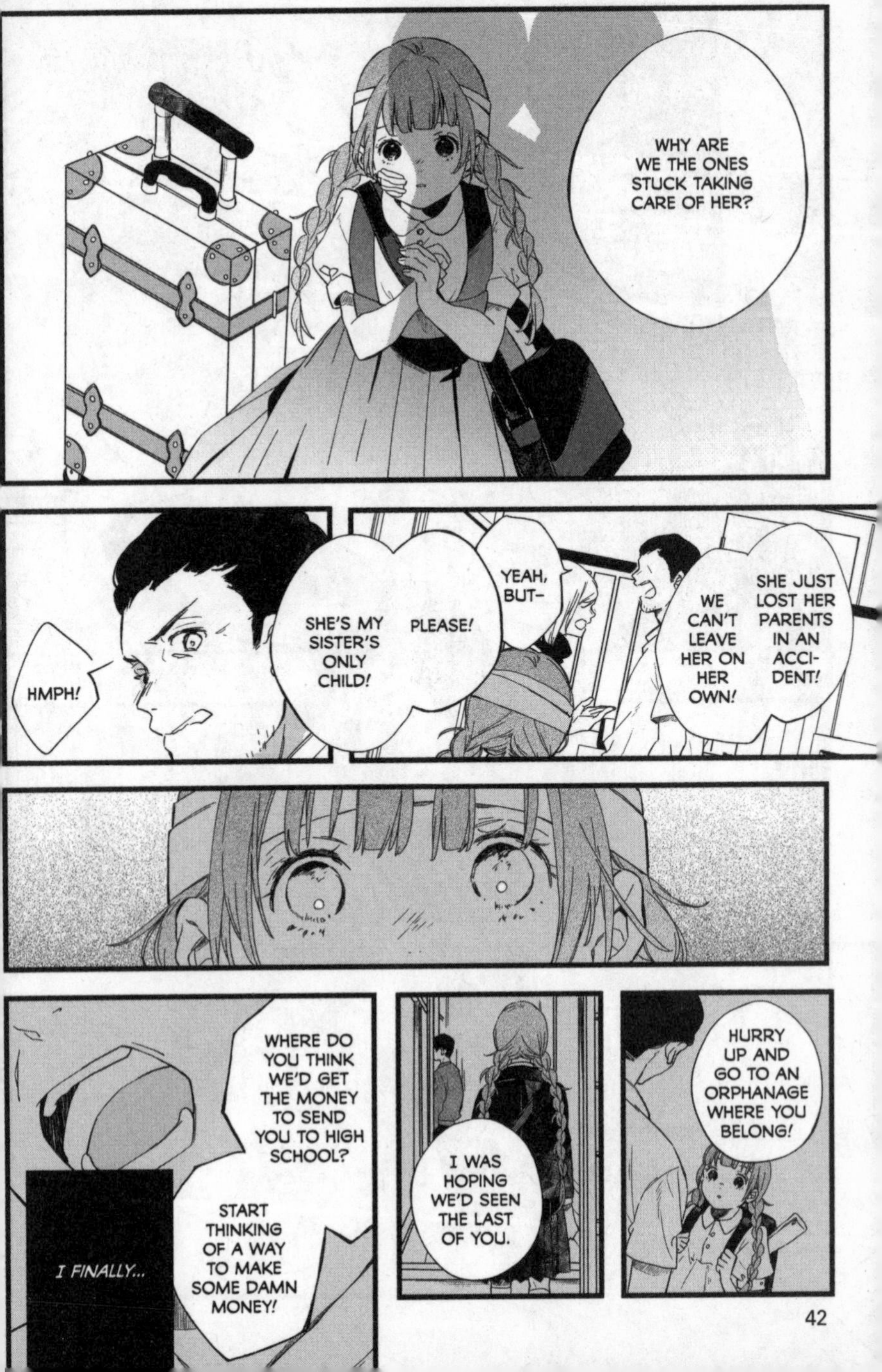
WHY ARE WE THE ONES STUCK TAKING CARE OF HER?
SHE JUST LOST HER PARENTS IN AN ACCIDENT!
WE CAN'T LEAVE HER ON HER OWN!
YEAH, BUT-
PLEASE!
SHE'S MY SISTER'S ONLY CHILD!
HMPH!
HURRY UP AND GO TO AN ORPHANAGE WHERE YOU BELONG!
I WAS HOPING WE'D SEEN THE LAST OF YOU.
WHERE DO YOU THINK WE'D GET THE MONEY TO SEND YOU TO HIGH SCHOOL?
START THINKING OF A WAY TO MAKE SOME DAMN MONEY!
I FINALLY...

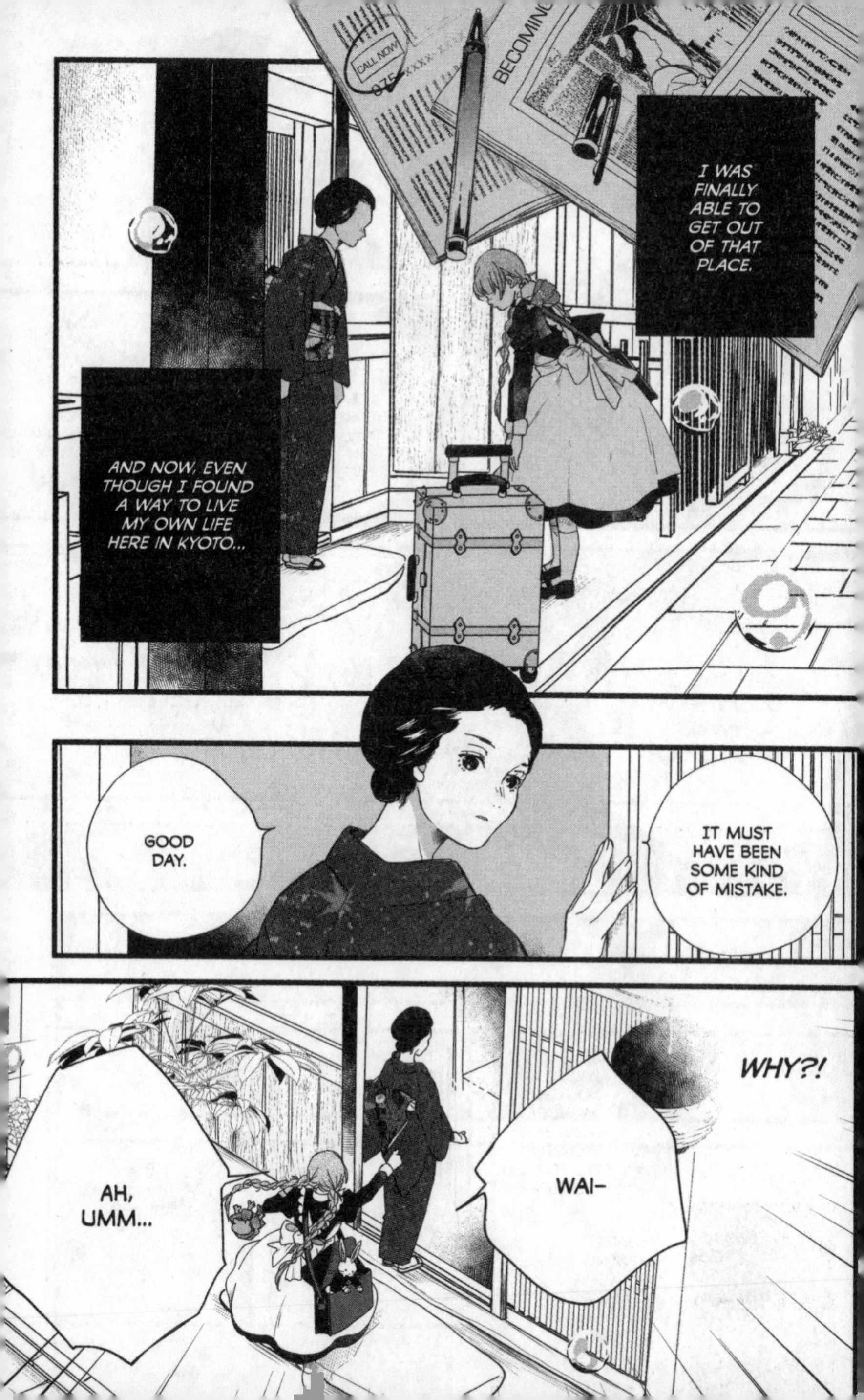
CALL NOW
BECOMING
I WAS FINALLY ABLE TO GET OUT OF THAT PLACE.
AND NOW, EVEN THOUGH I FOUND A WAY TO LIVE MY OWN LIFE HERE IN KYOTO...
IT MUST HAVE BEEN SOME KIND OF MISTAKE.
GOOD DAY.
WHY?!
WAI–
AH, UMM...

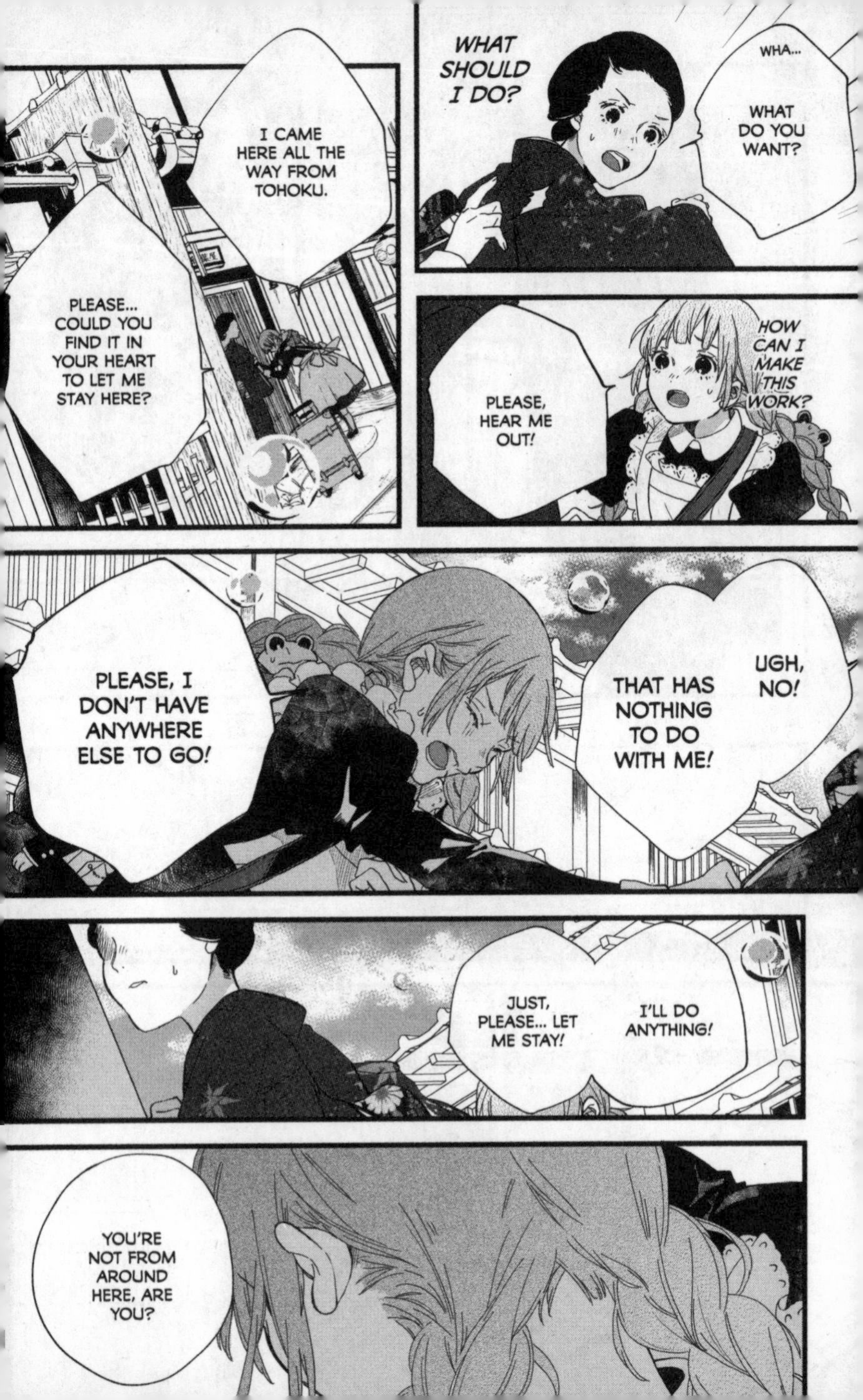
WHA... WHAT DO YOU WANT?
WHAT SHOULD I DO?
HOW CAN I MAKE THIS WORK?
PLEASE, HEAR ME OUT!
I CAME HERE ALL THE WAY FROM TOHOKU.
PLEASE... COULD YOU FIND IT IN YOUR HEART TO LET ME STAY HERE?
UGH, NO! THAT HAS NOTHING TO DO WITH ME!
PLEASE, I DON'T HAVE ANYWHERE ELSE TO GO!
I'LL DO ANYTHING! JUST, PLEASE... LET ME STAY!
YOU'RE NOT FROM AROUND HERE, ARE YOU?

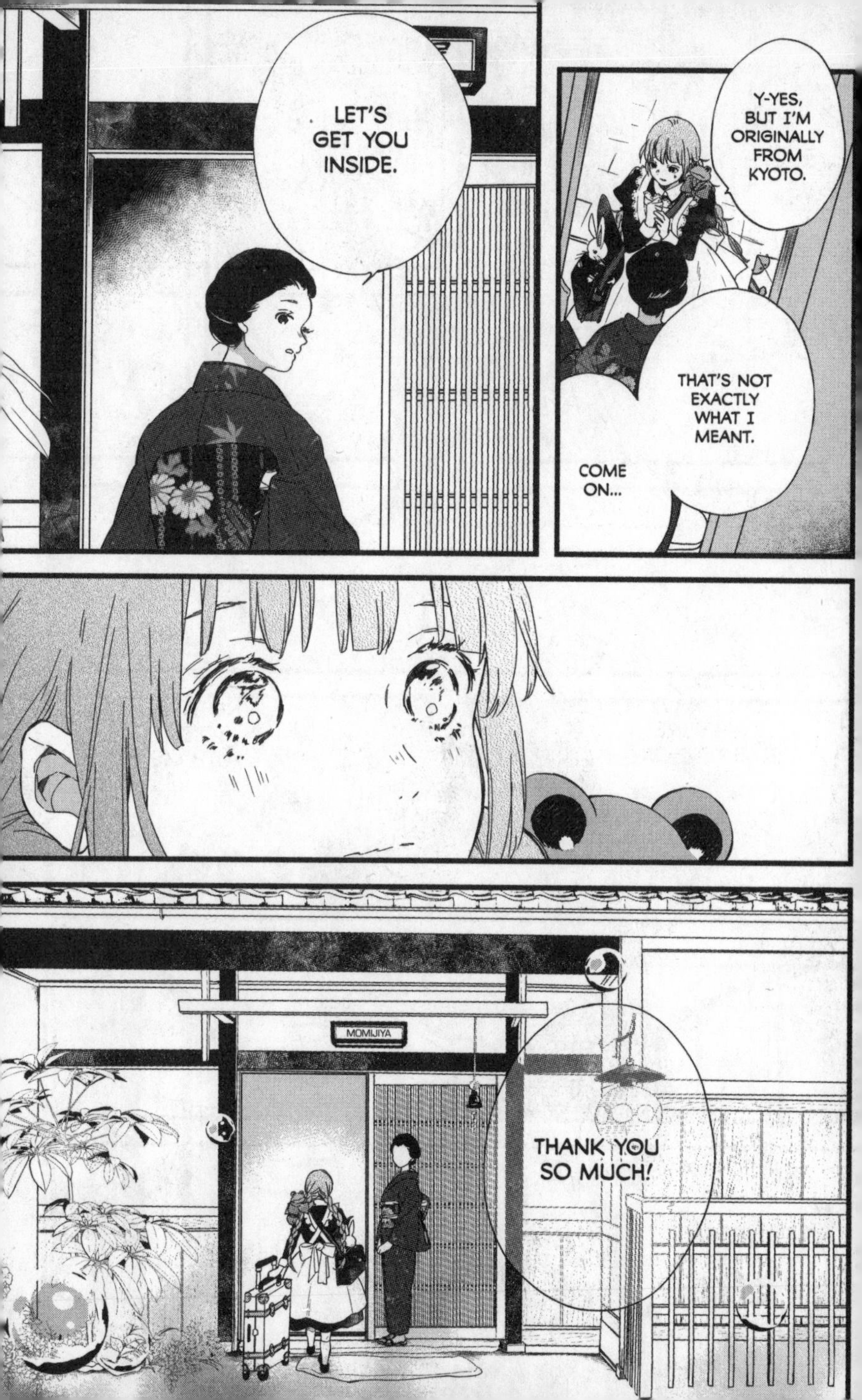
Y-YES, BUT I'M ORIGINALLY FROM KYOTO.
THAT'S NOT EXACTLY WHAT I MEANT.
COME ON...
LET'S GET YOU INSIDE.
MOMIJIYA
THANK YOU SO MUCH!

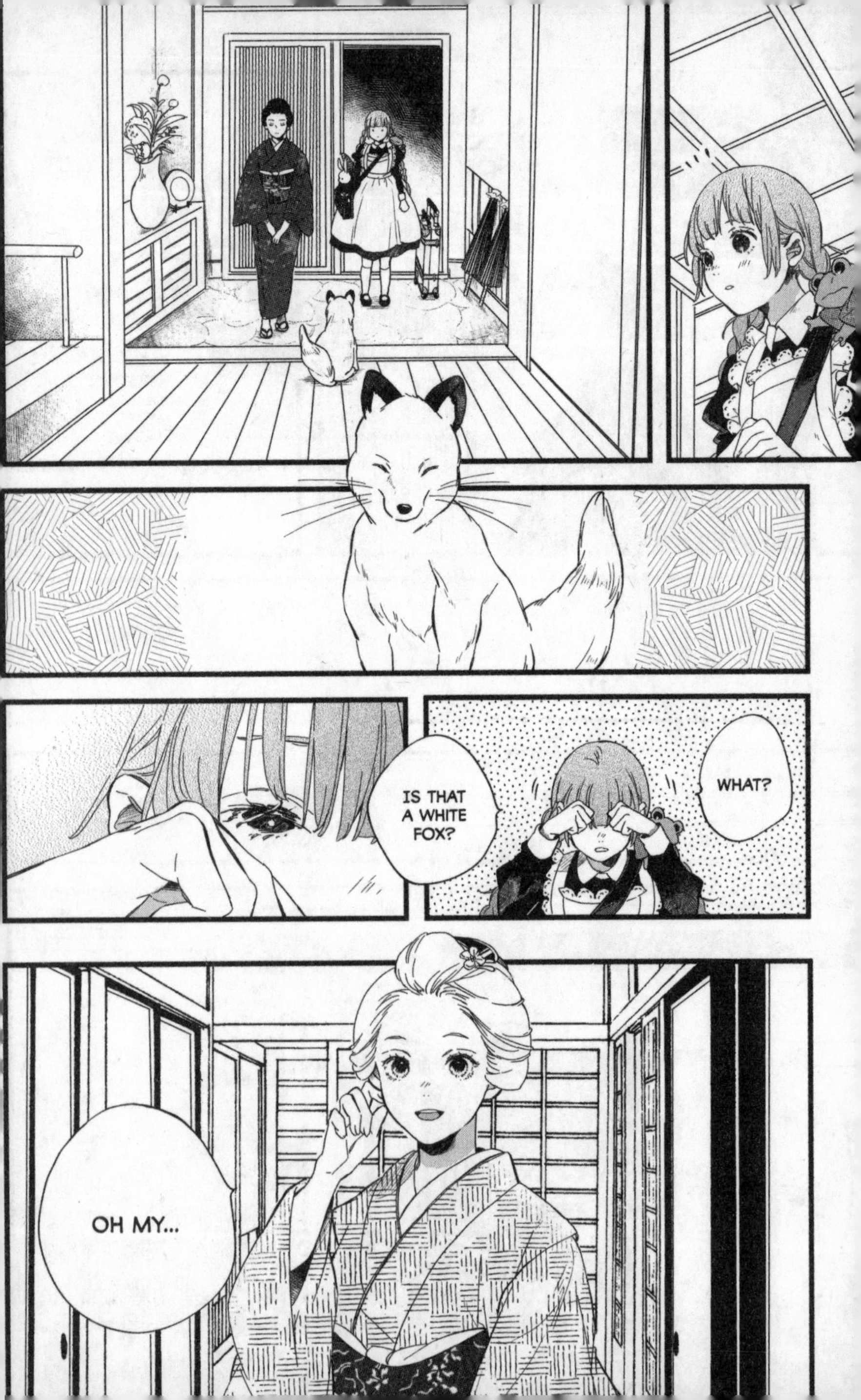
WHAT?
IS THAT A WHITE FOX?
OH MY...

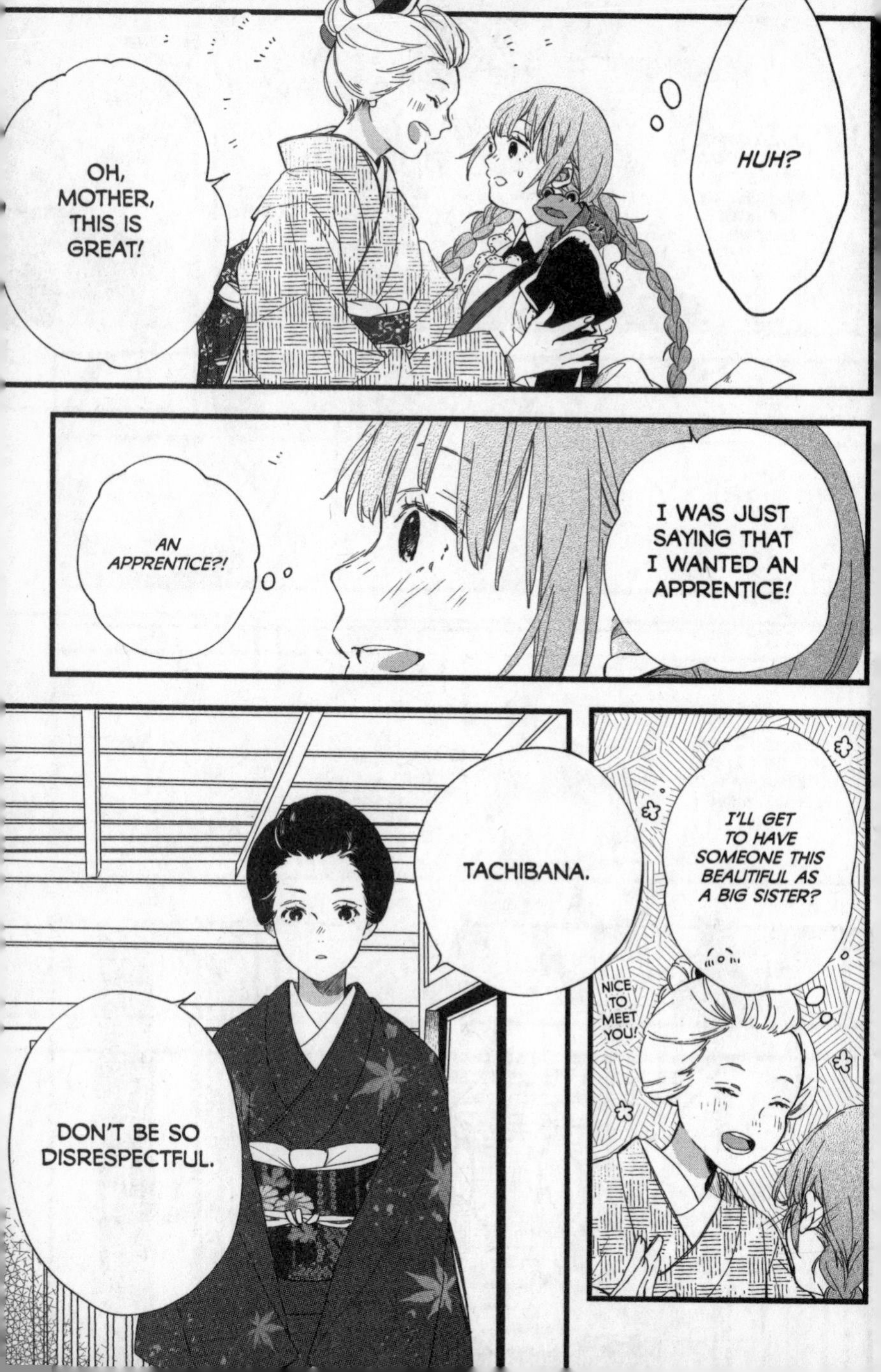
HUH?
OH, MOTHER, THIS IS GREAT!
I WAS JUST SAYING THAT I WANTED AN APPRENTICE!
AN APPRENTICE?!
I'LL GET TO HAVE SOMEONE THIS BEAUTIFUL AS A BIG SISTER?
NICE TO MEET YOU!
TACHIBANA.
DON'T BE SO DISRESPECTFUL.

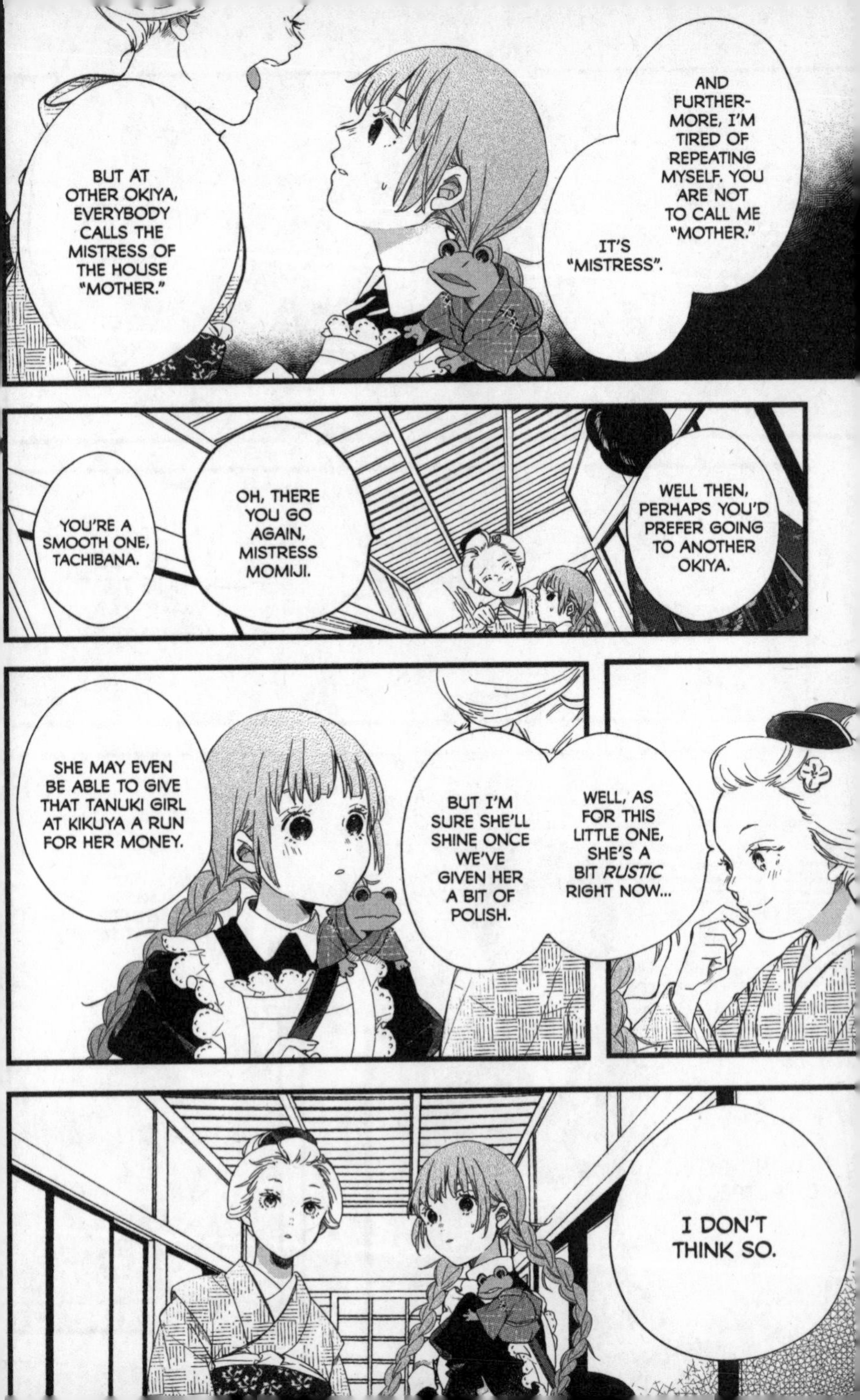
AND FURTHER-MORE, I'M TIRED OF REPEATING MYSELF. YOU ARE NOT TO CALL ME "MOTHER."
IT'S "MISTRESS".
BUT AT OTHER OKIYA, EVERYBODY CALLS THE MISTRESS OF THE HOUSE "MOTHER."
WELL THEN, PERHAPS YOU'D PREFER GOING TO ANOTHER OKIYA.
OH, THERE YOU GO AGAIN, MISTRESS MOMIJI.
YOU'RE A SMOOTH ONE, TACHIBANA.
WELL, AS FOR THIS LITTLE ONE, SHE'S A BIT *RUSTIC* RIGHT NOW...
BUT I'M SURE SHE'LL SHINE ONCE WE'VE GIVEN HER A BIT OF POLISH.
SHE MAY EVEN BE ABLE TO GIVE THAT TANUKI GIRL AT KIKUYA A RUN FOR HER MONEY.
I DON'T THINK SO.

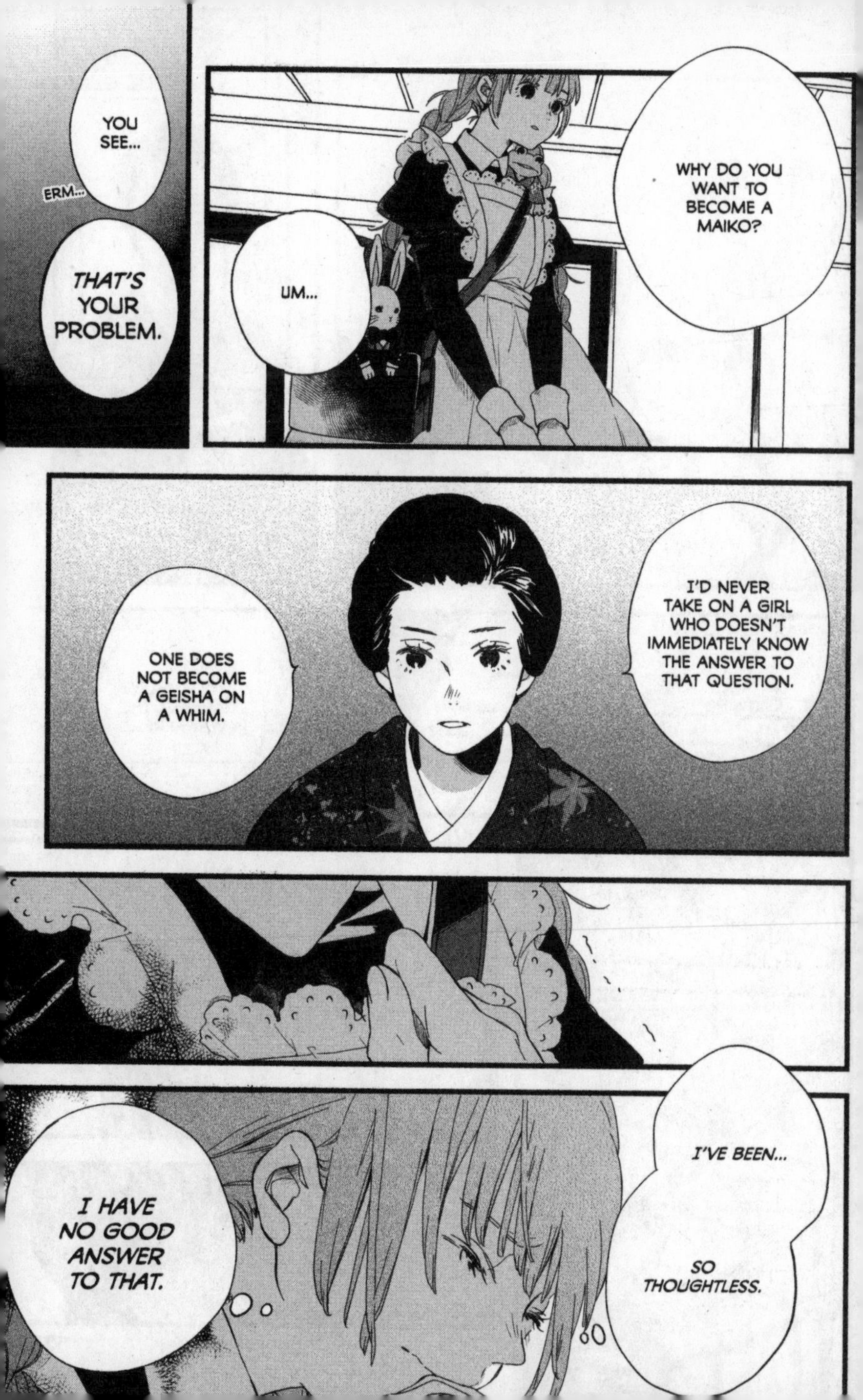
WHY DO YOU WANT TO BECOME A MAIKO?
UM...
YOU SEE...
ERM...
THAT'S YOUR PROBLEM.
I'D NEVER TAKE ON A GIRL WHO DOESN'T IMMEDIATELY KNOW THE ANSWER TO THAT QUESTION.
ONE DOES NOT BECOME A GEISHA ON A WHIM.
I'VE BEEN...
SO THOUGHTLESS.
I HAVE NO GOOD ANSWER TO THAT.

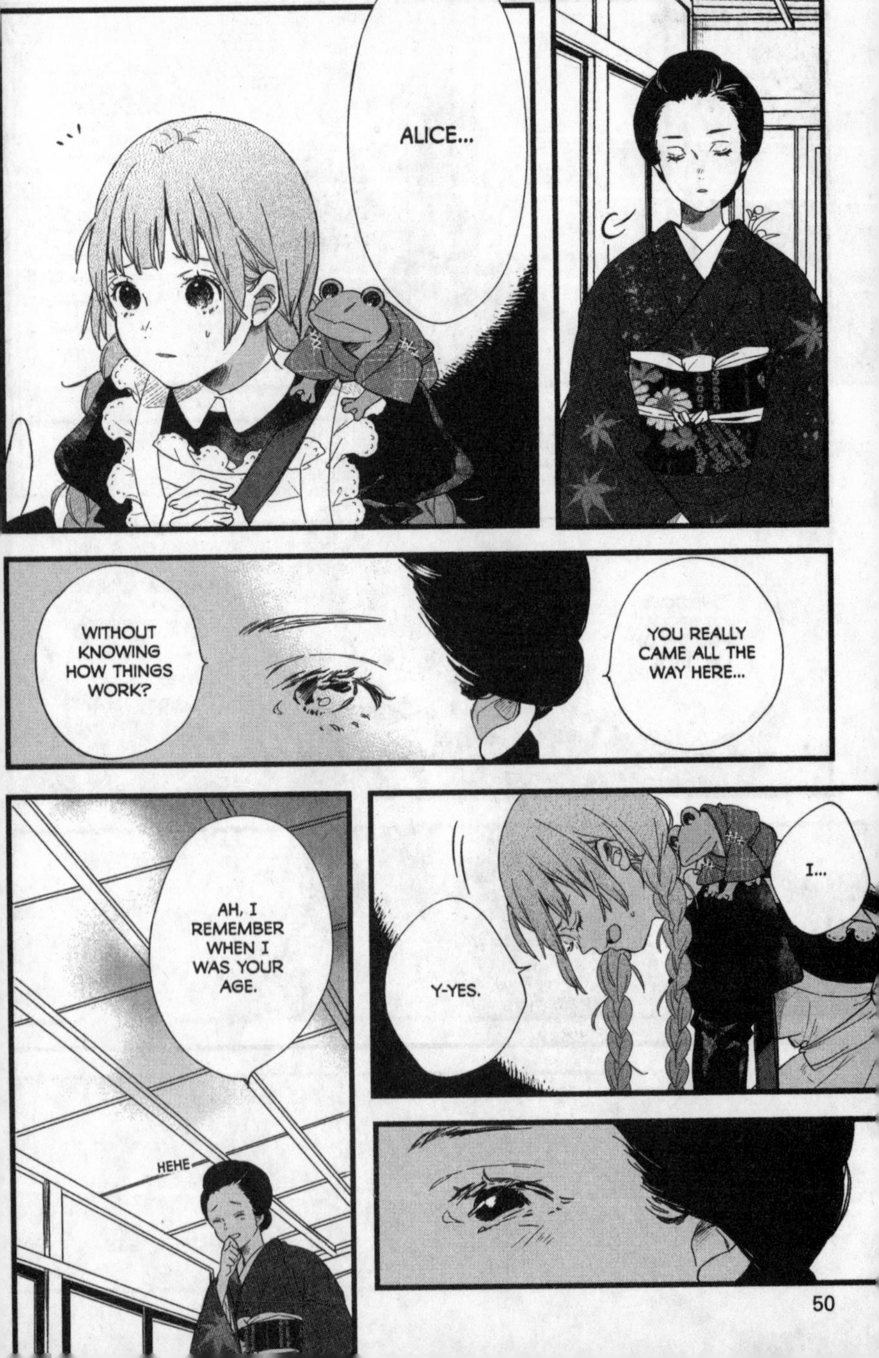
ALICE...
YOU REALLY CAME ALL THE WAY HERE...
WITHOUT KNOWING HOW THINGS WORK?
I...
Y-YES.
AH, I REMEMBER WHEN I WAS YOUR AGE.
HEHE

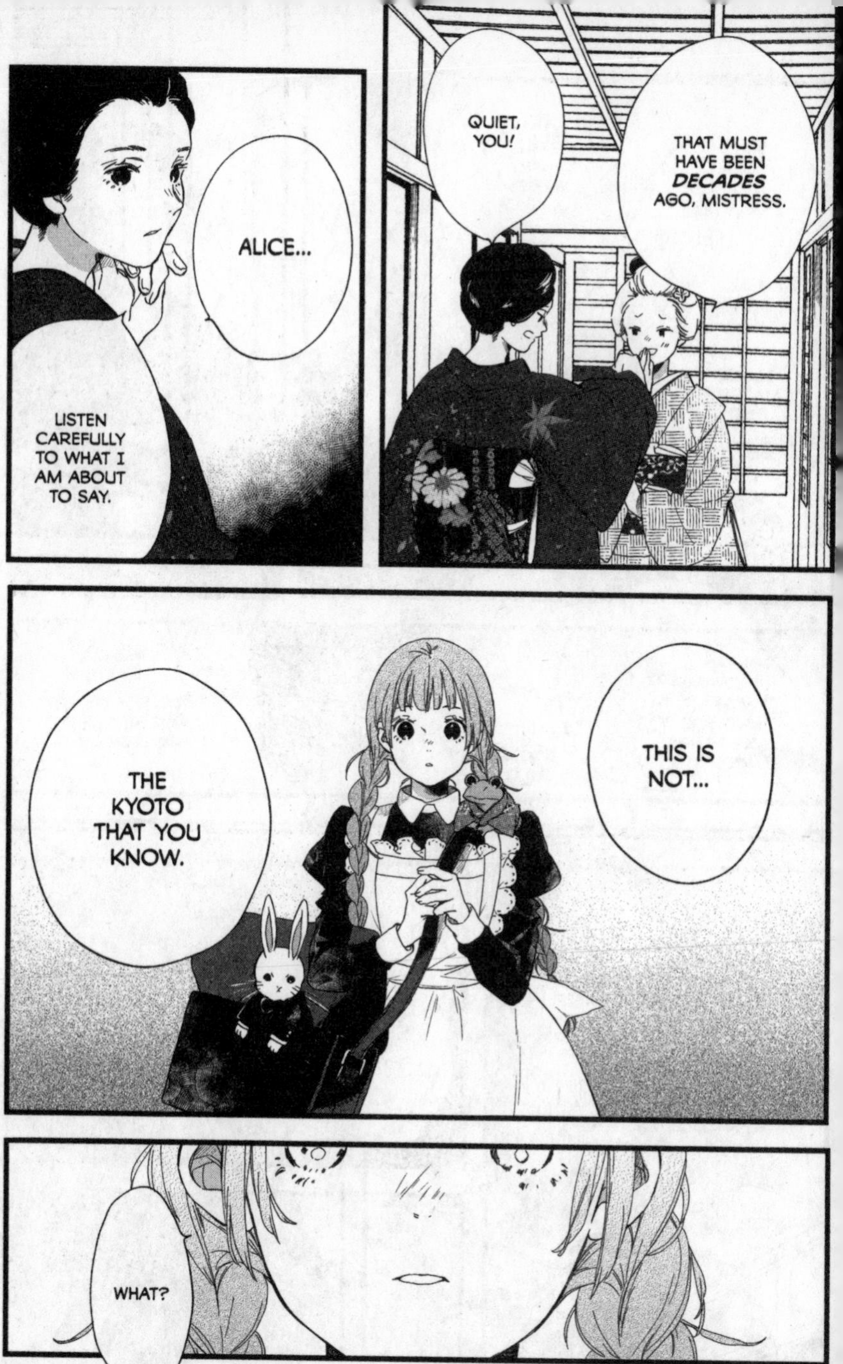
THAT MUST HAVE BEEN *DECADES* AGO, MISTRESS.
QUIET, YOU!
ALICE...
LISTEN CAREFULLY TO WHAT I AM ABOUT TO SAY.
THIS IS NOT...
THE KYOTO THAT YOU KNOW.
WHAT?

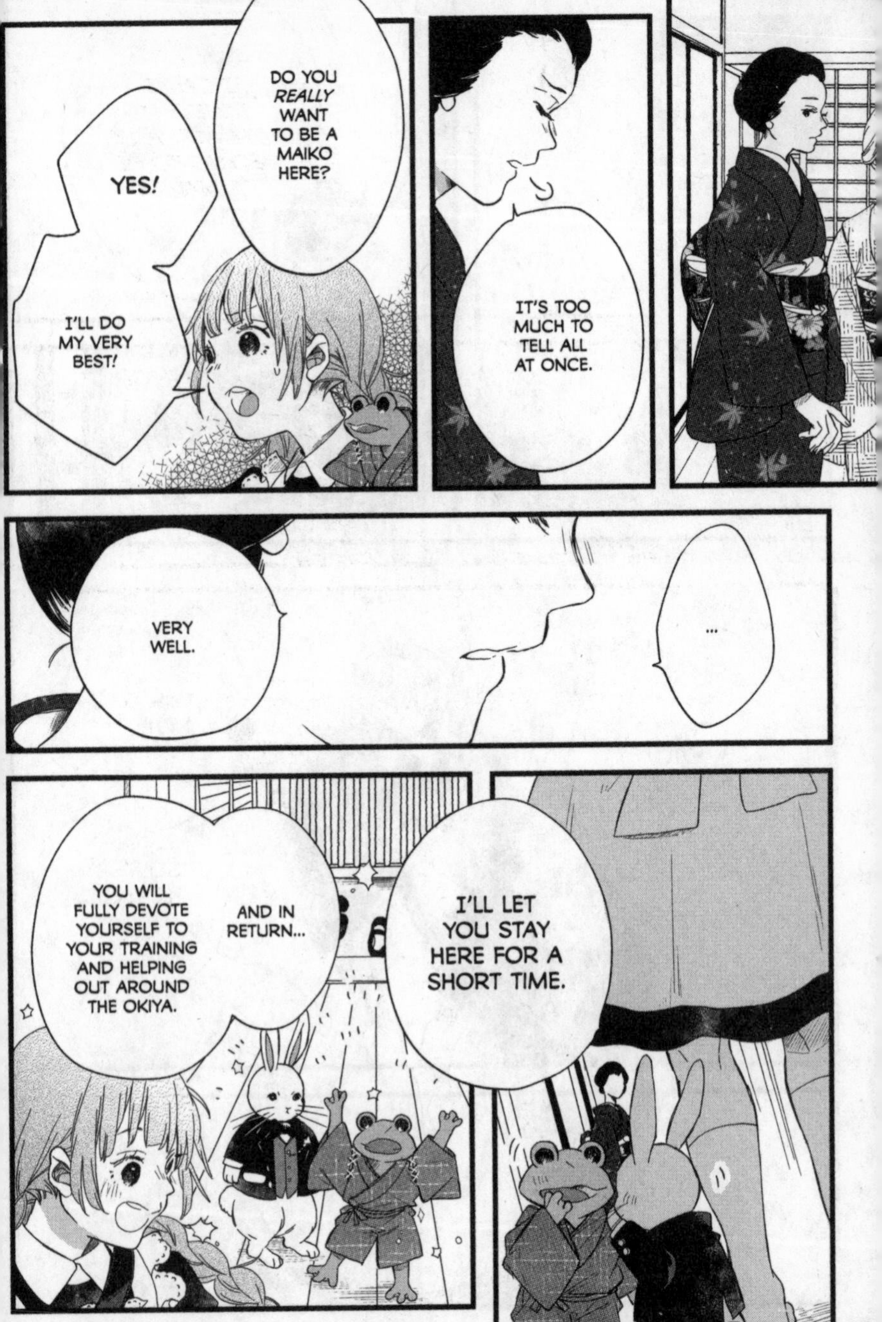
IT'S TOO MUCH TO TELL ALL AT ONCE.
DO YOU *REALLY* WANT TO BE A MAIKO HERE?
YES!
I'LL DO MY VERY BEST!
...
VERY WELL.
I'LL LET YOU STAY HERE FOR A SHORT TIME.
AND IN RETURN...
YOU WILL FULLY DEVOTE YOURSELF TO YOUR TRAINING AND HELPING OUT AROUND THE OKIYA.

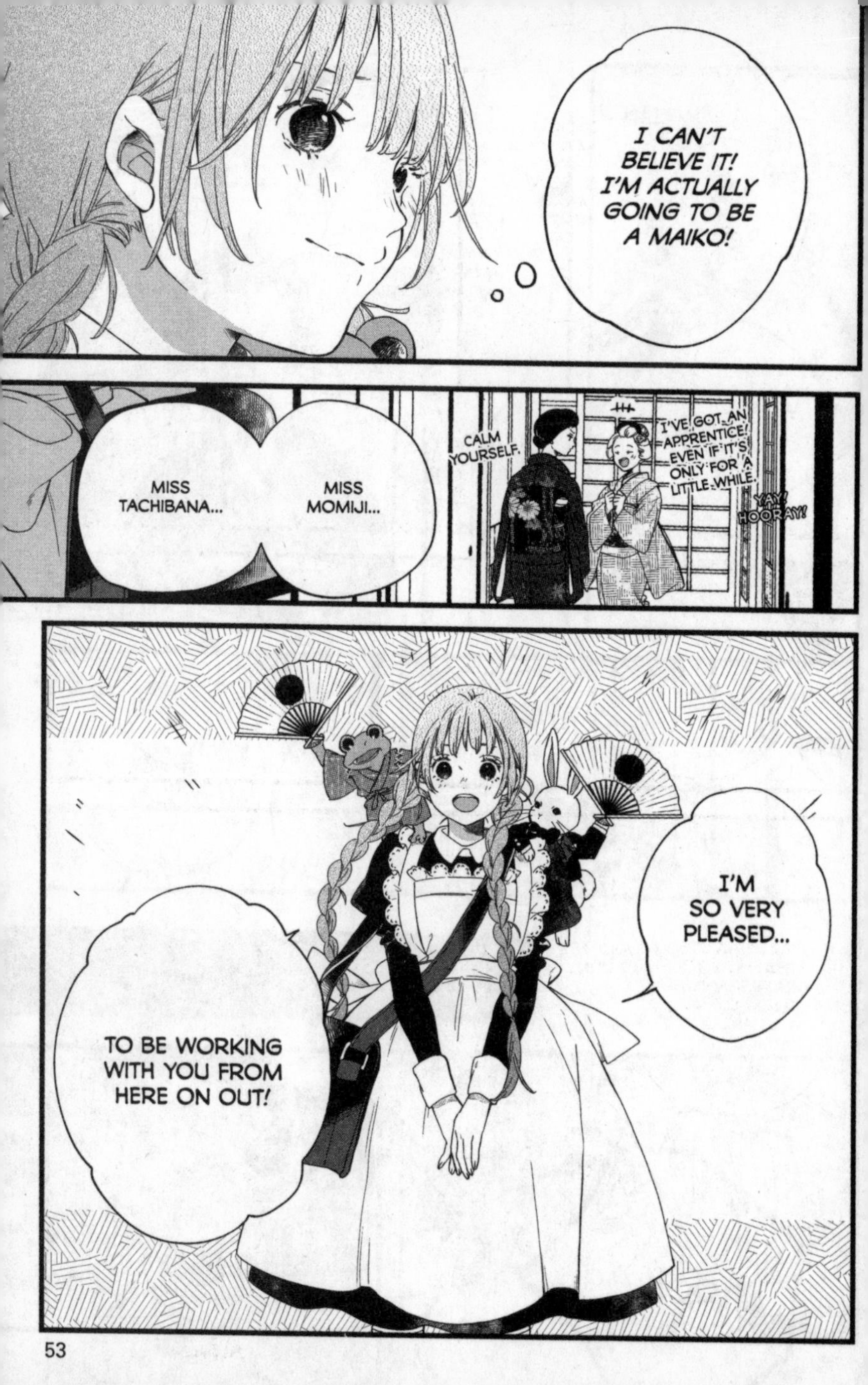
I CAN'T BELIEVE IT! I'M ACTUALLY GOING TO BE A MAIKO!
I'VE GOT AN APPRENTICE! EVEN IF IT'S ONLY FOR A LITTLE WHILE.
YAY! HOORAY!
CALM YOURSELF.
MISS MOMIJI...
MISS TACHIBANA...
I'M SO VERY PLEASED...
TO BE WORKING WITH YOU FROM HERE ON OUT!

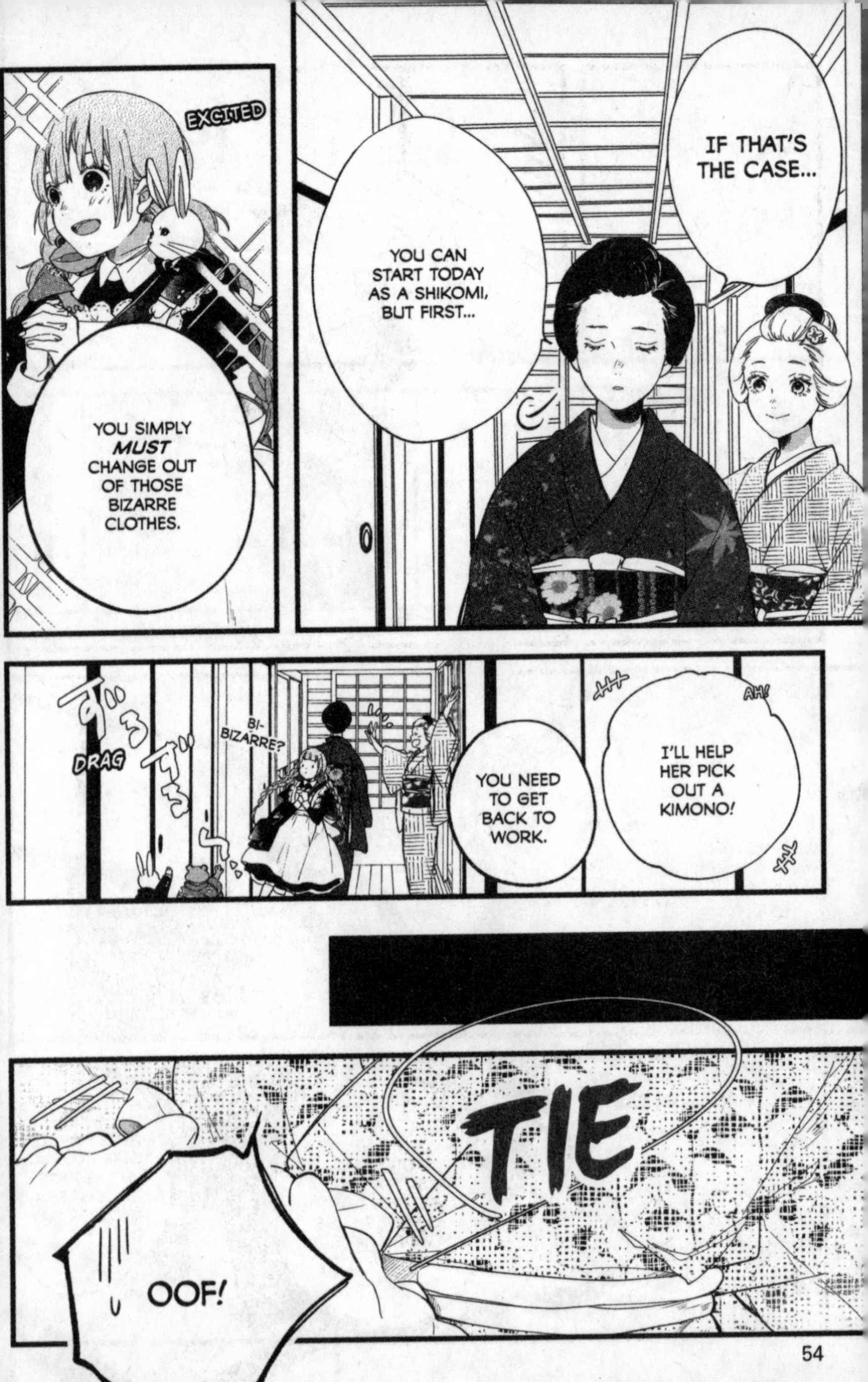
IF THAT'S THE CASE...
YOU CAN START TODAY AS A SHIKOMI, BUT FIRST...
EXCITED
YOU SIMPLY *MUST* CHANGE OUT OF THOSE BIZARRE CLOTHES.
AH!
I'LL HELP HER PICK OUT A KIMONO!
YOU NEED TO GET BACK TO WORK.
BI-BIZARRE?
DRAG
TIE
OOF!

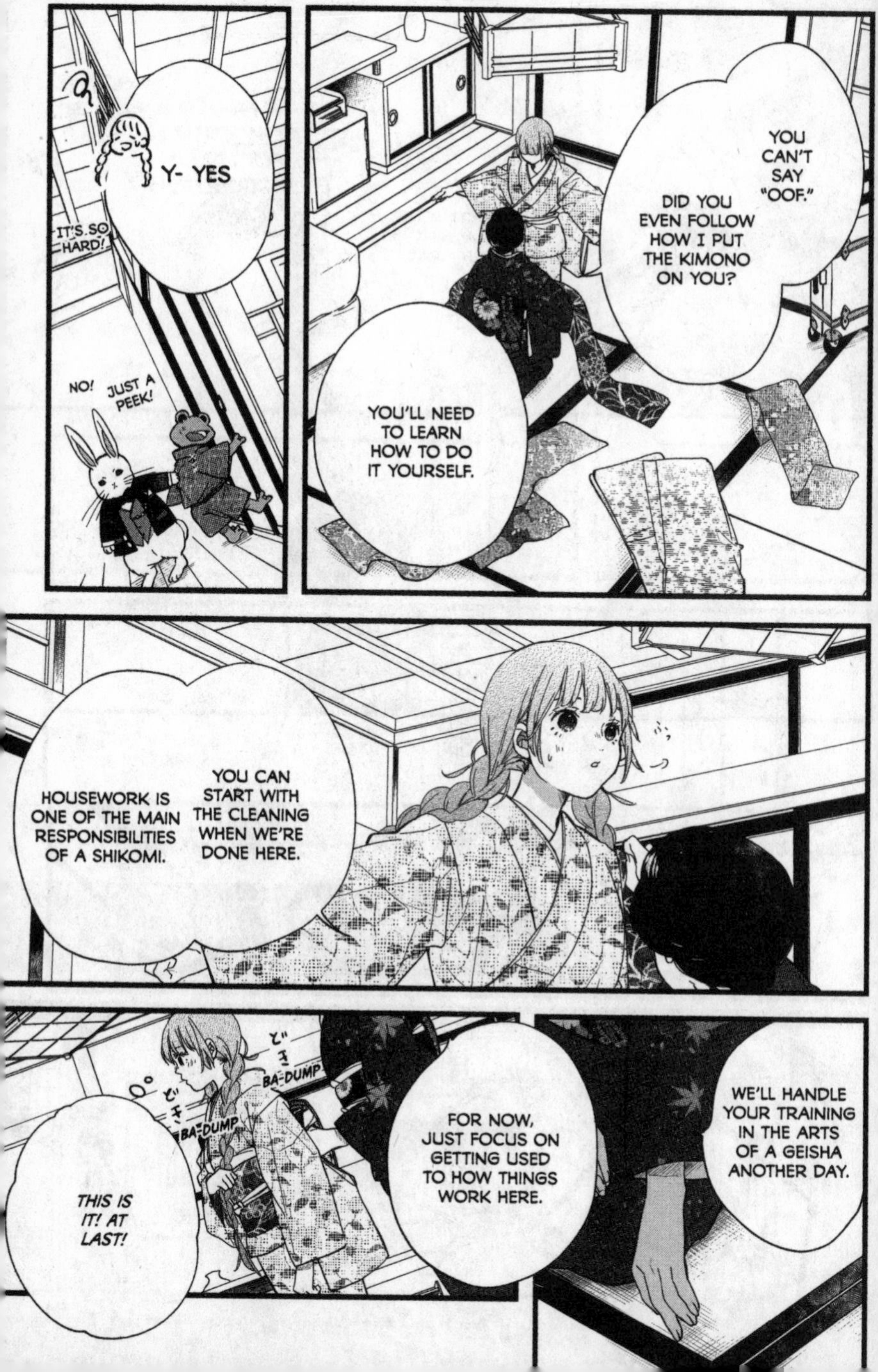
YOU CAN'T SAY "OOF."
DID YOU EVEN FOLLOW HOW I PUT THE KIMONO ON YOU?
YOU'LL NEED TO LEARN HOW TO DO IT YOURSELF.
Y- YES
IT'S SO HARD!
JUST A PEEK!
NO!
YOU CAN START WITH THE CLEANING WHEN WE'RE DONE HERE.
HOUSEWORK IS ONE OF THE MAIN RESPONSIBILITIES OF A SHIKOMI.
WE'LL HANDLE YOUR TRAINING IN THE ARTS OF A GEISHA ANOTHER DAY.
FOR NOW, JUST FOCUS ON GETTING USED TO HOW THINGS WORK HERE.
BA-DUMP
BA-DUMP
THIS IS IT! AT LAST!

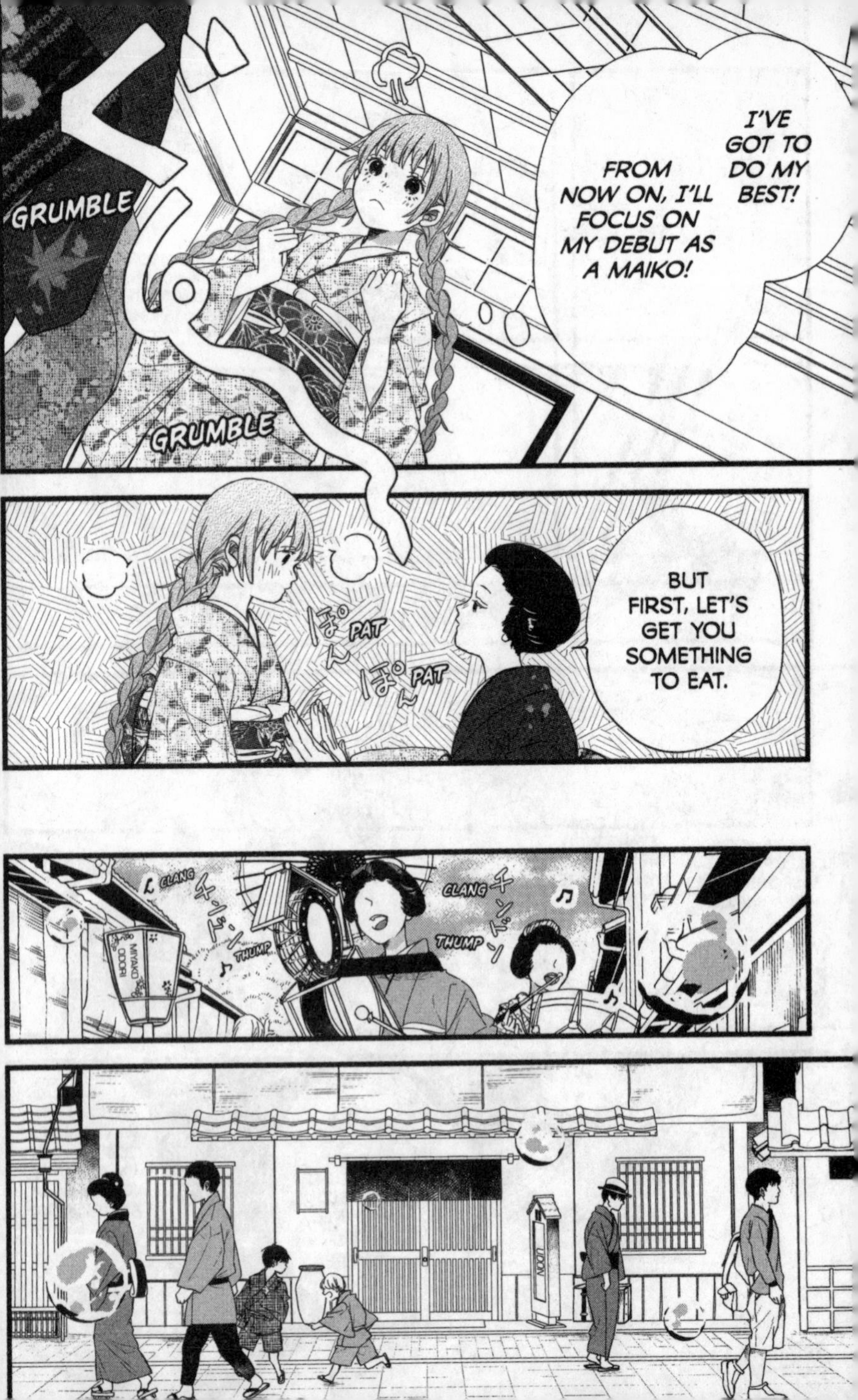

I'VE GOT TO DO MY BEST!
FROM NOW ON, I'LL FOCUS ON MY DEBUT AS A MAIKO!
GRUMBLE
GRUMBLE
BUT FIRST, LET'S GET YOU SOMETHING TO EAT.
PAT
PAT
CLANG
THUMP
CLANG
THUMP
MIYAKO ODORI
UDON

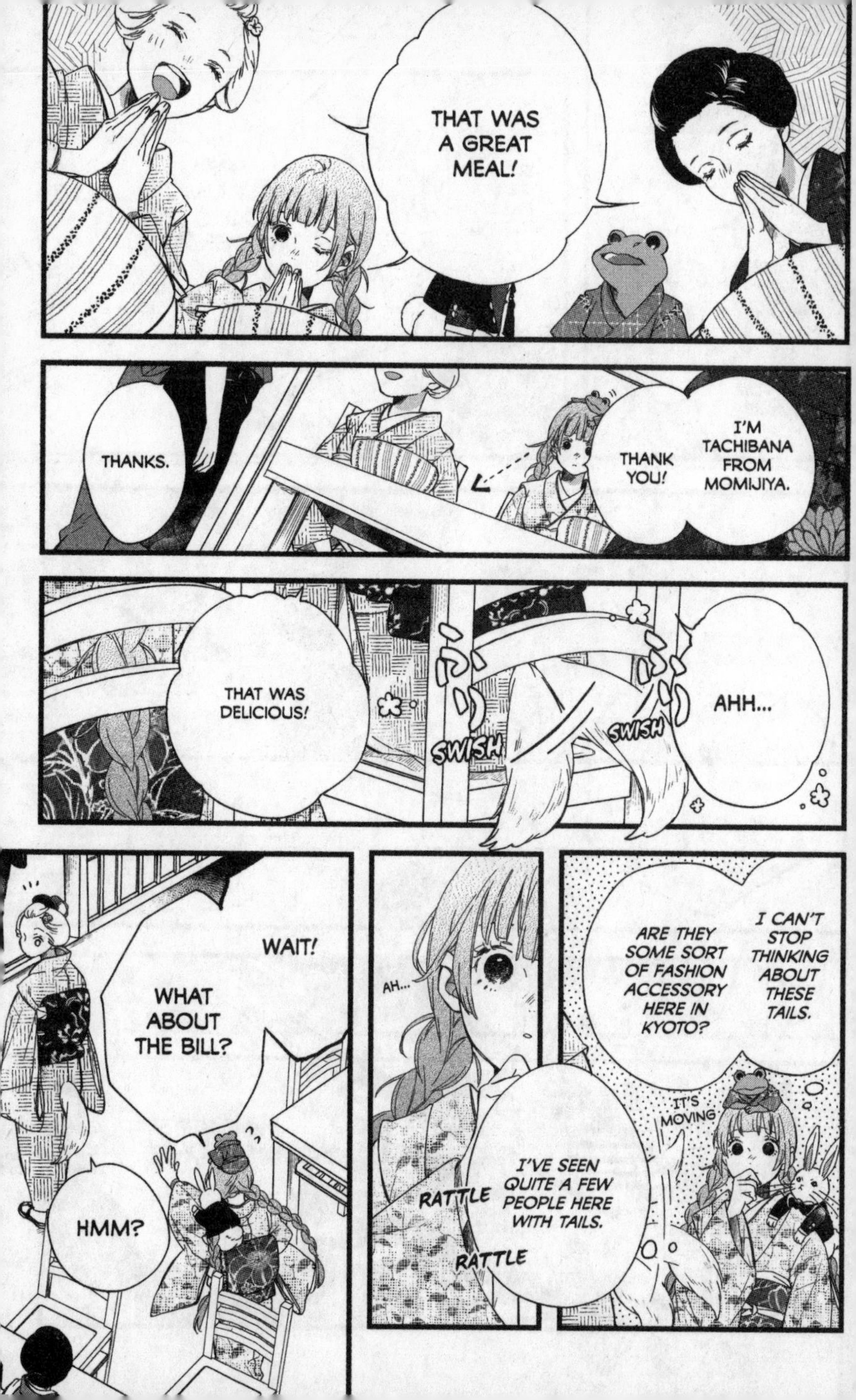
THAT WAS A GREAT MEAL!
I'M TACHIBANA FROM MOMIJIYA.
THANK YOU!
THANKS.
AHH...
SWISH
SWISH
THAT WAS DELICIOUS!
I CAN'T STOP THINKING ABOUT THESE TAILS.
ARE THEY SOME SORT OF FASHION ACCESSORY HERE IN KYOTO?
IT'S MOVING
AH...
I'VE SEEN QUITE A FEW PEOPLE HERE WITH TAILS.
RATTLE
RATTLE
WAIT!
WHAT ABOUT THE BILL?
HMM?

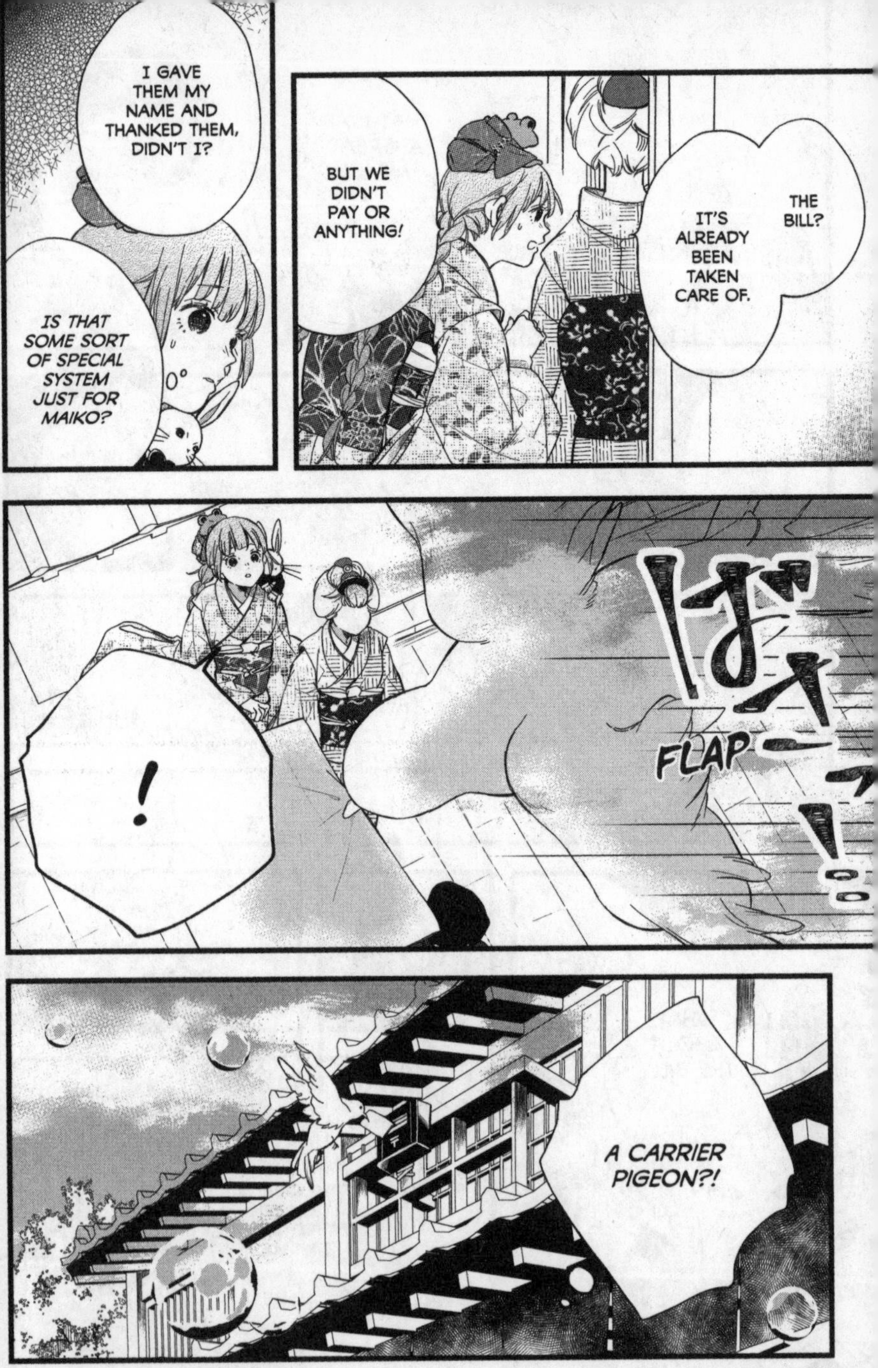
THE BILL?
IT'S ALREADY BEEN TAKEN CARE OF.
BUT WE DIDN'T PAY OR ANYTHING!
I GAVE THEM MY NAME AND THANKED THEM, DIDN'T I?
IS THAT SOME SORT OF SPECIAL SYSTEM JUST FOR MAIKO?
FLAP
!
A CARRIER PIGEON?!

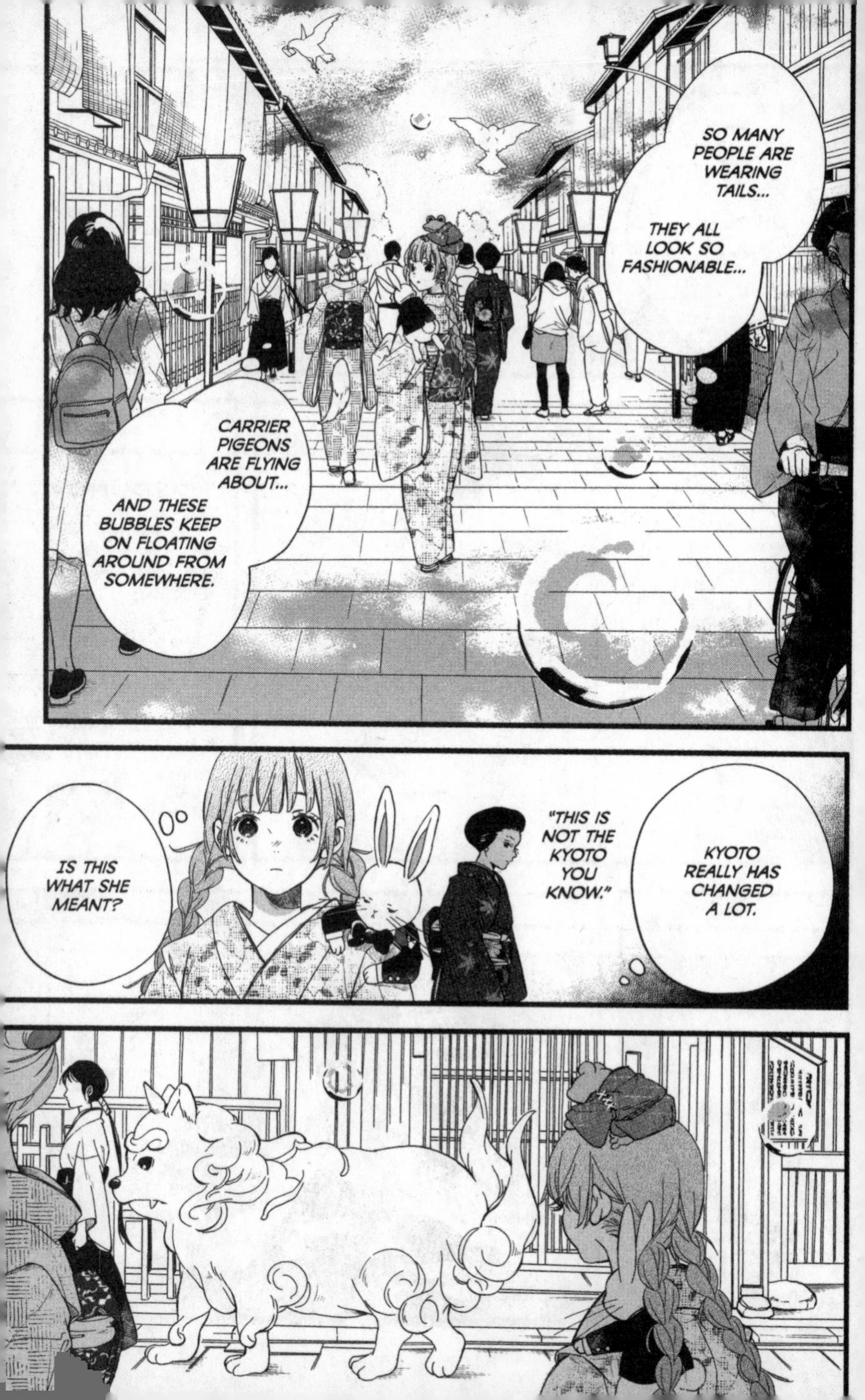
SO MANY PEOPLE ARE WEARING TAILS...
THEY ALL LOOK SO FASHIONABLE...
CARRIER PIGEONS ARE FLYING ABOUT...
AND THESE BUBBLES KEEP ON FLOATING AROUND FROM SOMEWHERE.
KYOTO REALLY HAS CHANGED A LOT.
"THIS IS NOT THE KYOTO YOU KNOW."
IS THIS WHAT SHE MEANT?

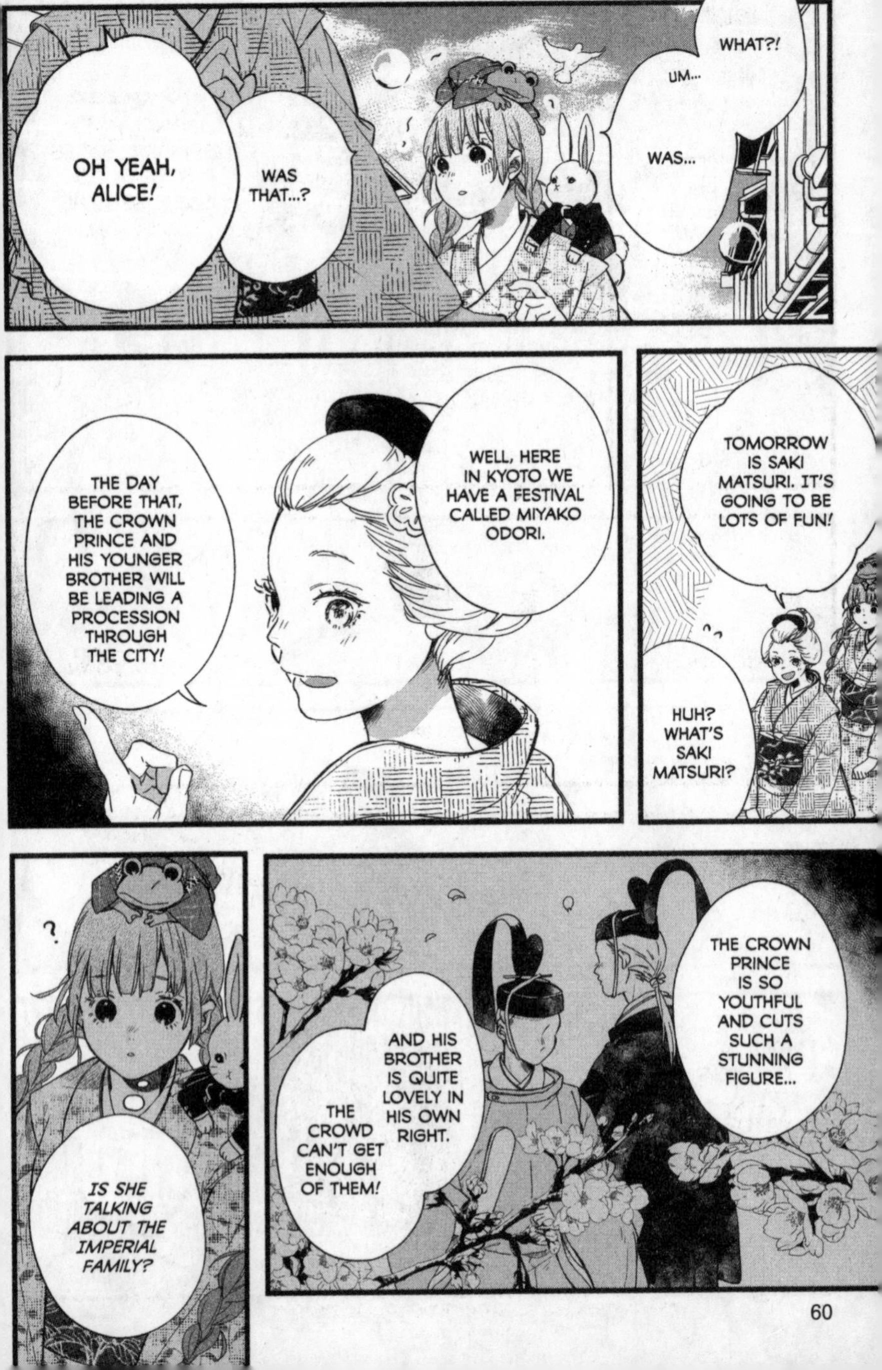
WHAT?!
UM...
WAS...
WAS THAT...?
OH YEAH, ALICE!
TOMORROW IS SAKI MATSURI. IT'S GOING TO BE LOTS OF FUN!
HUH? WHAT'S SAKI MATSURI?
WELL, HERE IN KYOTO WE HAVE A FESTIVAL CALLED MIYAKO ODORI.
THE DAY BEFORE THAT, THE CROWN PRINCE AND HIS YOUNGER BROTHER WILL BE LEADING A PROCESSION THROUGH THE CITY!
THE CROWN PRINCE IS SO YOUTHFUL AND CUTS SUCH A STUNNING FIGURE...
AND HIS BROTHER IS QUITE LOVELY IN HIS OWN RIGHT.
THE CROWD CAN'T GET ENOUGH OF THEM!
?
IS SHE TALKING ABOUT THE IMPERIAL FAMILY?

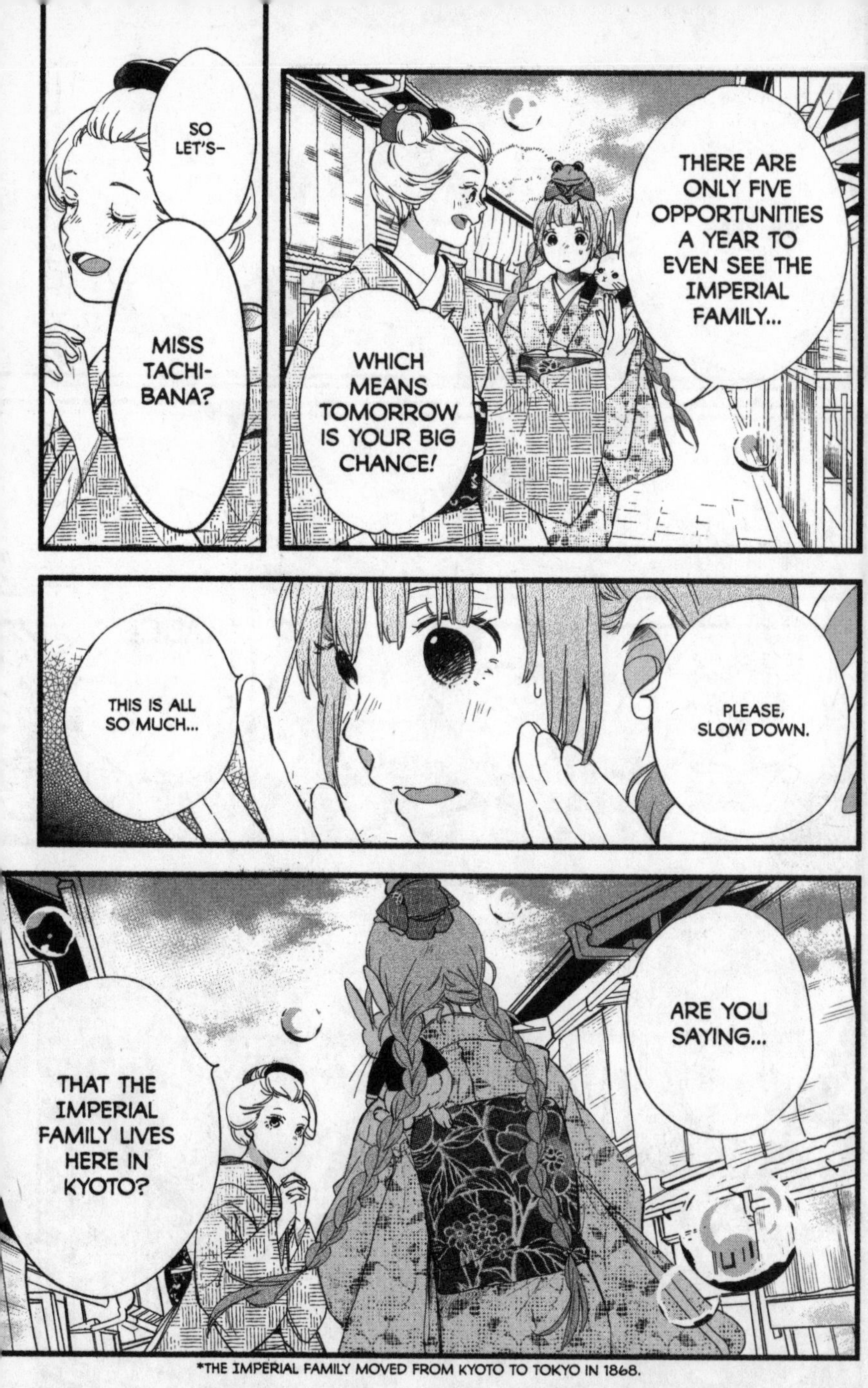
THERE ARE ONLY FIVE OPPORTUNITIES A YEAR TO EVEN SEE THE IMPERIAL FAMILY...
WHICH MEANS TOMORROW IS YOUR BIG CHANCE!
SO LET'S–
MISS TACHI-BANA?
PLEASE, SLOW DOWN.
THIS IS ALL SO MUCH...
ARE YOU SAYING...
THAT THE IMPERIAL FAMILY LIVES HERE IN KYOTO?

*THE IMPERIAL FAMILY MOVED FROM KYOTO TO TOKYO IN 1868.

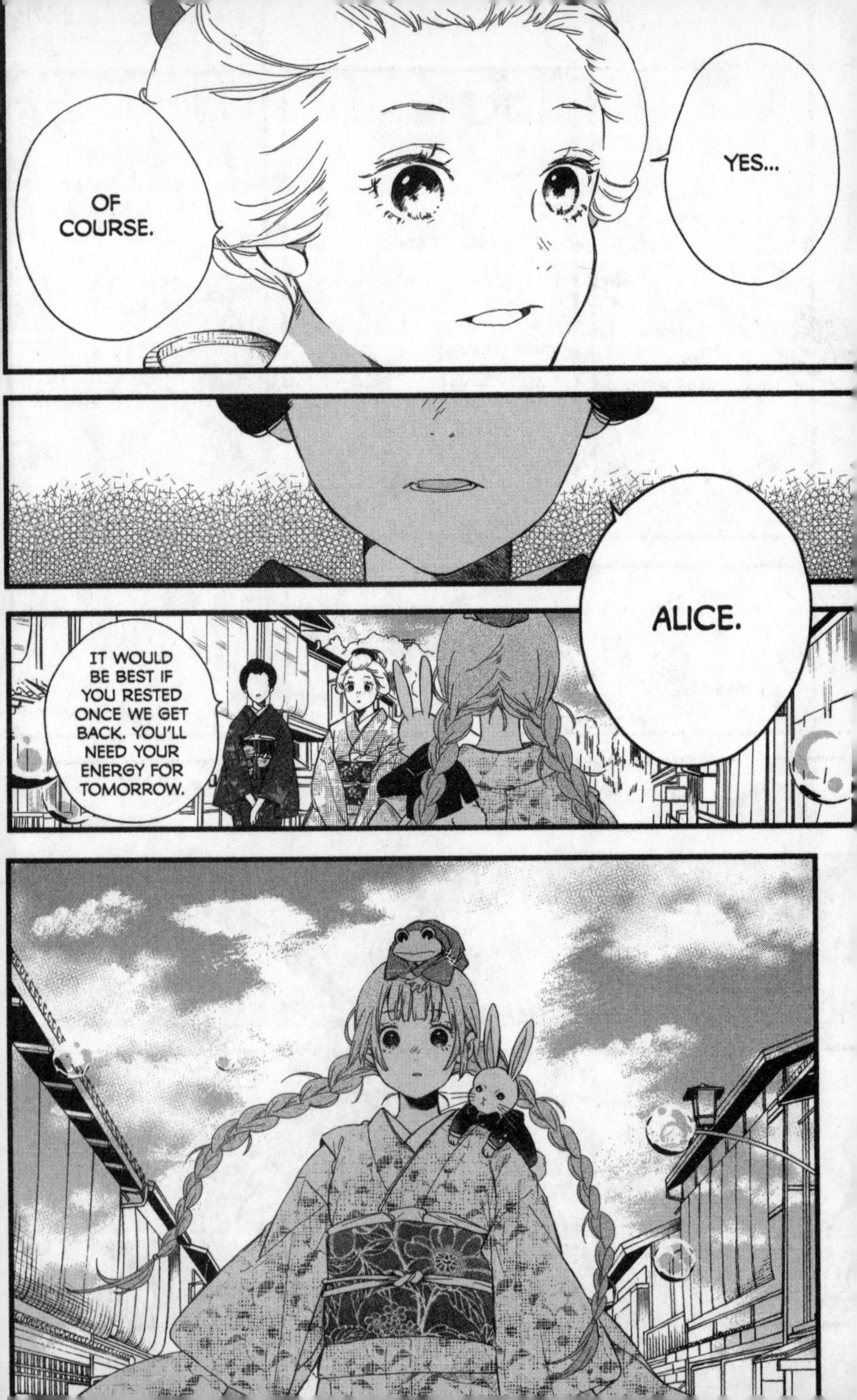
YES...
OF COURSE.
ALICE.
IT WOULD BE BEST IF YOU RESTED ONCE WE GET BACK. YOU'LL NEED YOUR ENERGY FOR TOMORROW.

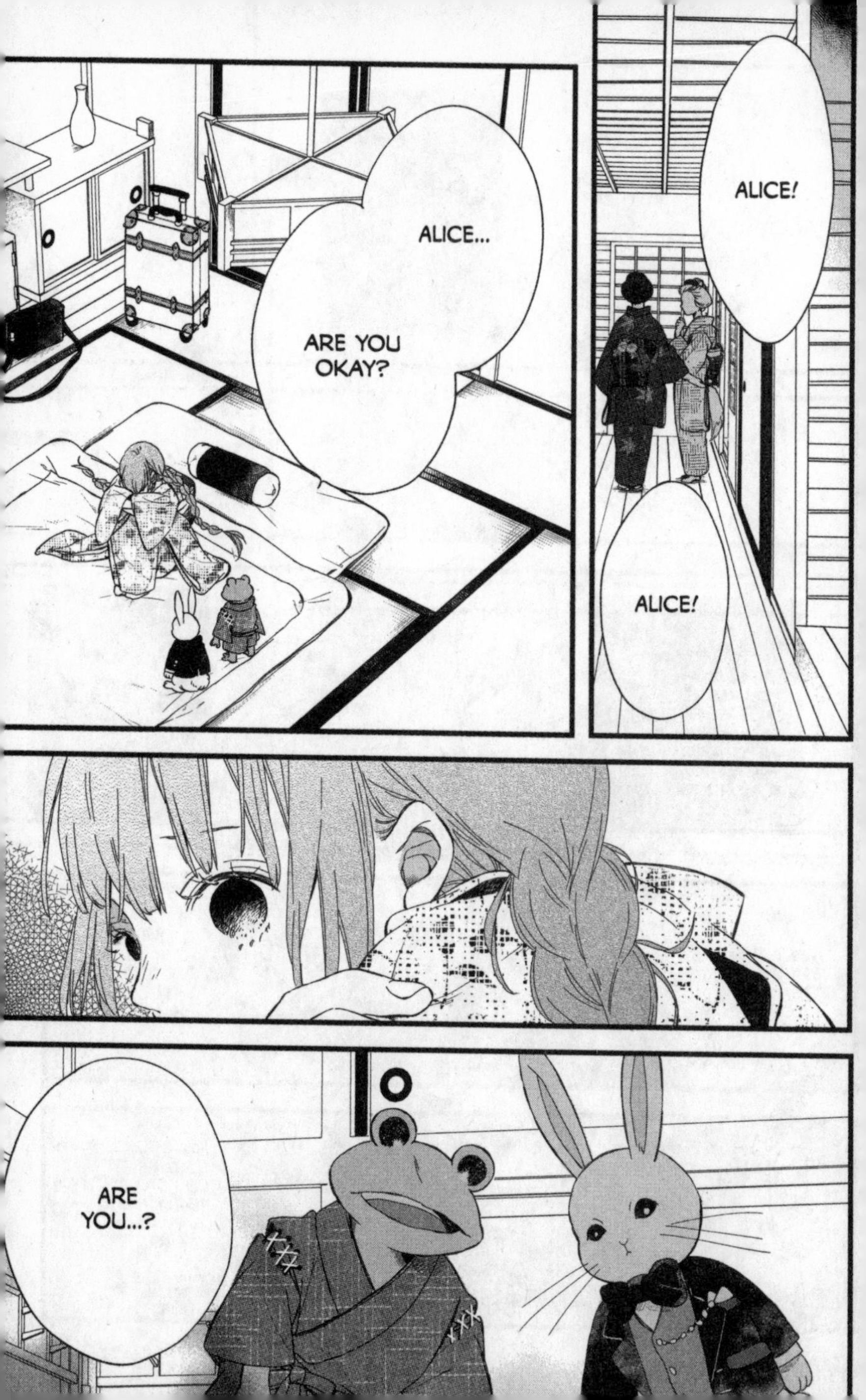
ALICE!
ALICE!
ALICE...
ARE YOU OKAY?
ARE YOU...?

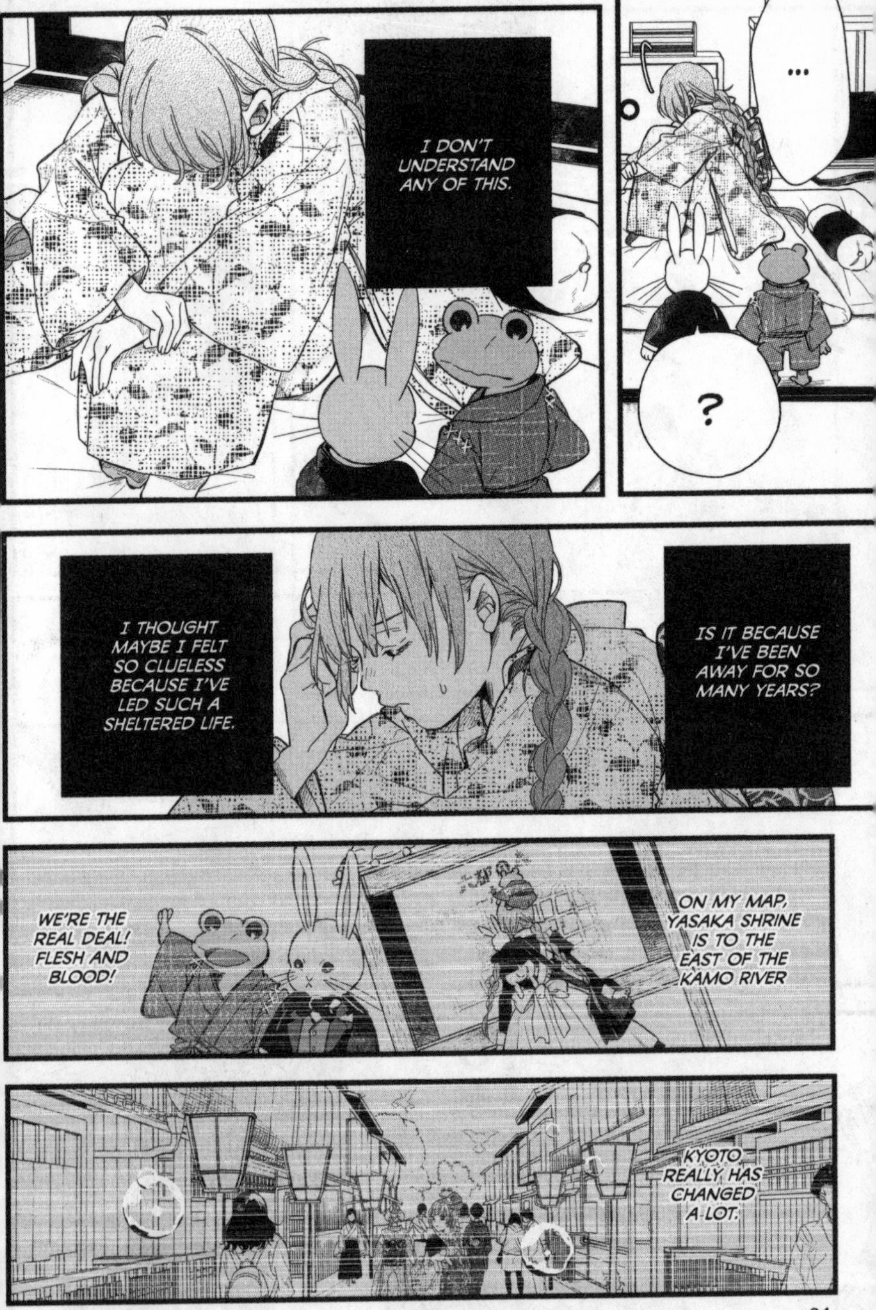
...
?
I DON'T UNDERSTAND ANY OF THIS.
IS IT BECAUSE I'VE BEEN AWAY FOR SO MANY YEARS?
I THOUGHT MAYBE I FELT SO CLUELESS BECAUSE I'VE LED SUCH A SHELTERED LIFE.
ON MY MAP, YASAKA SHRINE IS TO THE EAST OF THE KAMO RIVER
WE'RE THE REAL DEAL! FLESH AND BLOOD!
KYOTO REALLY HAS CHANGED A LOT.

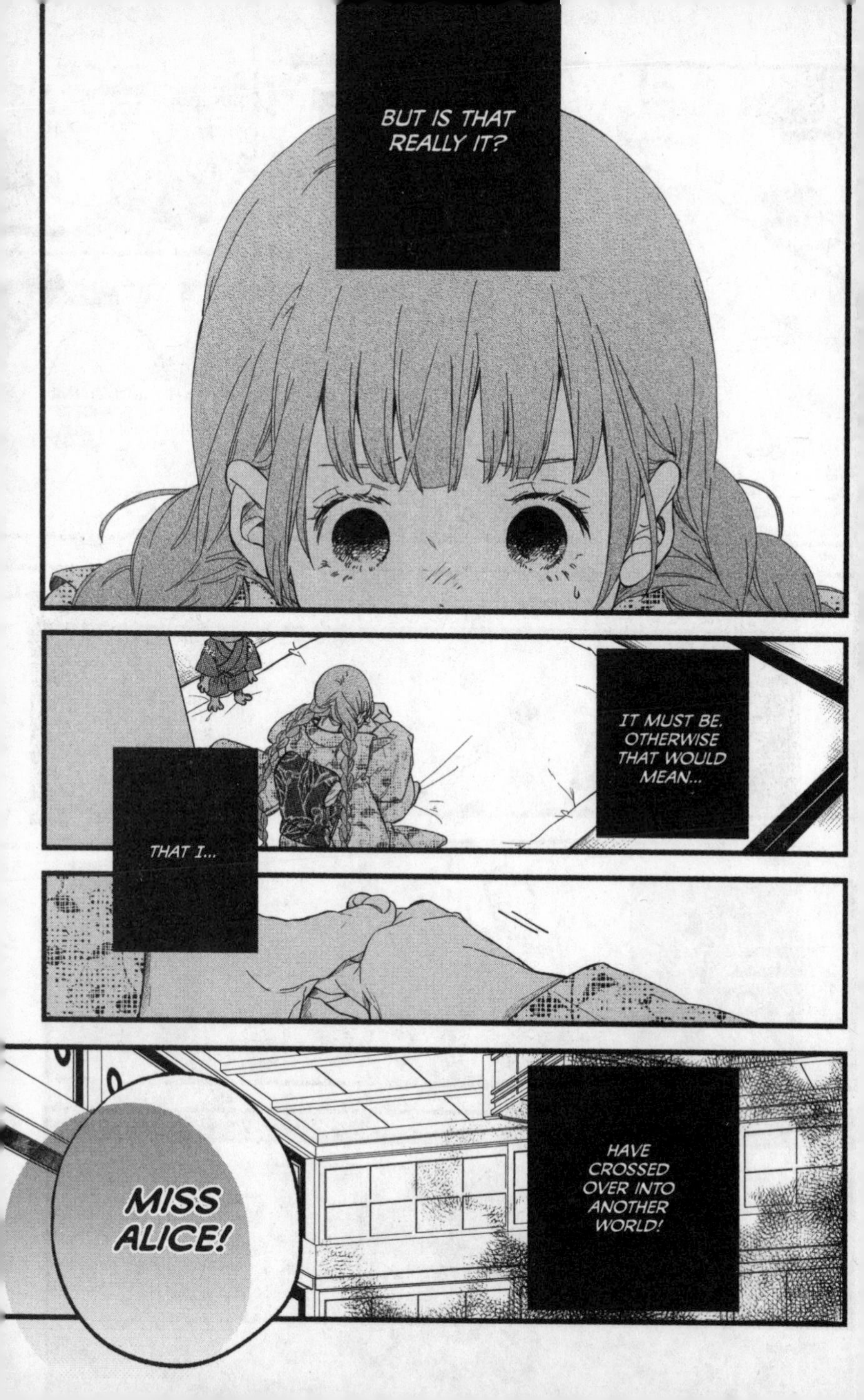
BUT IS THAT REALLY IT?
IT MUST BE. OTHERWISE THAT WOULD MEAN...
THAT I...
HAVE CROSSED OVER INTO ANOTHER WORLD!
MISS ALICE!

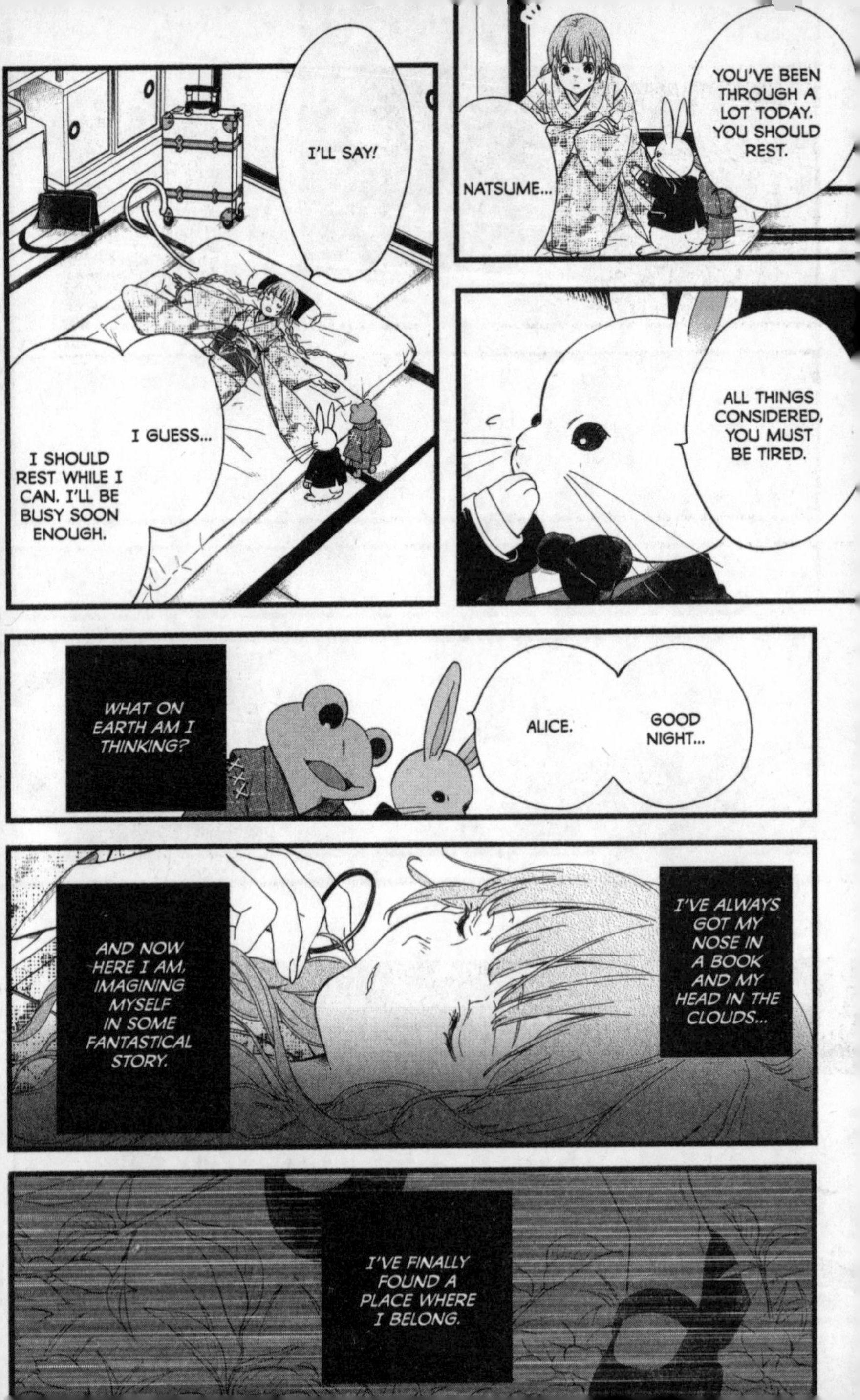
YOU'VE BEEN THROUGH A LOT TODAY. YOU SHOULD REST.
NATSUME...
ALL THINGS CONSIDERED, YOU MUST BE TIRED.
I'LL SAY!
I GUESS...
I SHOULD REST WHILE I CAN. I'LL BE BUSY SOON ENOUGH.
ALICE. GOOD NIGHT...
WHAT ON EARTH AM I THINKING?
I'VE ALWAYS GOT MY NOSE IN A BOOK AND MY HEAD IN THE CLOUDS...
AND NOW HERE I AM, IMAGINING MYSELF IN SOME FANTASTICAL STORY.
I'VE FINALLY FOUND A PLACE WHERE I BELONG.

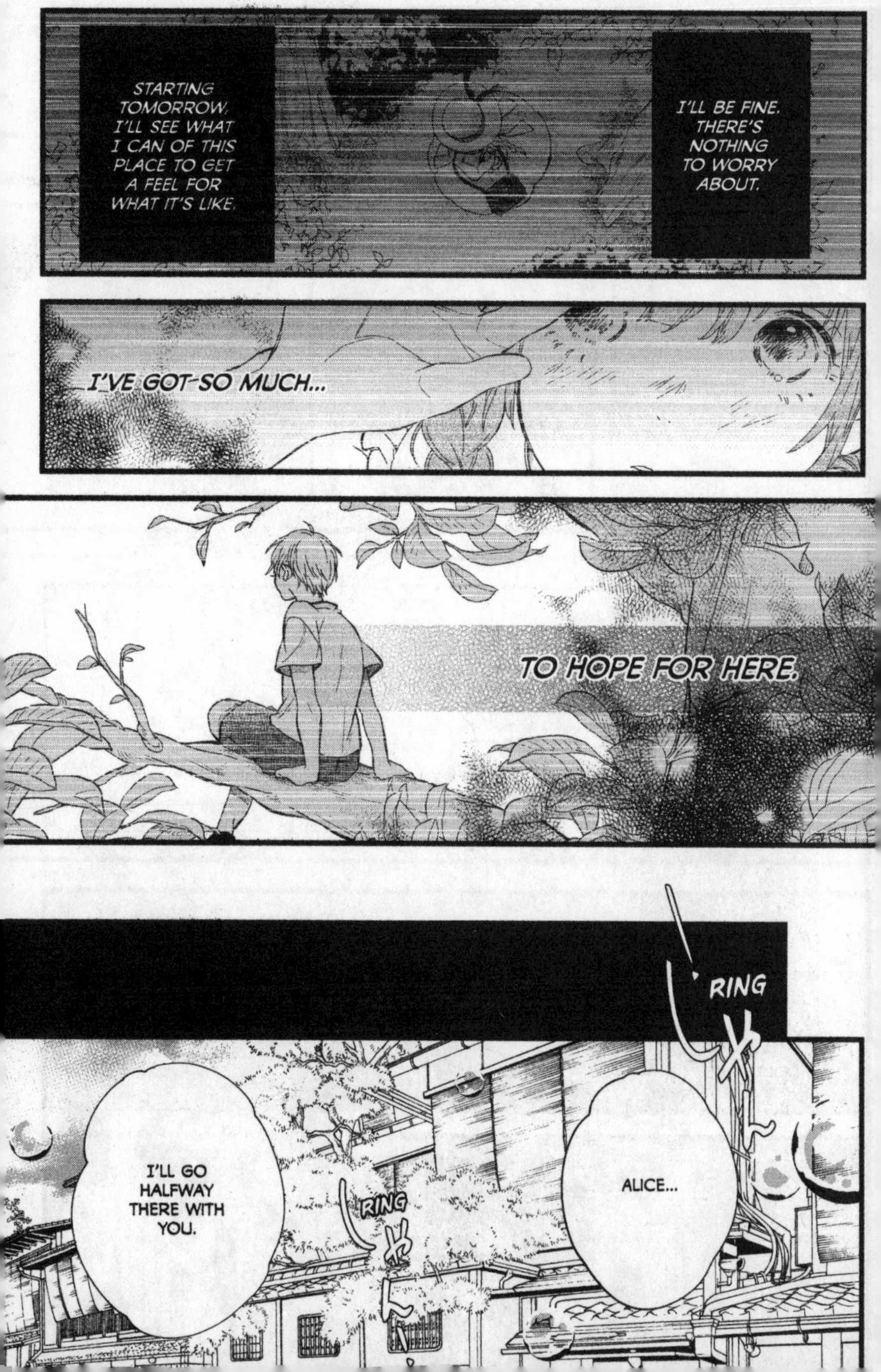
I'LL BE FINE. THERE'S NOTHING TO WORRY ABOUT.
STARTING TOMORROW, I'LL SEE WHAT I CAN OF THIS PLACE TO GET A FEEL FOR WHAT IT'S LIKE.
I'VE GOT SO MUCH...
TO HOPE FOR HERE.
RING
ALICE...
RING
I'LL GO HALFWAY THERE WITH YOU.

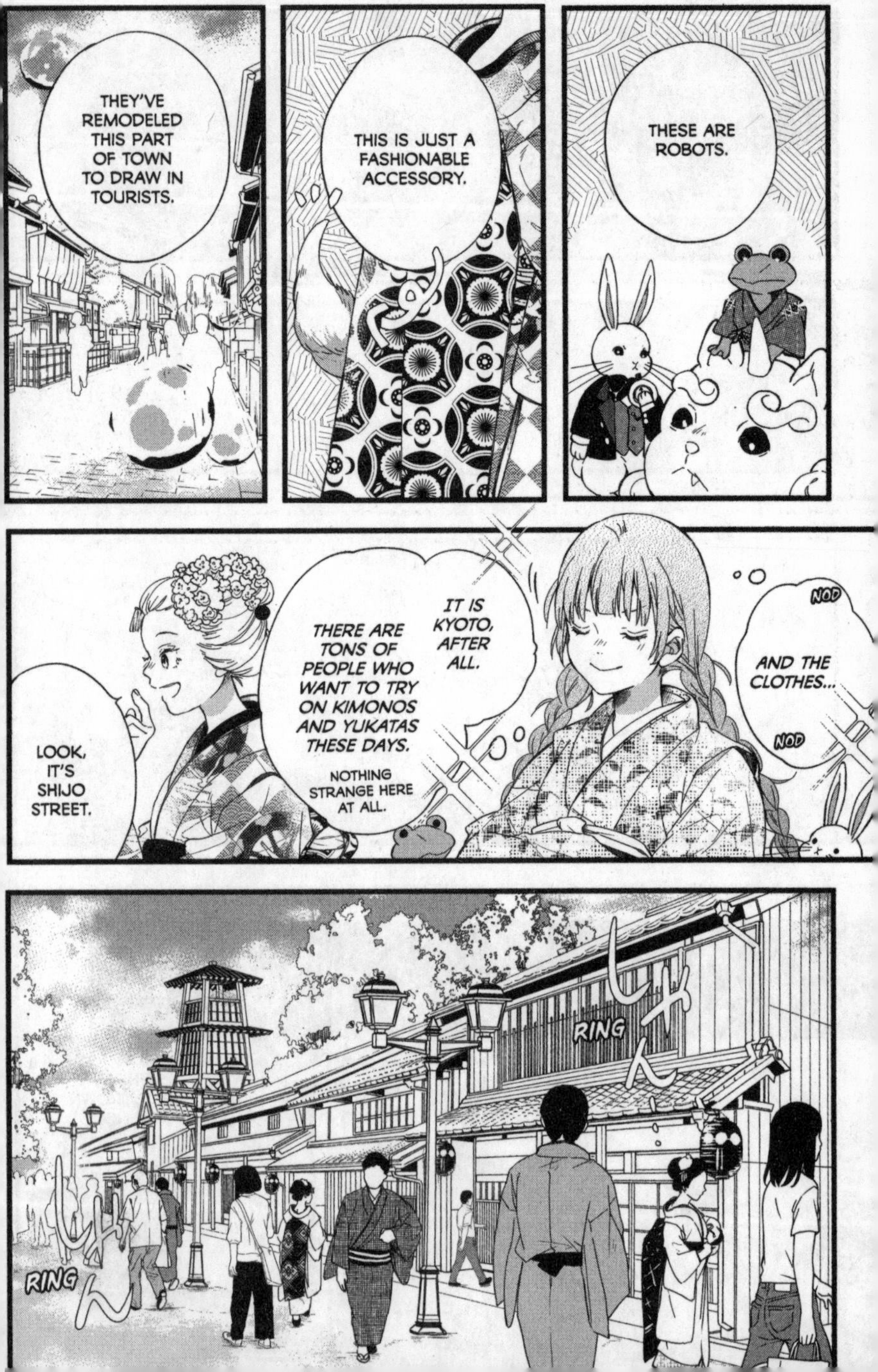
THESE ARE ROBOTS.
THIS IS JUST A FASHIONABLE ACCESSORY.
THEY'VE REMODELED THIS PART OF TOWN TO DRAW IN TOURISTS.
NOD
AND THE CLOTHES...
NOD
IT IS KYOTO, AFTER ALL.
THERE ARE TONS OF PEOPLE WHO WANT TO TRY ON KIMONOS AND YUKATAS THESE DAYS.
NOTHING STRANGE HERE AT ALL.
LOOK, IT'S SHIJO STREET.
RING
RING

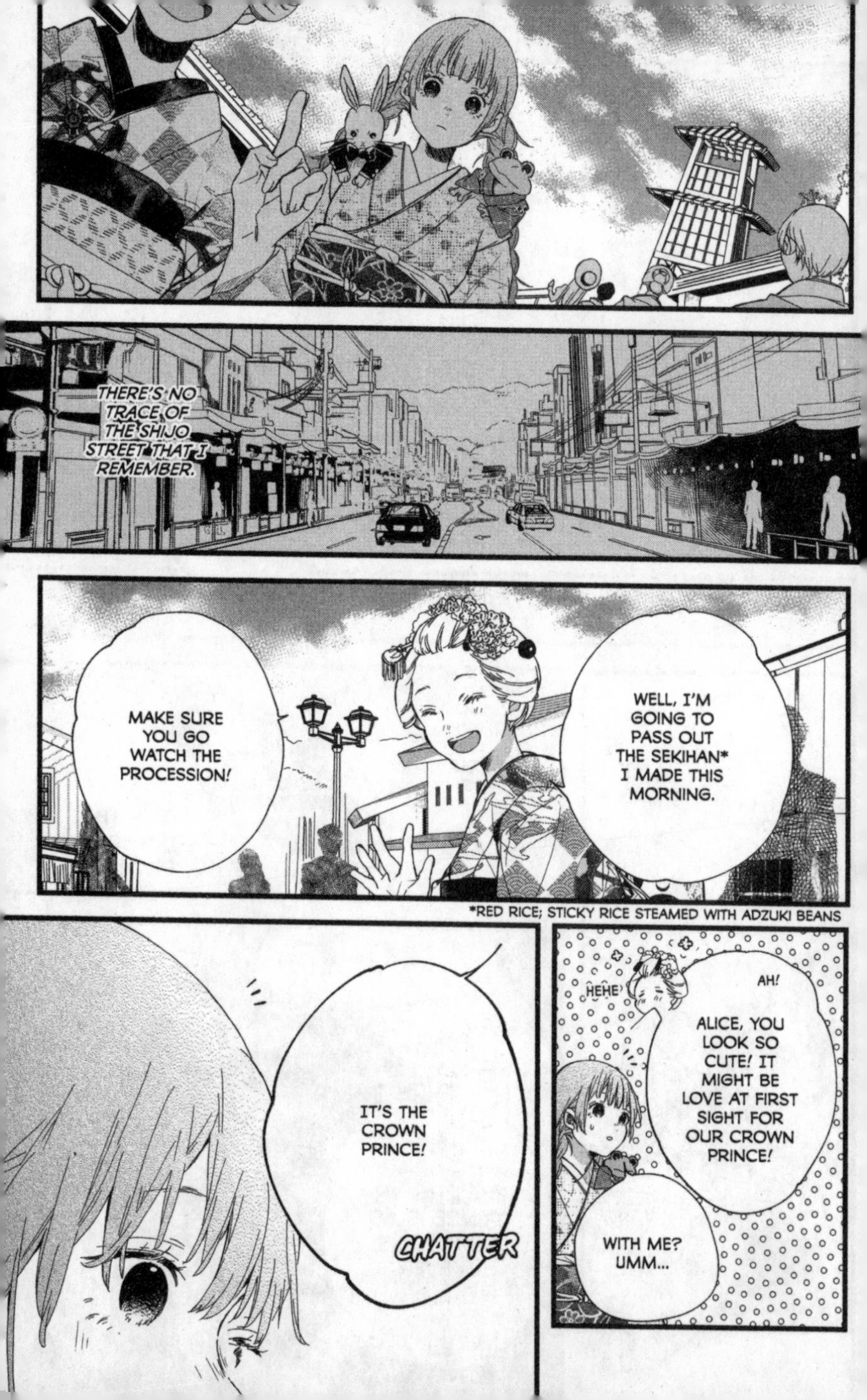
THERE'S NO TRACE OF THE SHIJO STREET THAT I REMEMBER.
WELL, I'M GOING TO PASS OUT THE SEKIHAN* I MADE THIS MORNING.
MAKE SURE YOU GO WATCH THE PROCESSION!
HEHE
AH!
ALICE, YOU LOOK SO CUTE! IT MIGHT BE LOVE AT FIRST SIGHT FOR OUR CROWN PRINCE!
WITH ME? UMM...
IT'S THE CROWN PRINCE!
CHATTER

*RED RICE; STICKY RICE STEAMED WITH ADZUKI BEANS

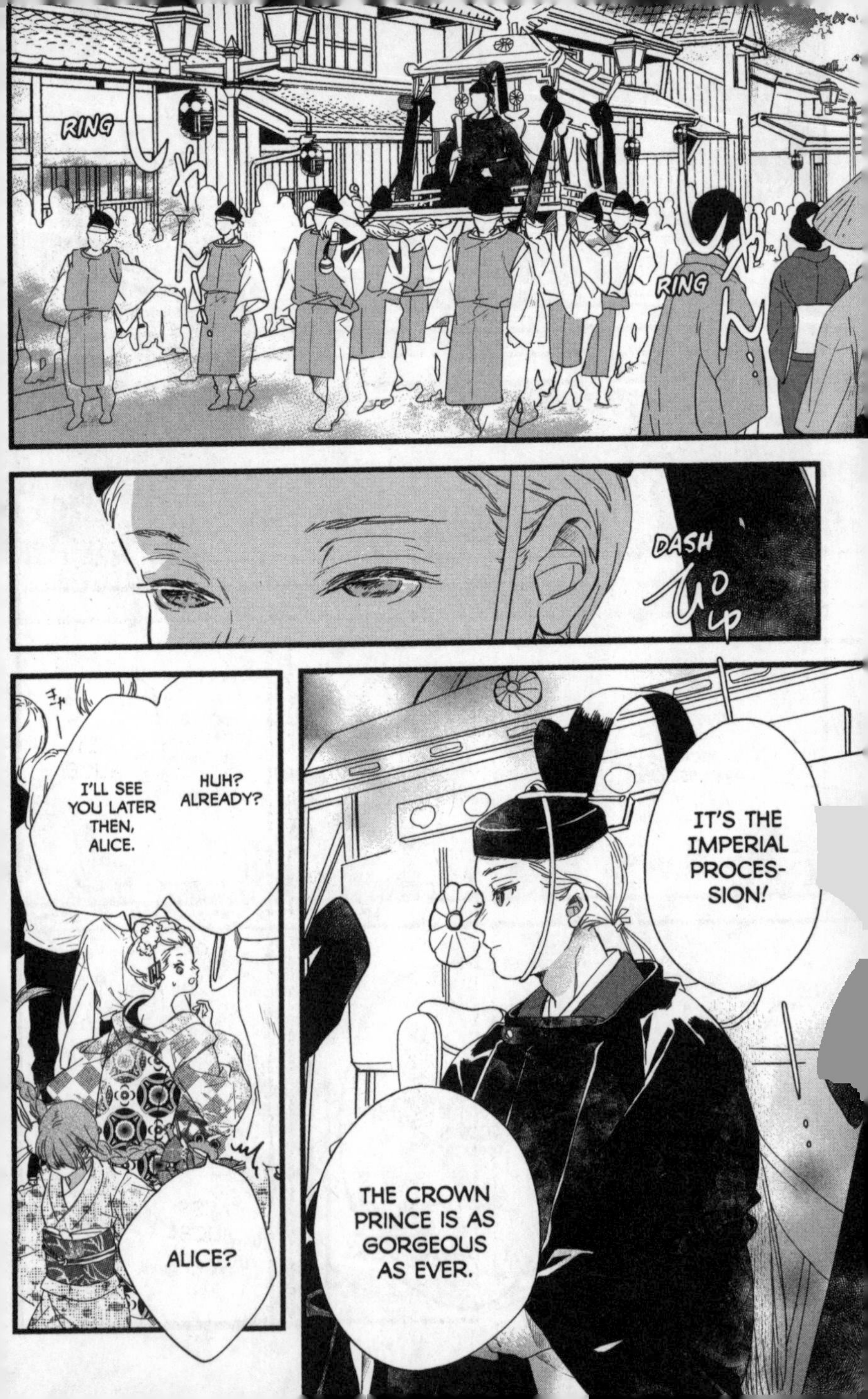

RING
RING
DASH
IT'S THE IMPERIAL PROCES-SION!
THE CROWN PRINCE IS AS GORGEOUS AS EVER.
HUH? ALREADY?
I'LL SEE YOU LATER THEN, ALICE.
ALICE?

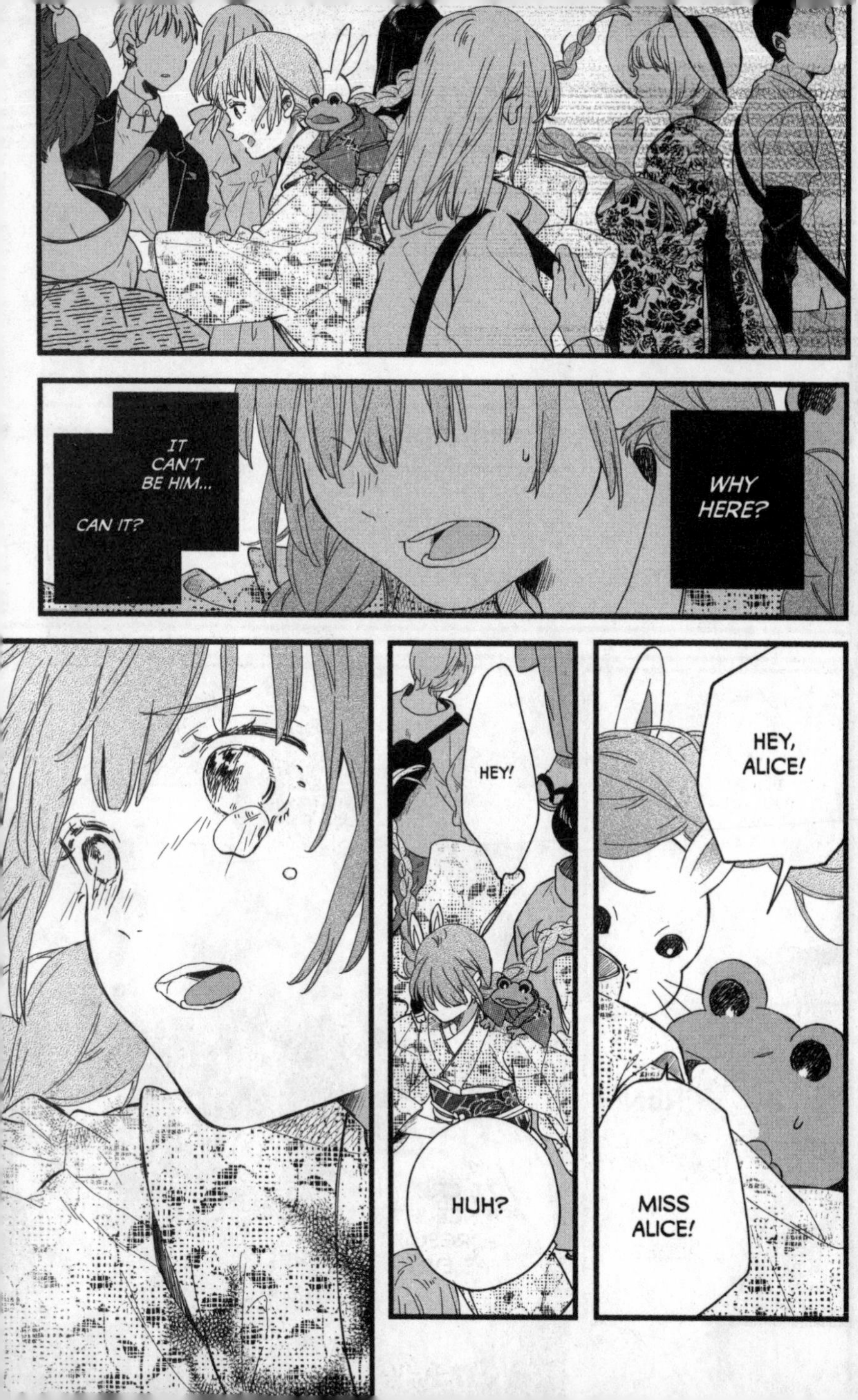
WHY HERE?
IT CAN'T BE HIM...
CAN IT?
HEY, ALICE!
MISS ALICE!
HEY!
HUH?

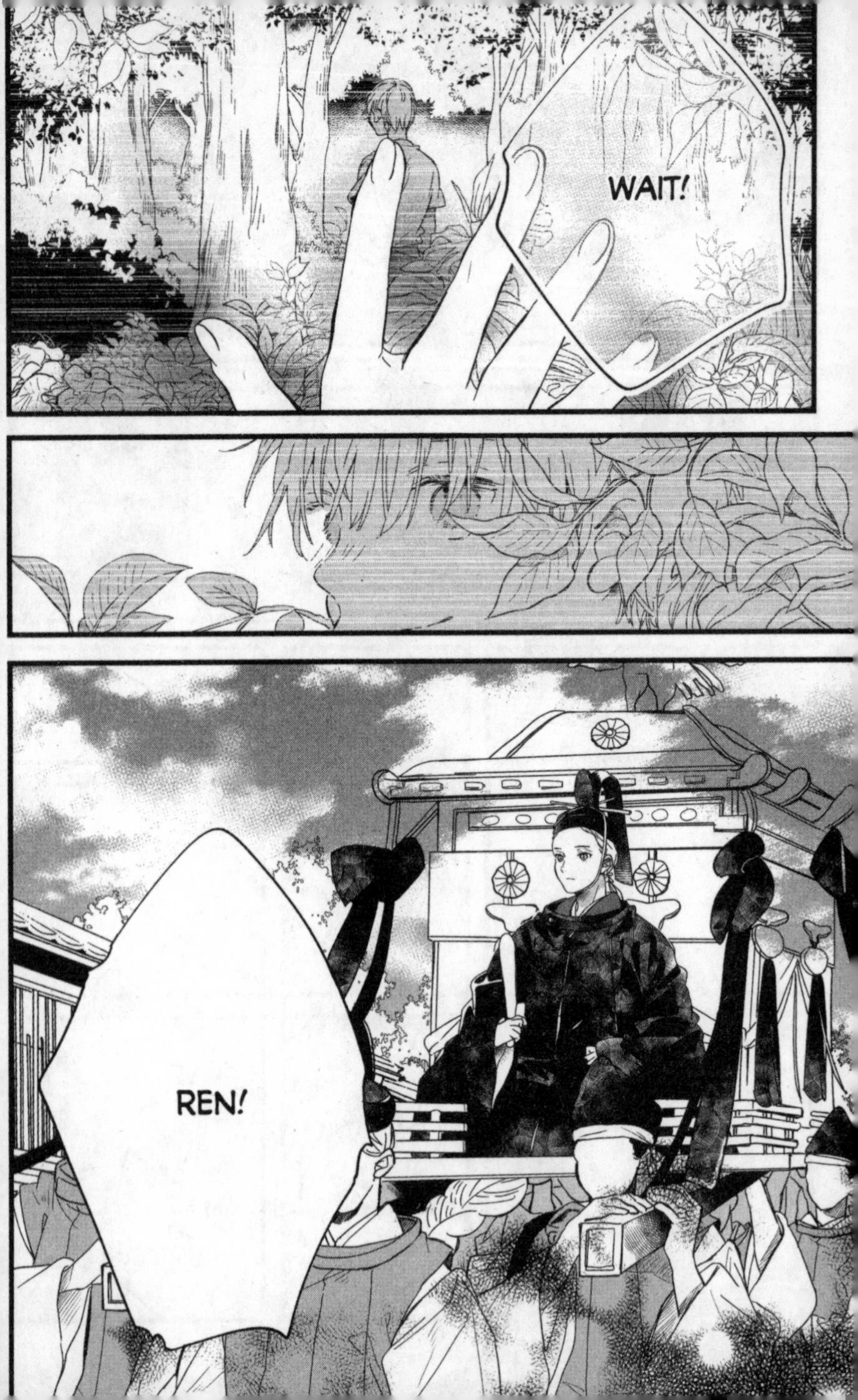
WAIT!
REN!

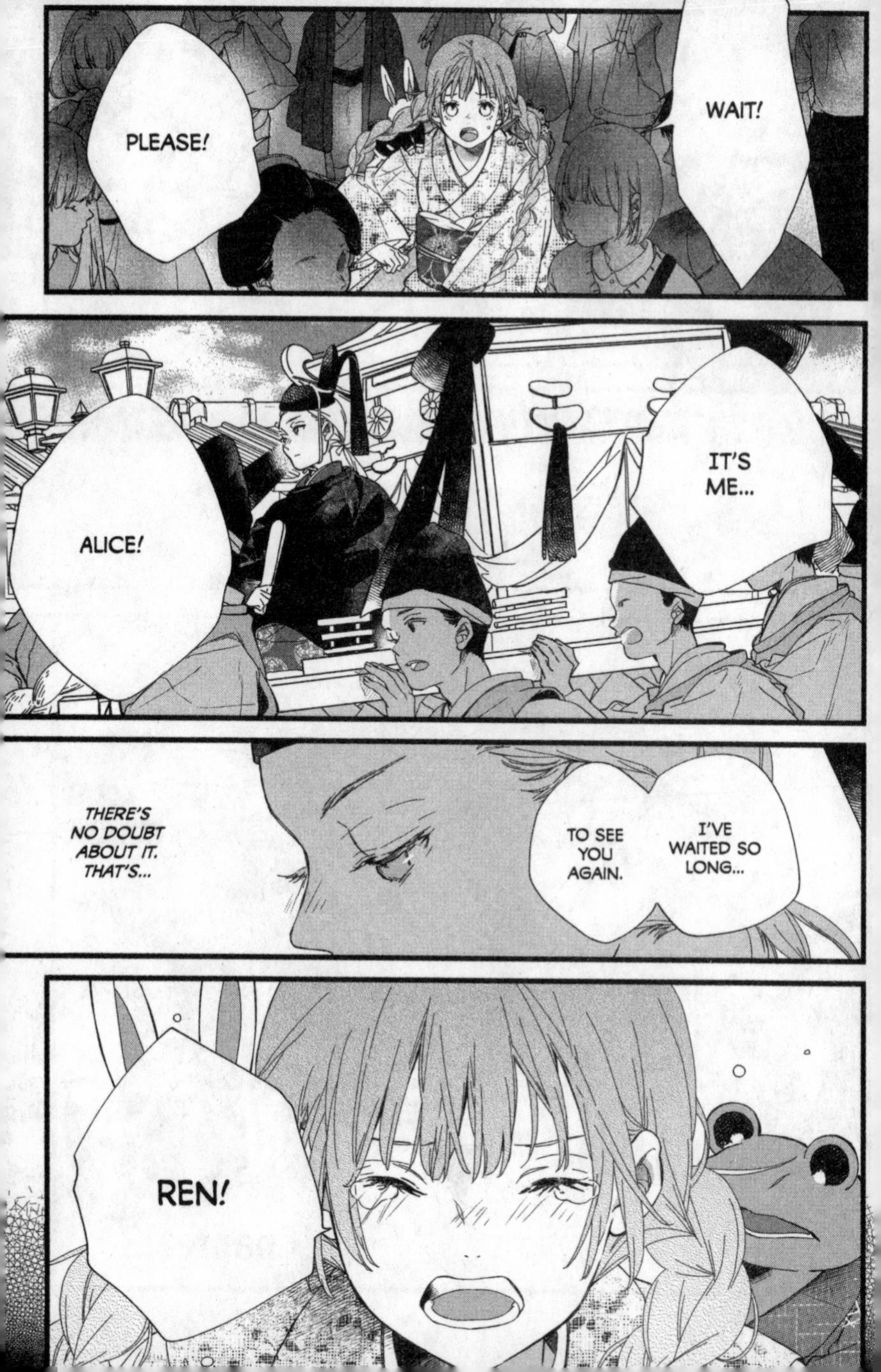
WAIT!
PLEASE!
IT'S ME...
ALICE!
I'VE WAITED SO LONG...
TO SEE YOU AGAIN.
THERE'S NO DOUBT ABOUT IT. THAT'S...
REN!

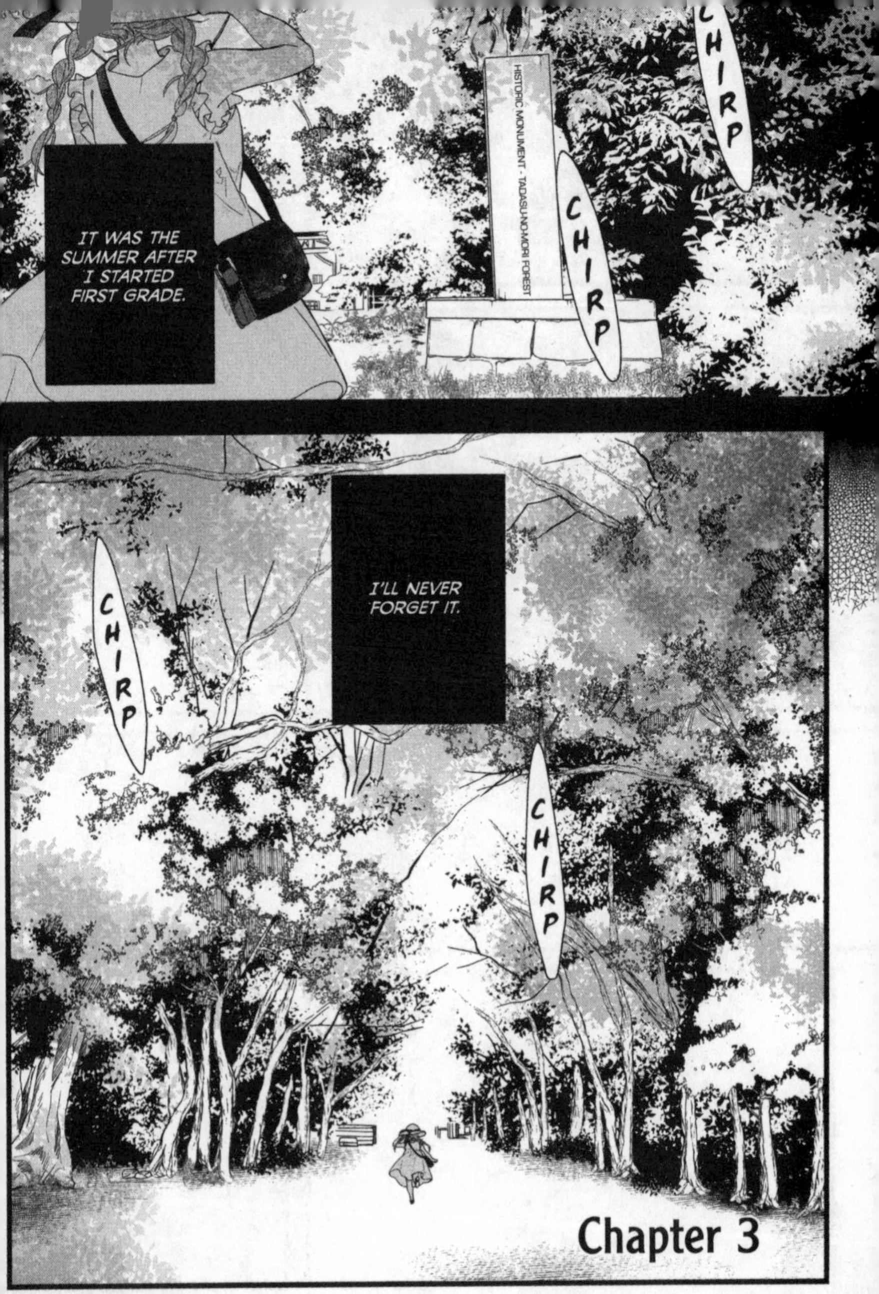
CHIRP
CHIRP
HISTORIC MONUMENT - TADASU-NO-MORI FOREST
IT WAS THE SUMMER AFTER I STARTED FIRST GRADE.
I'LL NEVER FORGET IT.
CHIRP
CHIRP
Chapter 3

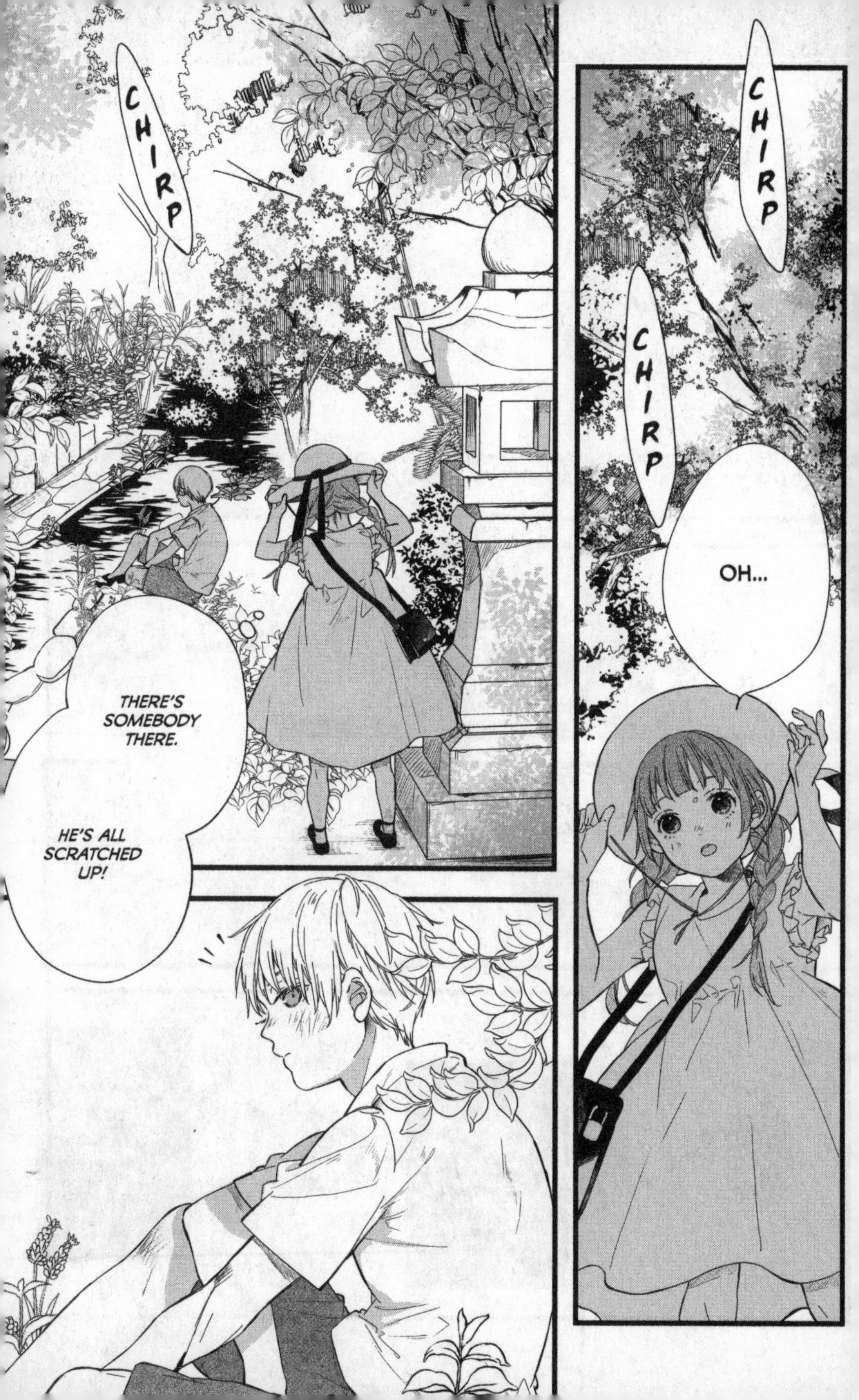
CHIRP
CHIRP
OH...
CHIRP
THERE'S SOMEBODY THERE.
HE'S ALL SCRATCHED UP!

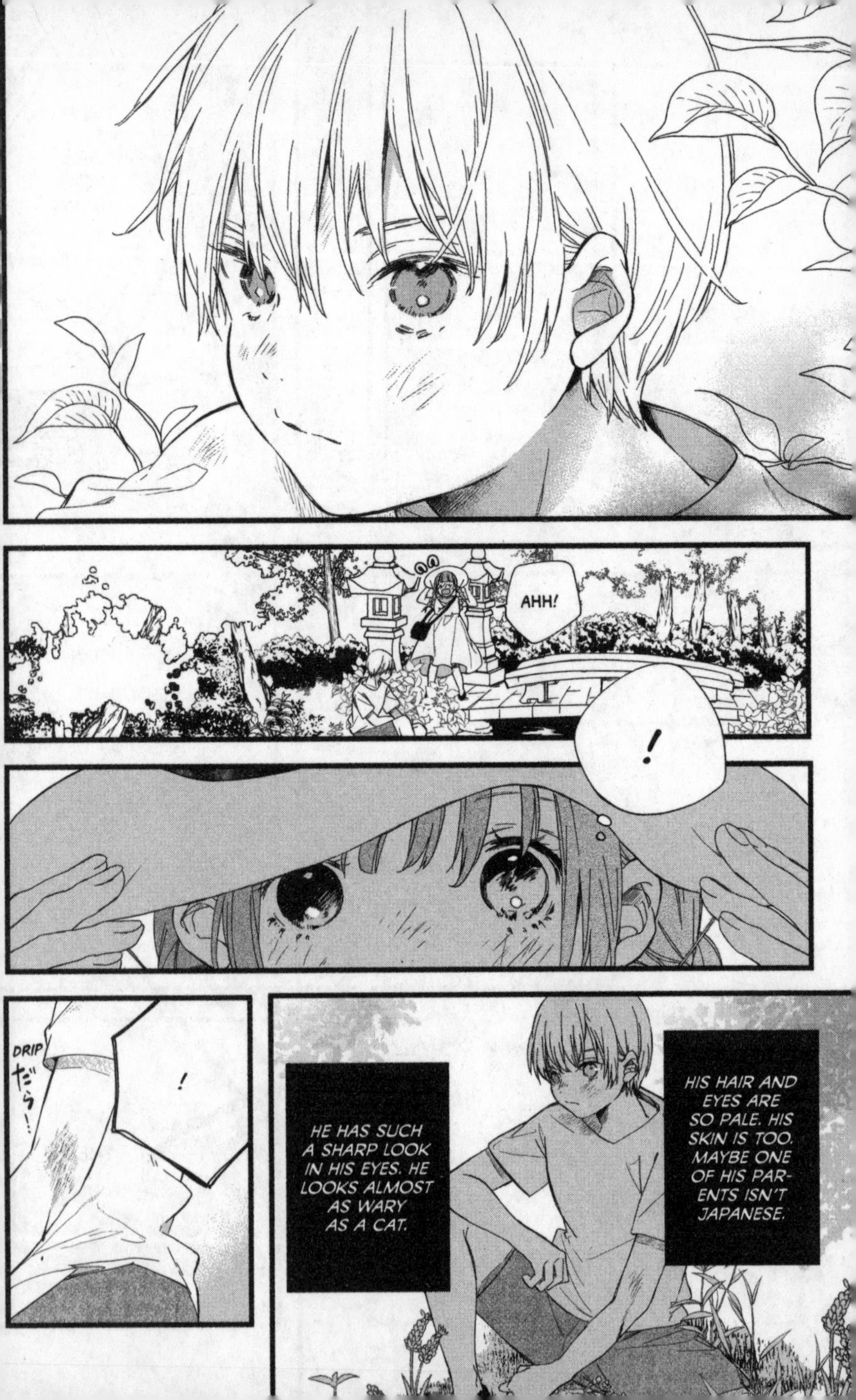
AHH!
!
HIS HAIR AND EYES ARE SO PALE. HIS SKIN IS TOO. MAYBE ONE OF HIS PAR-ENTS ISN'T JAPANESE.
HE HAS SUCH A SHARP LOOK IN HIS EYES. HE LOOKS ALMOST AS WARY AS A CAT.
DRIP
だら!!
!

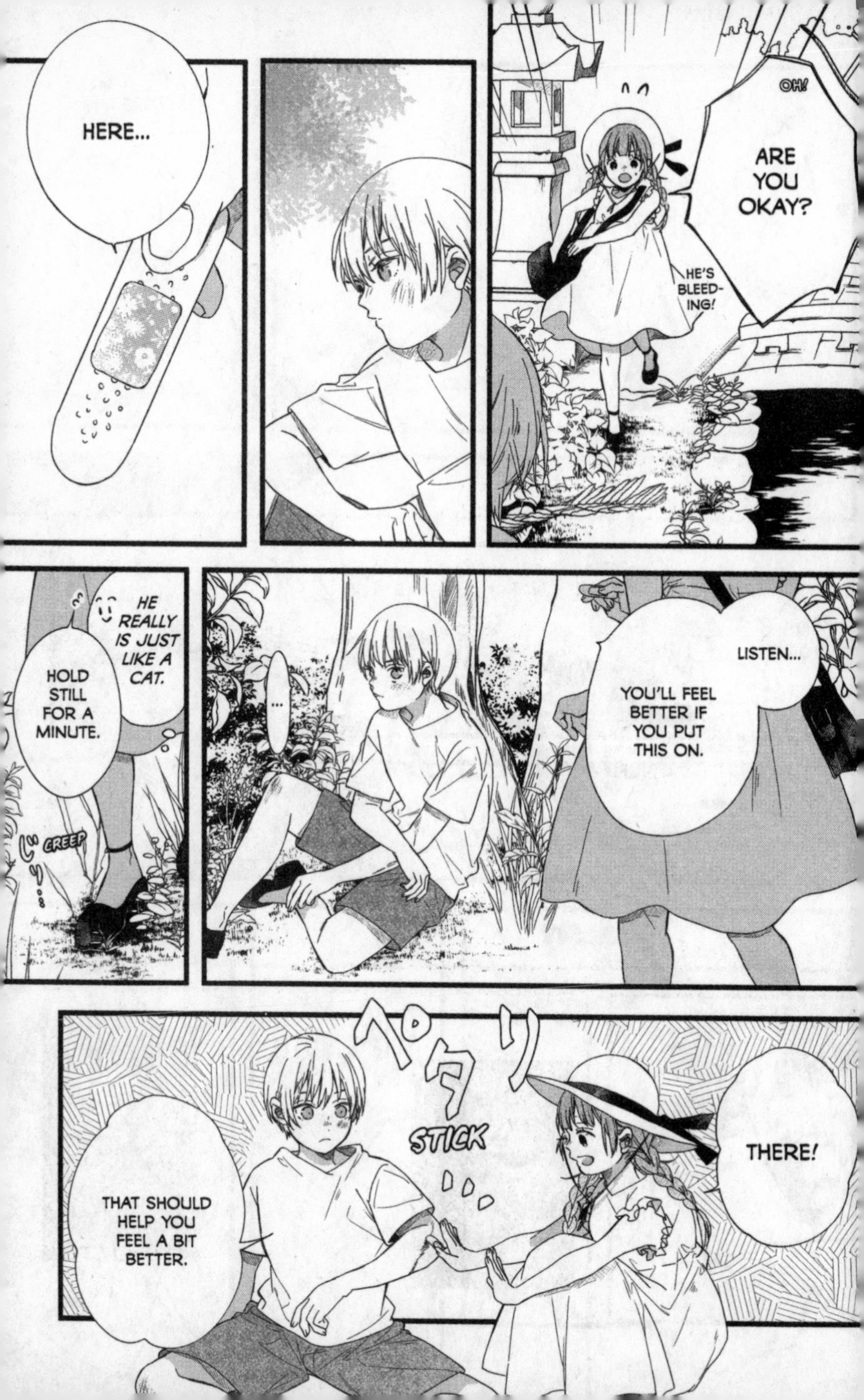
OH!
ARE YOU OKAY?
HE'S BLEEDING!
HERE...
LISTEN...
YOU'LL FEEL BETTER IF YOU PUT THIS ON.
...
HE REALLY IS JUST LIKE A CAT.
HOLD STILL FOR A MINUTE.
CREEP
THERE!
ペタリ
STICK
THAT SHOULD HELP YOU FEEL A BIT BETTER.

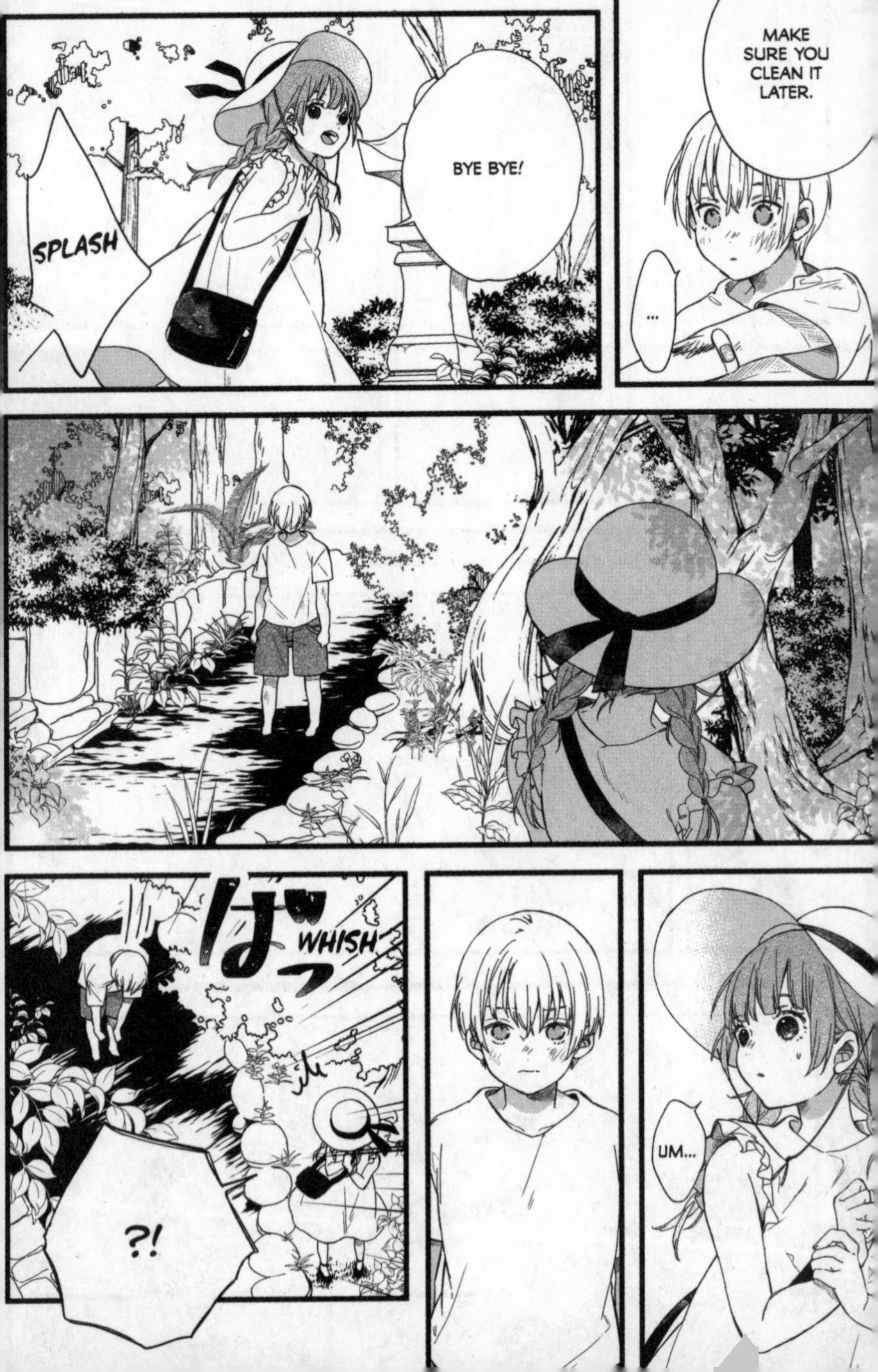
MAKE SURE YOU CLEAN IT LATER.
...
BYE BYE!
SPLASH
UM...
ばっ
WHISH
?!

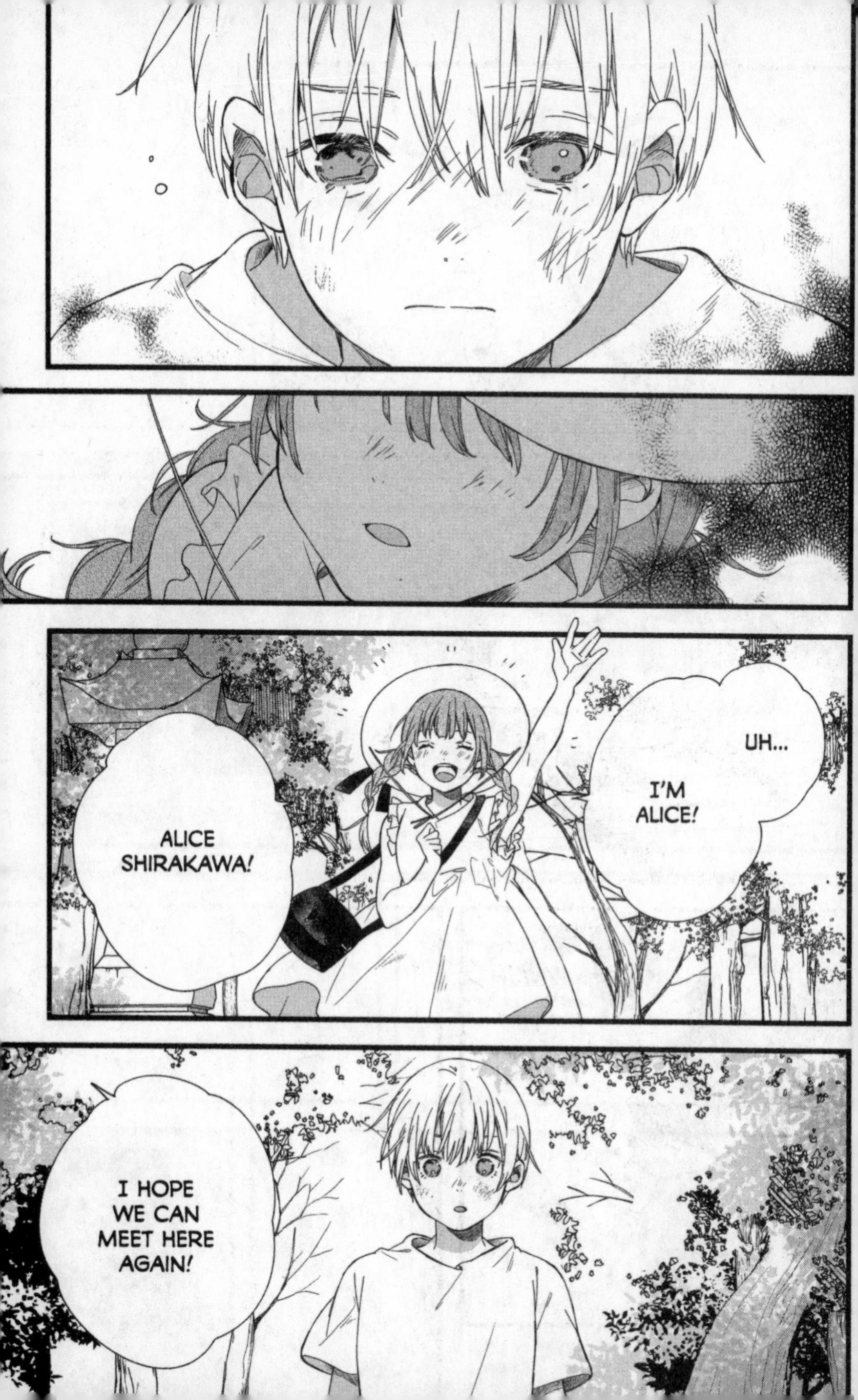
UH...
I'M ALICE!
ALICE SHIRAKAWA!
I HOPE WE CAN MEET HERE AGAIN!

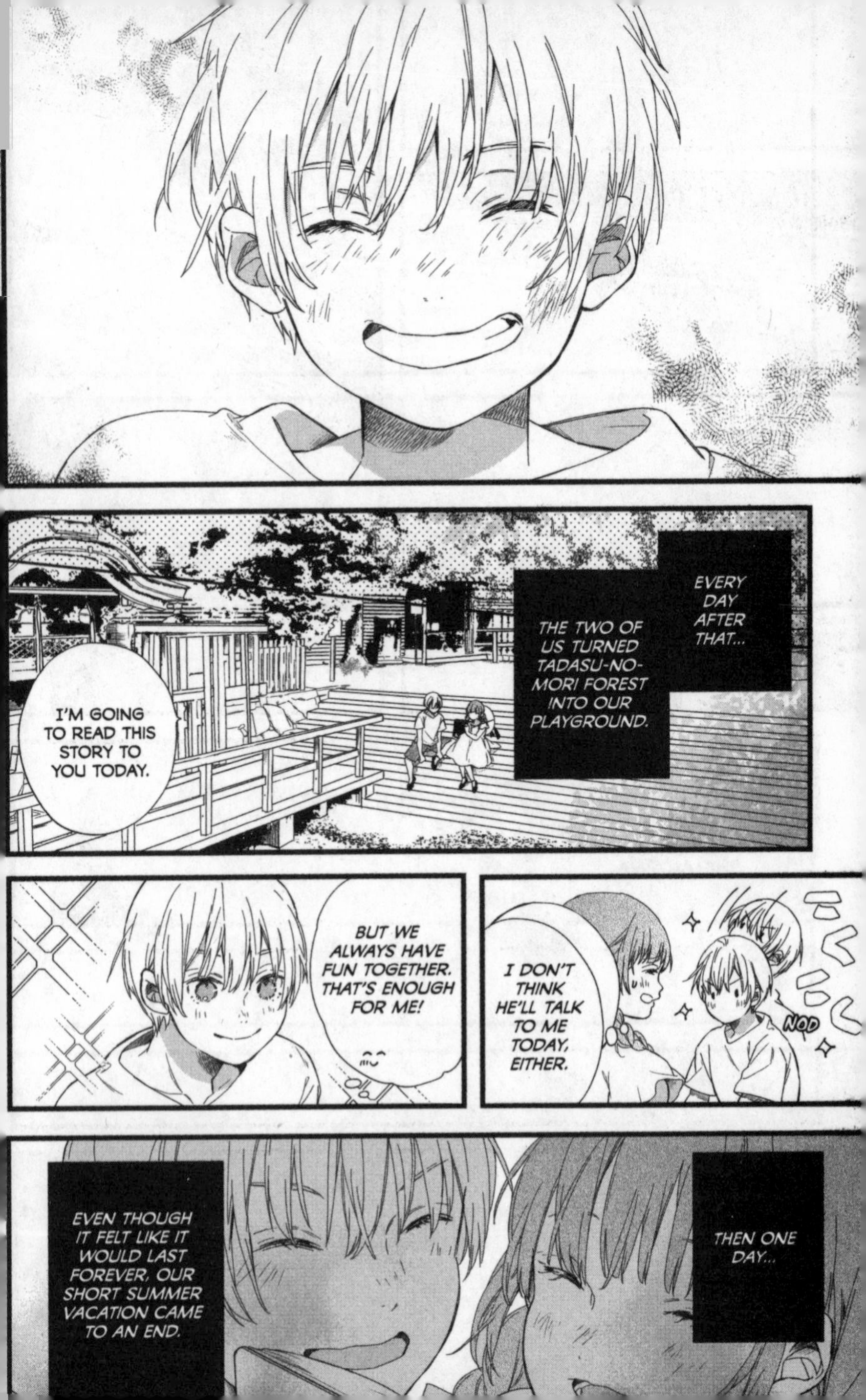
EVERY DAY AFTER THAT...
THE TWO OF US TURNED TADASU-NO-MORI FOREST INTO OUR PLAYGROUND.
I'M GOING TO READ THIS STORY TO YOU TODAY.
I DON'T THINK HE'LL TALK TO ME TODAY, EITHER.
NOD
BUT WE ALWAYS HAVE FUN TOGETHER. THAT'S ENOUGH FOR ME!
THEN ONE DAY...
EVEN THOUGH IT FELT LIKE IT WOULD LAST FOREVER, OUR SHORT SUMMER VACATION CAME TO AN END.

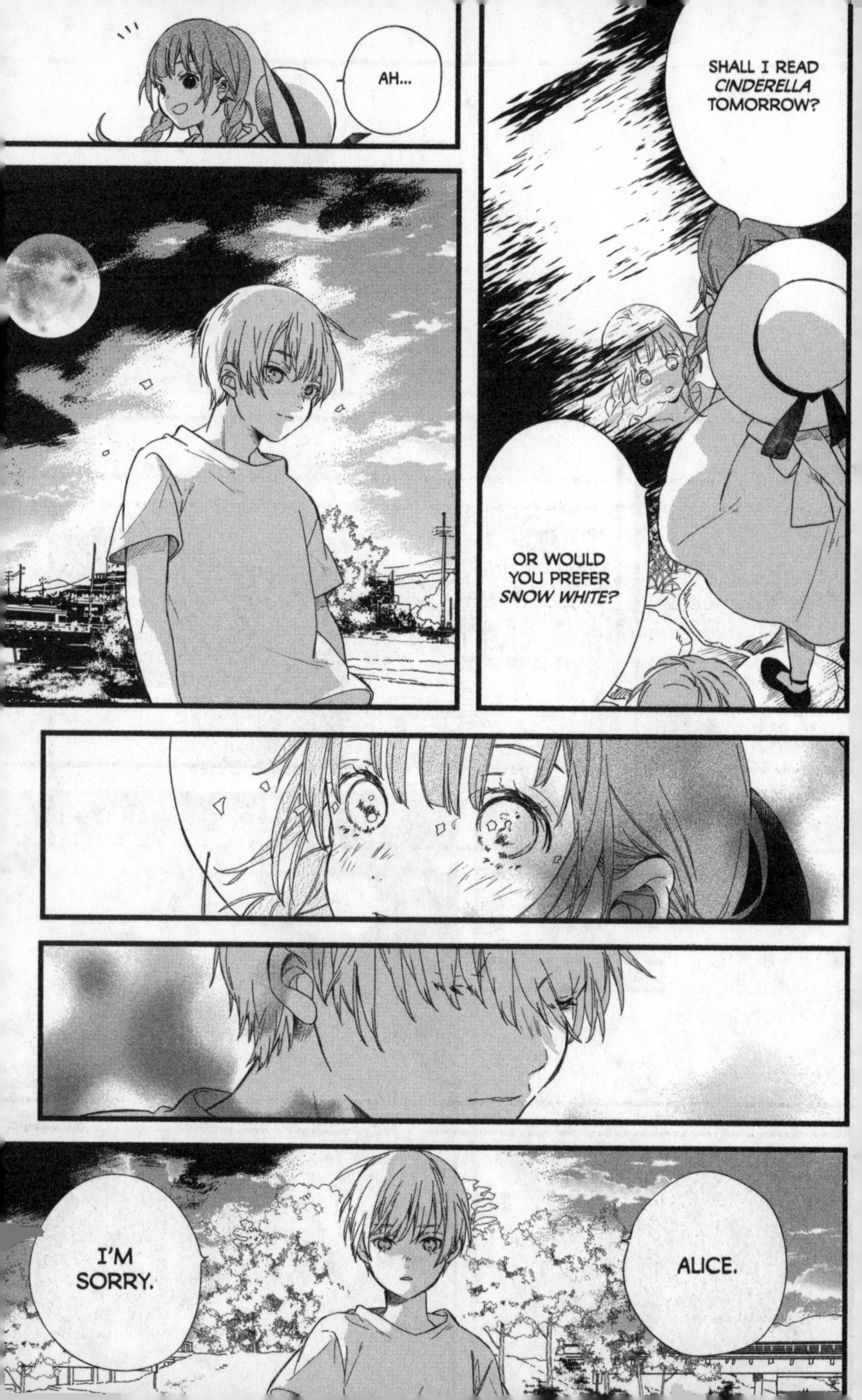
SHALL I READ *CINDERELLA* TOMORROW?
OR WOULD YOU PREFER *SNOW WHITE?*
AH...
ALICE.
I'M SORRY.

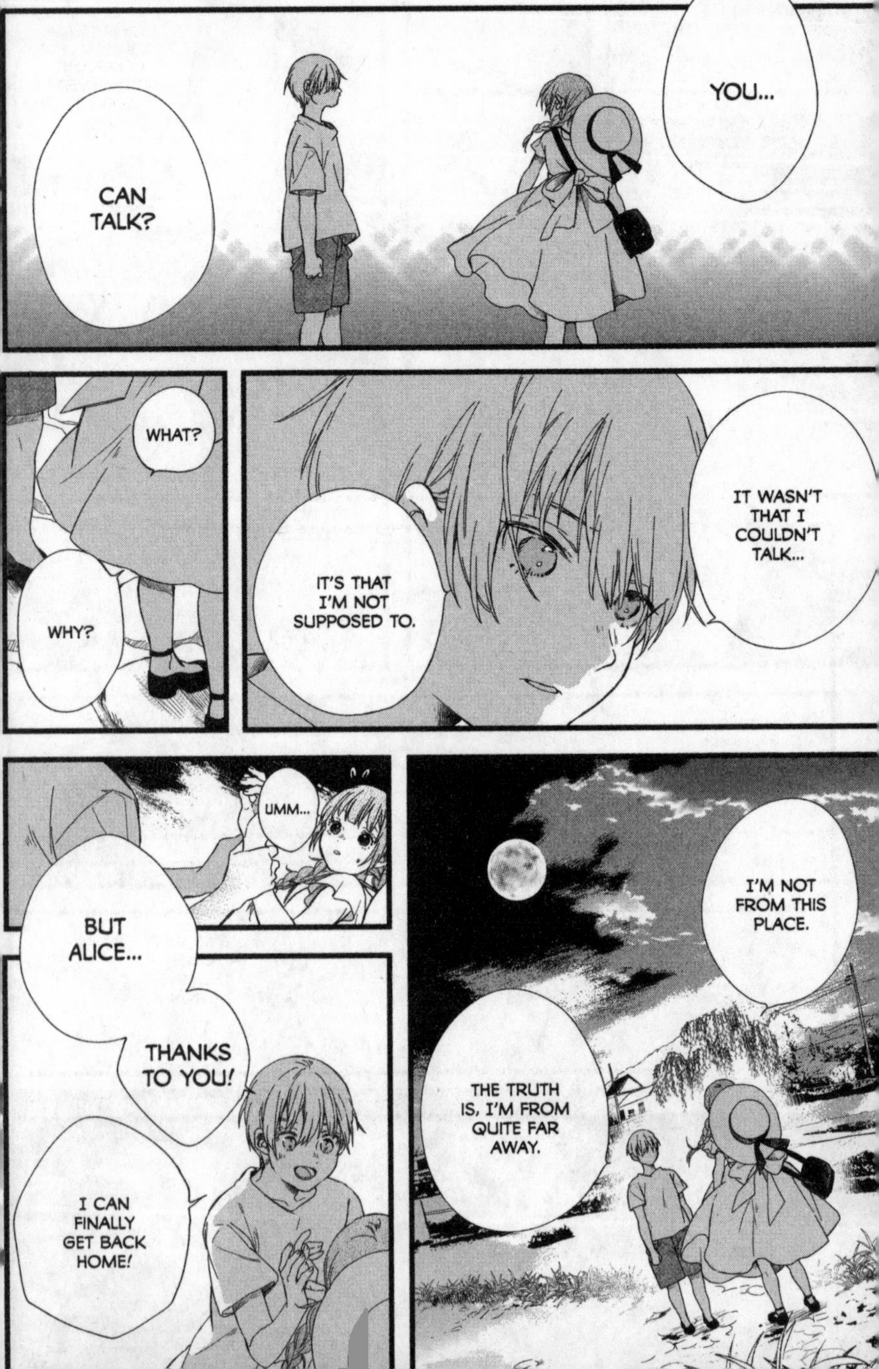
YOU...
CAN TALK?
IT WASN'T THAT I COULDN'T TALK...
IT'S THAT I'M NOT SUPPOSED TO.
WHAT?
WHY?
I'M NOT FROM THIS PLACE.
THE TRUTH IS, I'M FROM QUITE FAR AWAY.
UMM...
BUT ALICE...
THANKS TO YOU!
I CAN FINALLY GET BACK HOME!

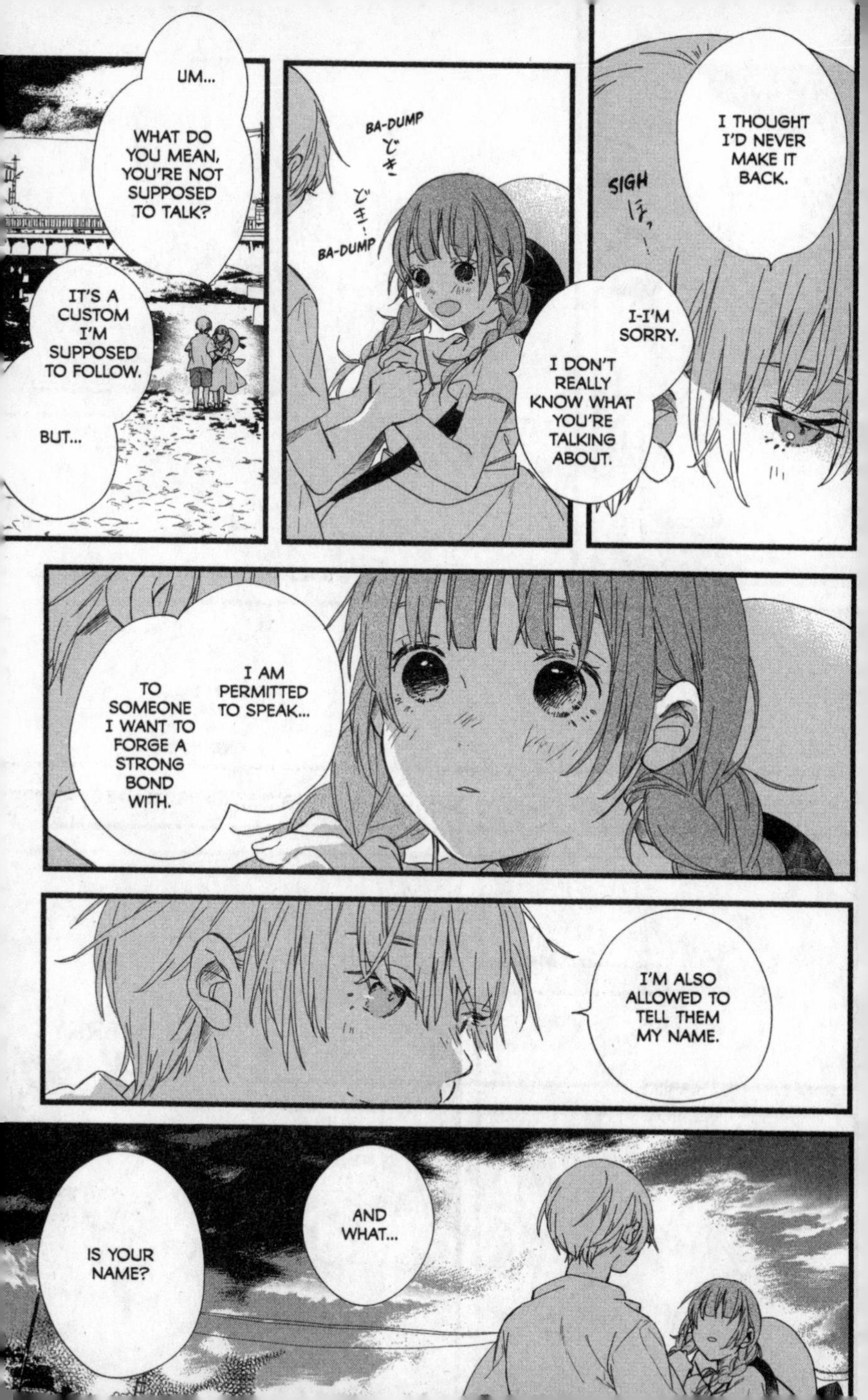
I THOUGHT I'D NEVER MAKE IT BACK.
SIGH
ほっ
I-I'M SORRY.
I DON'T REALLY KNOW WHAT YOU'RE TALKING ABOUT.
BA-DUMP
どき
どき…!
BA-DUMP
UM...
WHAT DO YOU MEAN, YOU'RE NOT SUPPOSED TO TALK?
IT'S A CUSTOM I'M SUPPOSED TO FOLLOW.
BUT...
I AM PERMITTED TO SPEAK...
TO SOMEONE I WANT TO FORGE A STRONG BOND WITH.
I'M ALSO ALLOWED TO TELL THEM MY NAME.
AND WHAT...
IS YOUR NAME?

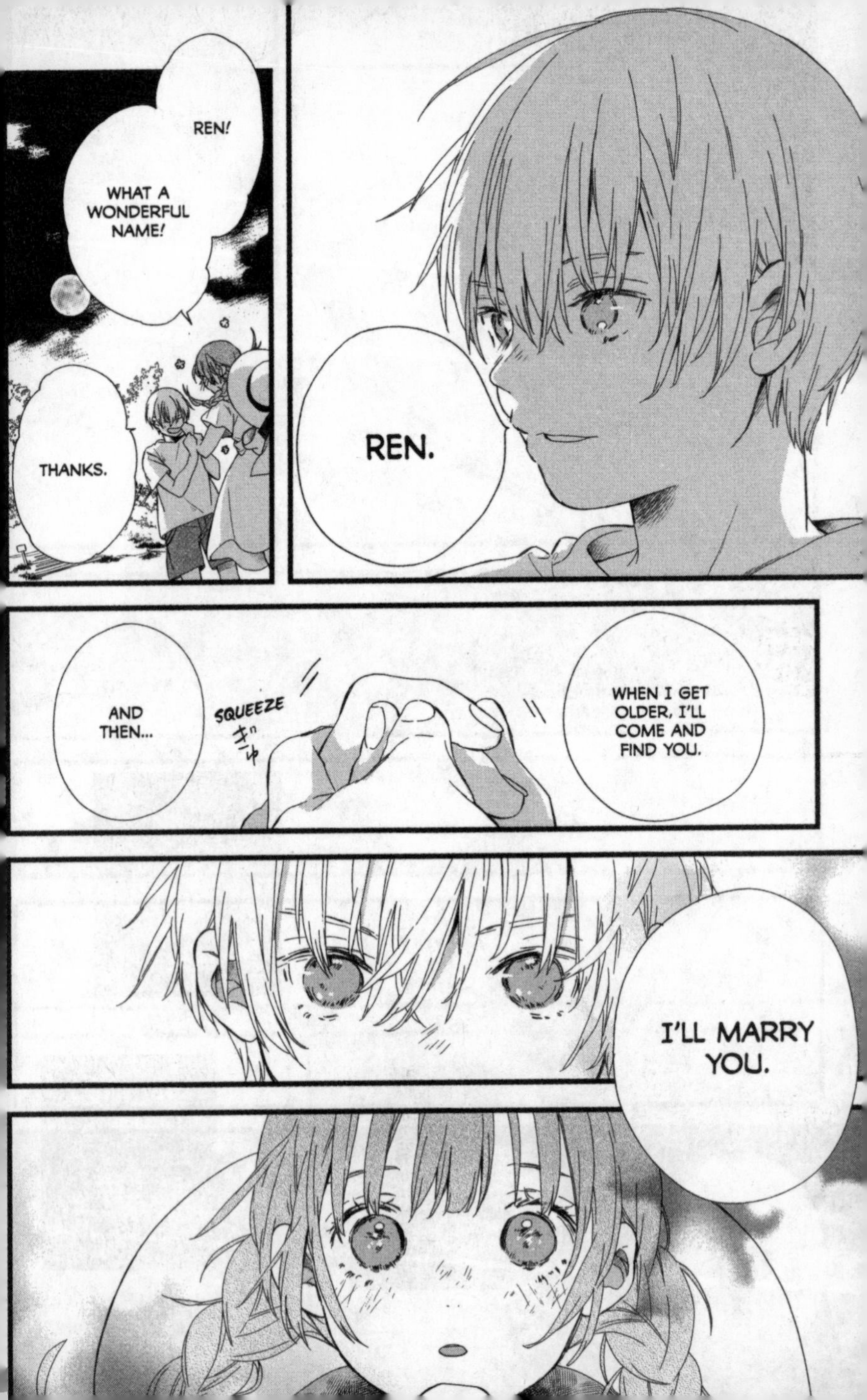
REN.
REN!
WHAT A WONDERFUL NAME!
THANKS.
WHEN I GET OLDER, I'LL COME AND FIND YOU.
SQUEEZE
ぎゅ
AND THEN...
I'LL MARRY YOU.

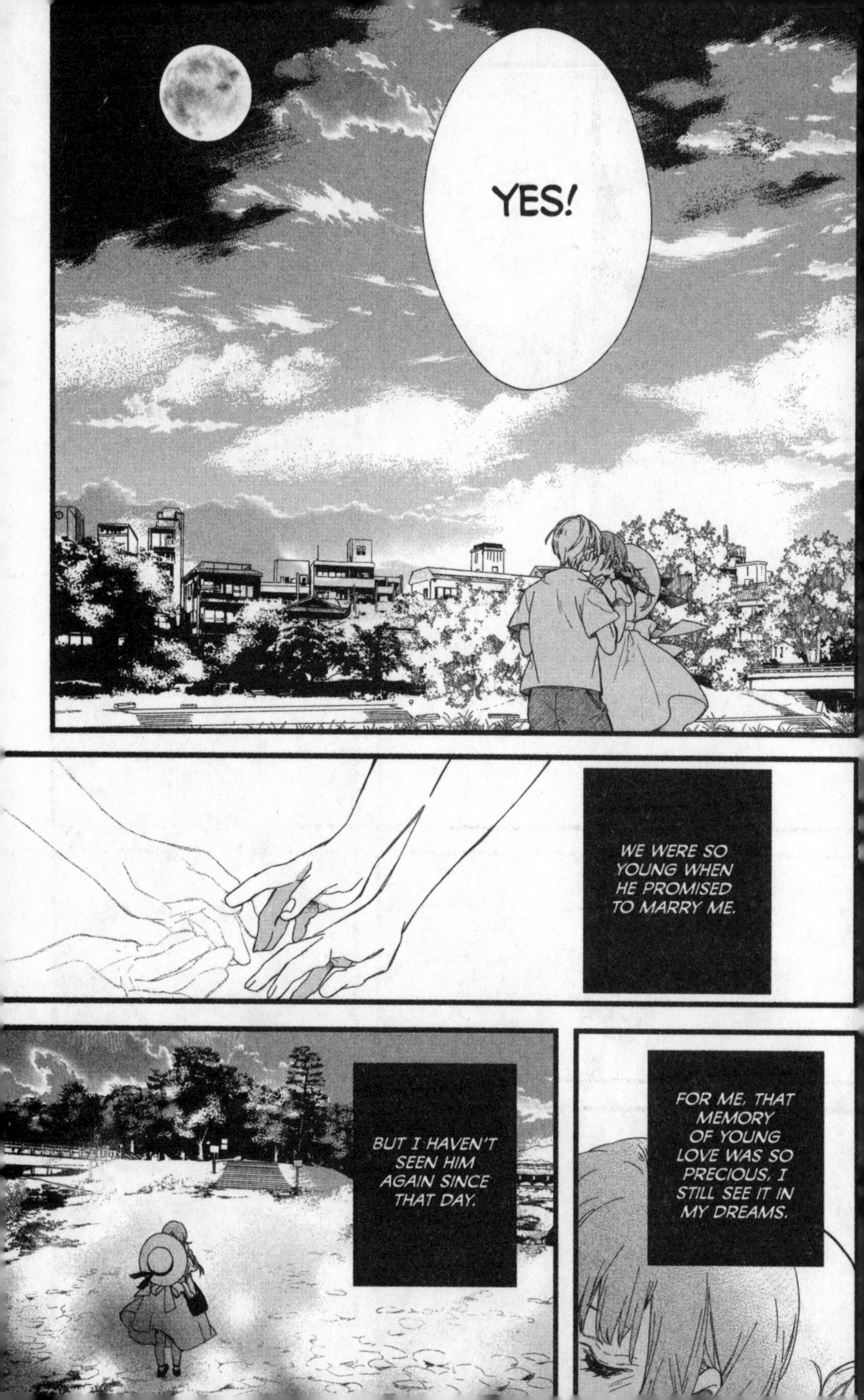
YES!
WE WERE SO YOUNG WHEN HE PROMISED TO MARRY ME.
FOR ME, THAT MEMORY OF YOUNG LOVE WAS SO PRECIOUS, I STILL SEE IT IN MY DREAMS.
BUT I HAVEN'T SEEN HIM AGAIN SINCE THAT DAY.

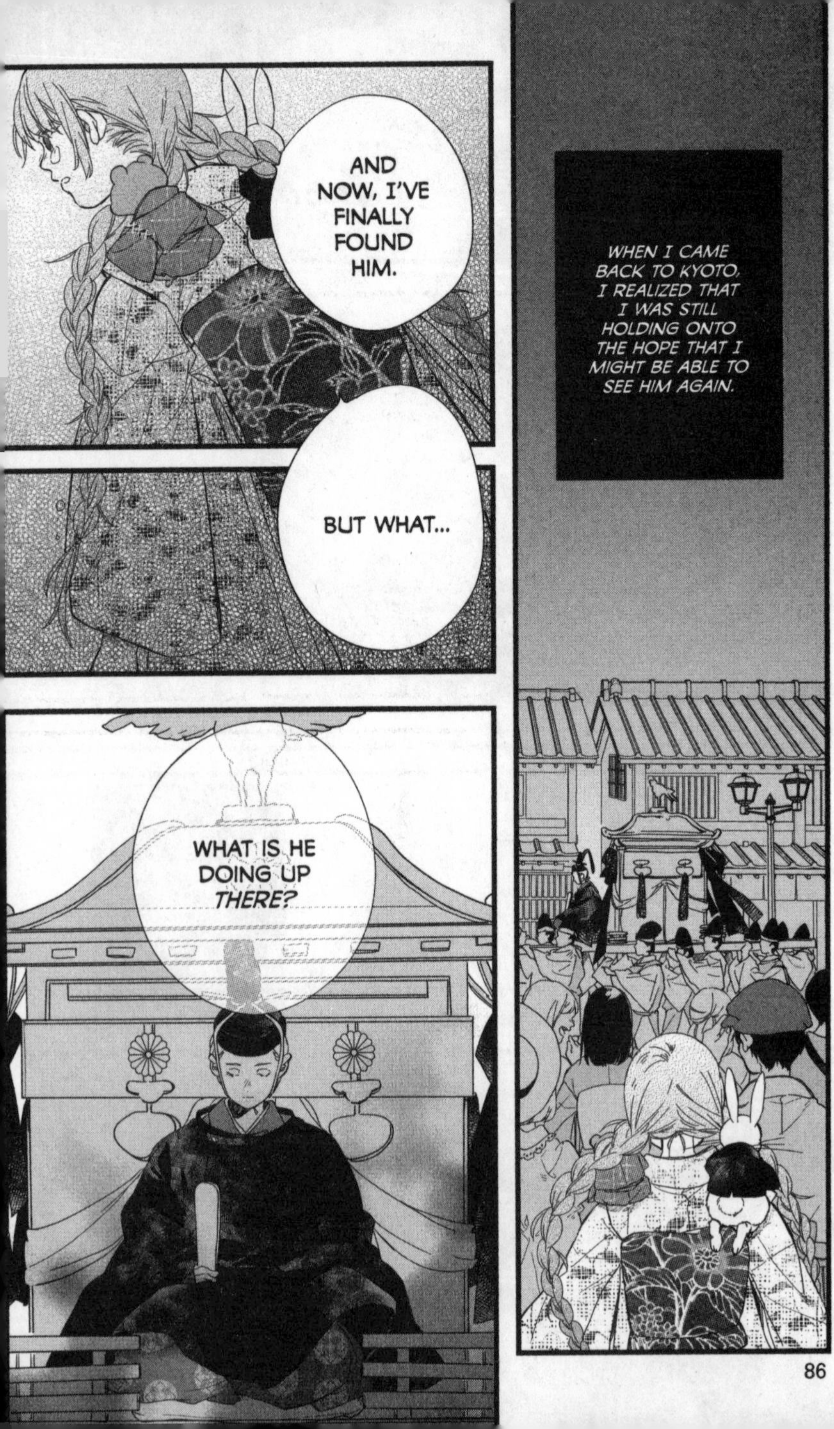
WHEN I CAME BACK TO KYOTO, I REALIZED THAT I WAS STILL HOLDING ONTO THE HOPE THAT I MIGHT BE ABLE TO SEE HIM AGAIN.
AND NOW, I'VE FINALLY FOUND HIM.
BUT WHAT...
WHAT IS HE DOING UP *THERE?*

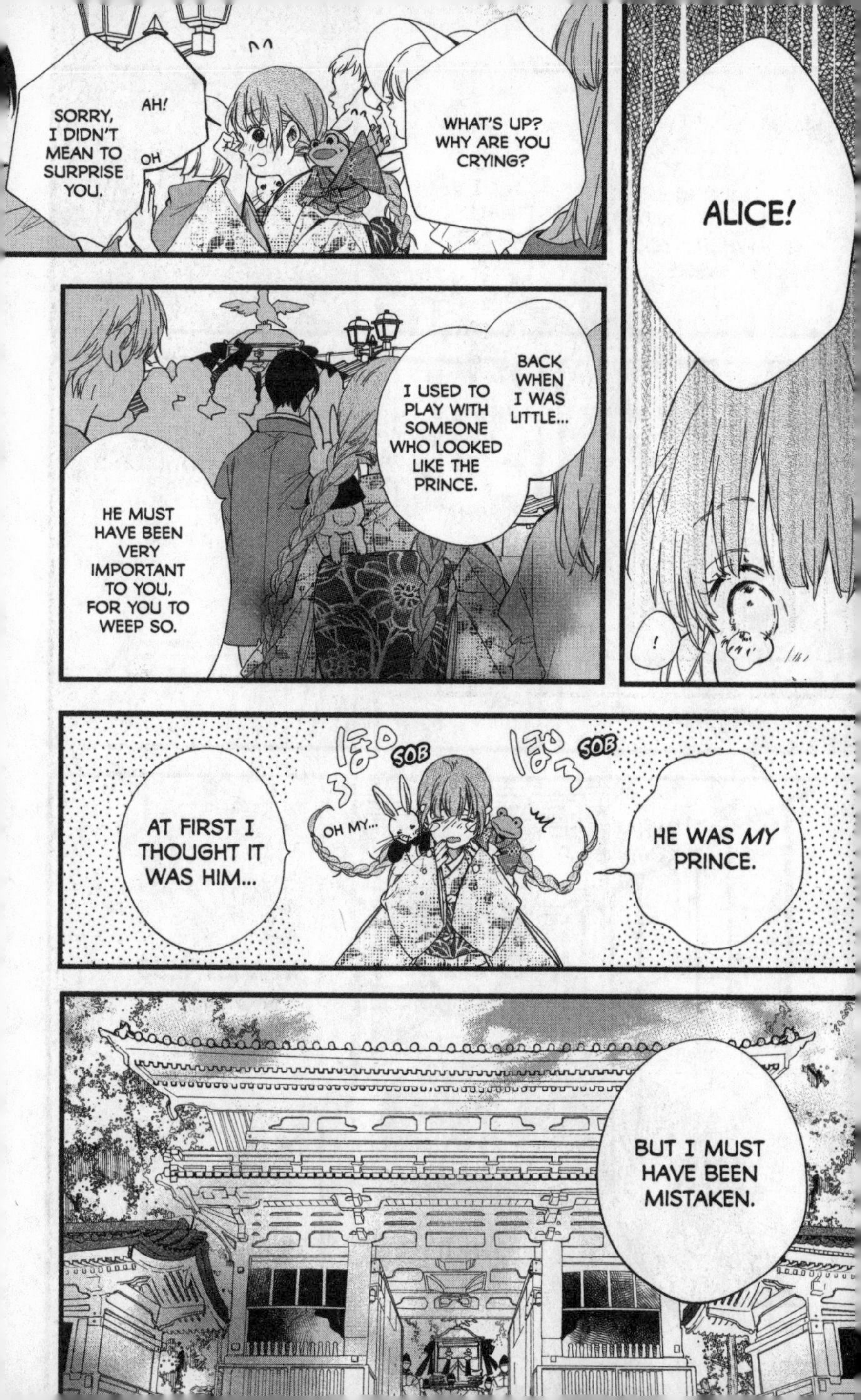
ALICE!
!
WHAT'S UP? WHY ARE YOU CRYING?
AH!
OH
SORRY, I DIDN'T MEAN TO SURPRISE YOU.
BACK WHEN I WAS LITTLE...
I USED TO PLAY WITH SOMEONE WHO LOOKED LIKE THE PRINCE.
HE MUST HAVE BEEN VERY IMPORTANT TO YOU, FOR YOU TO WEEP SO.
HE WAS *MY* PRINCE.
SOB
ほろ
SOB
ほろ
OH MY...
AT FIRST I THOUGHT IT WAS HIM...
BUT I MUST HAVE BEEN MISTAKEN.

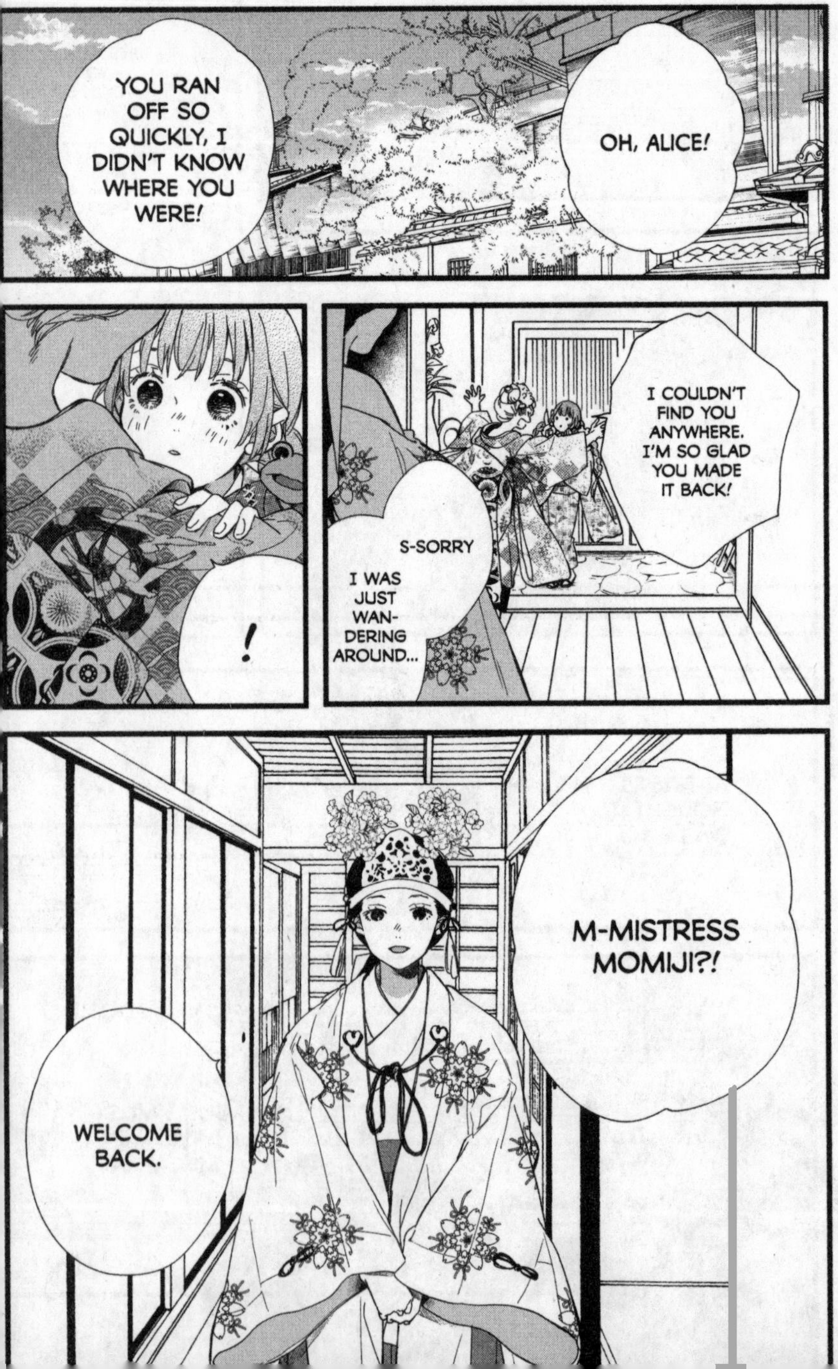
OH, ALICE!
YOU RAN OFF SO QUICKLY, I DIDN'T KNOW WHERE YOU WERE!
I COULDN'T FIND YOU ANYWHERE. I'M SO GLAD YOU MADE IT BACK!
S-SORRY
I WAS JUST WAN-DERING AROUND...
!
M-MISTRESS MOMIJI?!
WELCOME BACK.

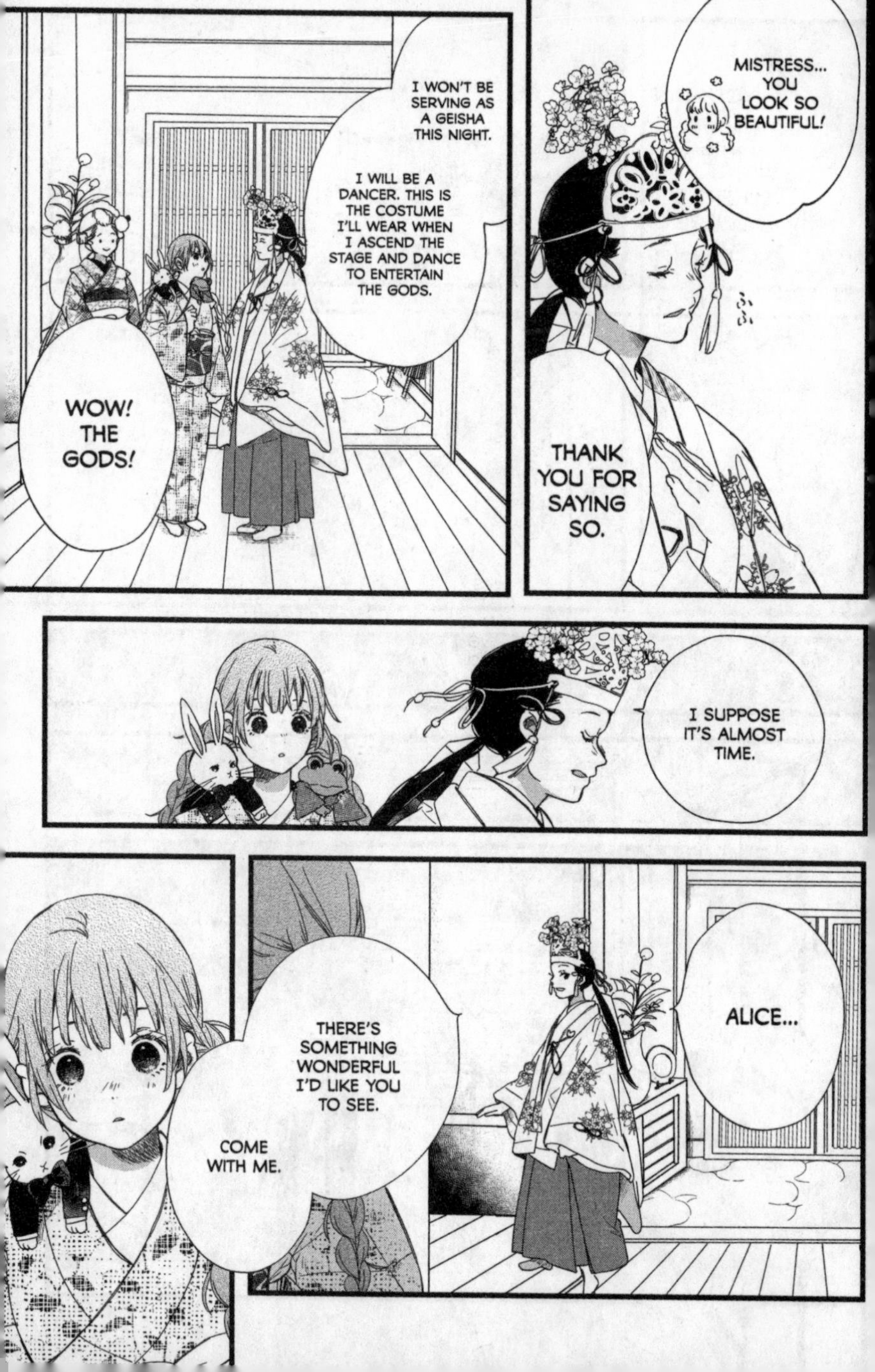
MISTRESS... YOU LOOK SO BEAUTIFUL!
ふふ
THANK YOU FOR SAYING SO.
I WON'T BE SERVING AS A GEISHA THIS NIGHT.
I WILL BE A DANCER. THIS IS THE COSTUME I'LL WEAR WHEN I ASCEND THE STAGE AND DANCE TO ENTERTAIN THE GODS.
WOW! THE GODS!
I SUPPOSE IT'S ALMOST TIME.
ALICE...
THERE'S SOMETHING WONDERFUL I'D LIKE YOU TO SEE.
COME WITH ME.

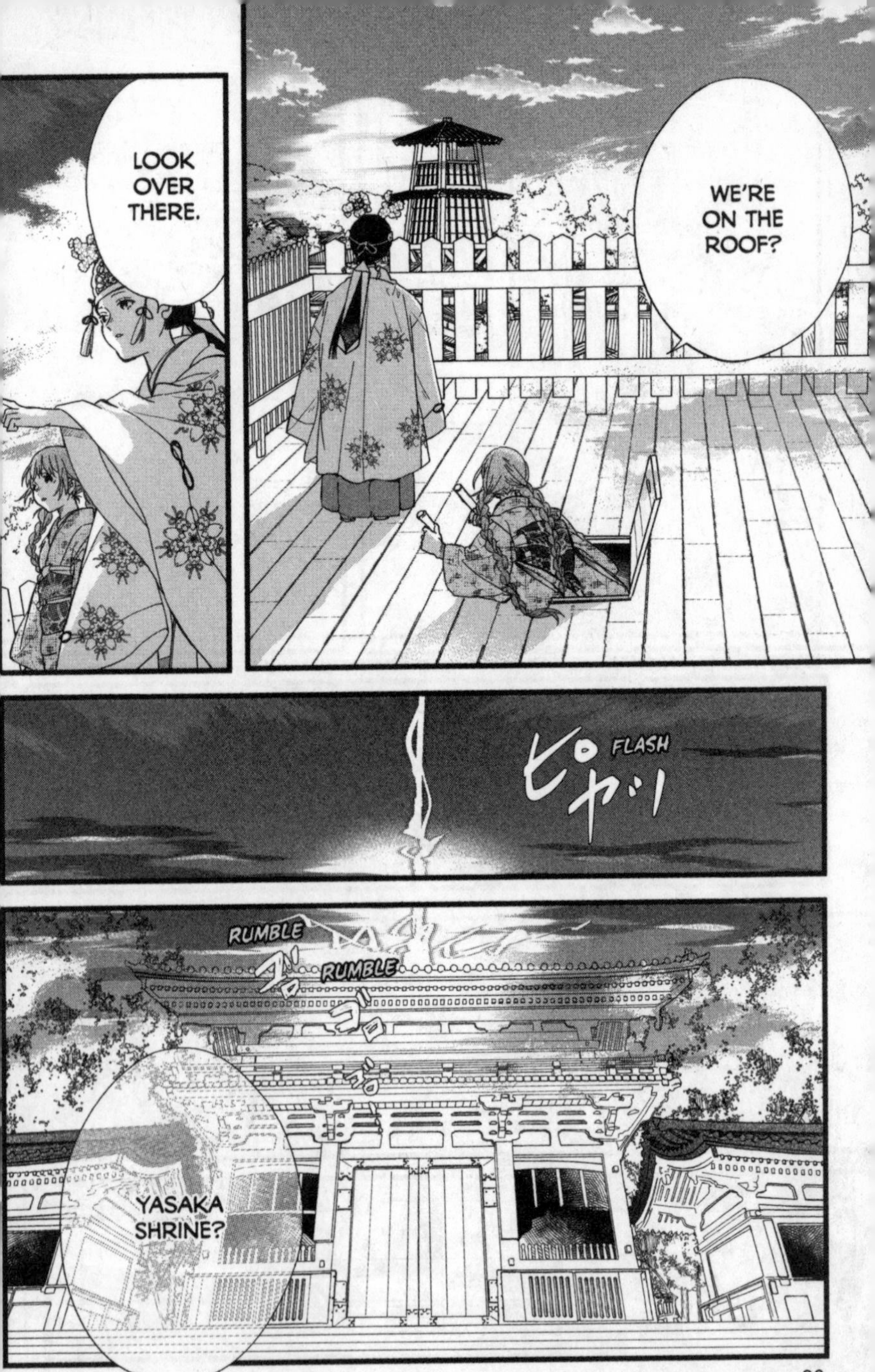
WE'RE ON THE ROOF?
LOOK OVER THERE.
FLASH
RUMBLE
RUMBLE
YASAKA SHRINE?

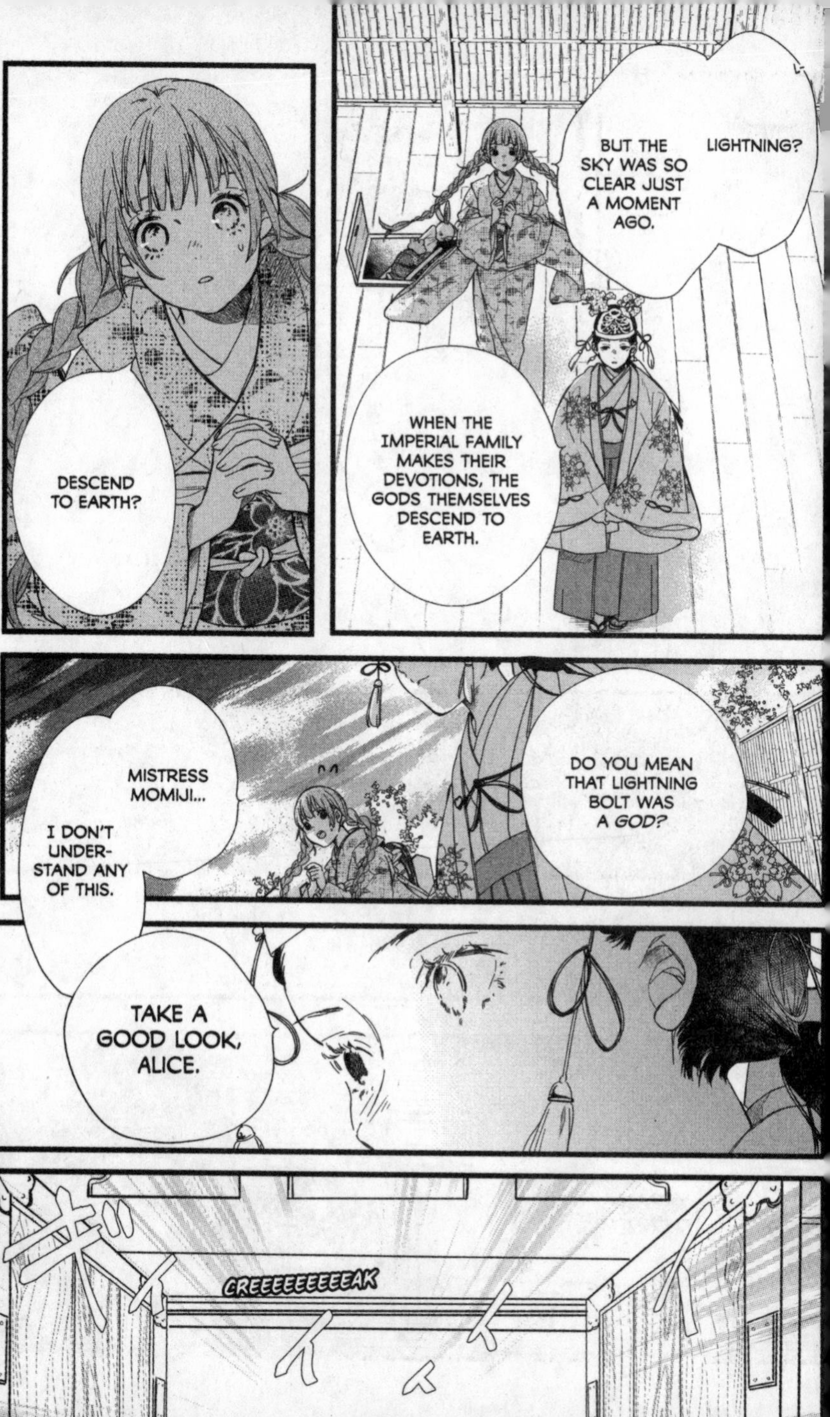
LIGHTNING?
BUT THE SKY WAS SO CLEAR JUST A MOMENT AGO.
WHEN THE IMPERIAL FAMILY MAKES THEIR DEVOTIONS, THE GODS THEMSELVES DESCEND TO EARTH.
DESCEND TO EARTH?
DO YOU MEAN THAT LIGHTNING BOLT WAS A *GOD?*
MISTRESS MOMIJI...
I DON'T UNDERSTAND ANY OF THIS.
TAKE A GOOD LOOK, ALICE.
CREEEEEEEEEEAK

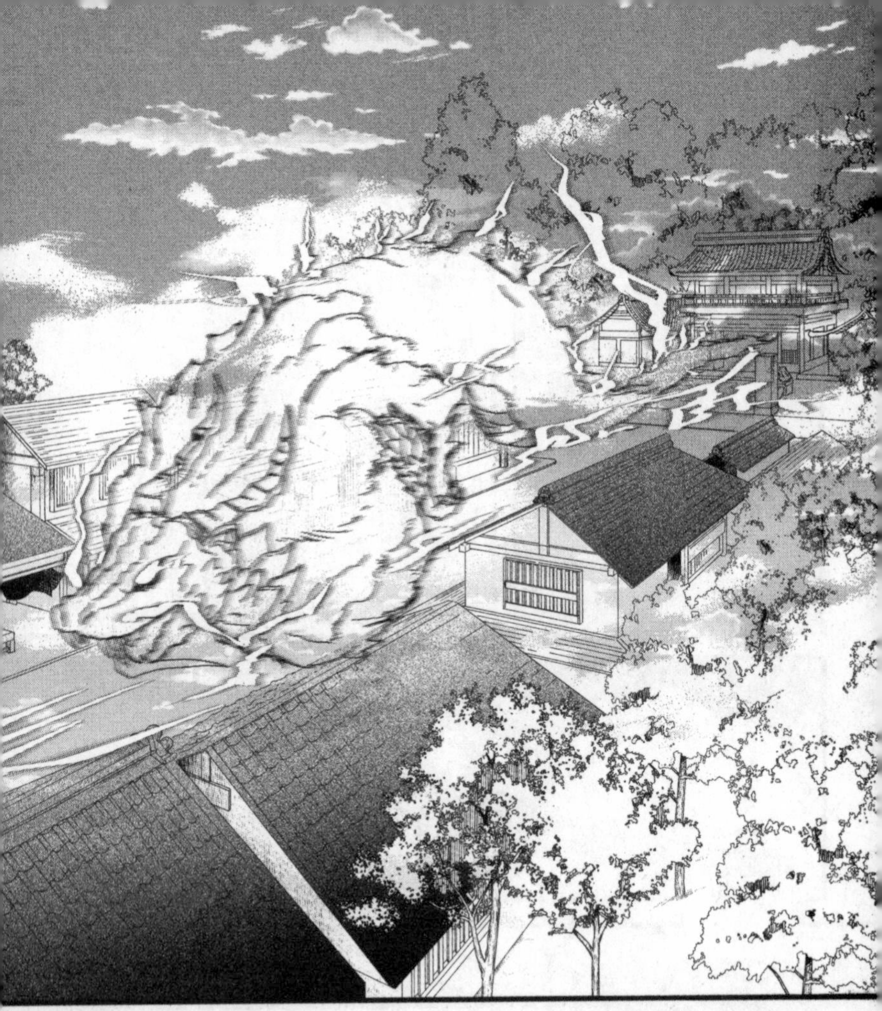
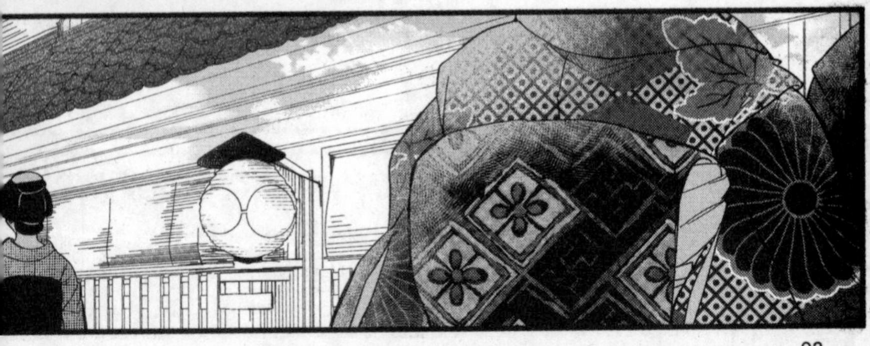

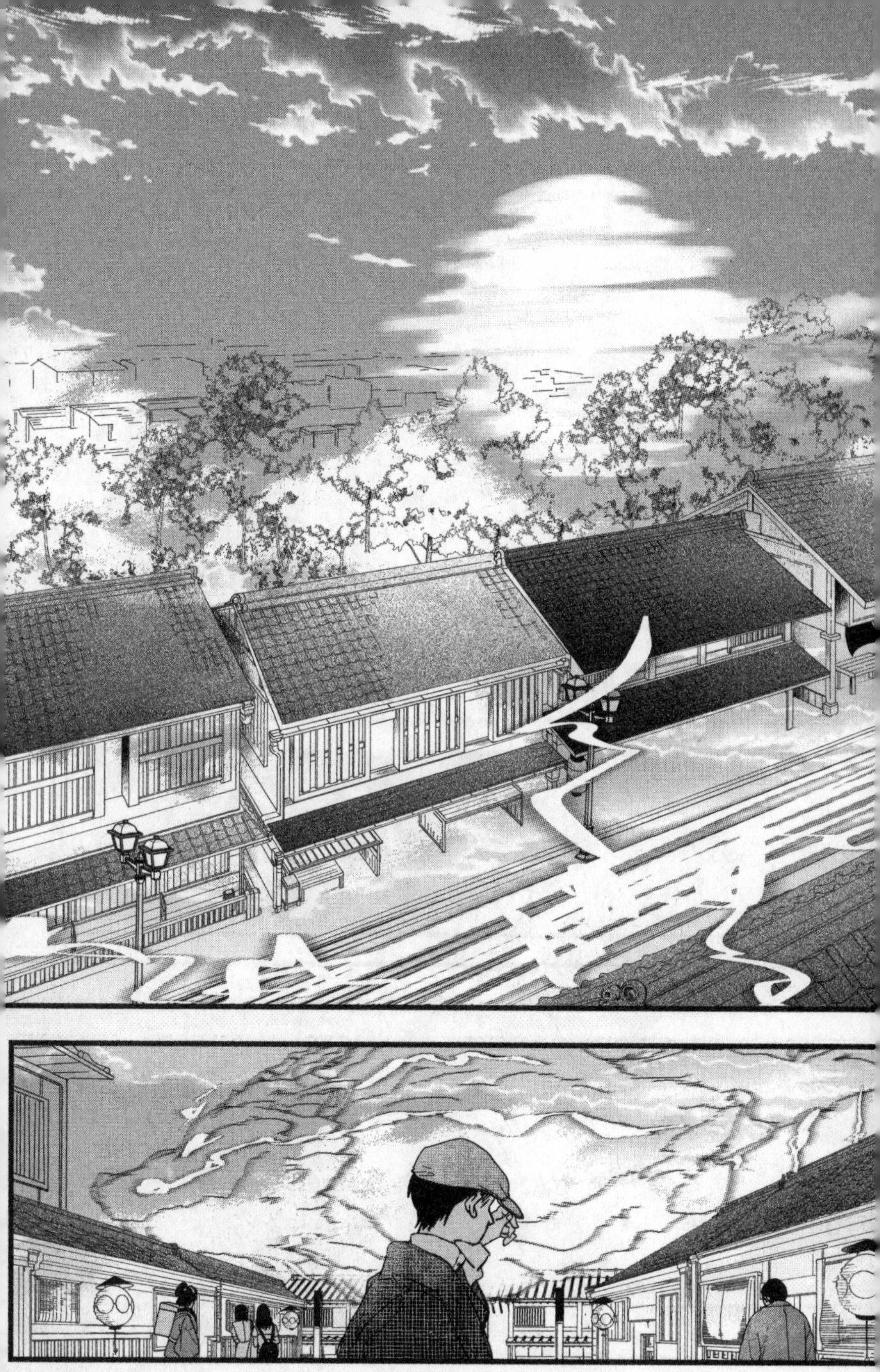

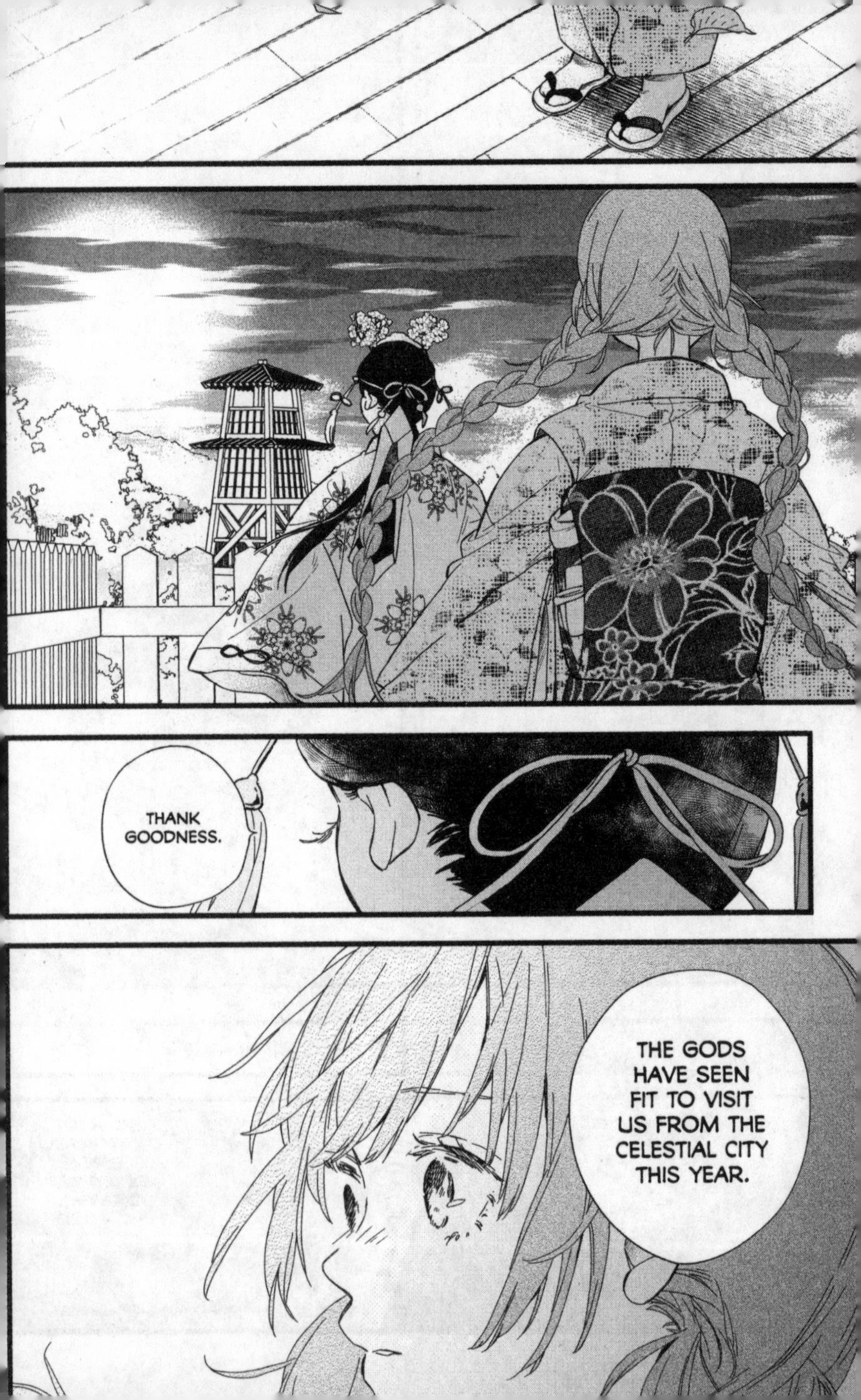
THANK GOODNESS.
THE GODS HAVE SEEN FIT TO VISIT US FROM THE CELESTIAL CITY THIS YEAR.

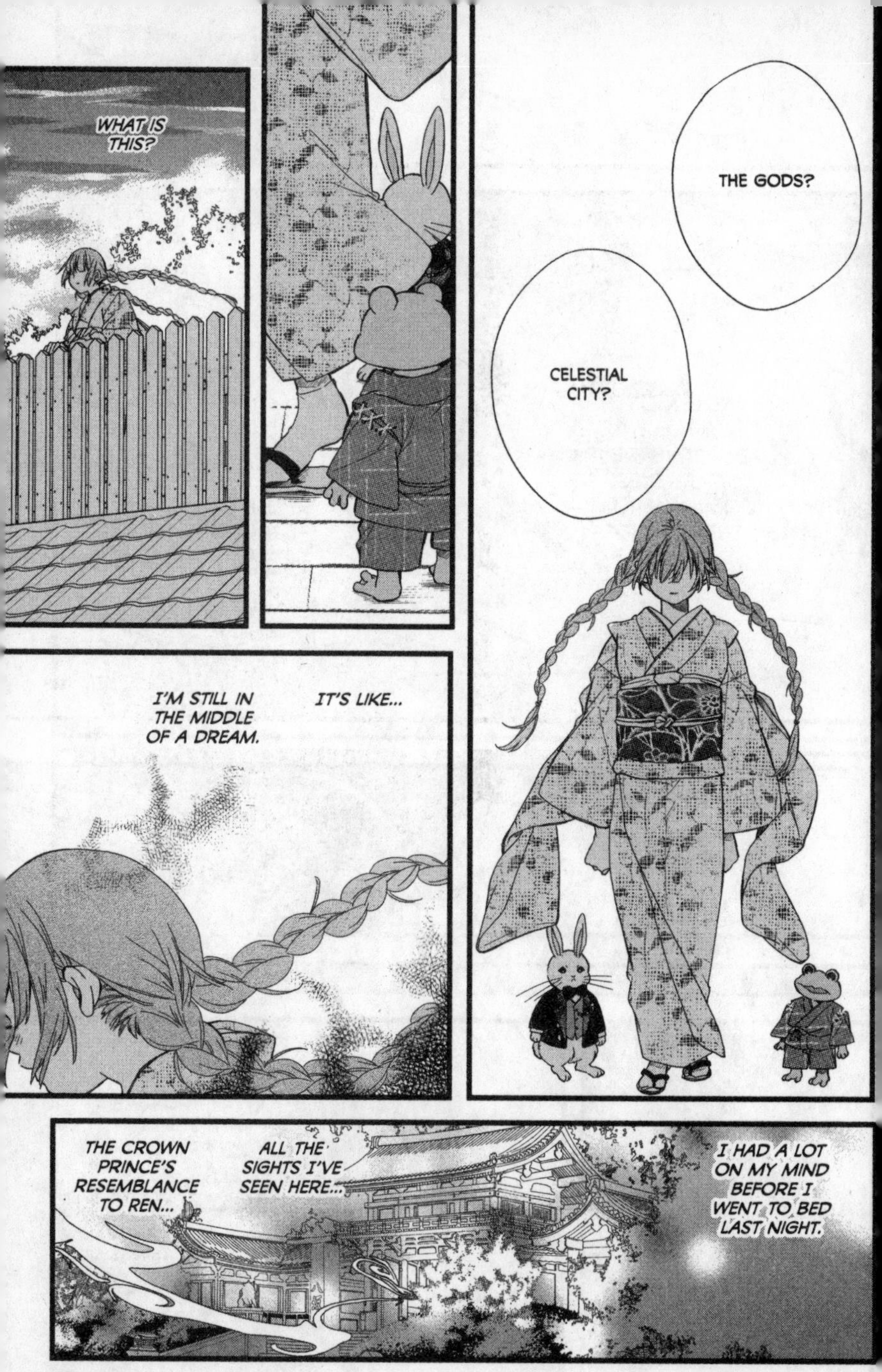
THE GODS?
CELESTIAL CITY?
WHAT IS THIS?
IT'S LIKE...
I'M STILL IN THE MIDDLE OF A DREAM.
I HAD A LOT ON MY MIND BEFORE I WENT TO BED LAST NIGHT.
ALL THE SIGHTS I'VE SEEN HERE...
THE CROWN PRINCE'S RESEMBLANCE TO REN...

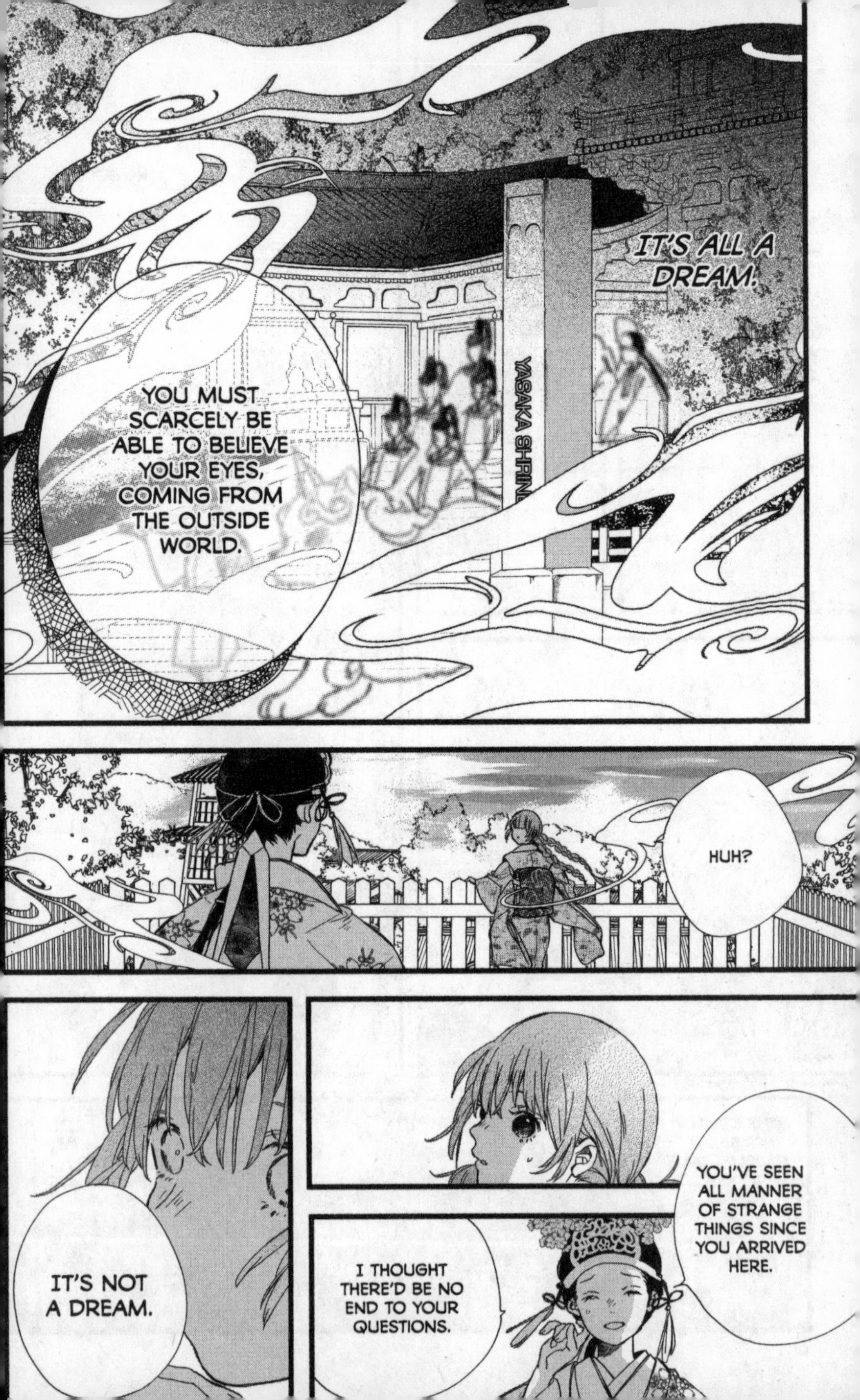

IT'S ALL A DREAM.
YASAKA SHRIN
YOU MUST SCARCELY BE ABLE TO BELIEVE YOUR EYES, COMING FROM THE OUTSIDE WORLD.
HUH?
YOU'VE SEEN ALL MANNER OF STRANGE THINGS SINCE YOU ARRIVED HERE.
I THOUGHT THERE'D BE NO END TO YOUR QUESTIONS.
IT'S NOT A DREAM.

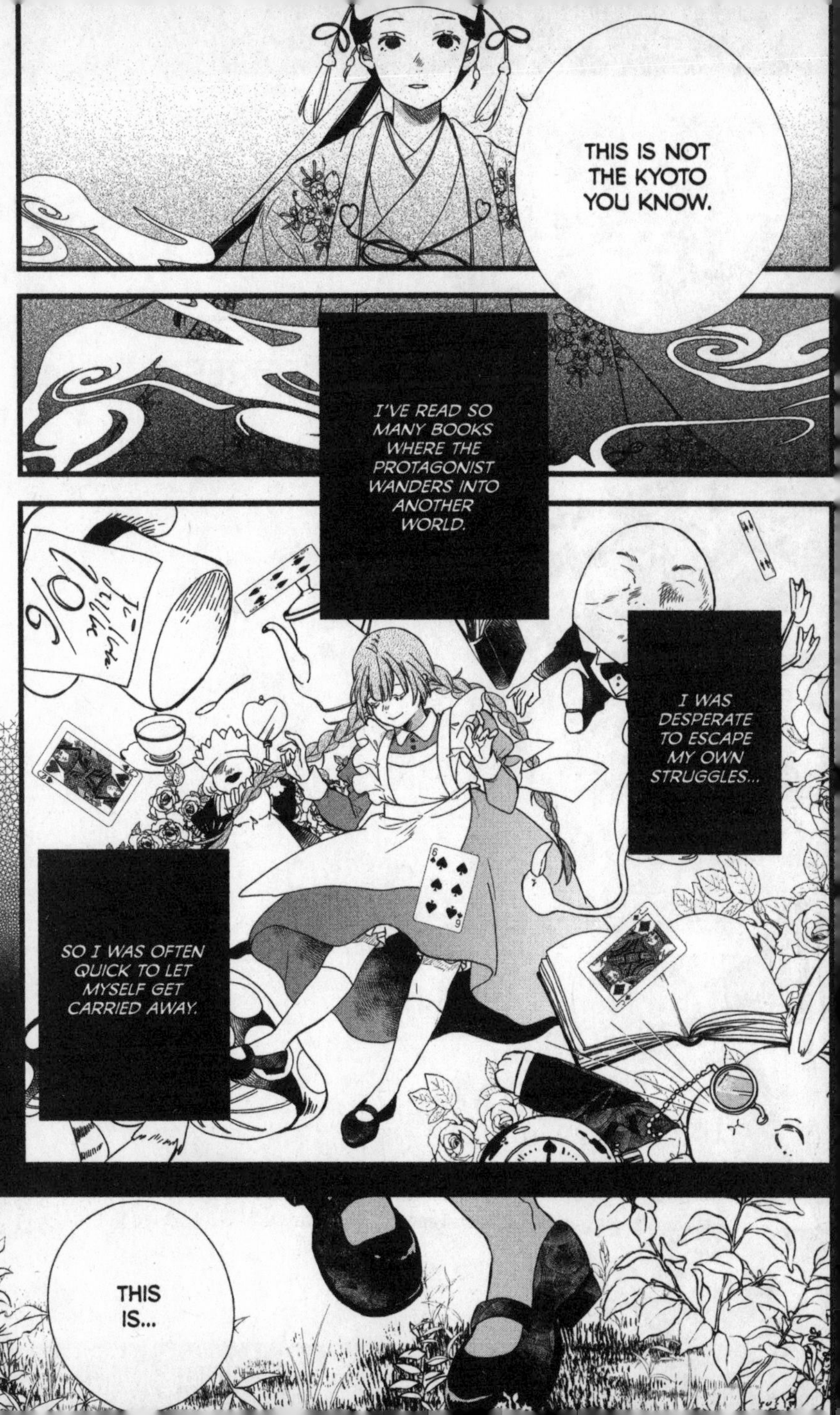
THIS IS NOT THE KYOTO YOU KNOW.
I'VE READ SO MANY BOOKS WHERE THE PROTAGONIST WANDERS INTO ANOTHER WORLD.
I WAS DESPERATE TO ESCAPE MY OWN STRUGGLES...
SO I WAS OFTEN QUICK TO LET MYSELF GET CARRIED AWAY.
THIS IS...

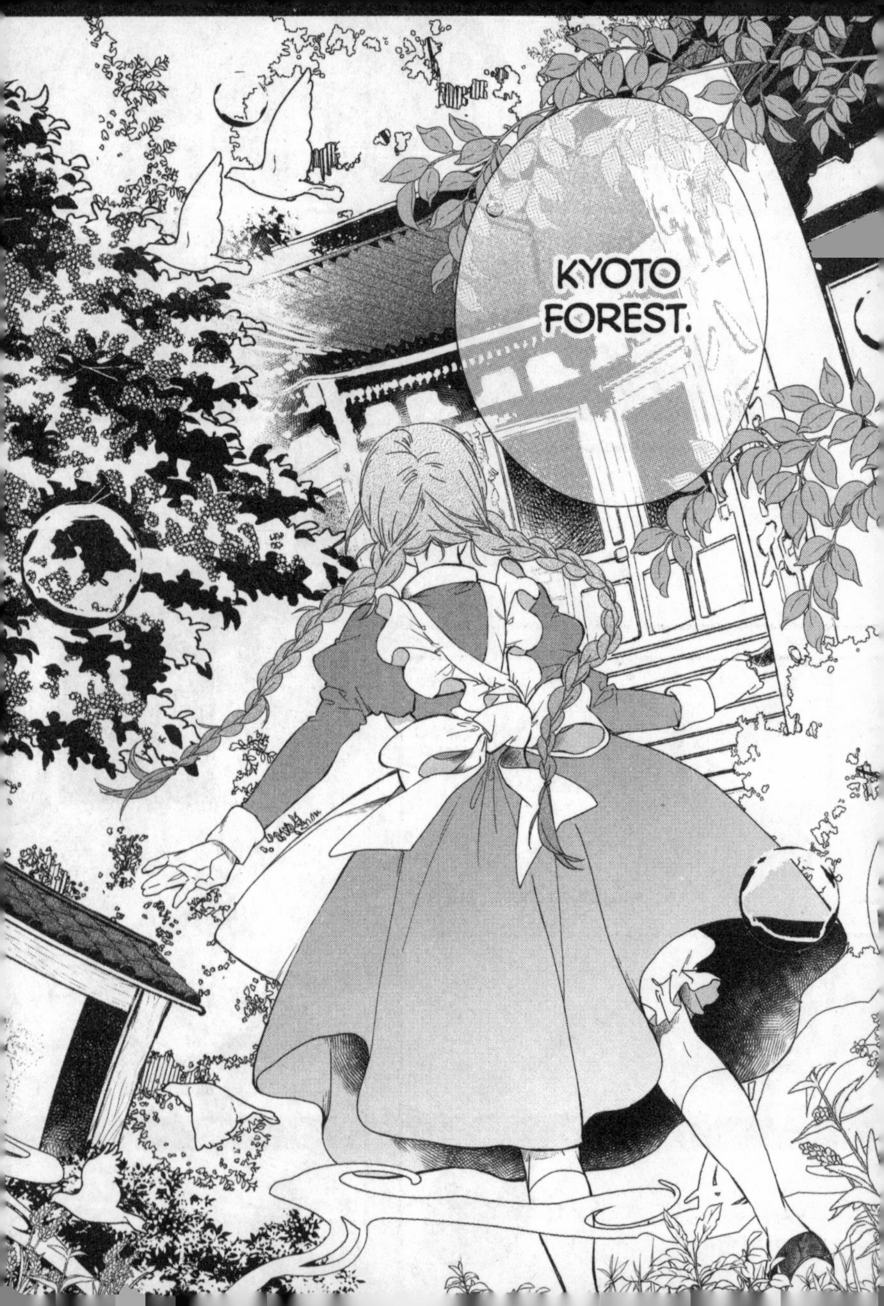
KYOTO FOREST.

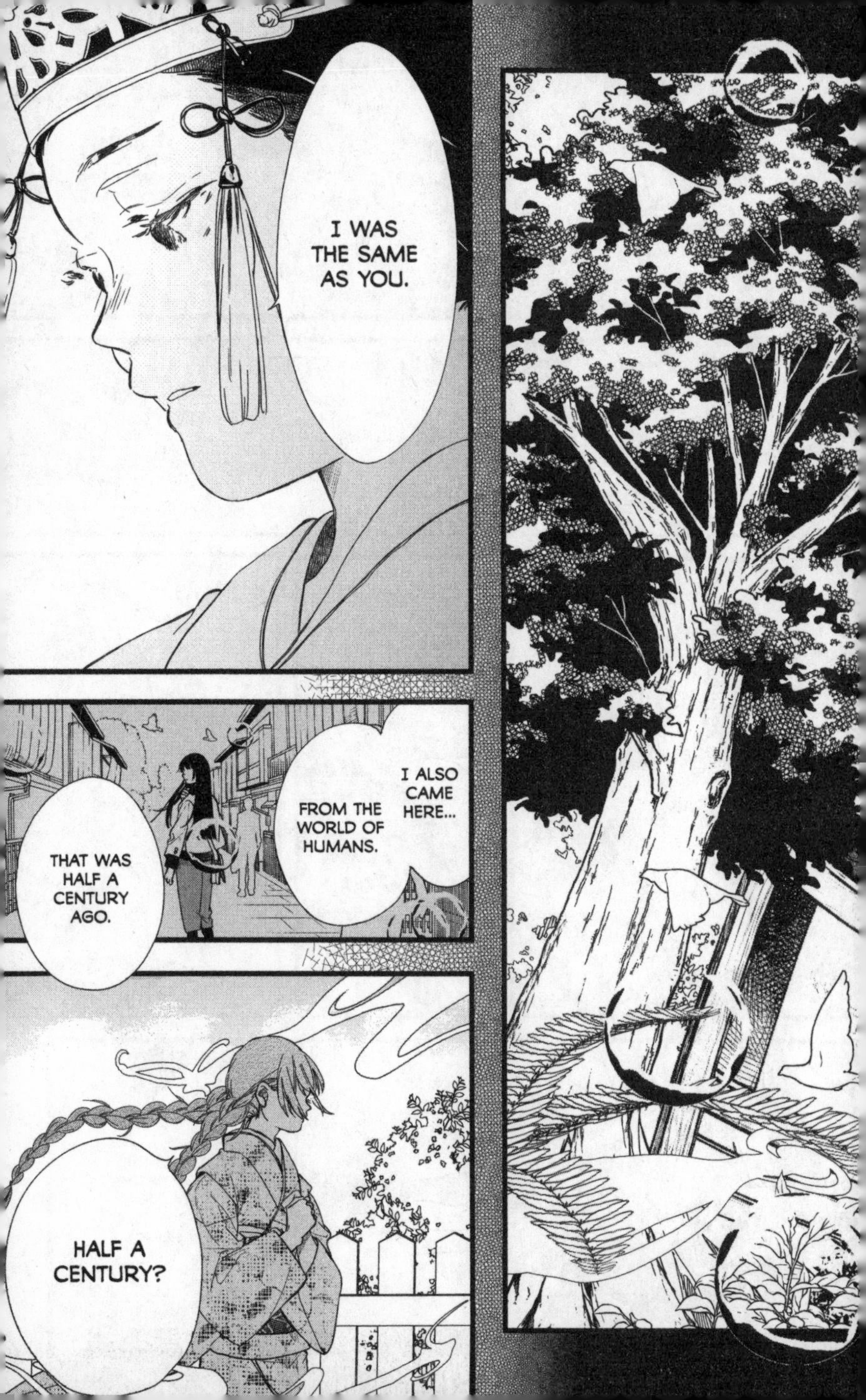
I WAS THE SAME AS YOU.
I ALSO CAME HERE...
FROM THE WORLD OF HUMANS.
THAT WAS HALF A CENTURY AGO.
HALF A CENTURY?

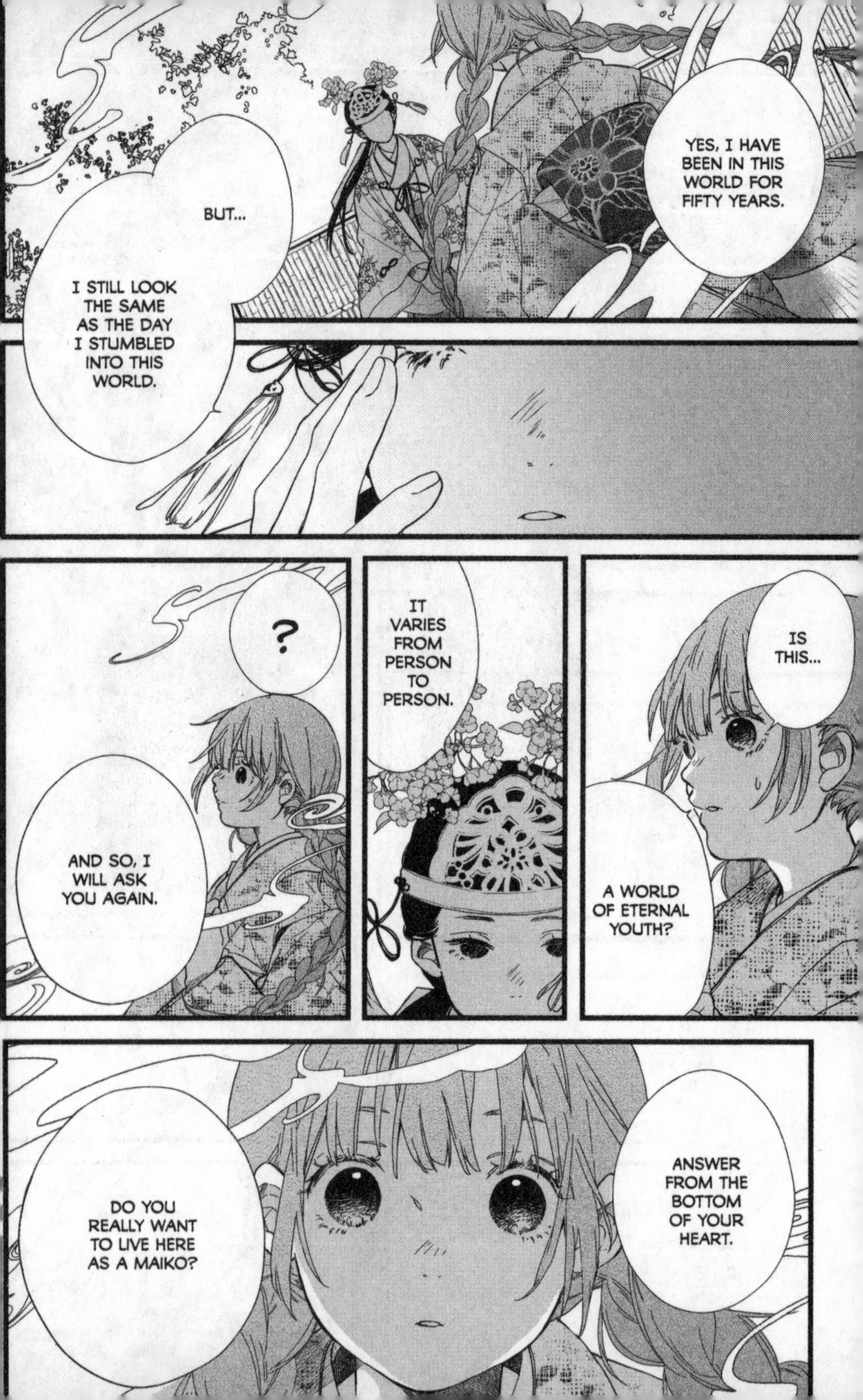
YES, I HAVE BEEN IN THIS WORLD FOR FIFTY YEARS.
BUT...
I STILL LOOK THE SAME AS THE DAY I STUMBLED INTO THIS WORLD.
IS THIS...
A WORLD OF ETERNAL YOUTH?
IT VARIES FROM PERSON TO PERSON.
?
AND SO, I WILL ASK YOU AGAIN.
ANSWER FROM THE BOTTOM OF YOUR HEART.
DO YOU REALLY WANT TO LIVE HERE AS A MAIKO?

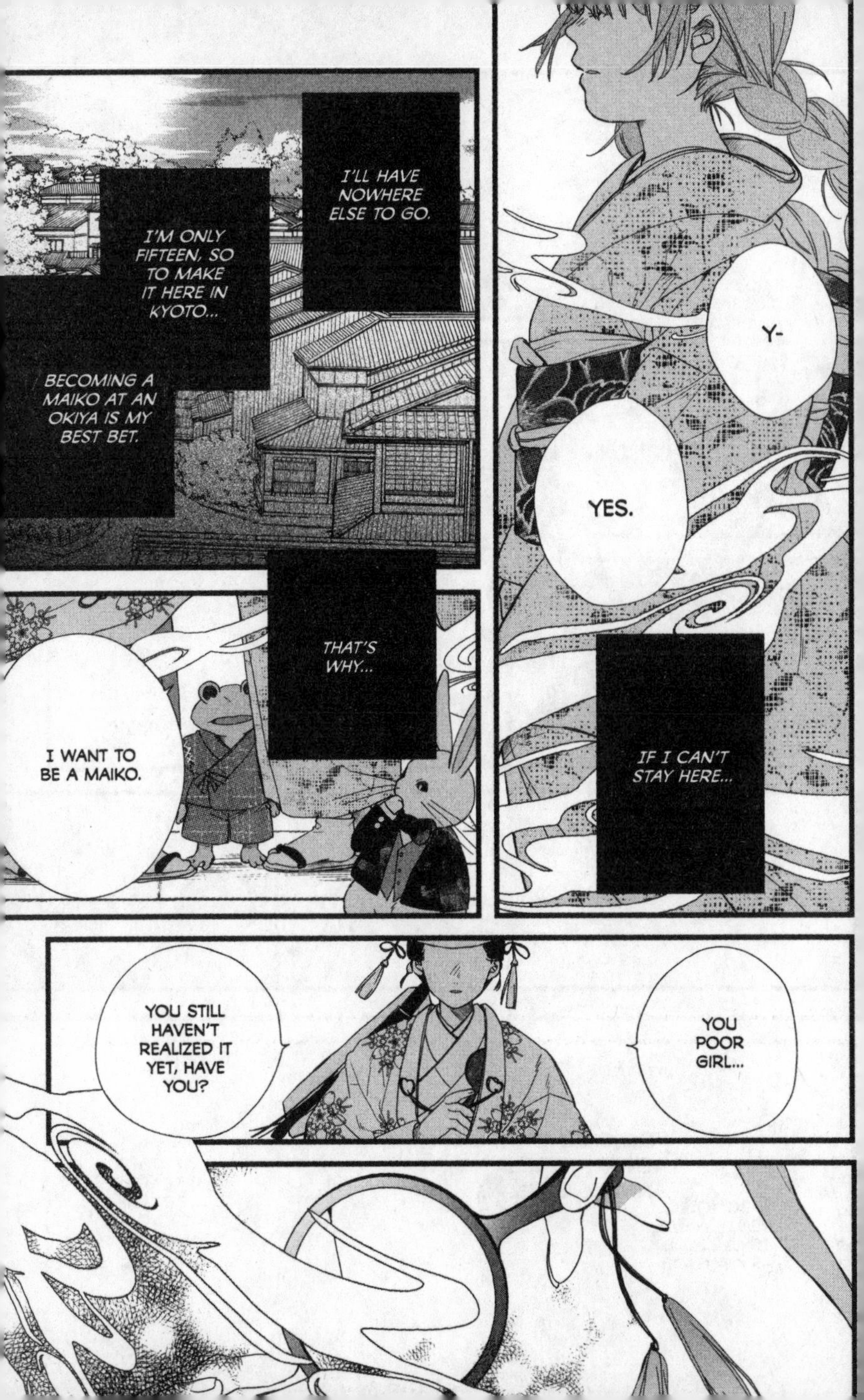
Y-
YES.
IF I CAN'T STAY HERE...
I'LL HAVE NOWHERE ELSE TO GO.
I'M ONLY FIFTEEN, SO TO MAKE IT HERE IN KYOTO...
BECOMING A MAIKO AT AN OKIYA IS MY BEST BET.
THAT'S WHY...
I WANT TO BE A MAIKO.
YOU POOR GIRL...
YOU STILL HAVEN'T REALIZED IT YET, HAVE YOU?

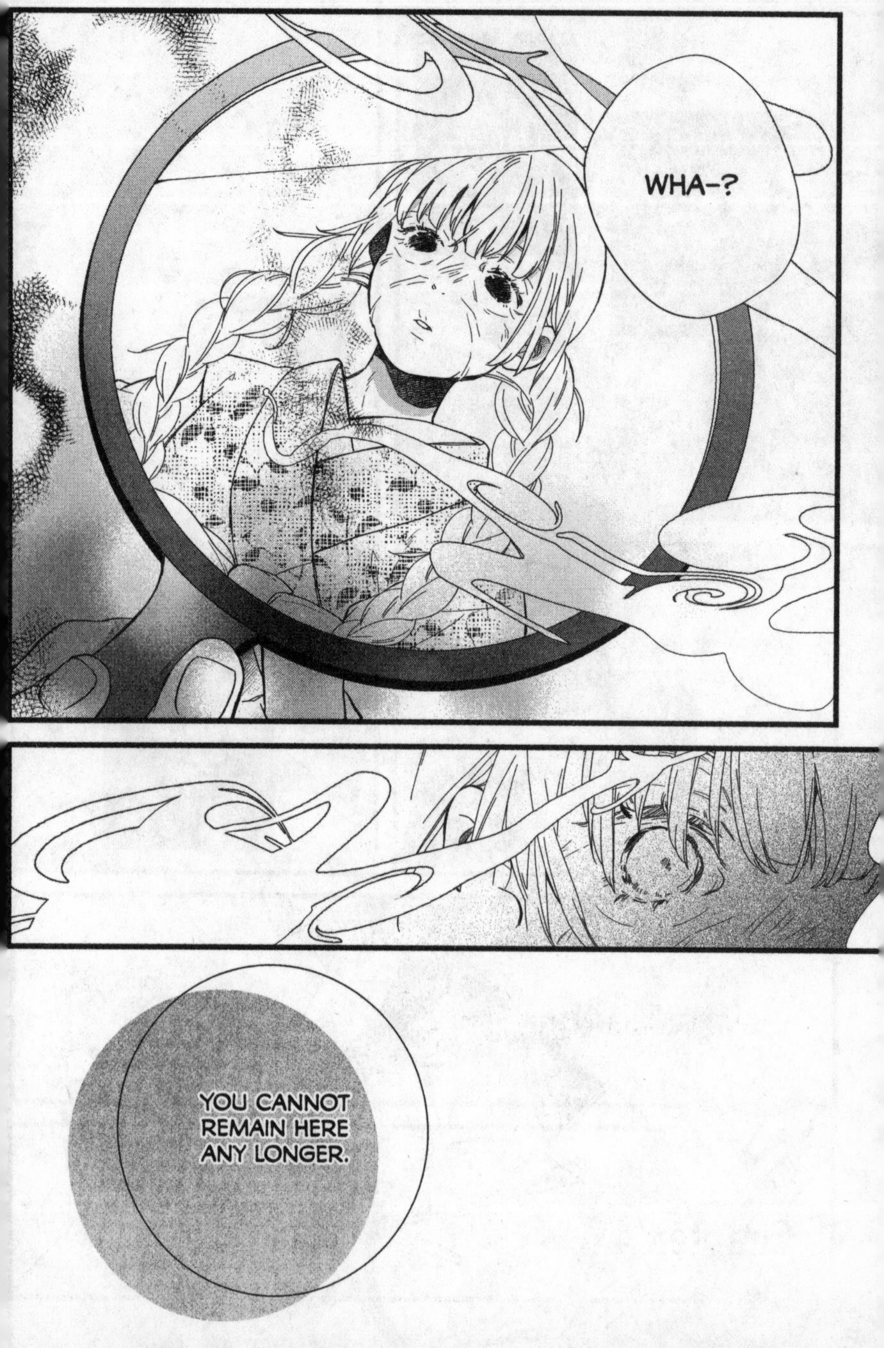
WHA-?
YOU CANNOT REMAIN HERE ANY LONGER.

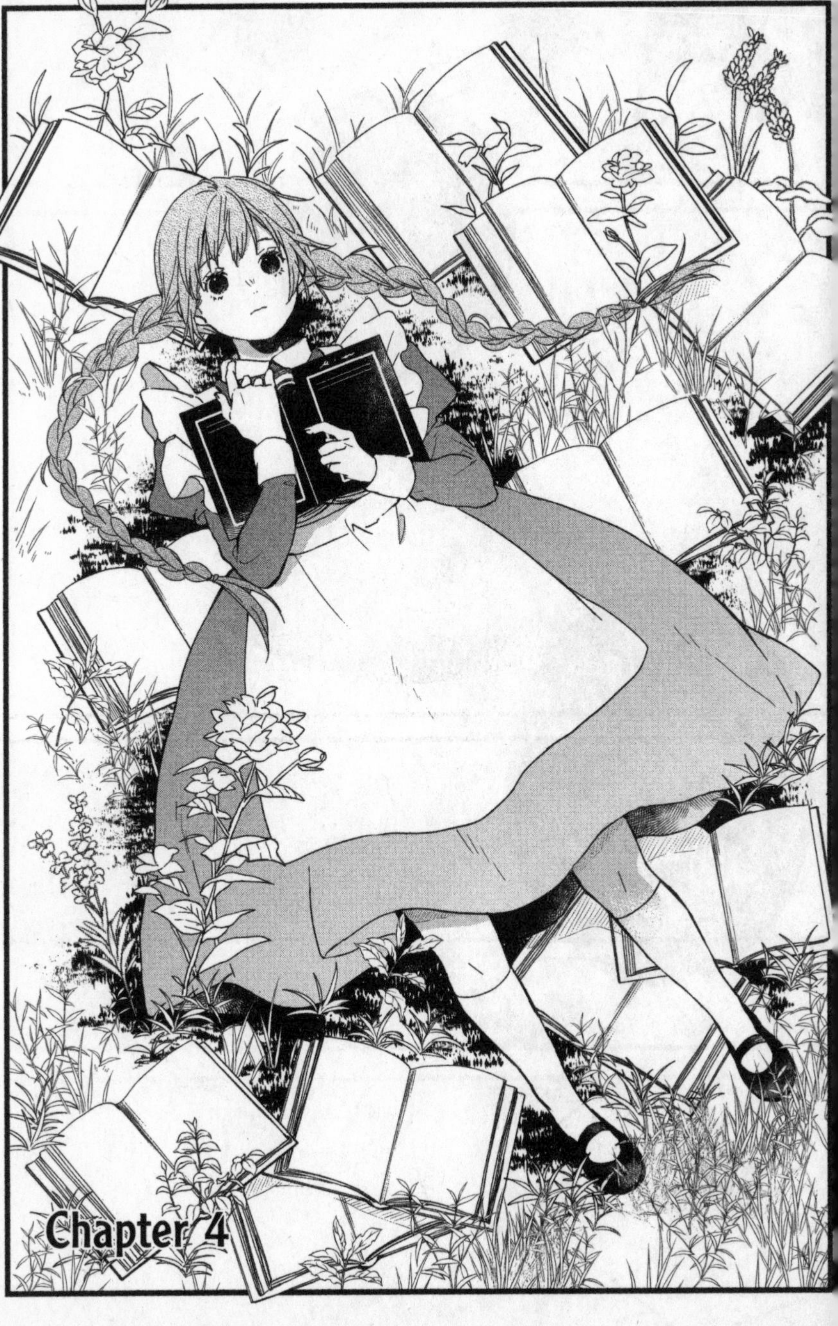
Chapter 4

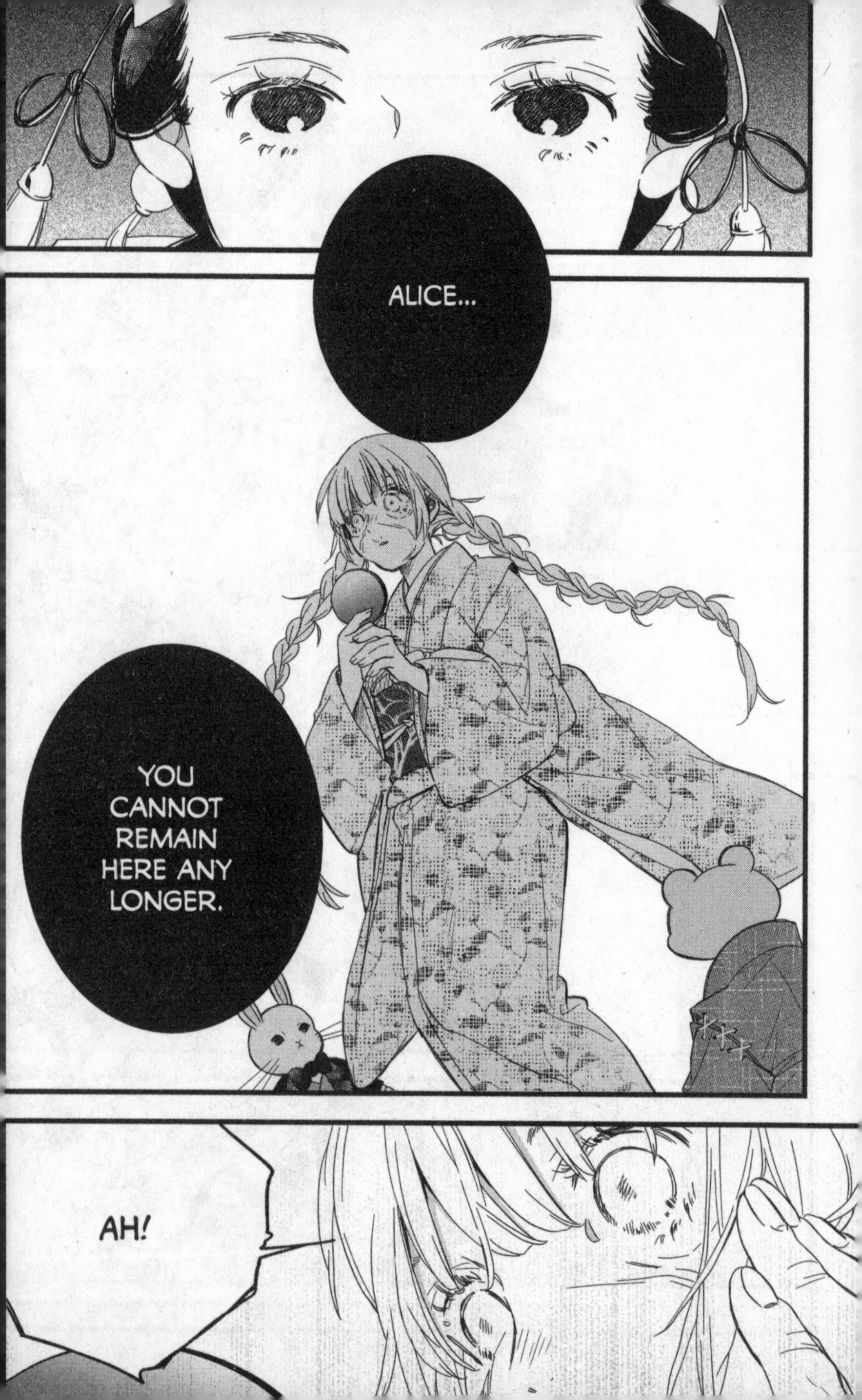
ALICE...
YOU CANNOT REMAIN HERE ANY LONGER.
AH!

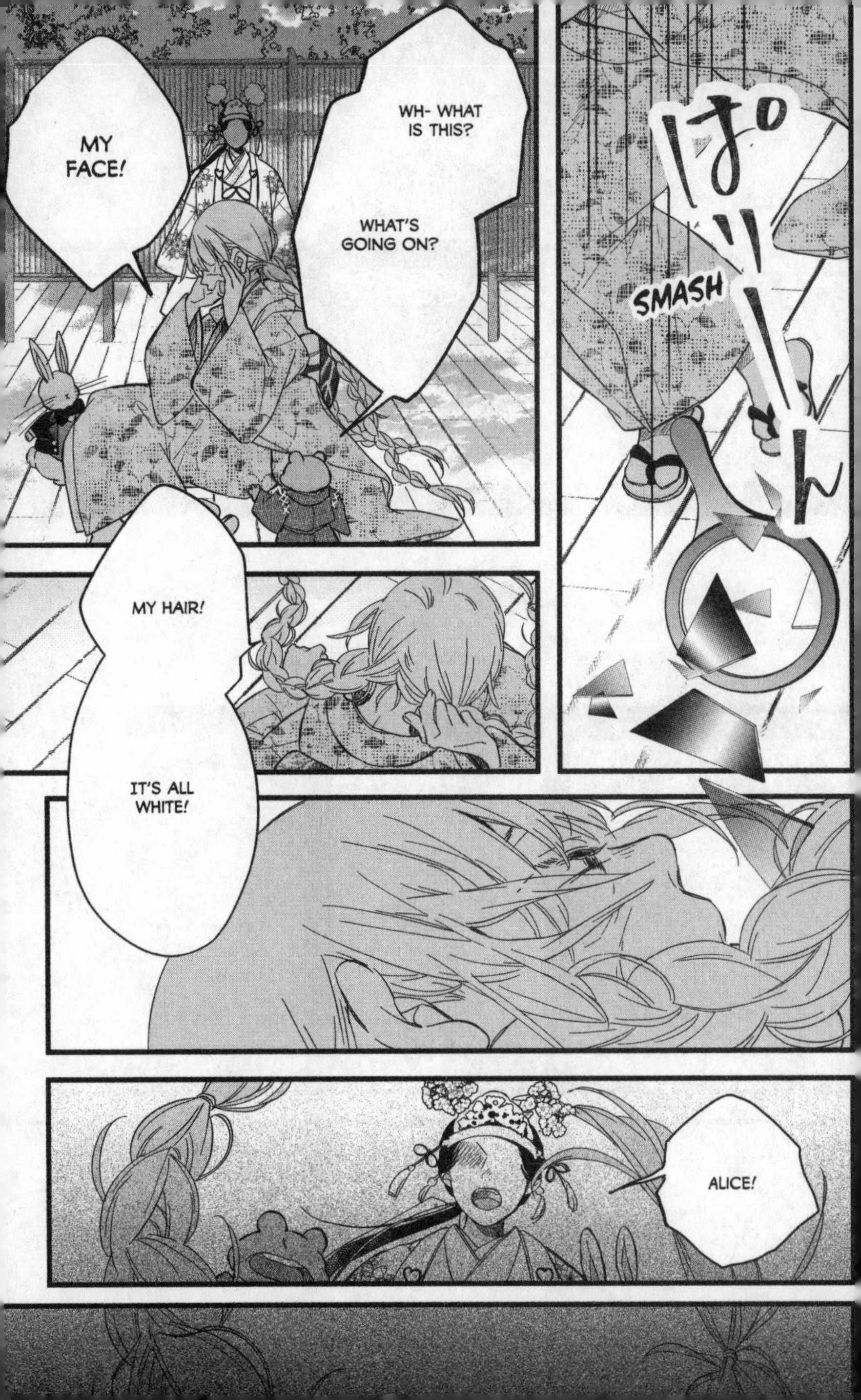
ぱリーん
SMASH
WH- WHAT IS THIS?
WHAT'S GOING ON?
MY FACE!
MY HAIR!
IT'S ALL WHITE!
ALICE!

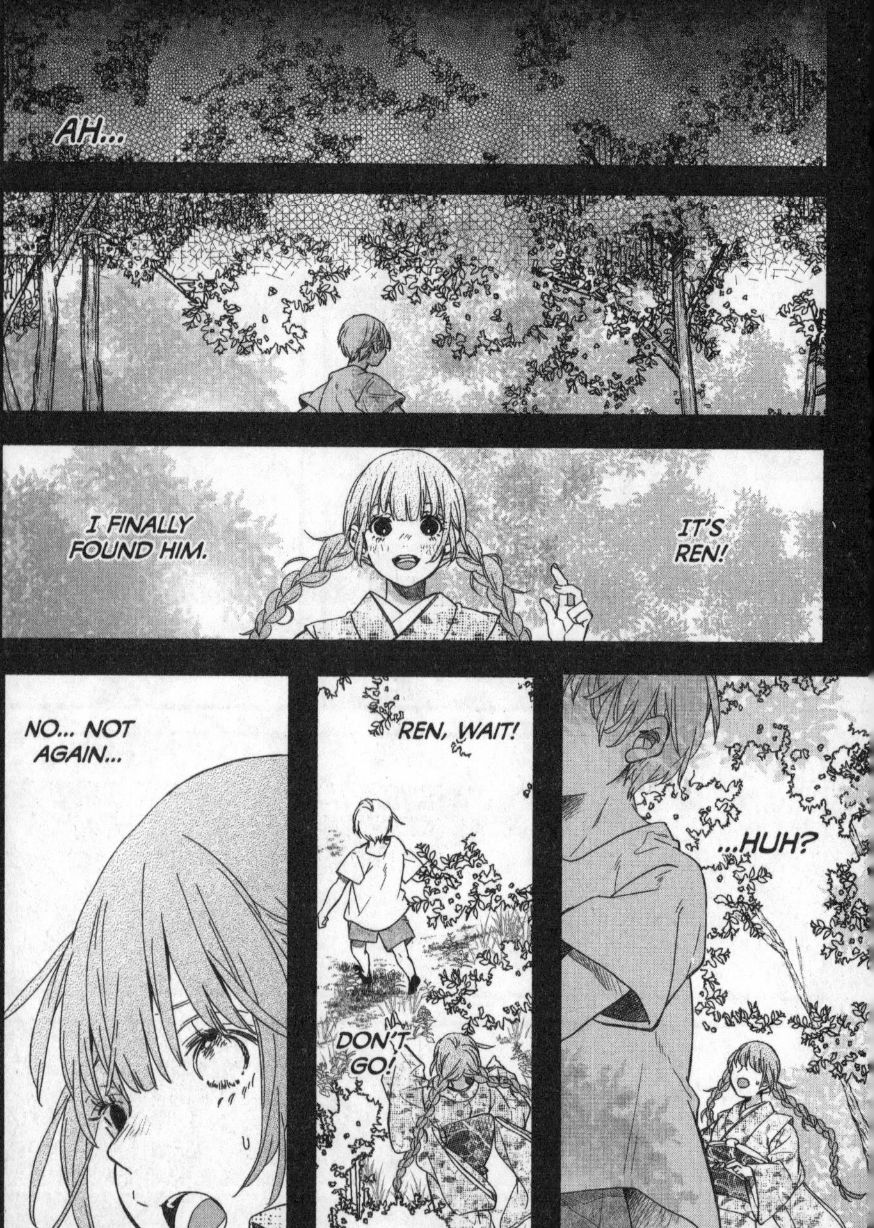
AH...
IT'S REN!
I FINALLY FOUND HIM.
...HUH?
REN, WAIT!
DON'T GO!
NO... NOT AGAIN...

NOT AGAIN...

MY BODY FEELS SO HEAVY ALL OF A SUDDEN.

HUH?

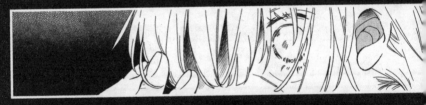

WHAT?

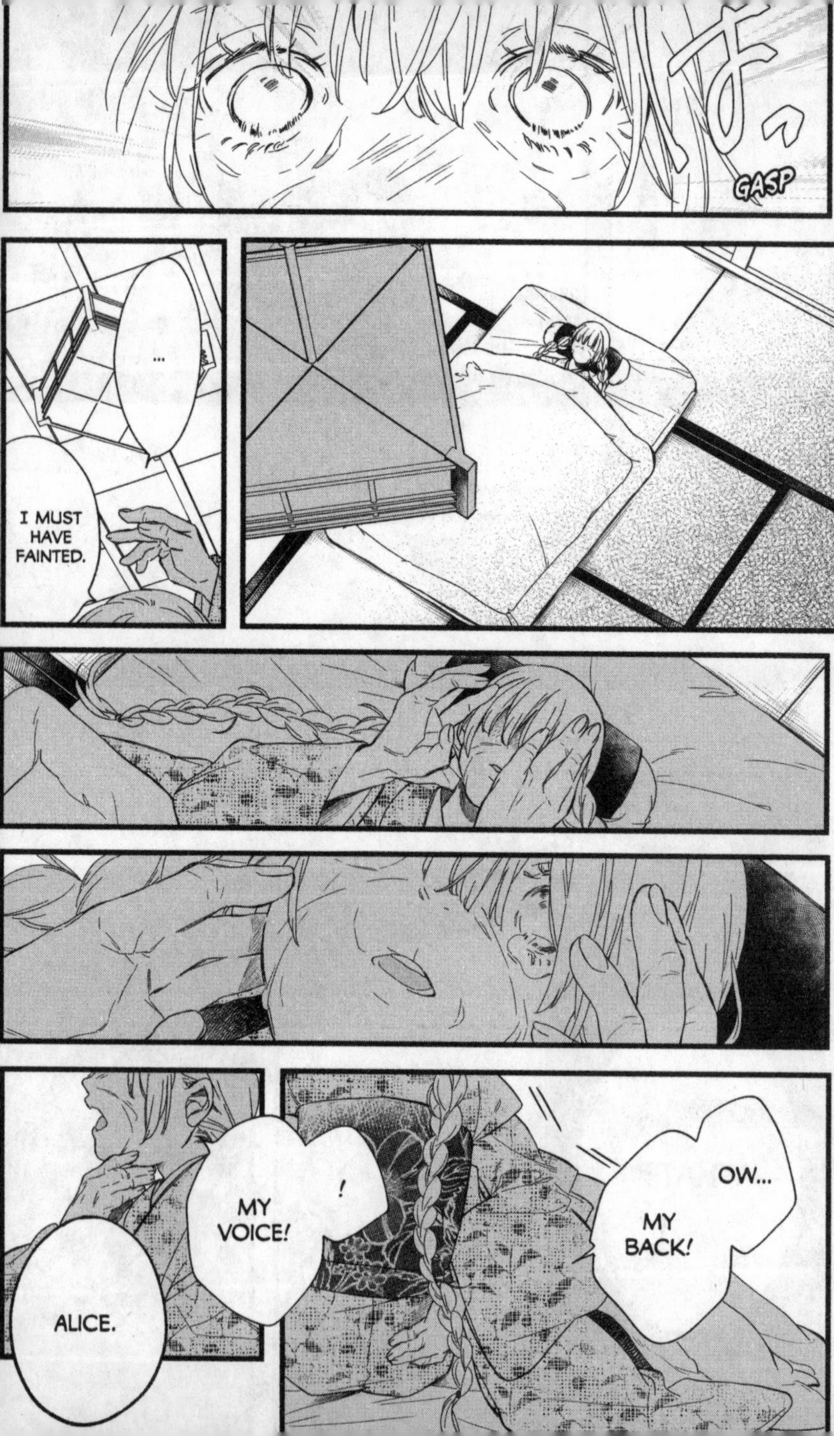
GASP
...
I MUST HAVE FAINTED.
OW...
MY BACK!
!
MY VOICE!
ALICE.

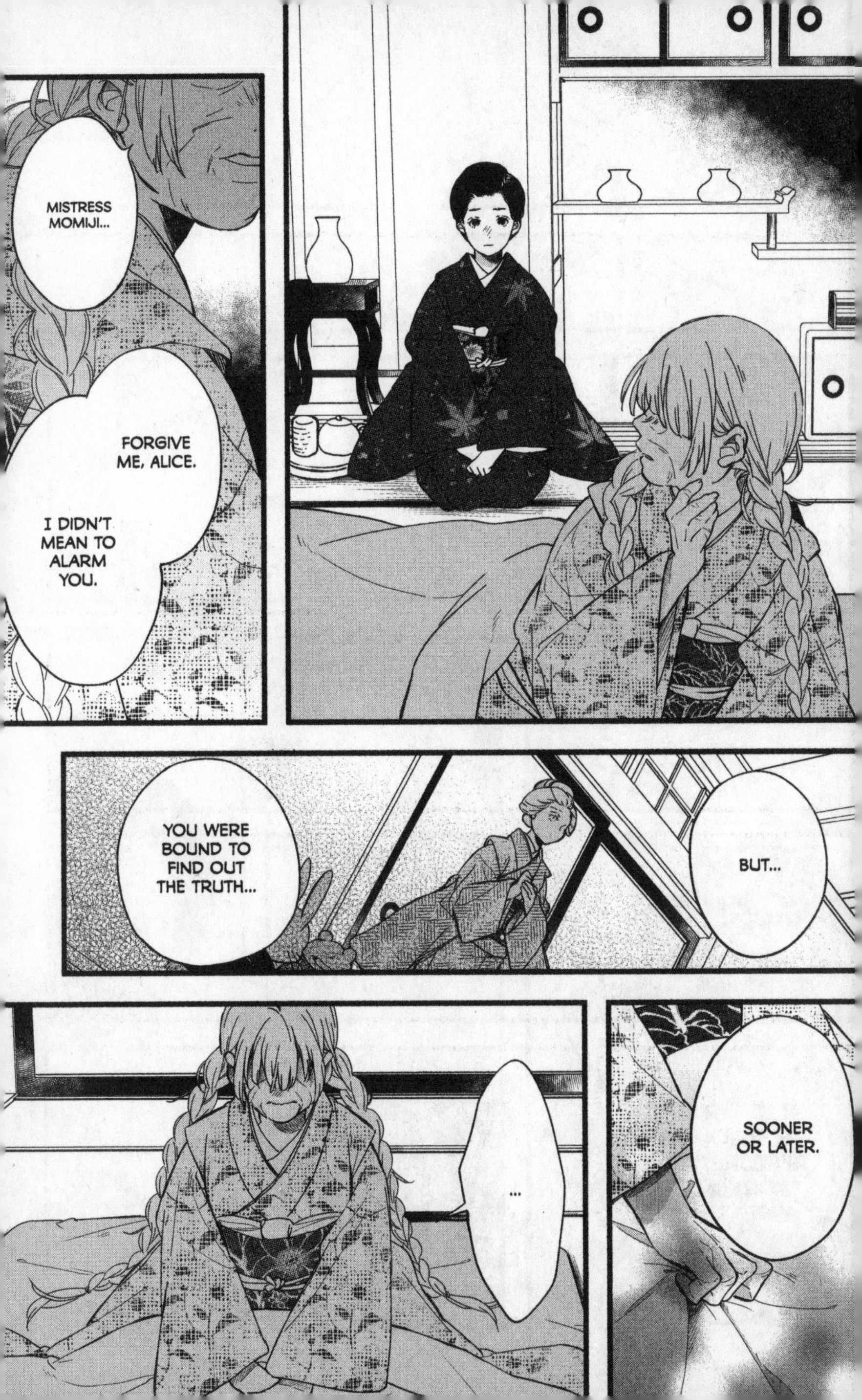
MISTRESS MOMIJI...
FORGIVE ME, ALICE.
I DIDN'T MEAN TO ALARM YOU.
BUT...
YOU WERE BOUND TO FIND OUT THE TRUTH...
SOONER OR LATER.
...

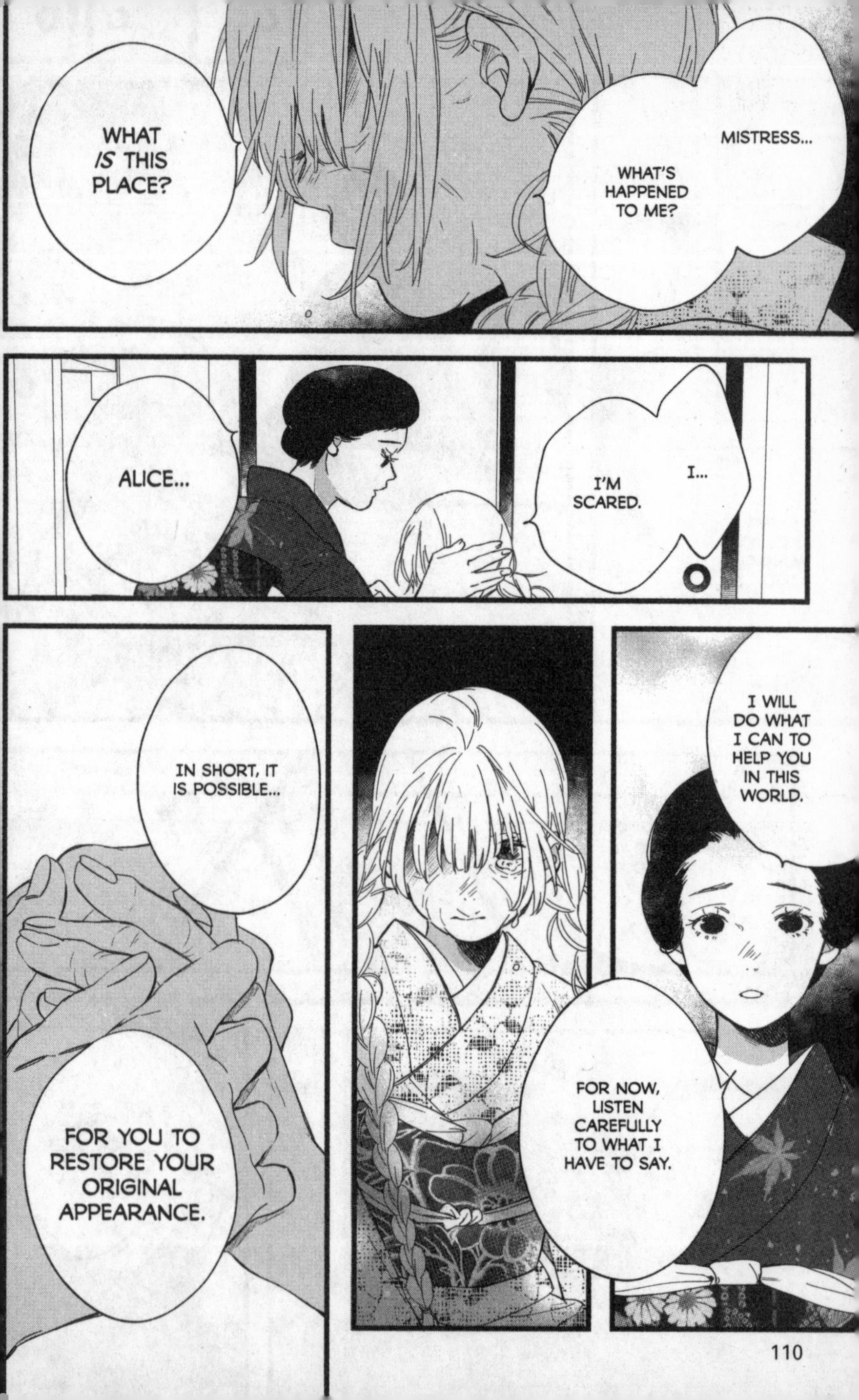
MISTRESS...
WHAT'S HAPPENED TO ME?
WHAT *IS* THIS PLACE?
I...
I'M SCARED.
ALICE...
I WILL DO WHAT I CAN TO HELP YOU IN THIS WORLD.
FOR NOW, LISTEN CAREFULLY TO WHAT I HAVE TO SAY.
IN SHORT, IT IS POSSIBLE...
FOR YOU TO RESTORE YOUR ORIGINAL APPEARANCE.

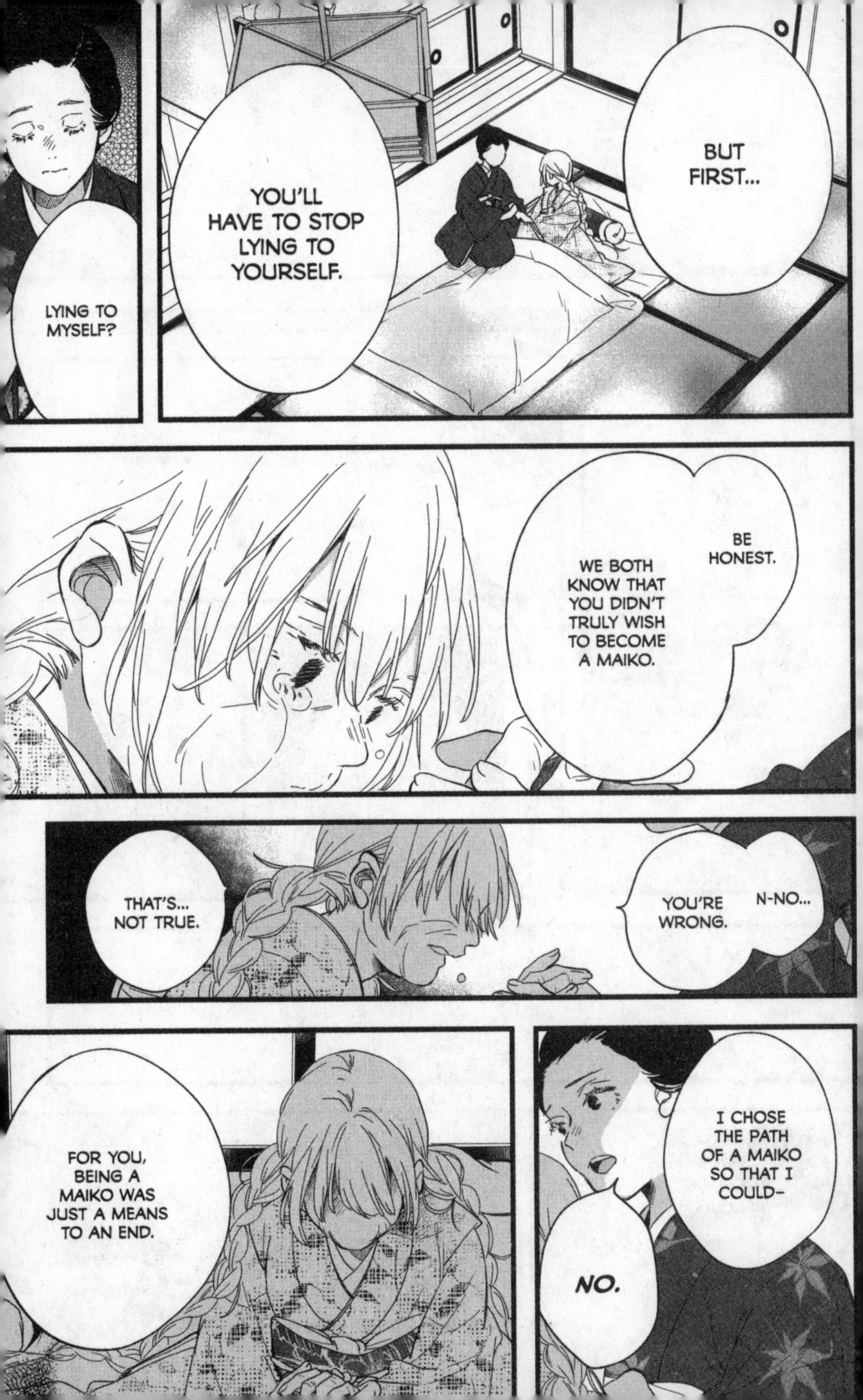
BUT FIRST...
YOU'LL HAVE TO STOP LYING TO YOURSELF.
LYING TO MYSELF?
BE HONEST.
WE BOTH KNOW THAT YOU DIDN'T TRULY WISH TO BECOME A MAIKO.
N-NO...
YOU'RE WRONG.
THAT'S... NOT TRUE.
I CHOSE THE PATH OF A MAIKO SO THAT I COULD-
NO.
FOR YOU, BEING A MAIKO WAS JUST A MEANS TO AN END.

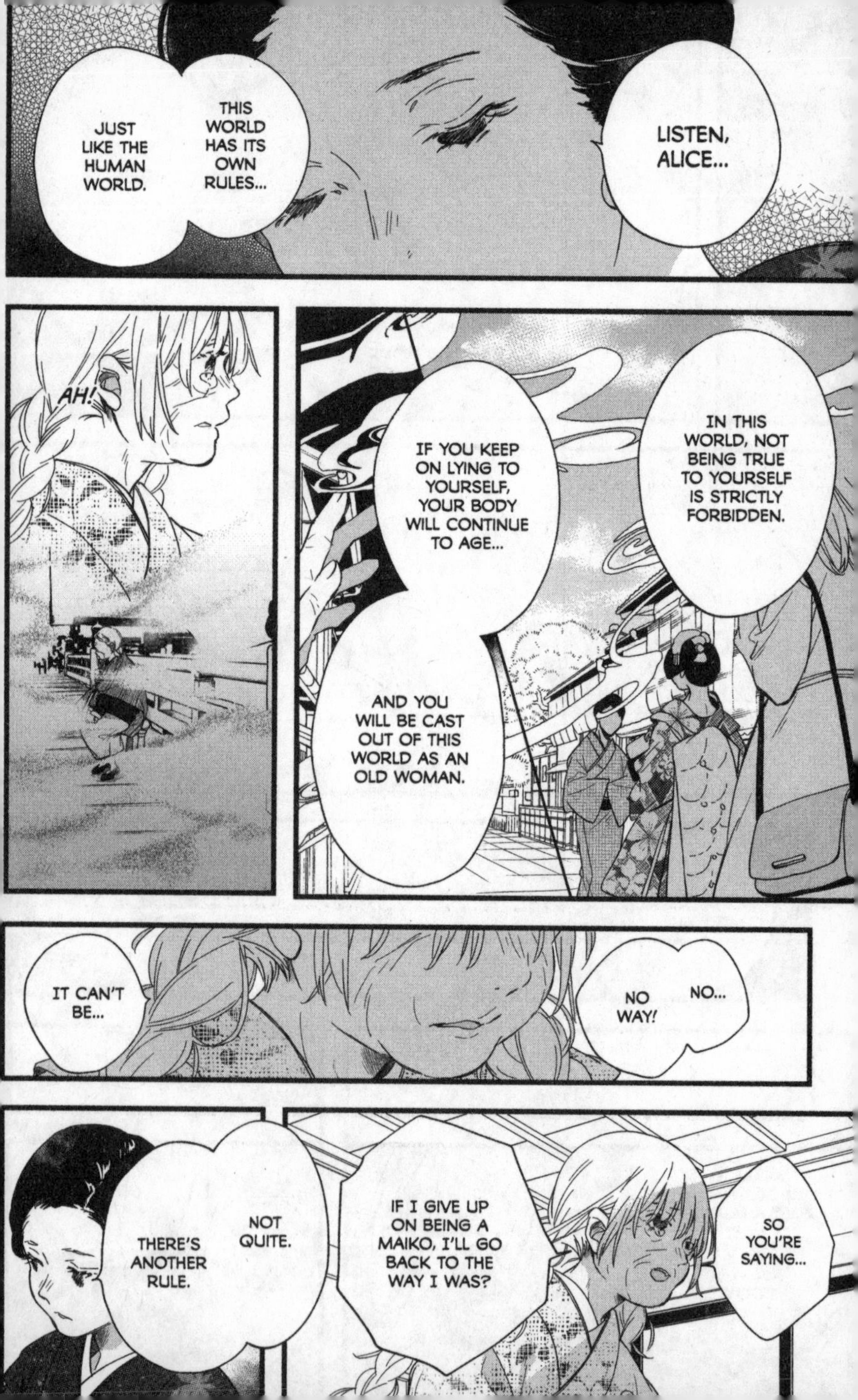
LISTEN, ALICE...
THIS WORLD HAS ITS OWN RULES...
JUST LIKE THE HUMAN WORLD.
IN THIS WORLD, NOT BEING TRUE TO YOURSELF IS STRICTLY FORBIDDEN.
IF YOU KEEP ON LYING TO YOURSELF, YOUR BODY WILL CONTINUE TO AGE...
AND YOU WILL BE CAST OUT OF THIS WORLD AS AN OLD WOMAN.
AH!
NO...
NO WAY!
IT CAN'T BE...
SO YOU'RE SAYING...
IF I GIVE UP ON BEING A MAIKO, I'LL GO BACK TO THE WAY I WAS?
NOT QUITE.
THERE'S ANOTHER RULE.

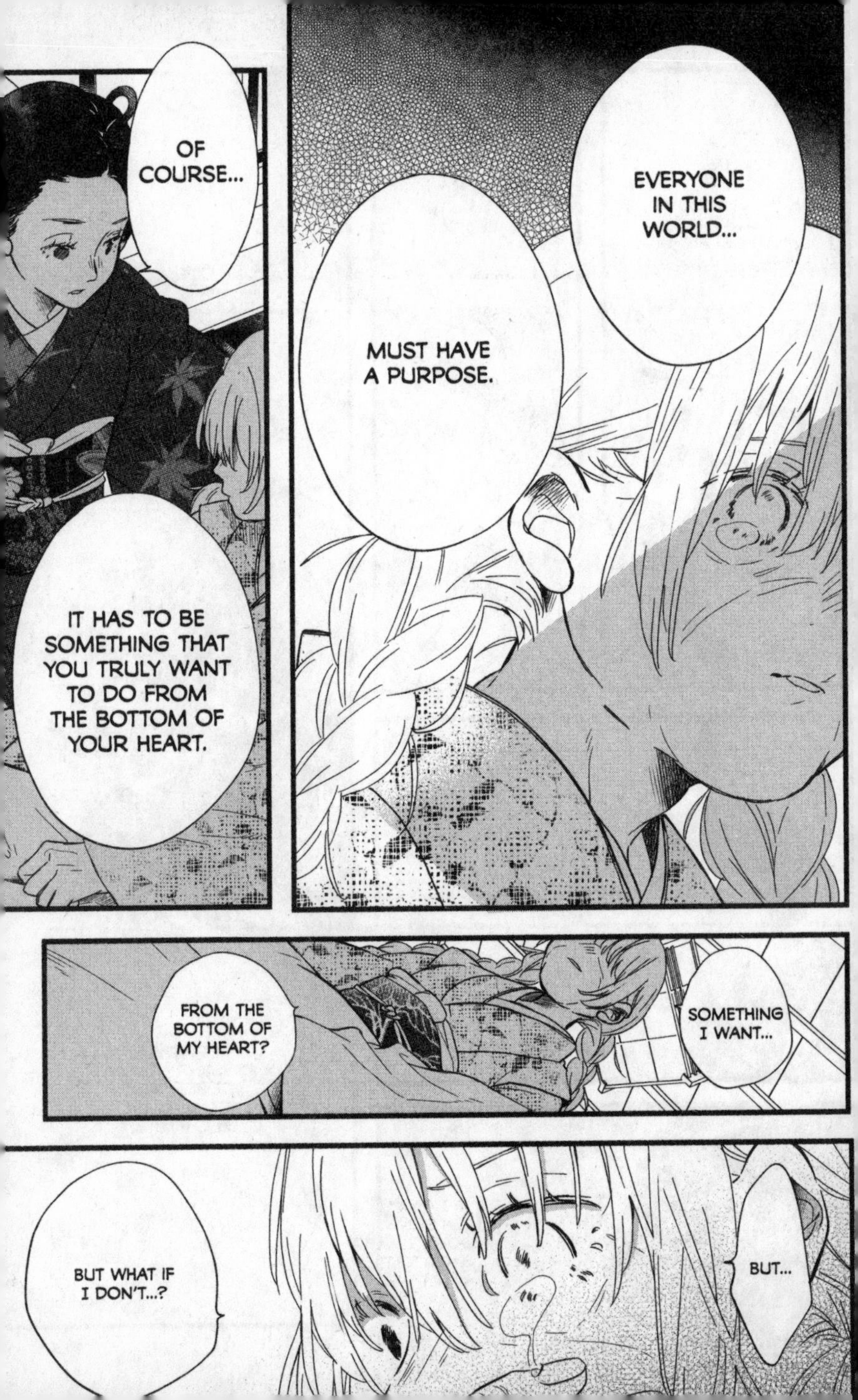
EVERYONE IN THIS WORLD...
MUST HAVE A PURPOSE.
OF COURSE...
IT HAS TO BE SOMETHING THAT YOU TRULY WANT TO DO FROM THE BOTTOM OF YOUR HEART.
SOMETHING I WANT...
FROM THE BOTTOM OF MY HEART?
BUT...
BUT WHAT IF I DON'T...?

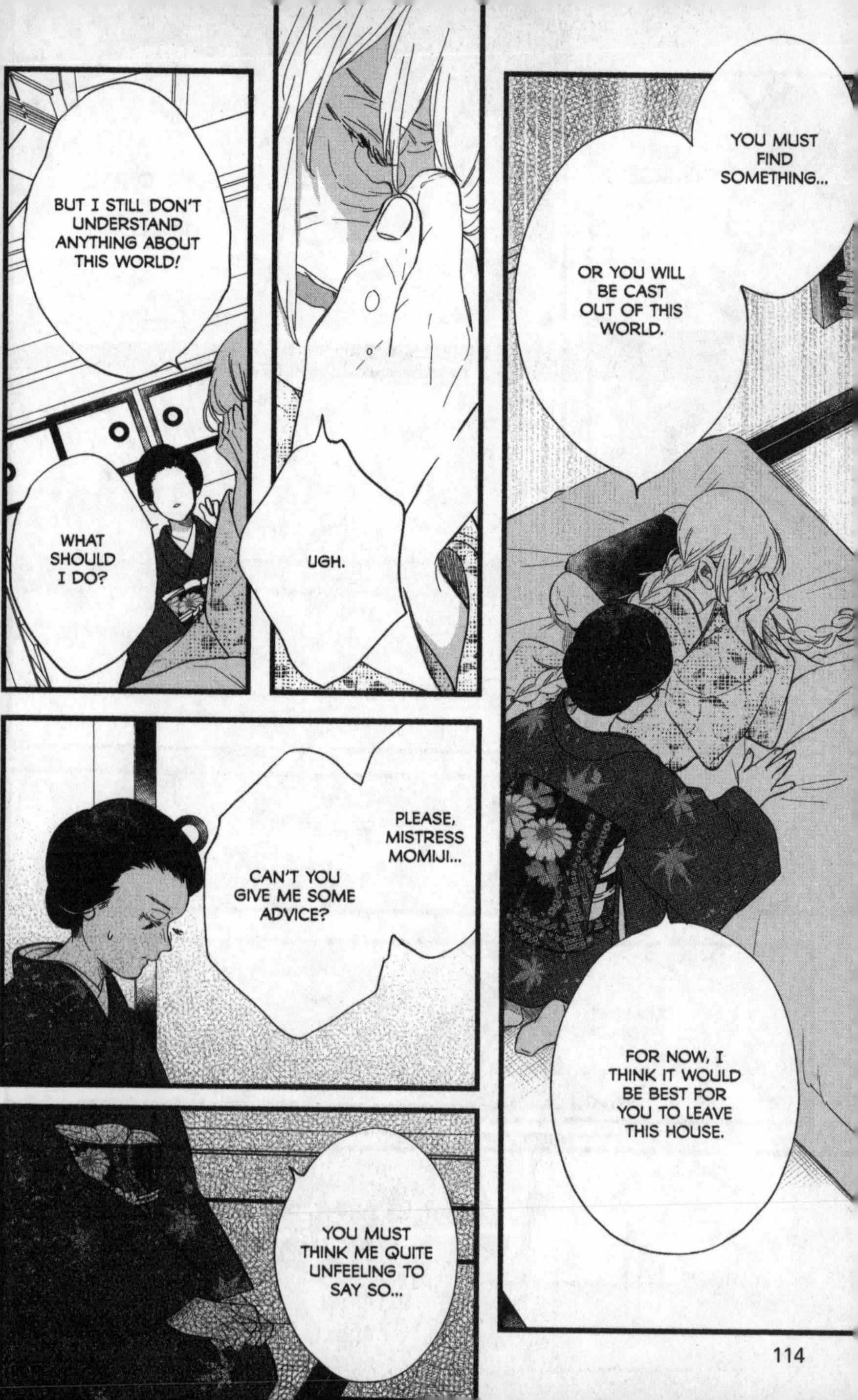
YOU MUST FIND SOMETHING...
OR YOU WILL BE CAST OUT OF THIS WORLD.
FOR NOW, I THINK IT WOULD BE BEST FOR YOU TO LEAVE THIS HOUSE.
UGH.
BUT I STILL DON'T UNDERSTAND ANYTHING ABOUT THIS WORLD!
WHAT SHOULD I DO?
PLEASE, MISTRESS MOMIJI...
CAN'T YOU GIVE ME SOME ADVICE?
YOU MUST THINK ME QUITE UNFEELING TO SAY SO...

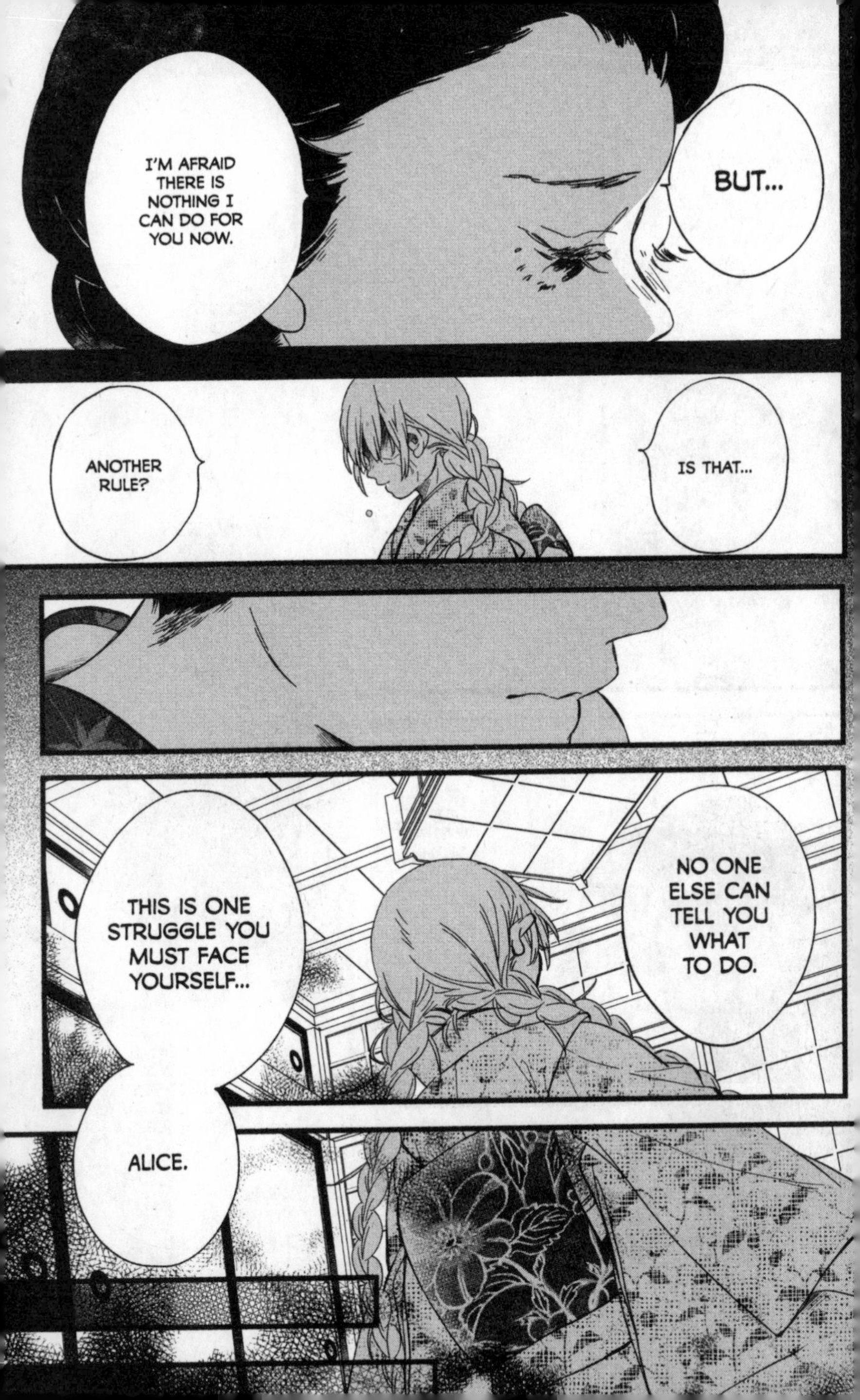
BUT...
I'M AFRAID THERE IS NOTHING I CAN DO FOR YOU NOW.
IS THAT...
ANOTHER RULE?
NO ONE ELSE CAN TELL YOU WHAT TO DO.
THIS IS ONE STRUGGLE YOU MUST FACE YOURSELF...
ALICE.

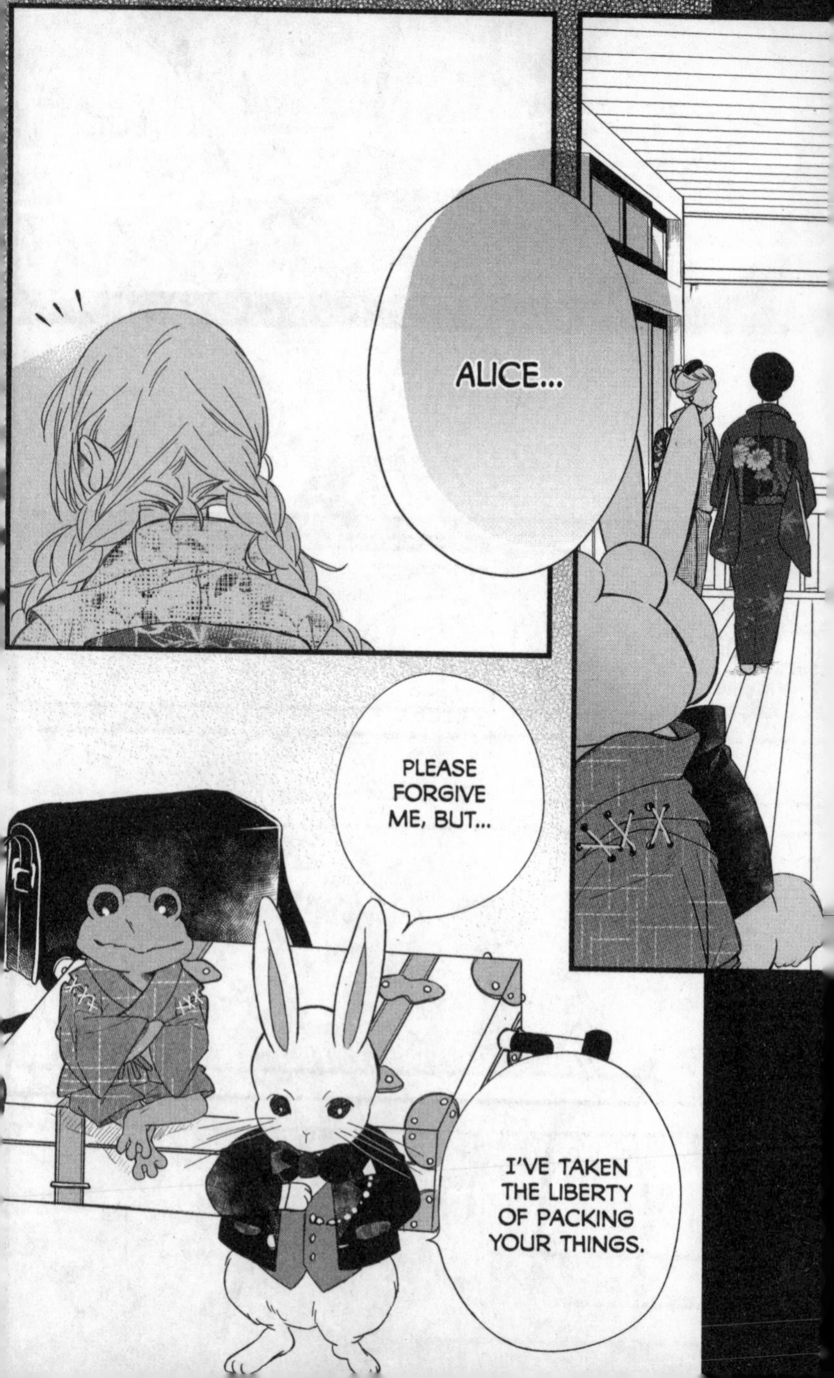
ALICE...
PLEASE FORGIVE ME, BUT...
I'VE TAKEN THE LIBERTY OF PACKING YOUR THINGS.

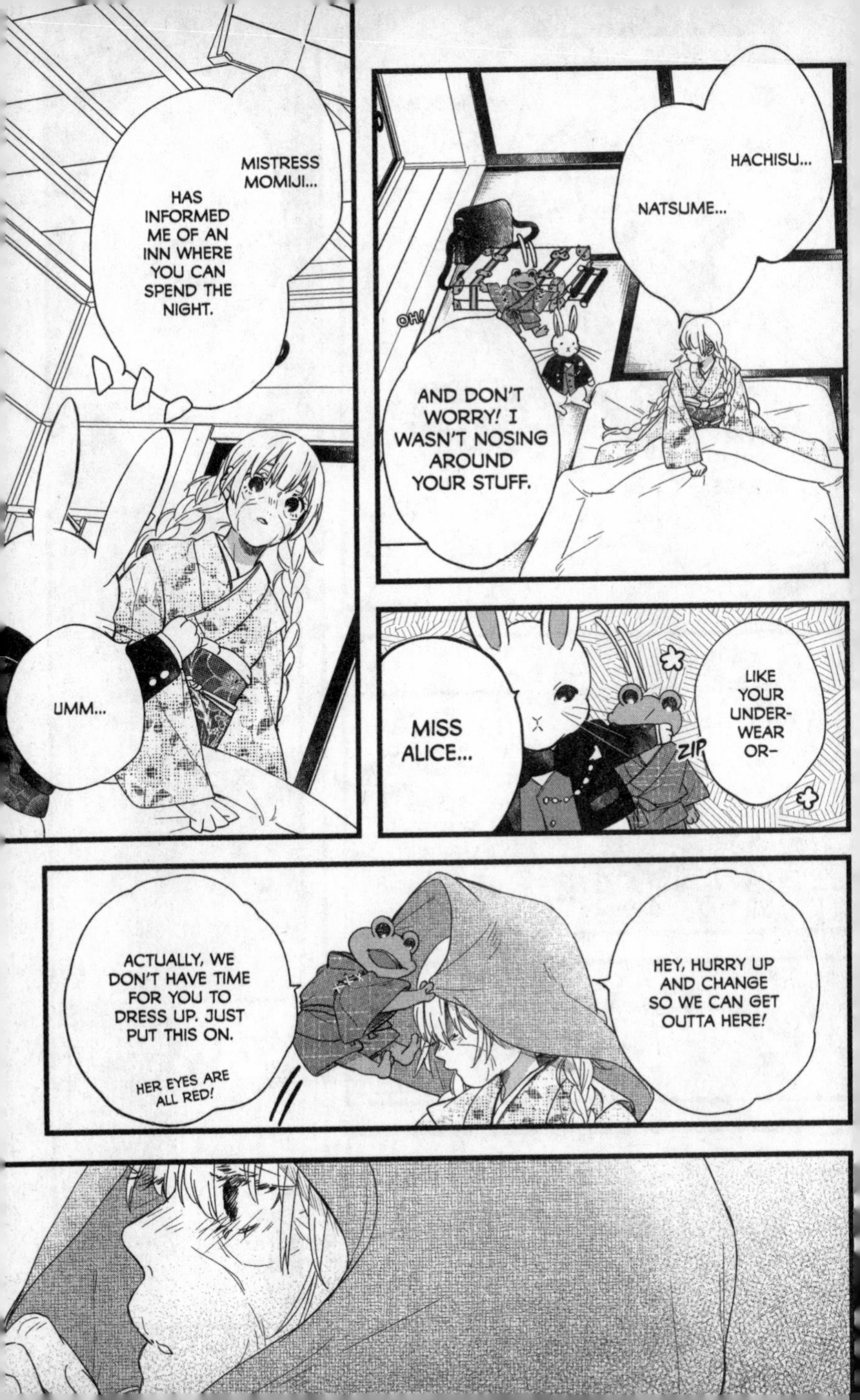
HACHISU...
NATSUME...
OH!
AND DON'T WORRY! I WASN'T NOSING AROUND YOUR STUFF.
LIKE YOUR UNDER-WEAR OR–
ZIP
MISS ALICE...
MISTRESS MOMIJI...
HAS INFORMED ME OF AN INN WHERE YOU CAN SPEND THE NIGHT.
UMM...
HEY, HURRY UP AND CHANGE SO WE CAN GET OUTTA HERE!
ACTUALLY, WE DON'T HAVE TIME FOR YOU TO DRESS UP. JUST PUT THIS ON.
HER EYES ARE ALL RED!

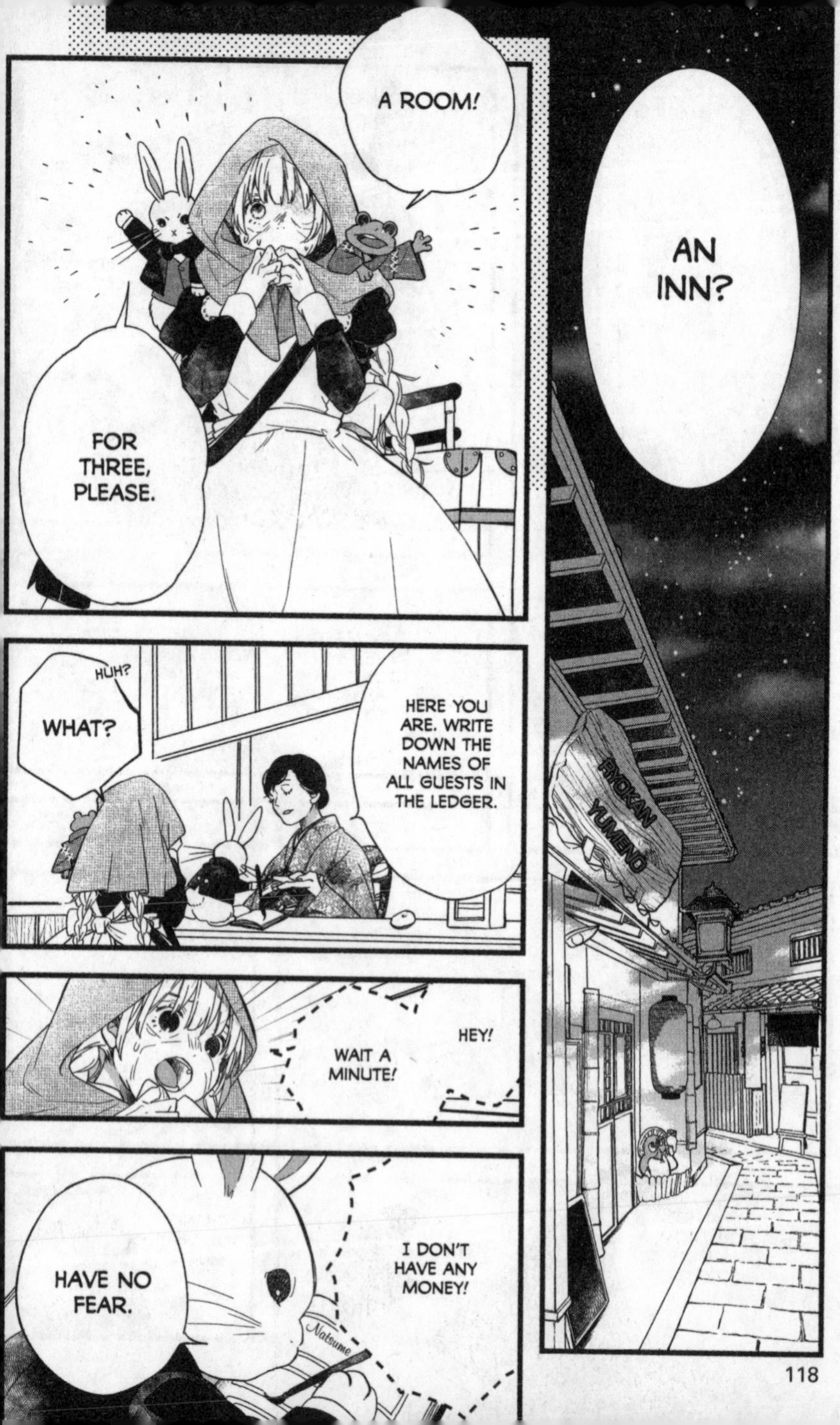
AN INN?
RYOKAN YUMENO
A ROOM!
FOR THREE, PLEASE.
HERE YOU ARE. WRITE DOWN THE NAMES OF ALL GUESTS IN THE LEDGER.
HUH?
WHAT?
HEY!
WAIT A MINUTE!
I DON'T HAVE ANY MONEY!
HAVE NO FEAR.
Natsume

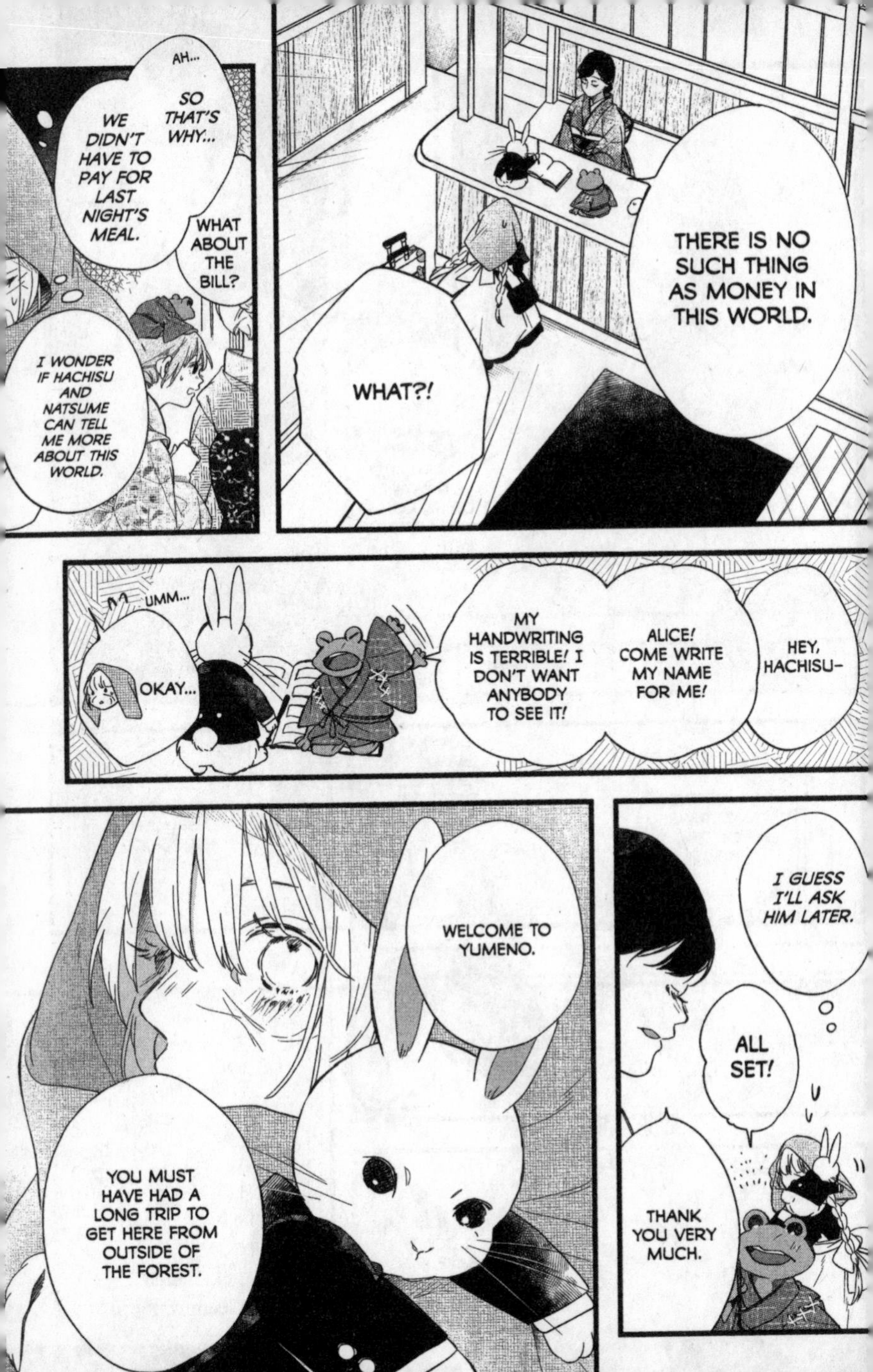
THERE IS NO SUCH THING AS MONEY IN THIS WORLD.
WHAT?!
AH... SO THAT'S WHY...
WE DIDN'T HAVE TO PAY FOR LAST NIGHT'S MEAL.
WHAT ABOUT THE BILL?
I WONDER IF HACHISU AND NATSUME CAN TELL ME MORE ABOUT THIS WORLD.
HEY, HACHISU–
ALICE! COME WRITE MY NAME FOR ME!
MY HANDWRITING IS TERRIBLE! I DON'T WANT ANYBODY TO SEE IT!
UMM...
OKAY...
I GUESS I'LL ASK HIM LATER.
ALL SET!
THANK YOU VERY MUCH.
WELCOME TO YUMENO.
YOU MUST HAVE HAD A LONG TRIP TO GET HERE FROM OUTSIDE OF THE FOREST.

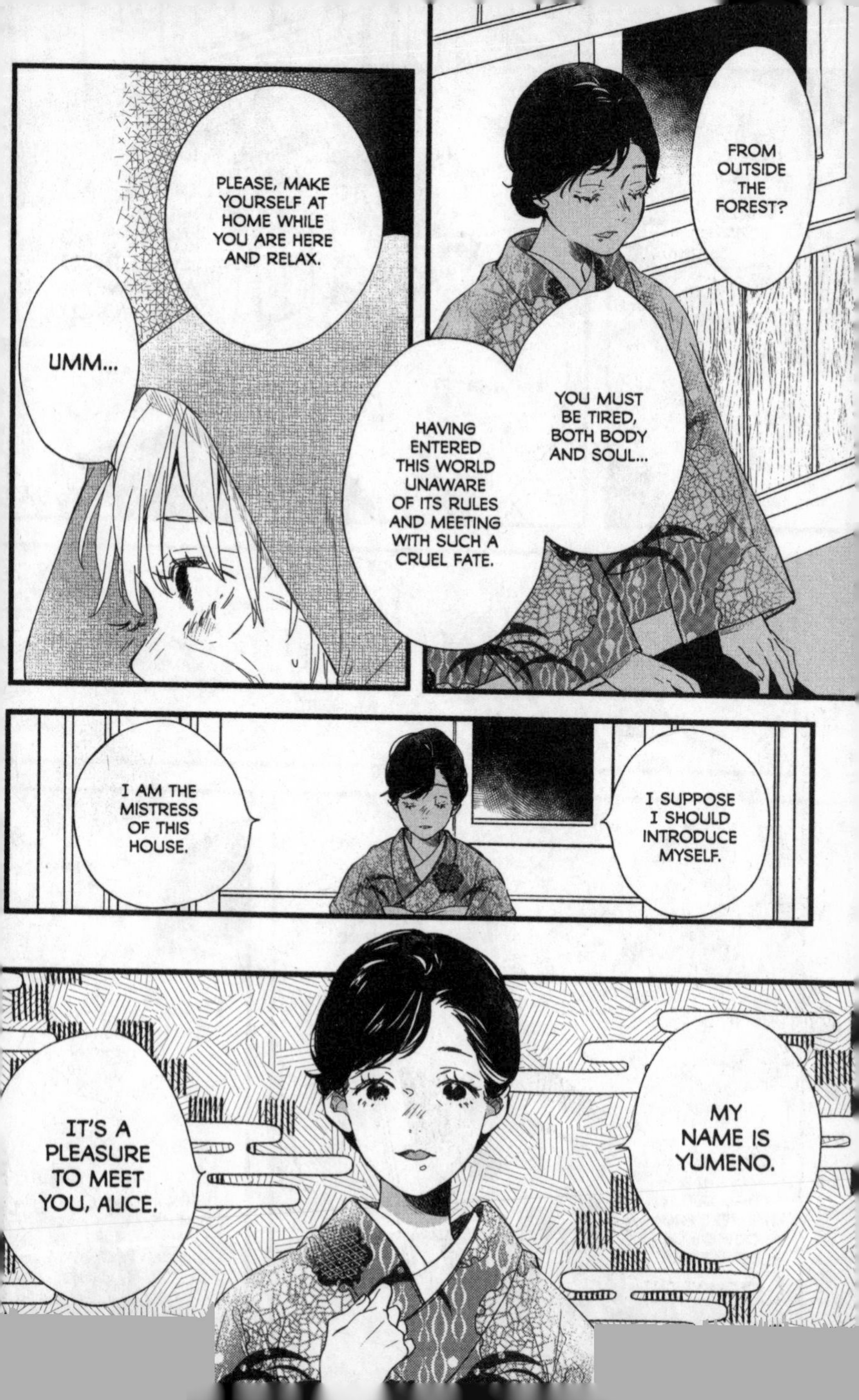
FROM OUTSIDE THE FOREST?
YOU MUST BE TIRED, BOTH BODY AND SOUL...
HAVING ENTERED THIS WORLD UNAWARE OF ITS RULES AND MEETING WITH SUCH A CRUEL FATE.
PLEASE, MAKE YOURSELF AT HOME WHILE YOU ARE HERE AND RELAX.
UMM...
I SUPPOSE I SHOULD INTRODUCE MYSELF.
I AM THE MISTRESS OF THIS HOUSE.
MY NAME IS YUMENO.
IT'S A PLEASURE TO MEET YOU, ALICE.

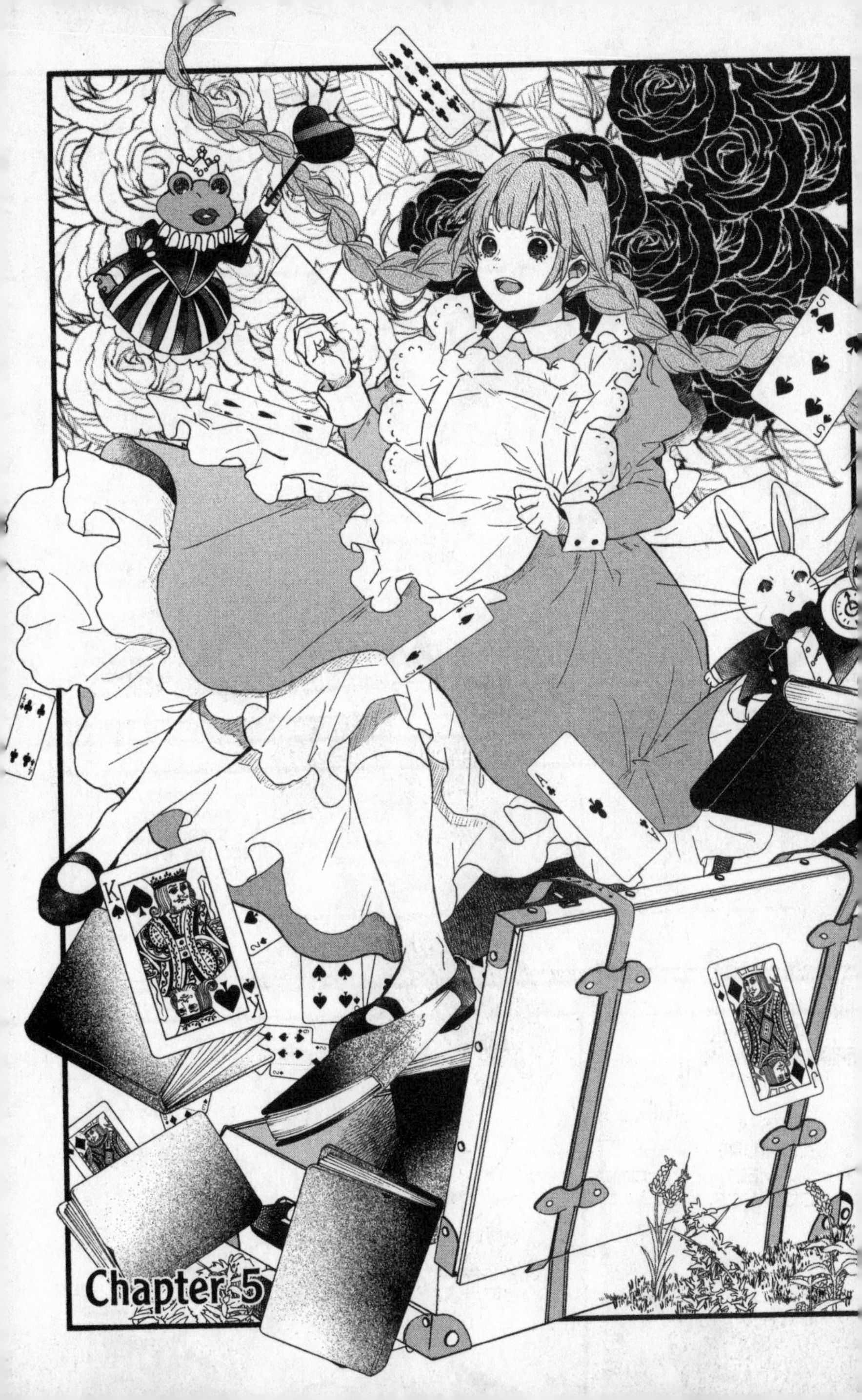
Chapter 5

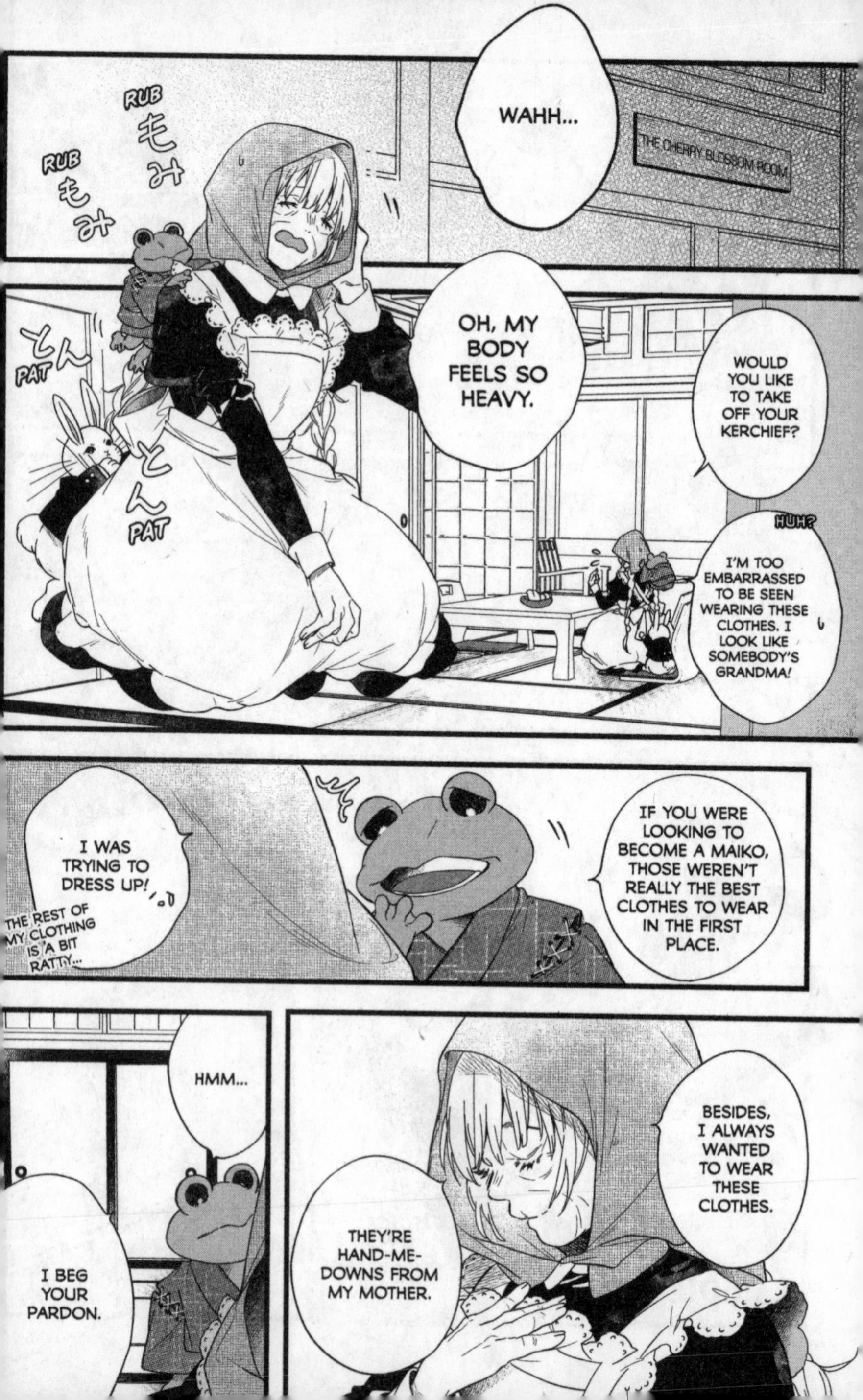
THE CHERRY BLOSSOM ROOM
WAHH...
RUB もみ
RUB もみ
OH, MY BODY FEELS SO HEAVY.
WOULD YOU LIKE TO TAKE OFF YOUR KERCHIEF?
HUH?
I'M TOO EMBARRASSED TO BE SEEN WEARING THESE CLOTHES. I LOOK LIKE SOMEBODY'S GRANDMA!
とん PAT
とん PAT
IF YOU WERE LOOKING TO BECOME A MAIKO, THOSE WEREN'T REALLY THE BEST CLOTHES TO WEAR IN THE FIRST PLACE.
I WAS TRYING TO DRESS UP!
THE REST OF MY CLOTHING IS A BIT RATTY...
BESIDES, I ALWAYS WANTED TO WEAR THESE CLOTHES.
THEY'RE HAND-ME-DOWNS FROM MY MOTHER.
HMM...
I BEG YOUR PARDON.

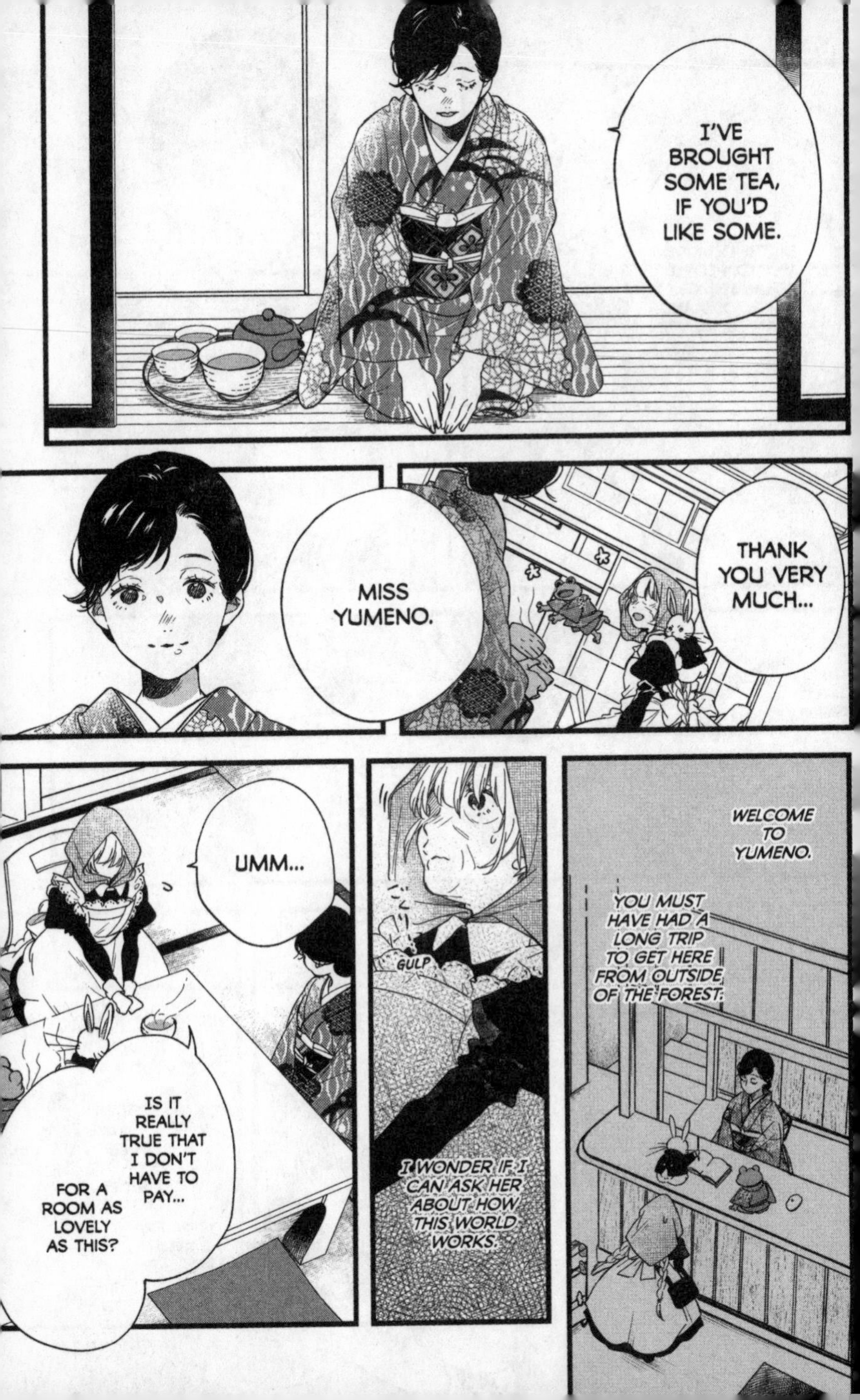
I'VE BROUGHT SOME TEA, IF YOU'D LIKE SOME.
THANK YOU VERY MUCH...
MISS YUMENO.
WELCOME TO YUMENO.
YOU MUST HAVE HAD A LONG TRIP TO GET HERE FROM OUTSIDE OF THE FOREST.
GULP
I WONDER IF I CAN ASK HER ABOUT HOW THIS WORLD WORKS.
UMM...
IS IT REALLY TRUE THAT I DON'T HAVE TO PAY...
FOR A ROOM AS LOVELY AS THIS?

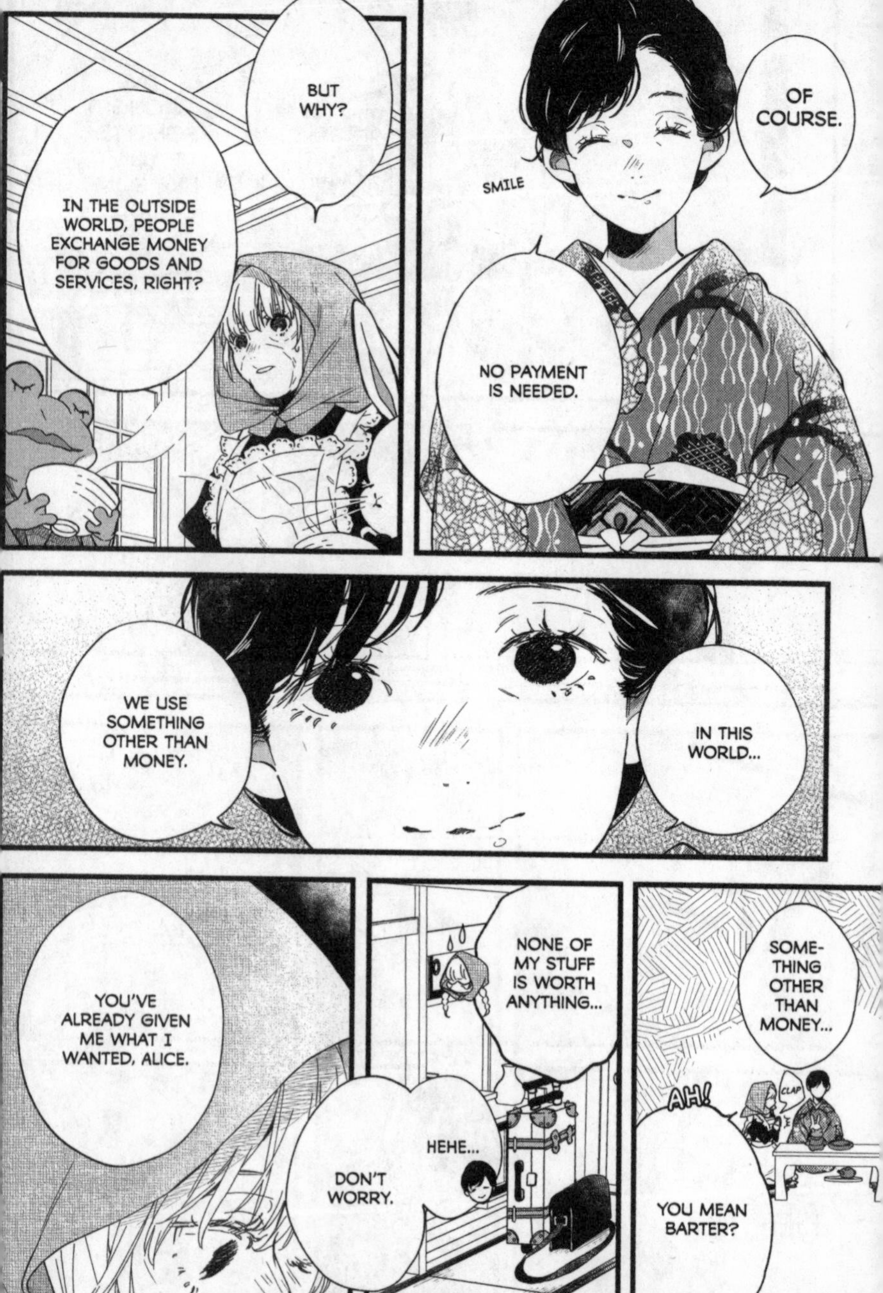
OF COURSE.
SMILE
NO PAYMENT IS NEEDED.
BUT WHY?
IN THE OUTSIDE WORLD, PEOPLE EXCHANGE MONEY FOR GOODS AND SERVICES, RIGHT?
IN THIS WORLD...
WE USE SOMETHING OTHER THAN MONEY.
SOME-THING OTHER THAN MONEY...
AH!
CLAP
YOU MEAN BARTER?
NONE OF MY STUFF IS WORTH ANYTHING...
HEHE...
DON'T WORRY.
YOU'VE ALREADY GIVEN ME WHAT I WANTED, ALICE.

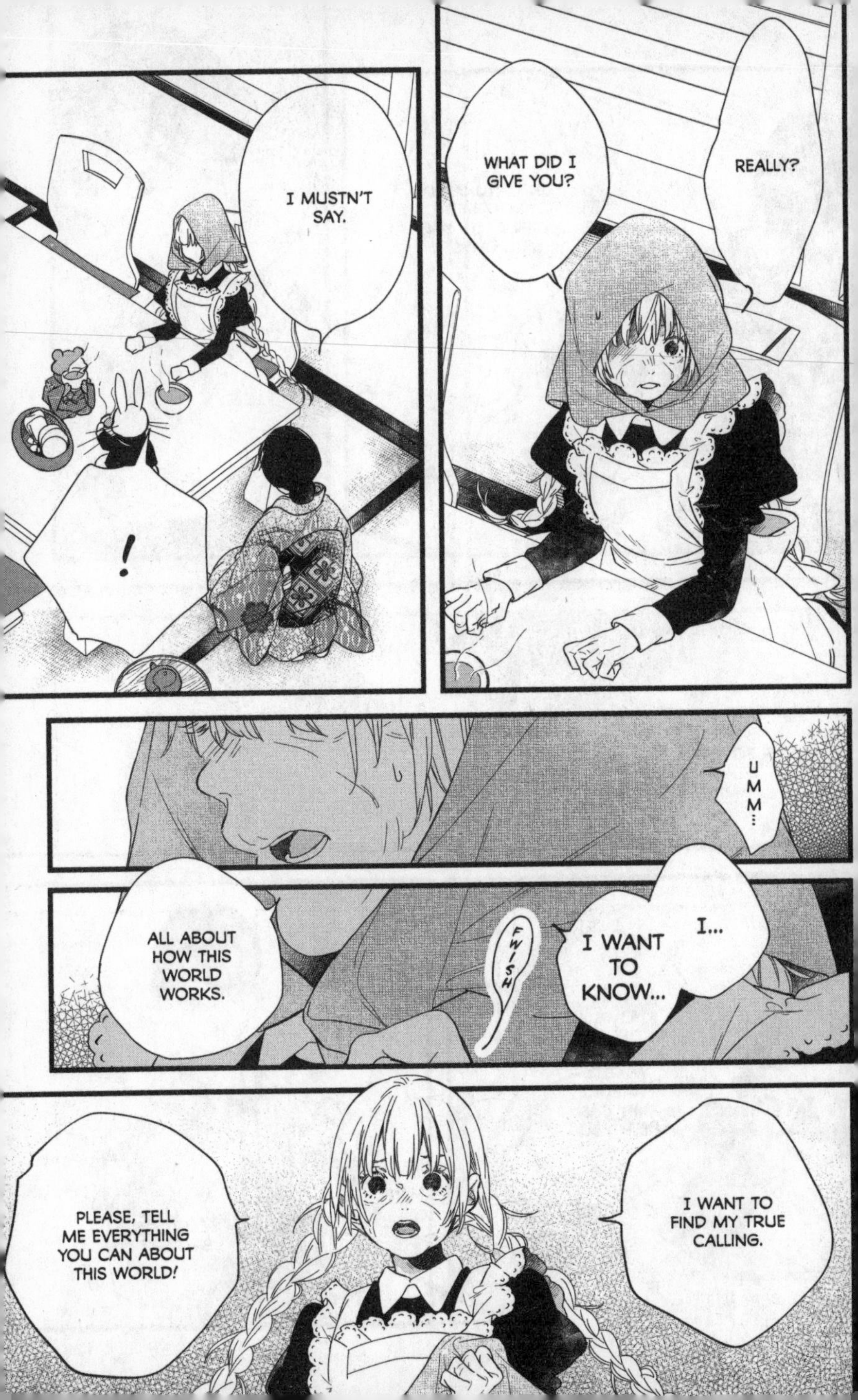
REALLY?
WHAT DID I GIVE YOU?
I MUSTN'T SAY.
!
UMM...
I...
I WANT TO KNOW...
FWISH
ALL ABOUT HOW THIS WORLD WORKS.
I WANT TO FIND MY TRUE CALLING.
PLEASE, TELL ME EVERYTHING YOU CAN ABOUT THIS WORLD!

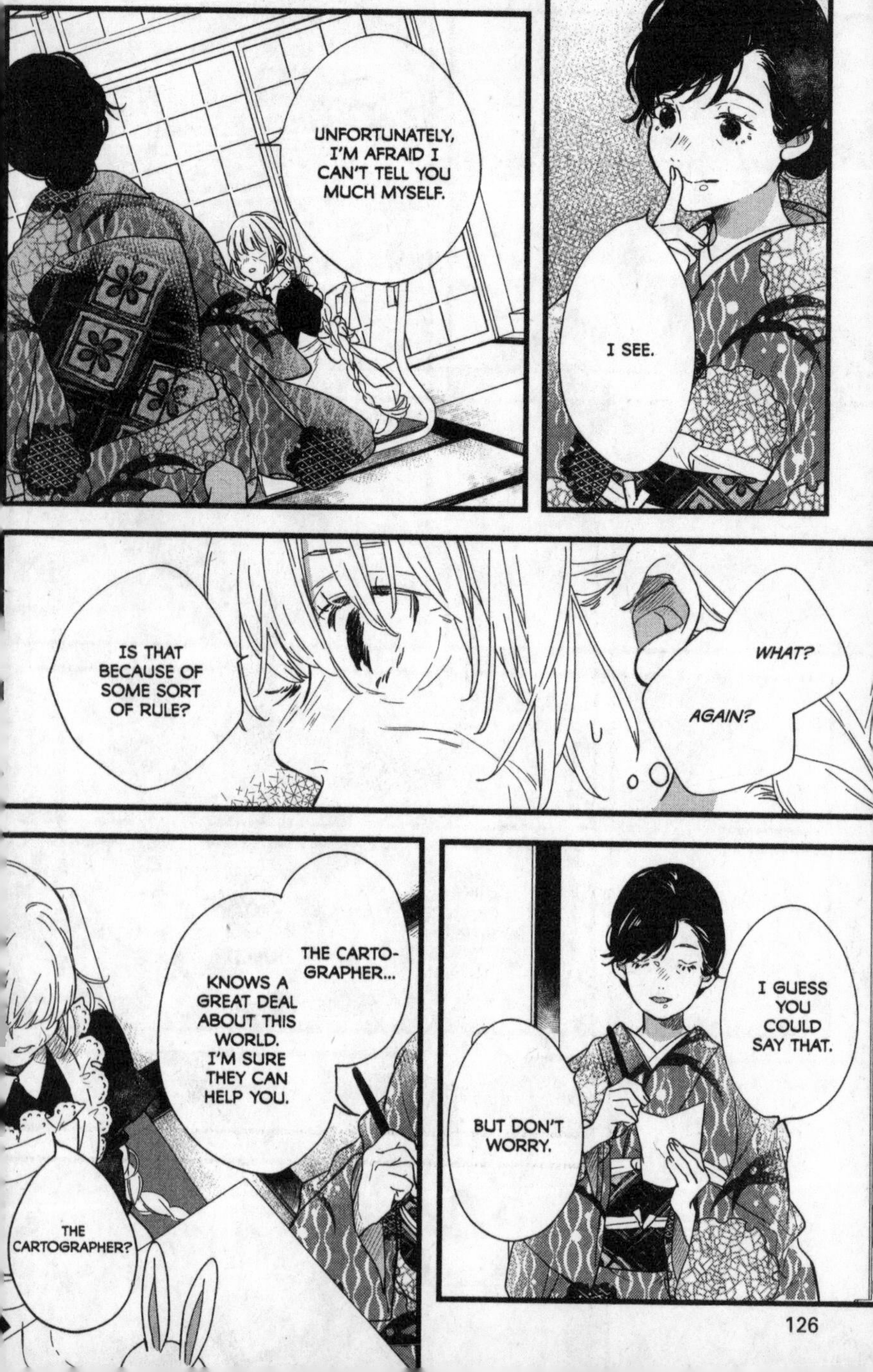
I SEE.
UNFORTUNATELY, I'M AFRAID I CAN'T TELL YOU MUCH MYSELF.
WHAT? AGAIN?
IS THAT BECAUSE OF SOME SORT OF RULE?
I GUESS YOU COULD SAY THAT.
BUT DON'T WORRY.
THE CARTOGRAPHER...
KNOWS A GREAT DEAL ABOUT THIS WORLD. I'M SURE THEY CAN HELP YOU.
THE CARTOGRAPHER?

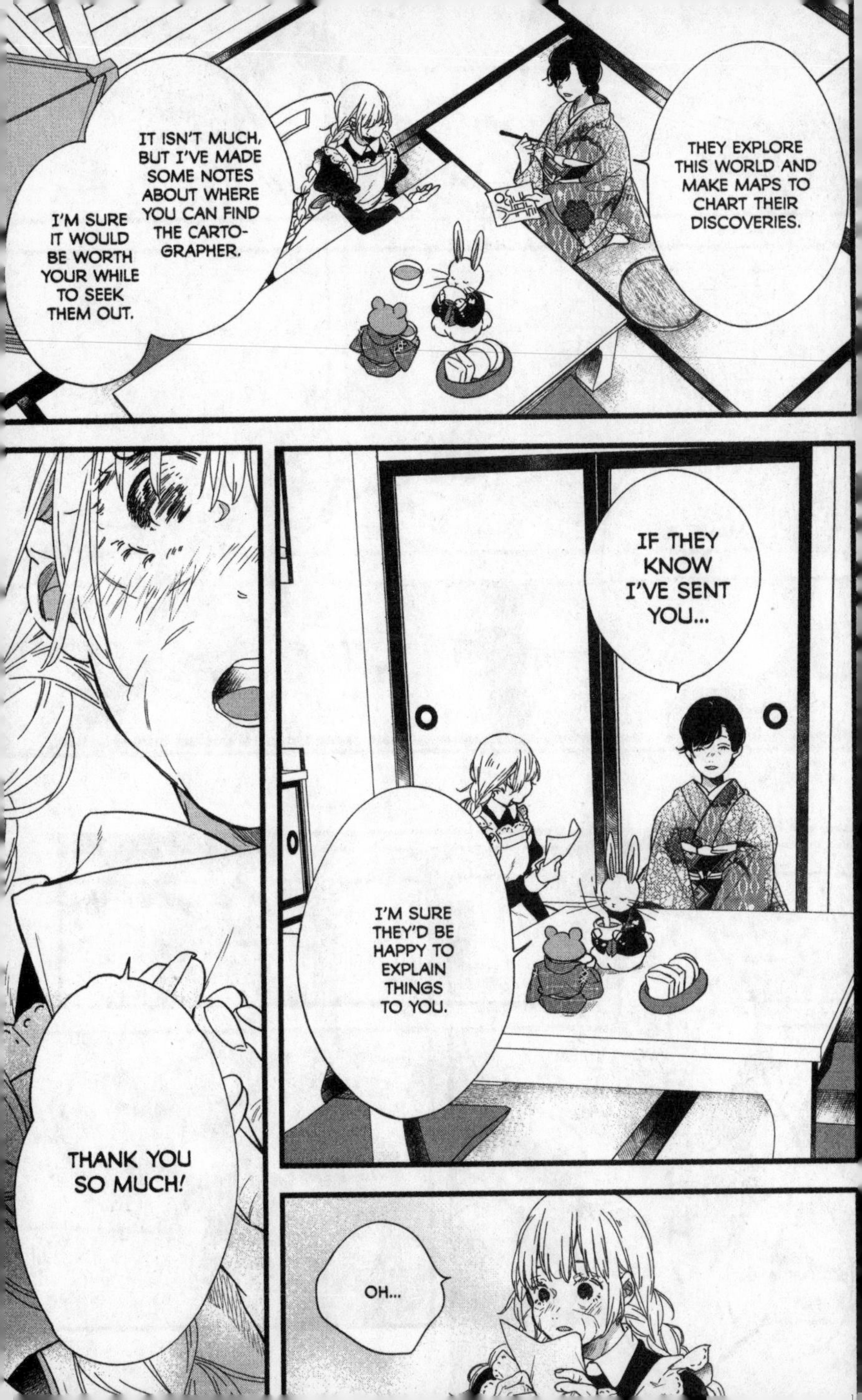
THEY EXPLORE THIS WORLD AND MAKE MAPS TO CHART THEIR DISCOVERIES.
IT ISN'T MUCH, BUT I'VE MADE SOME NOTES ABOUT WHERE YOU CAN FIND THE CARTOGRAPHER.
I'M SURE IT WOULD BE WORTH YOUR WHILE TO SEEK THEM OUT.
IF THEY KNOW I'VE SENT YOU...
I'M SURE THEY'D BE HAPPY TO EXPLAIN THINGS TO YOU.
OH...
THANK YOU SO MUCH!

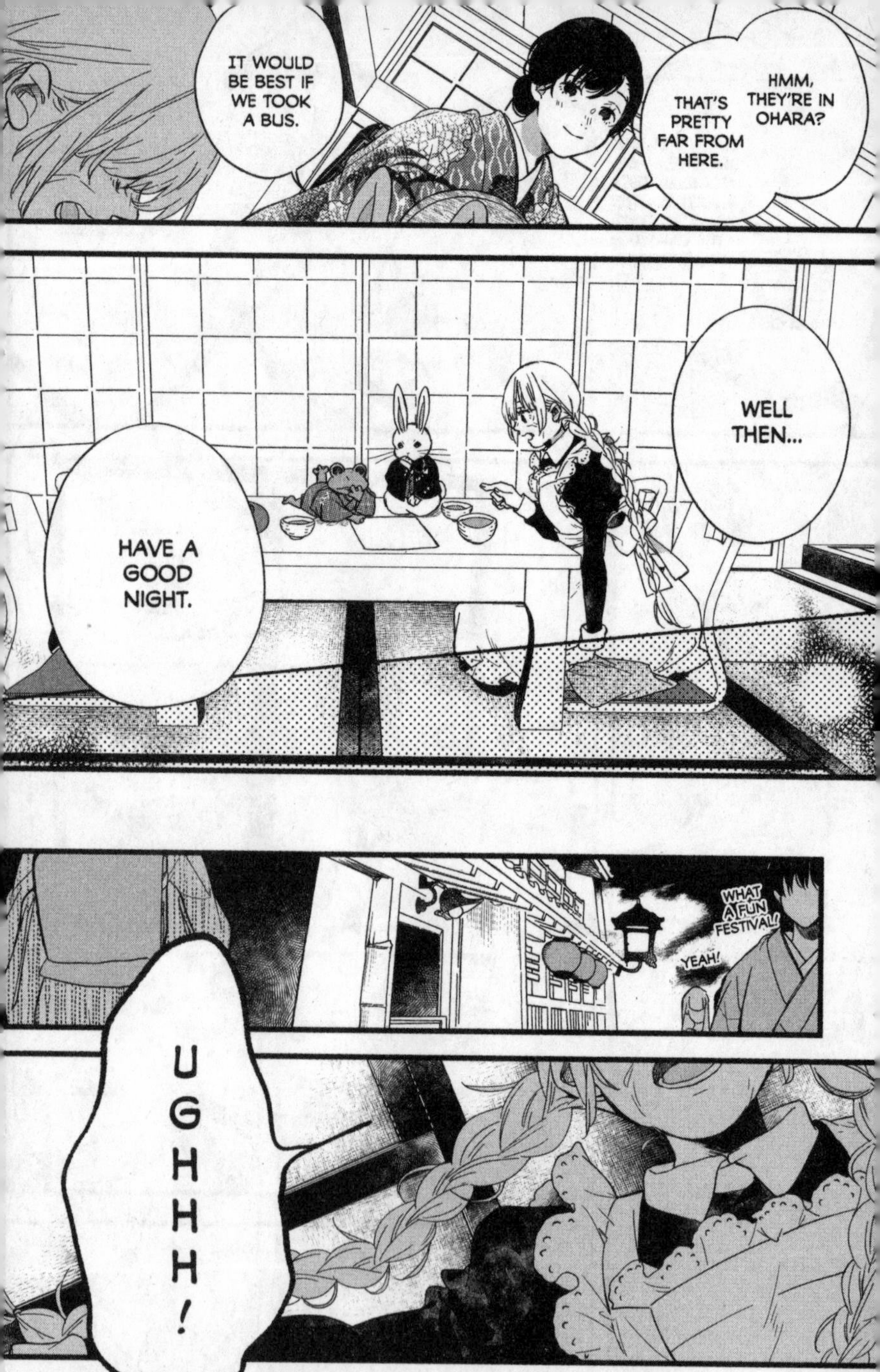
HMM, THEY'RE IN OHARA?
THAT'S PRETTY FAR FROM HERE.
IT WOULD BE BEST IF WE TOOK A BUS.
WELL THEN...
HAVE A GOOD NIGHT.
WHAT A FUN FESTIVAL!
YEAH!
UGHHH!

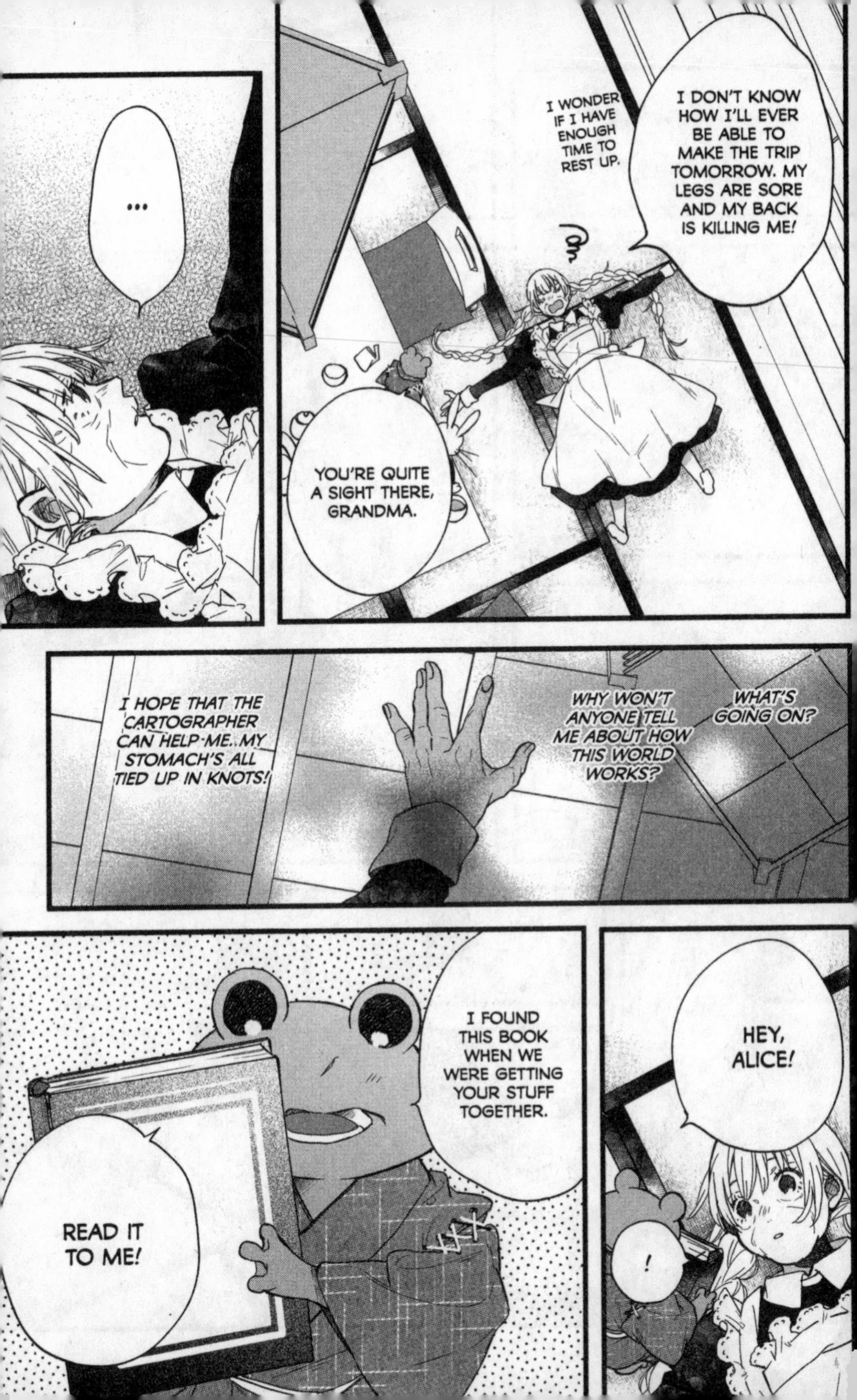
I DON'T KNOW HOW I'LL EVER BE ABLE TO MAKE THE TRIP TOMORROW. MY LEGS ARE SORE AND MY BACK IS KILLING ME!
I WONDER IF I HAVE ENOUGH TIME TO REST UP.
YOU'RE QUITE A SIGHT THERE, GRANDMA.
...
WHAT'S GOING ON?
WHY WON'T ANYONE TELL ME ABOUT HOW THIS WORLD WORKS?
I HOPE THAT THE CARTOGRAPHER CAN HELP ME..MY STOMACH'S ALL TIED UP IN KNOTS!
HEY, ALICE!
!
I FOUND THIS BOOK WHEN WE WERE GETTING YOUR STUFF TOGETHER.
READ IT TO ME!

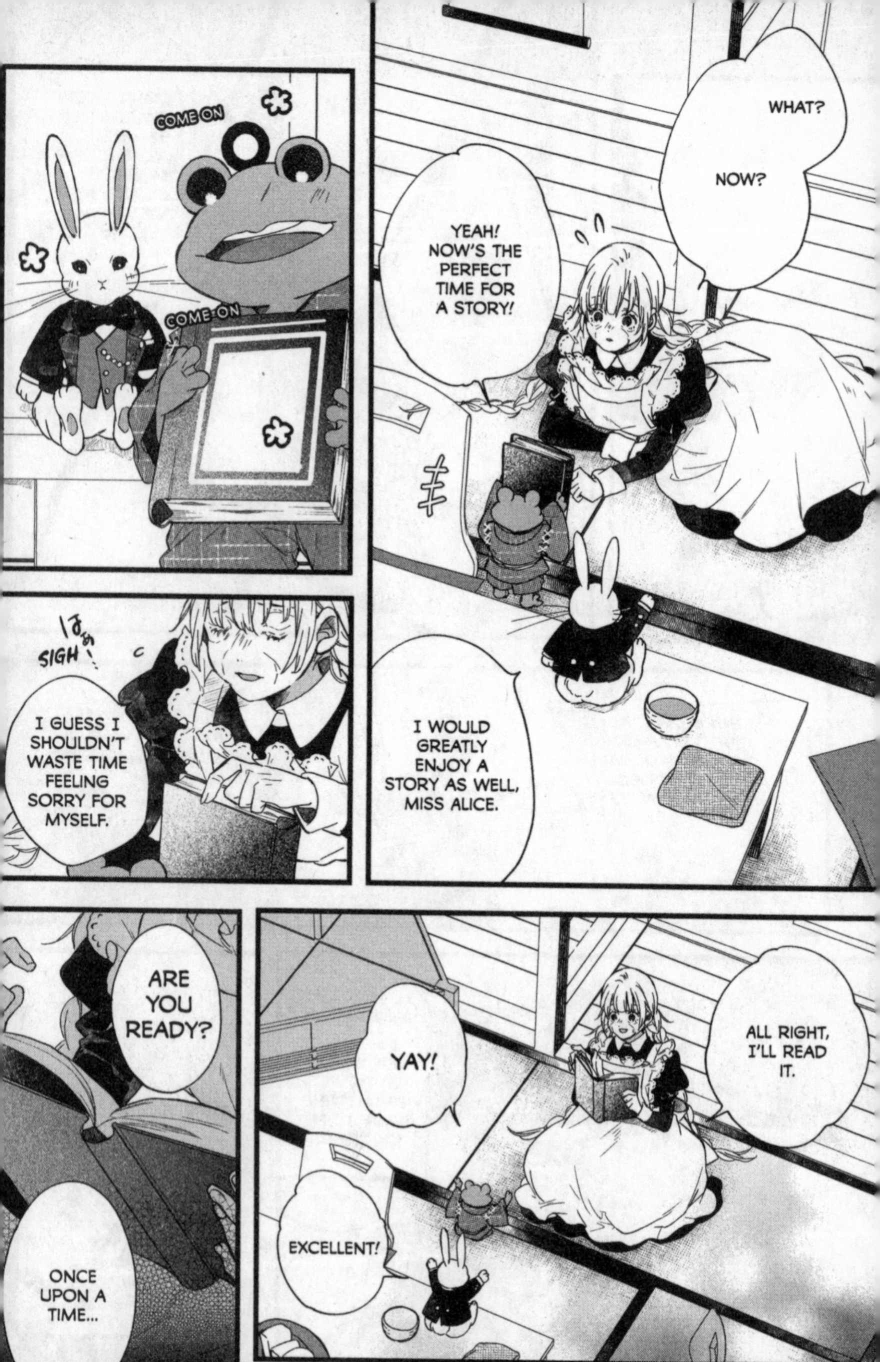
WHAT?
NOW?
YEAH! NOW'S THE PERFECT TIME FOR A STORY!
I WOULD GREATLY ENJOY A STORY AS WELL, MISS ALICE.
COME ON
COME ON
SIGH
I GUESS I SHOULDN'T WASTE TIME FEELING SORRY FOR MYSELF.
ALL RIGHT, I'LL READ IT.
YAY!
EXCELLENT!
ARE YOU READY?
ONCE UPON A TIME...

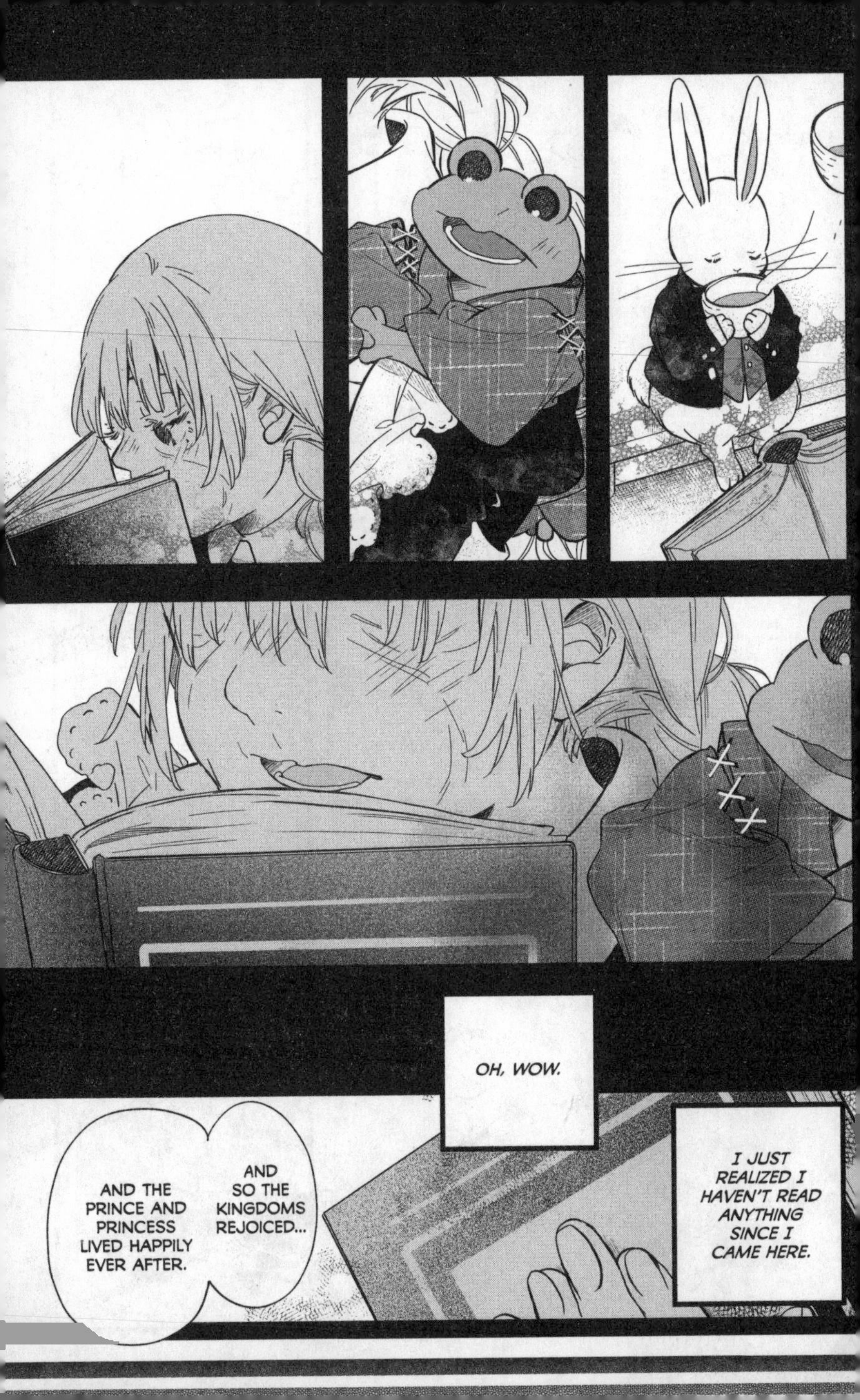

OH, WOW.
I JUST REALIZED I HAVEN'T READ ANYTHING SINCE I CAME HERE.
AND SO THE KINGDOMS REJOICED...
AND THE PRINCE AND PRINCESS LIVED HAPPILY EVER AFTER.

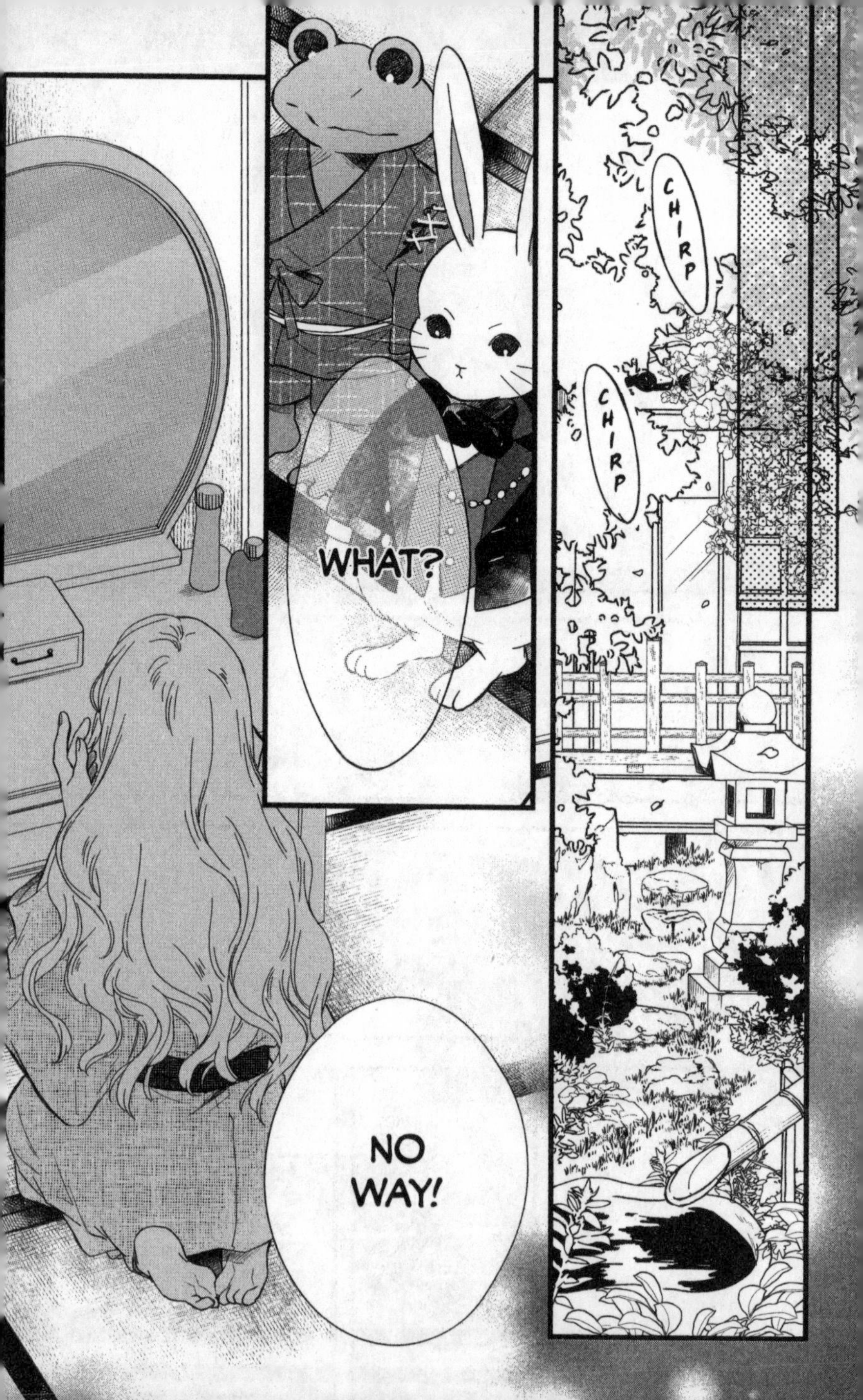
CHIRP
CHIRP
WHAT?
NO WAY!

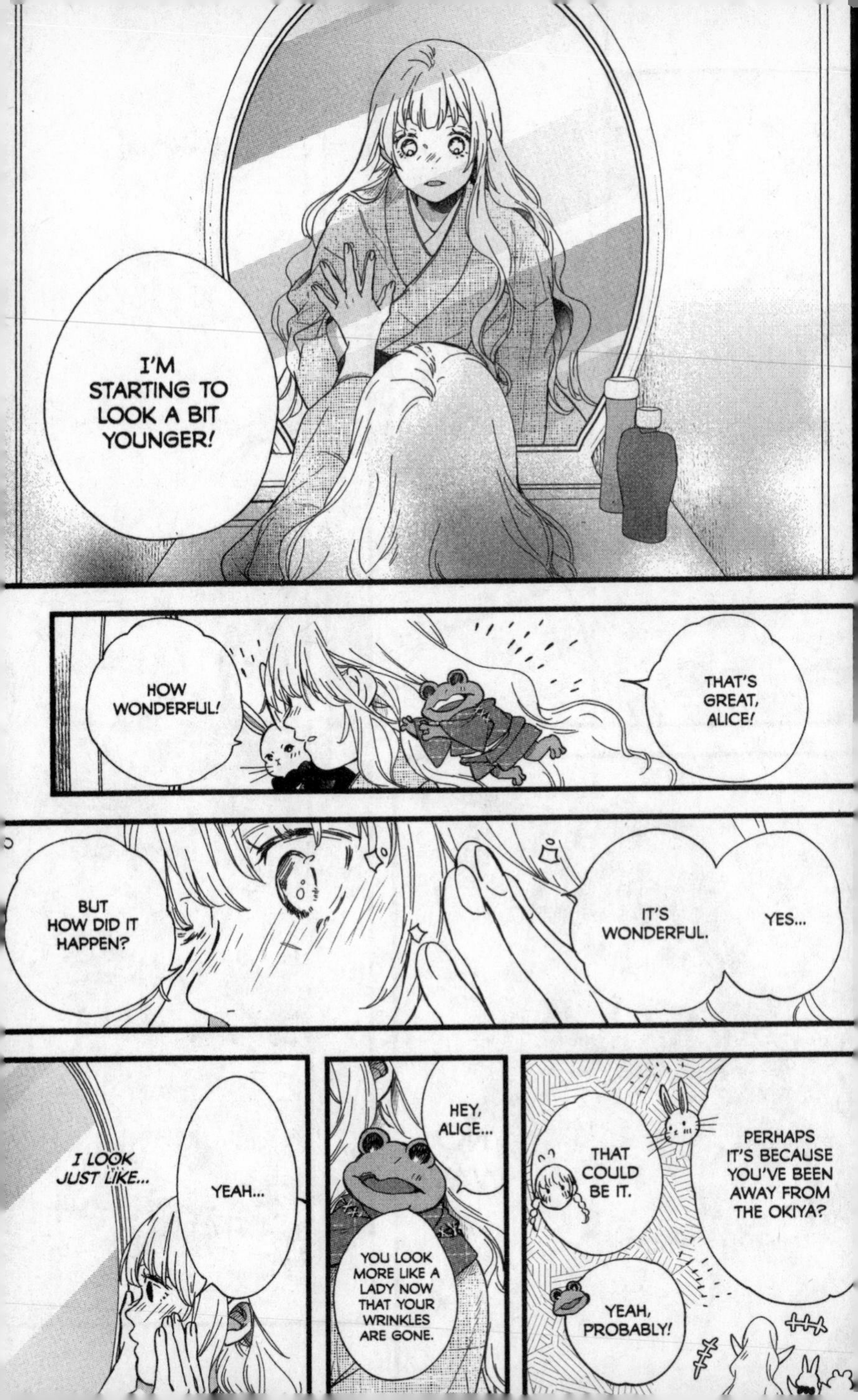
I'M STARTING TO LOOK A BIT YOUNGER!
THAT'S GREAT, ALICE!
HOW WONDERFUL!
YES...
IT'S WONDERFUL.
BUT HOW DID IT HAPPEN?
PERHAPS IT'S BECAUSE YOU'VE BEEN AWAY FROM THE OKIYA?
THAT COULD BE IT.
YEAH, PROBABLY!
HEY, ALICE...
YOU LOOK MORE LIKE A LADY NOW THAT YOUR WRINKLES ARE GONE.
YEAH...
I LOOK JUST LIKE...

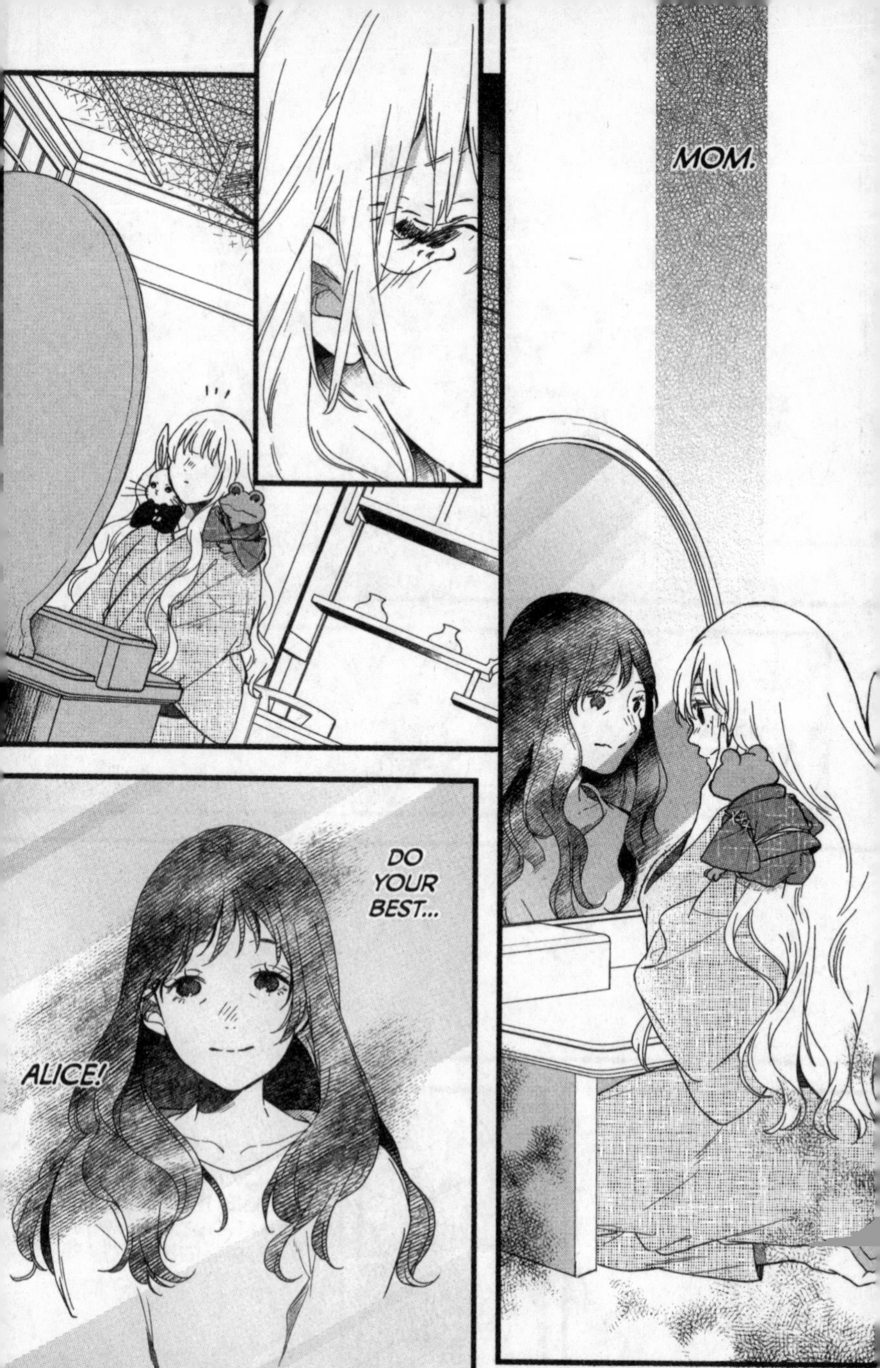
MOM.
DO YOUR BEST...
ALICE!

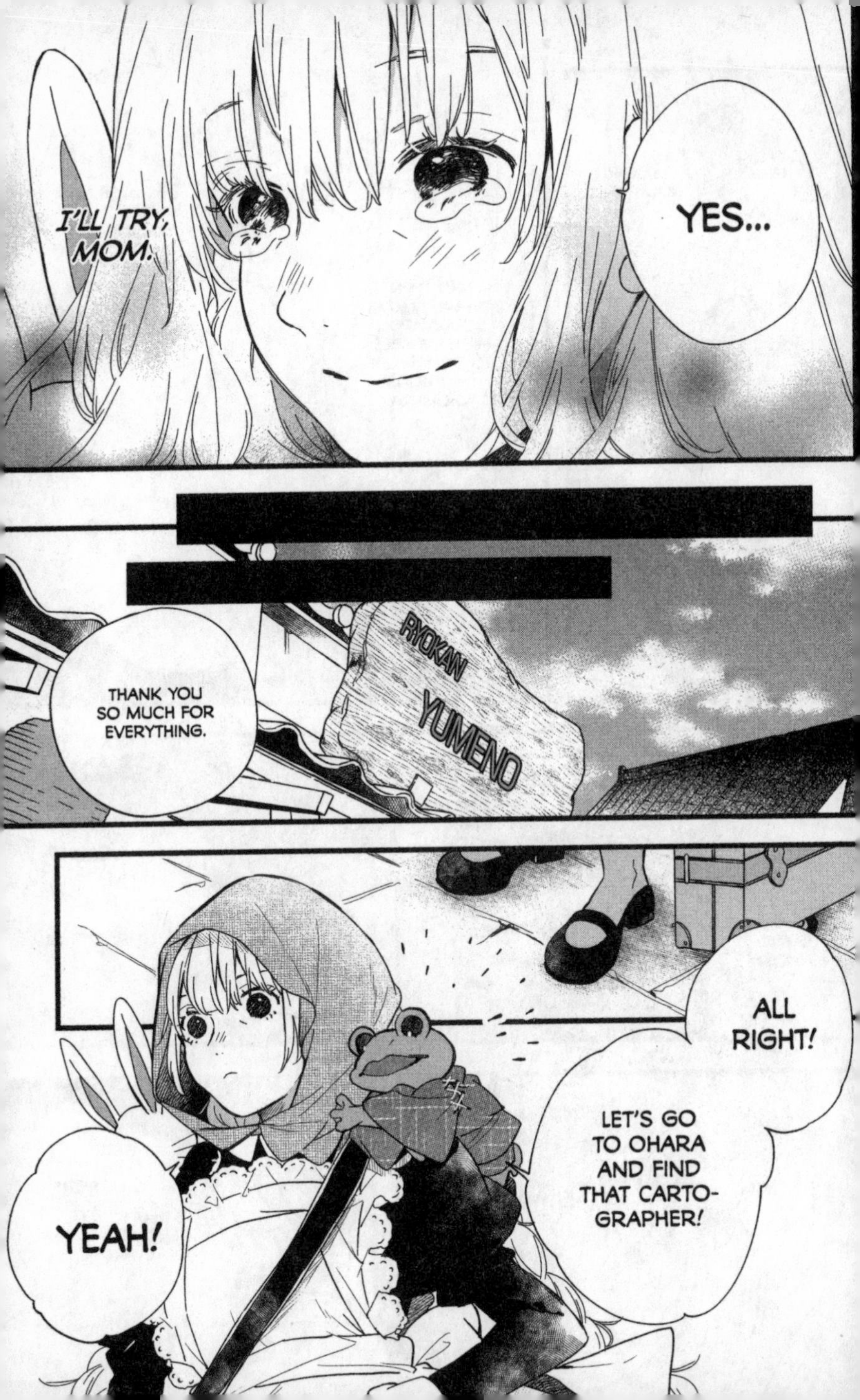
YES...
I'LL TRY, MOM.
[redacted]
RYOKAN YUMENO
THANK YOU SO MUCH FOR EVERYTHING.
ALL RIGHT!
LET'S GO TO OHARA AND FIND THAT CARTO-GRAPHER!
YEAH!

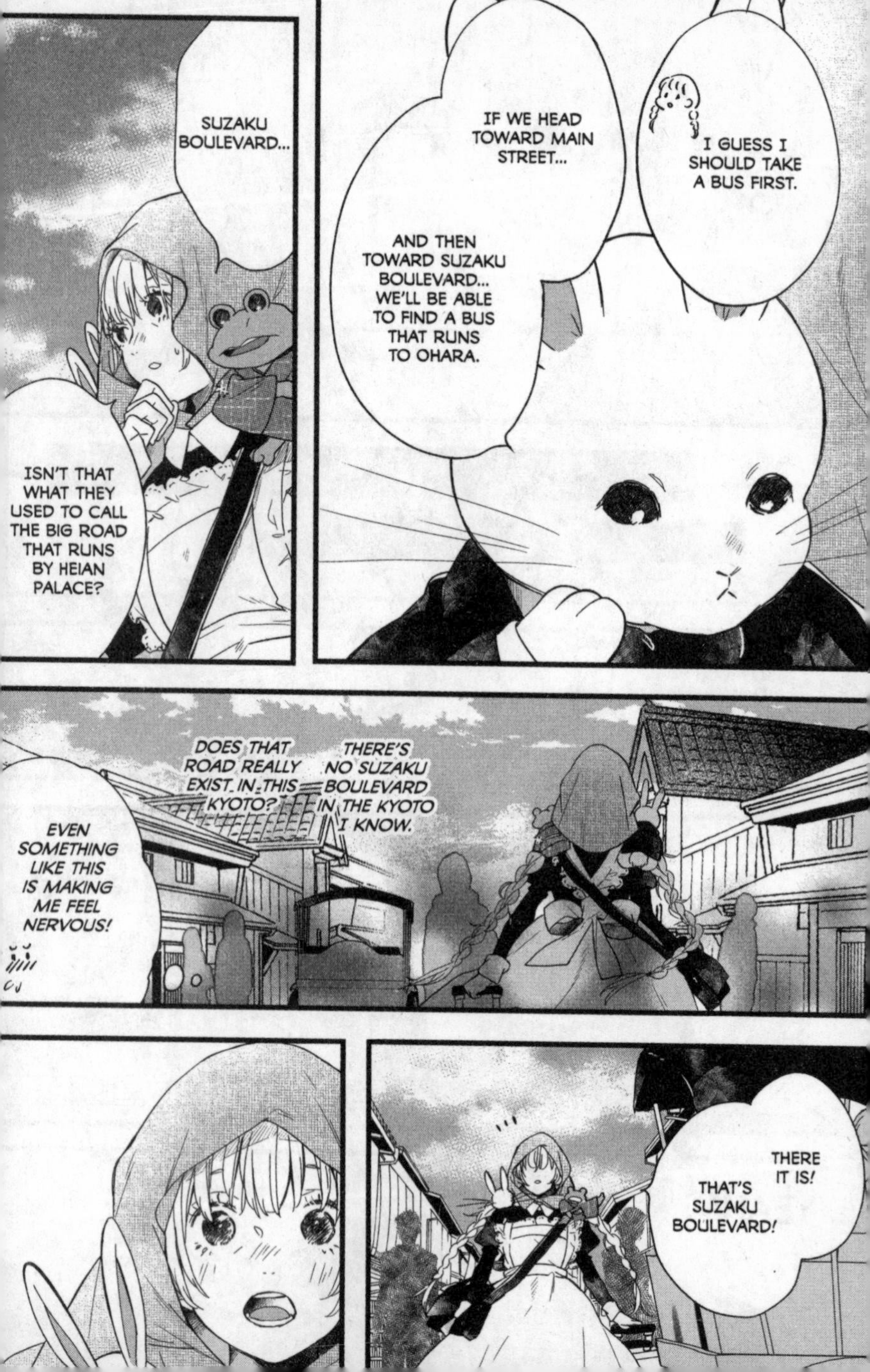
I GUESS I SHOULD TAKE A BUS FIRST.
IF WE HEAD TOWARD MAIN STREET...
AND THEN TOWARD SUZAKU BOULEVARD... WE'LL BE ABLE TO FIND A BUS THAT RUNS TO OHARA.
SUZAKU BOULEVARD...
ISN'T THAT WHAT THEY USED TO CALL THE BIG ROAD THAT RUNS BY HEIAN PALACE?
THERE'S NO SUZAKU BOULEVARD IN THE KYOTO I KNOW.
DOES THAT ROAD REALLY EXIST IN THIS KYOTO?
EVEN SOMETHING LIKE THIS IS MAKING ME FEEL NERVOUS!
THERE IT IS!
THAT'S SUZAKU BOULEVARD!

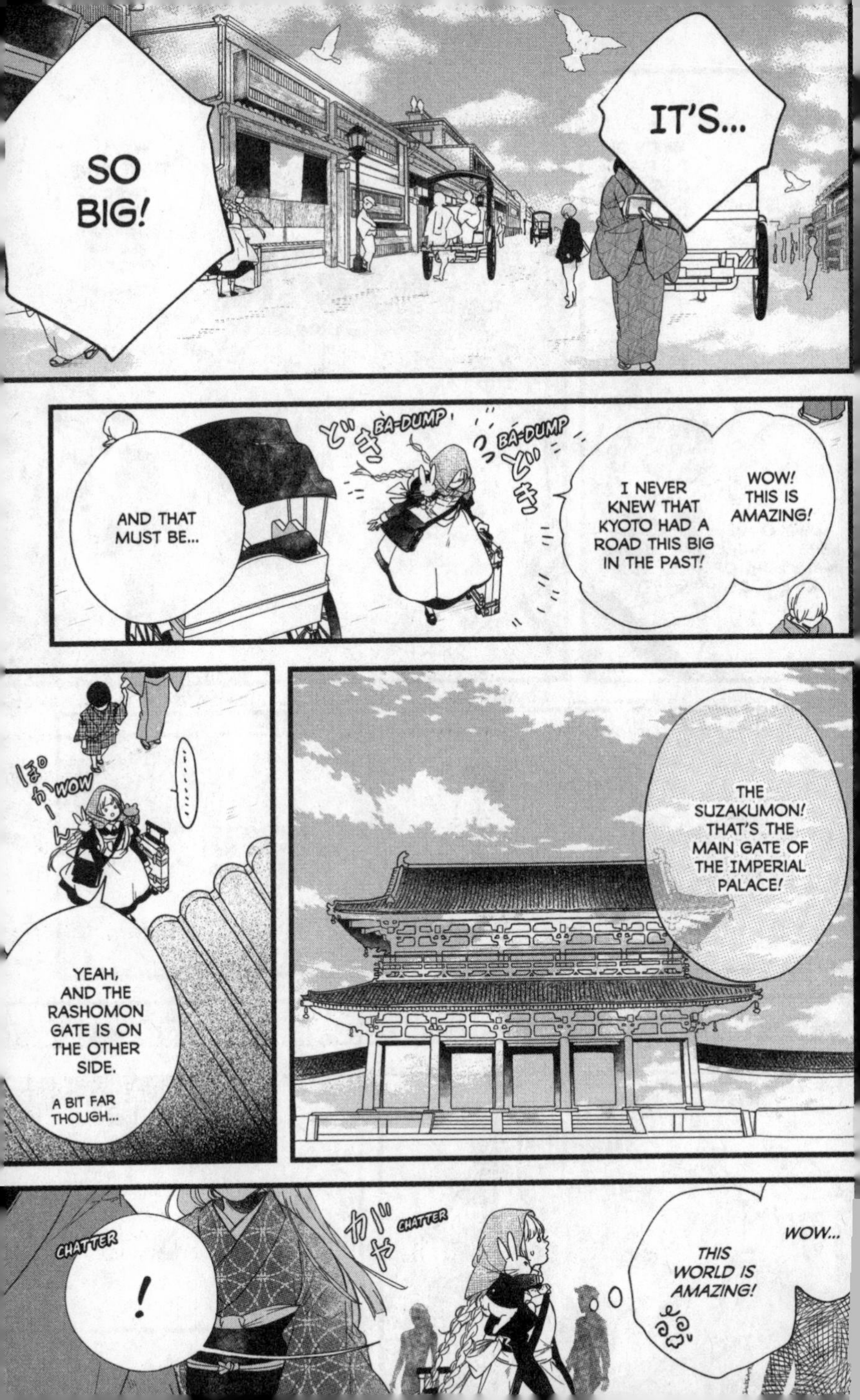
IT'S...
SO BIG!
WOW! THIS IS AMAZING!
I NEVER KNEW THAT KYOTO HAD A ROAD THIS BIG IN THE PAST!
BA-DUMP
BA-DUMP
AND THAT MUST BE...
THE SUZAKUMON! THAT'S THE MAIN GATE OF THE IMPERIAL PALACE!
......
WOW
YEAH, AND THE RASHOMON GATE IS ON THE OTHER SIDE.
A BIT FAR THOUGH...
WOW...
THIS WORLD IS AMAZING!
CHATTER
CHATTER
!

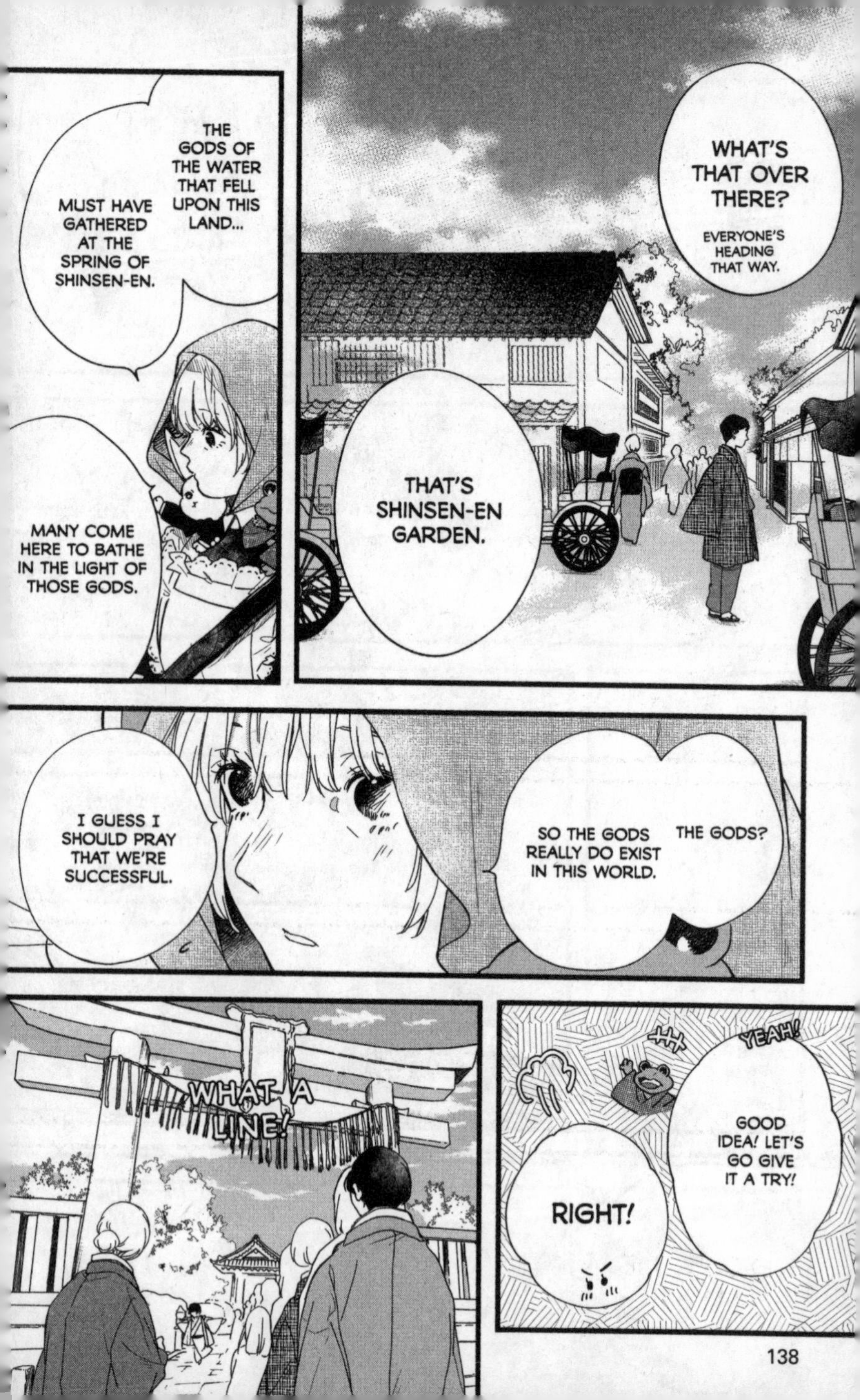
WHAT'S THAT OVER THERE?
EVERYONE'S HEADING THAT WAY.
THAT'S SHINSEN-EN GARDEN.
THE GODS OF THE WATER THAT FELL UPON THIS LAND...
MUST HAVE GATHERED AT THE SPRING OF SHINSEN-EN.
MANY COME HERE TO BATHE IN THE LIGHT OF THOSE GODS.
THE GODS?
SO THE GODS REALLY DO EXIST IN THIS WORLD.
I GUESS I SHOULD PRAY THAT WE'RE SUCCESSFUL.
YEAH!
GOOD IDEA! LET'S GO GIVE IT A TRY!
RIGHT!
WHAT A LINE!

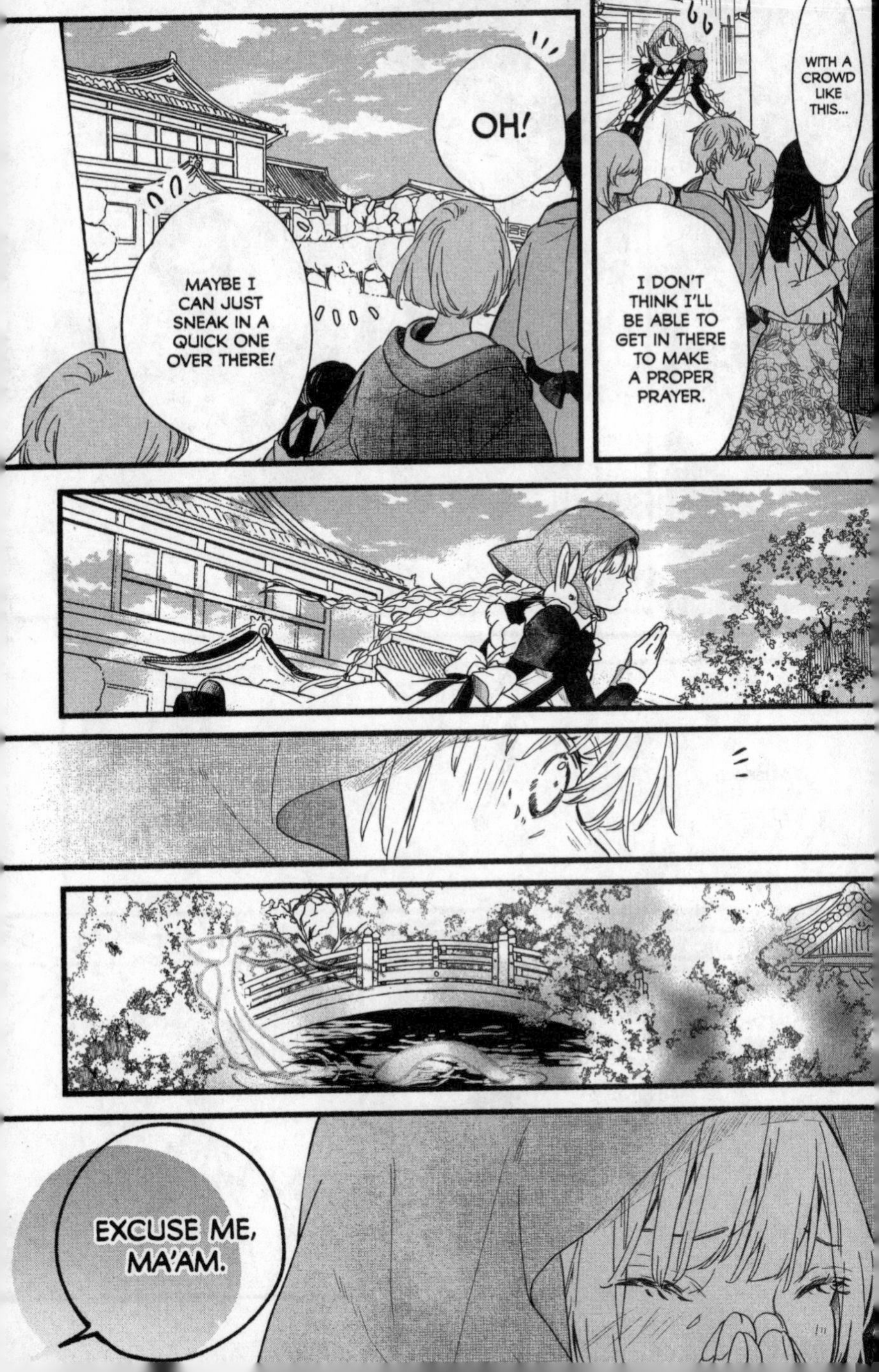
WITH A CROWD LIKE THIS...
I DON'T THINK I'LL BE ABLE TO GET IN THERE TO MAKE A PROPER PRAYER.
OH!
MAYBE I CAN JUST SNEAK IN A QUICK ONE OVER THERE!
EXCUSE ME, MA'AM.

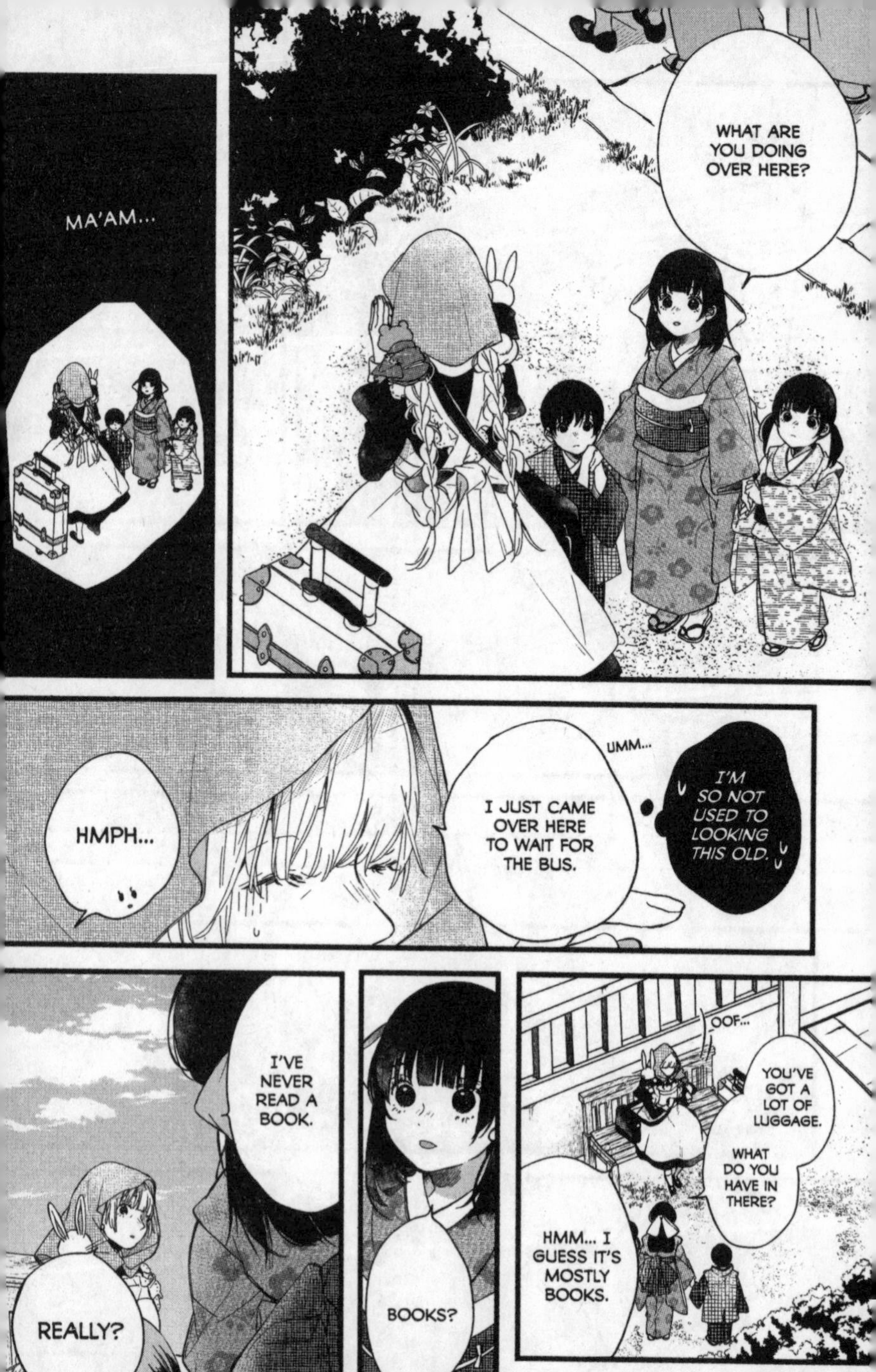
WHAT ARE YOU DOING OVER HERE?
MA'AM...
I'M SO NOT USED TO LOOKING THIS OLD.
UMM...
I JUST CAME OVER HERE TO WAIT FOR THE BUS.
HMPH...
OOF...
YOU'VE GOT A LOT OF LUGGAGE.
WHAT DO YOU HAVE IN THERE?
HMM... I GUESS IT'S MOSTLY BOOKS.
BOOKS?
I'VE NEVER READ A BOOK.
REALLY?

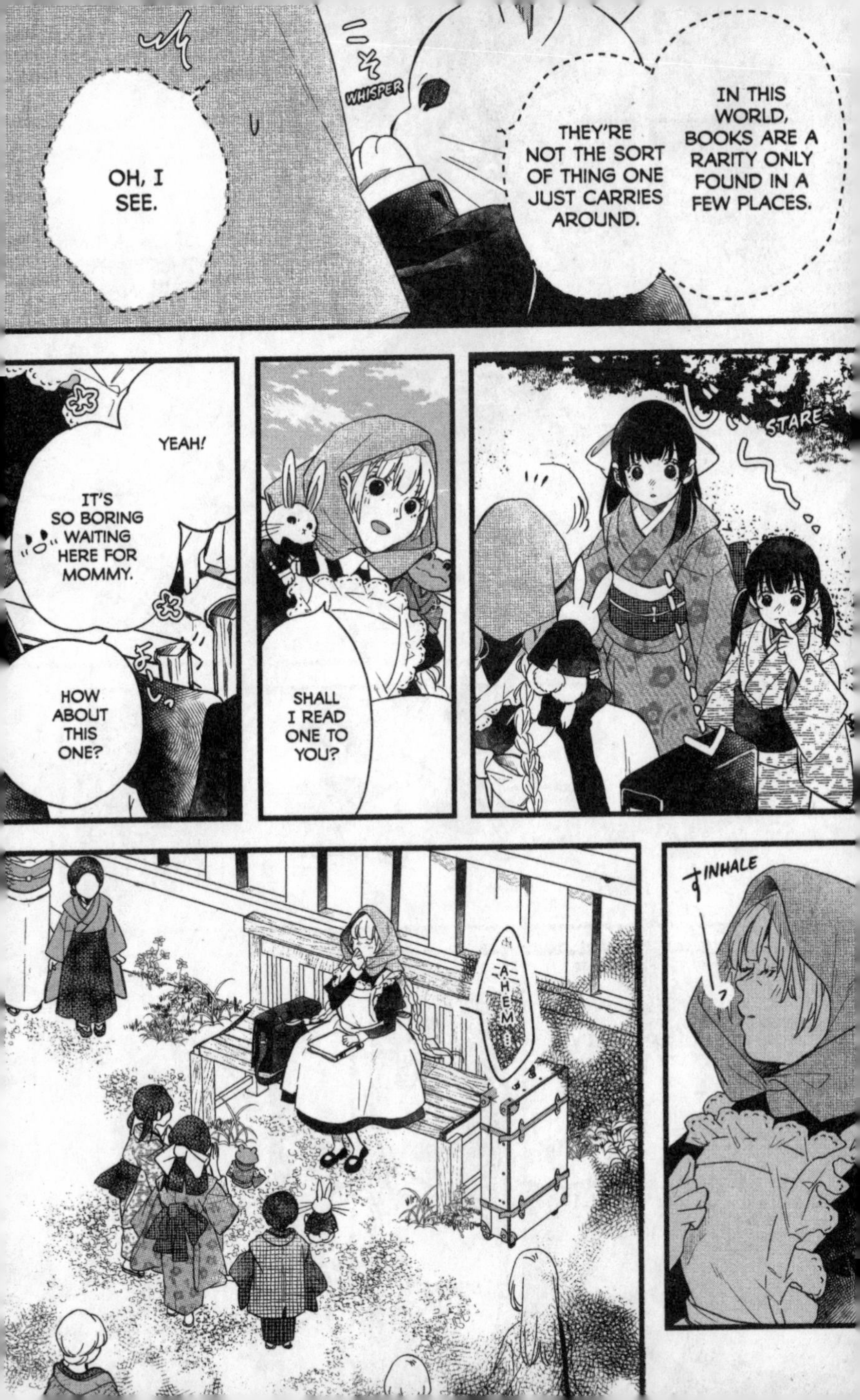
IN THIS WORLD, BOOKS ARE A RARITY ONLY FOUND IN A FEW PLACES.
THEY'RE NOT THE SORT OF THING ONE JUST CARRIES AROUND.
WHISPER
OH, I SEE.
STARE
SHALL I READ ONE TO YOU?
YEAH!
IT'S SO BORING WAITING HERE FOR MOMMY.
HOW ABOUT THIS ONE?
INHALE
AHEM...

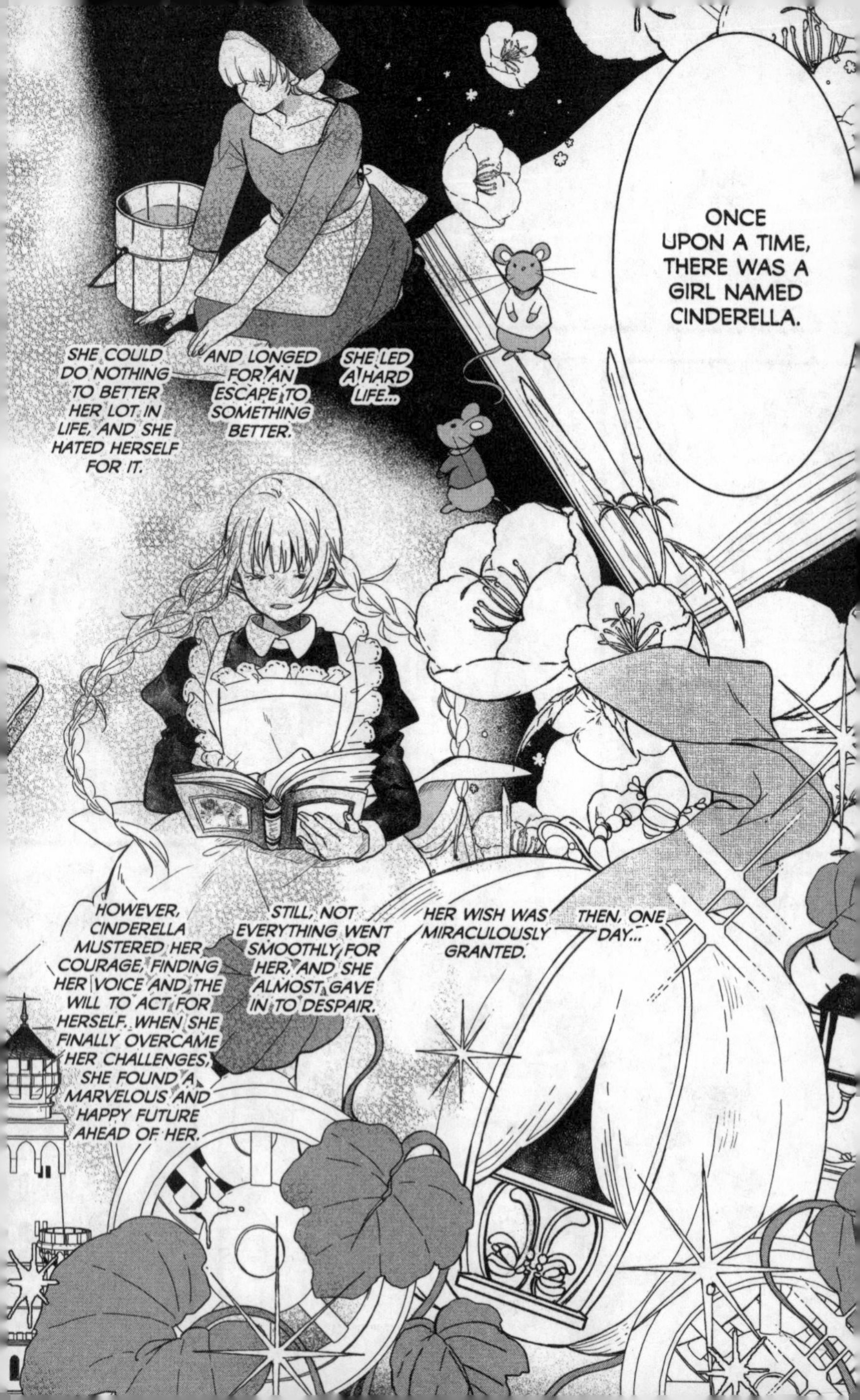
ONCE UPON A TIME, THERE WAS A GIRL NAMED CINDERELLA.
SHE LED A HARD LIFE...
AND LONGED FOR AN ESCAPE TO SOMETHING BETTER.
SHE COULD DO NOTHING TO BETTER HER LOT IN LIFE, AND SHE HATED HERSELF FOR IT.
THEN, ONE DAY...
HER WISH WAS MIRACULOUSLY GRANTED.
STILL, NOT EVERYTHING WENT SMOOTHLY FOR HER, AND SHE ALMOST GAVE IN TO DESPAIR.
HOWEVER, CINDERELLA MUSTERED HER COURAGE, FINDING HER VOICE AND THE WILL TO ACT FOR HERSELF. WHEN SHE FINALLY OVERCAME HER CHALLENGES, SHE FOUND A MARVELOUS AND HAPPY FUTURE AHEAD OF HER.

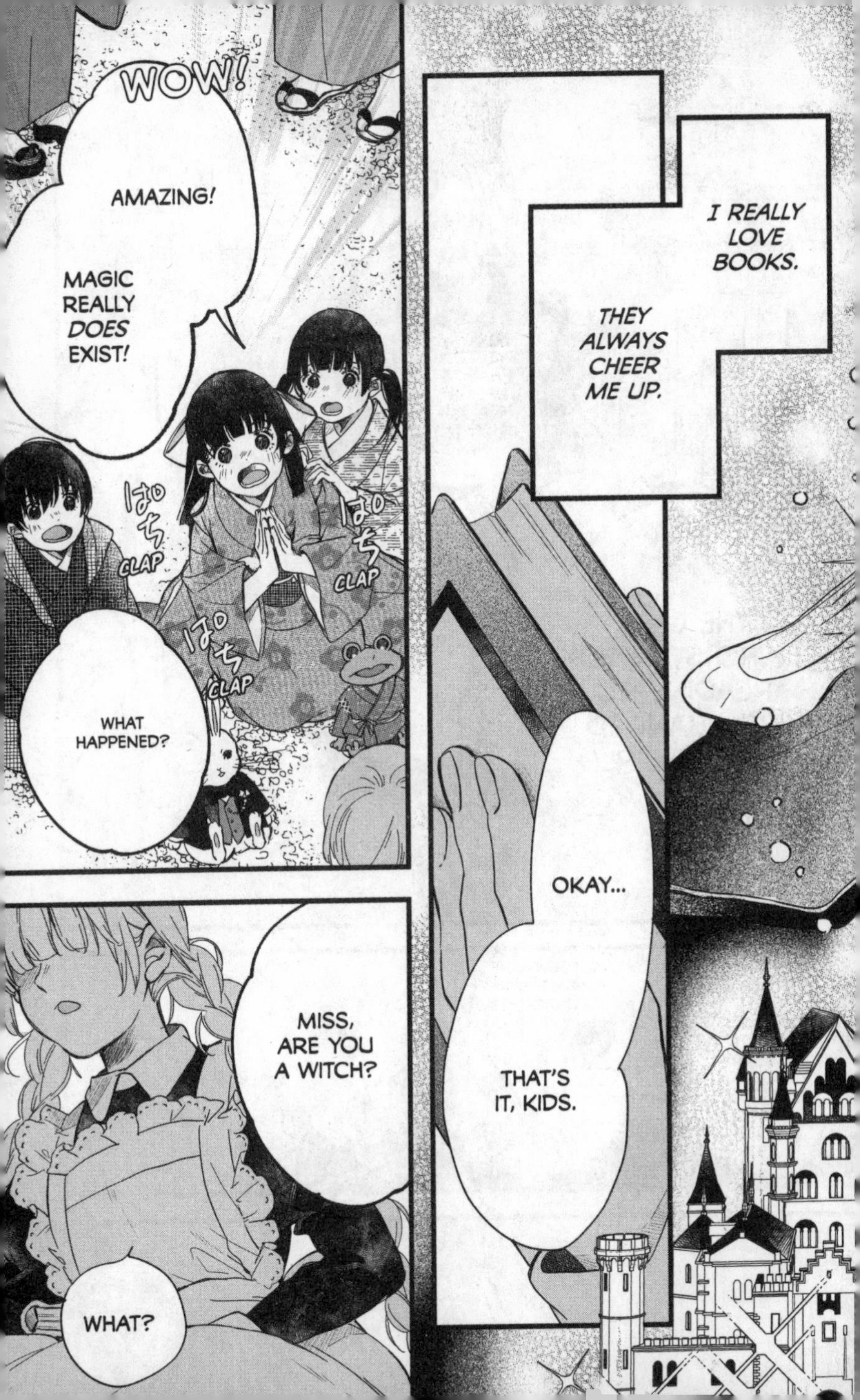
I REALLY LOVE BOOKS.
THEY ALWAYS CHEER ME UP.
OKAY...
THAT'S IT, KIDS.
WOW!
AMAZING!
MAGIC REALLY *DOES* EXIST!
ぱち
CLAP
ぱち
CLAP
ぱち
CLAP
WHAT HAPPENED?
MISS, ARE YOU A WITCH?
WHAT?

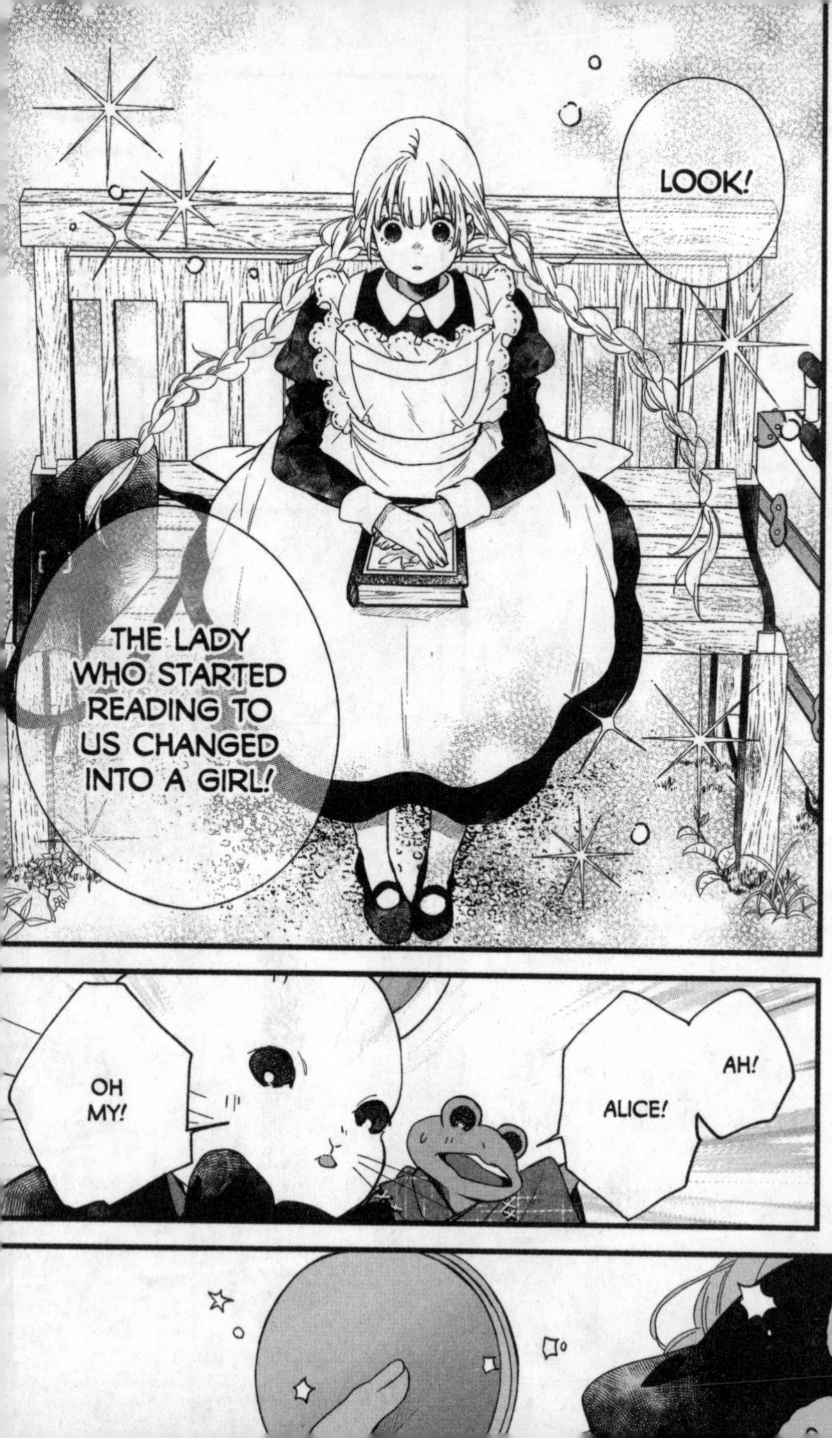
LOOK!
THE LADY WHO STARTED READING TO US CHANGED INTO A GIRL!
AH! ALICE!
OH MY!

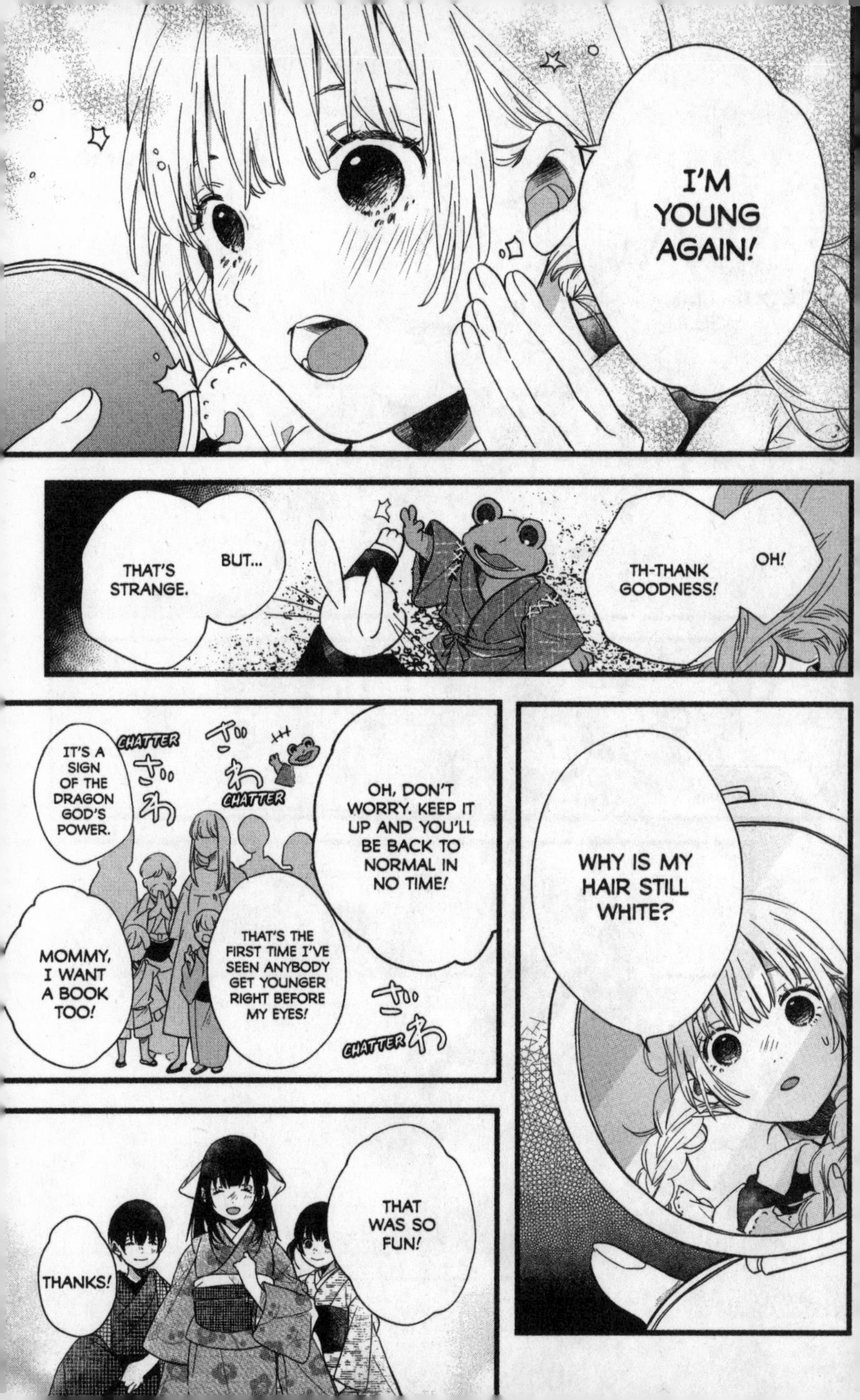
I'M YOUNG AGAIN!
OH!
TH-THANK GOODNESS!
BUT...
THAT'S STRANGE.
WHY IS MY HAIR STILL WHITE?
OH, DON'T WORRY. KEEP IT UP AND YOU'LL BE BACK TO NORMAL IN NO TIME!
CHATTER
THAT'S THE FIRST TIME I'VE SEEN ANYBODY GET YOUNGER RIGHT BEFORE MY EYES!
CHATTER
IT'S A SIGN OF THE DRAGON GOD'S POWER.
CHATTER
MOMMY, I WANT A BOOK TOO!
THAT WAS SO FUN!
THANKS!

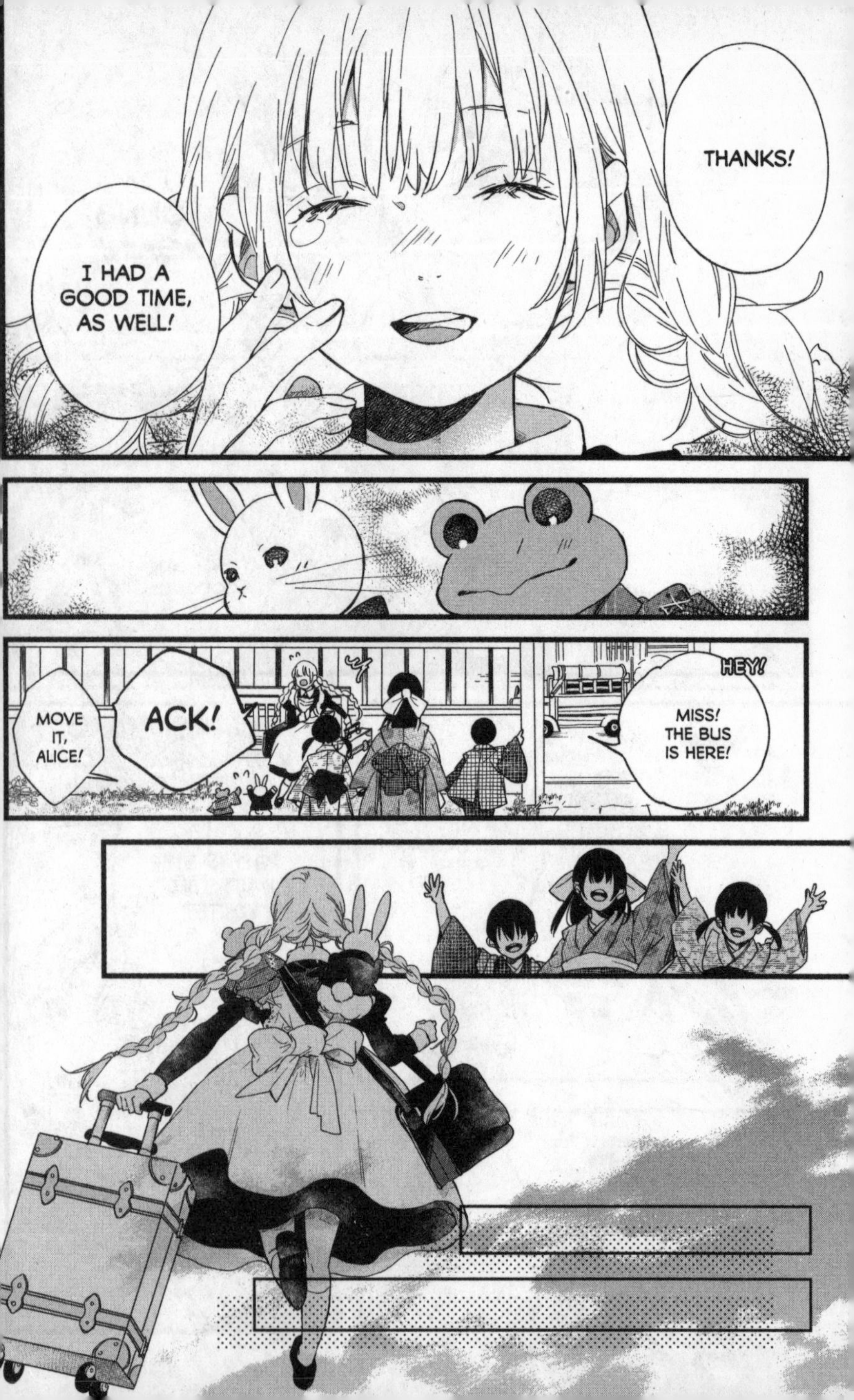
THANKS!
I HAD A GOOD TIME, AS WELL!
HEY!
MISS! THE BUS IS HERE!
ACK!
MOVE IT, ALICE!

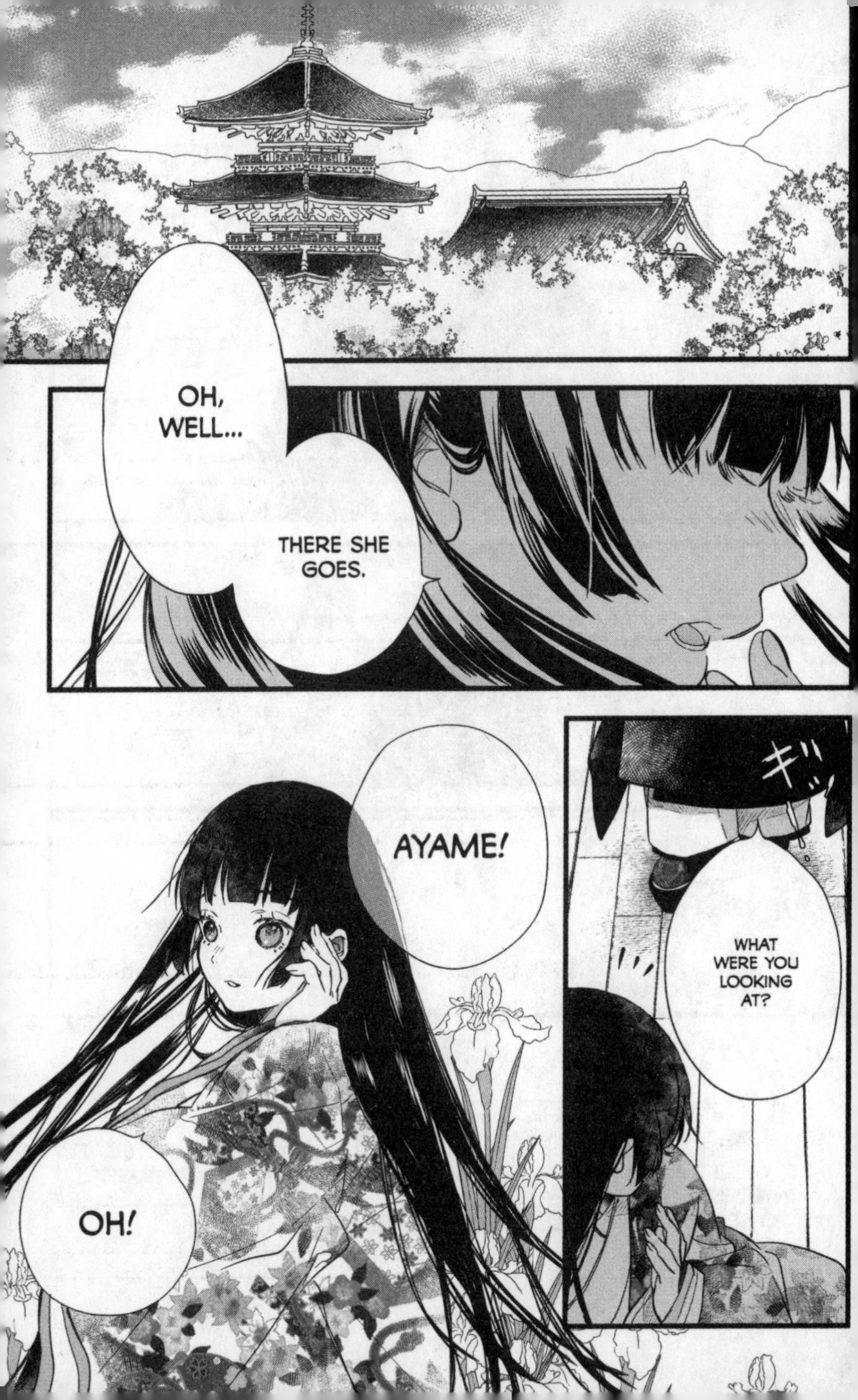
OH, WELL...
THERE SHE GOES.
ギ
WHAT WERE YOU LOOKING AT?
AYAME!
OH!

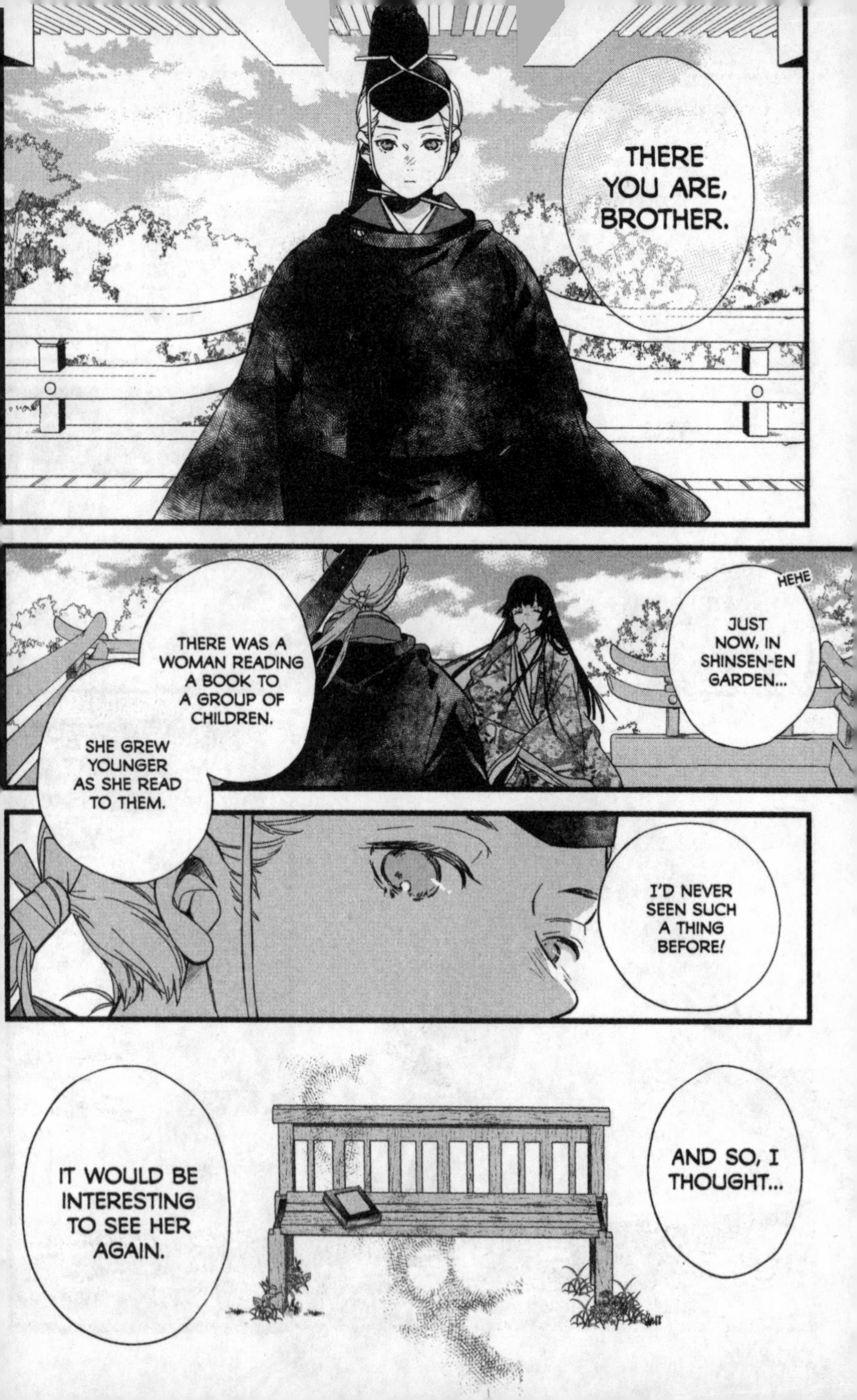
THERE YOU ARE, BROTHER.
HEHE
JUST NOW, IN SHINSEN-EN GARDEN...
THERE WAS A WOMAN READING A BOOK TO A GROUP OF CHILDREN.
SHE GREW YOUNGER AS SHE READ TO THEM.
I'D NEVER SEEN SUCH A THING BEFORE!
AND SO, I THOUGHT...
IT WOULD BE INTERESTING TO SEE HER AGAIN.

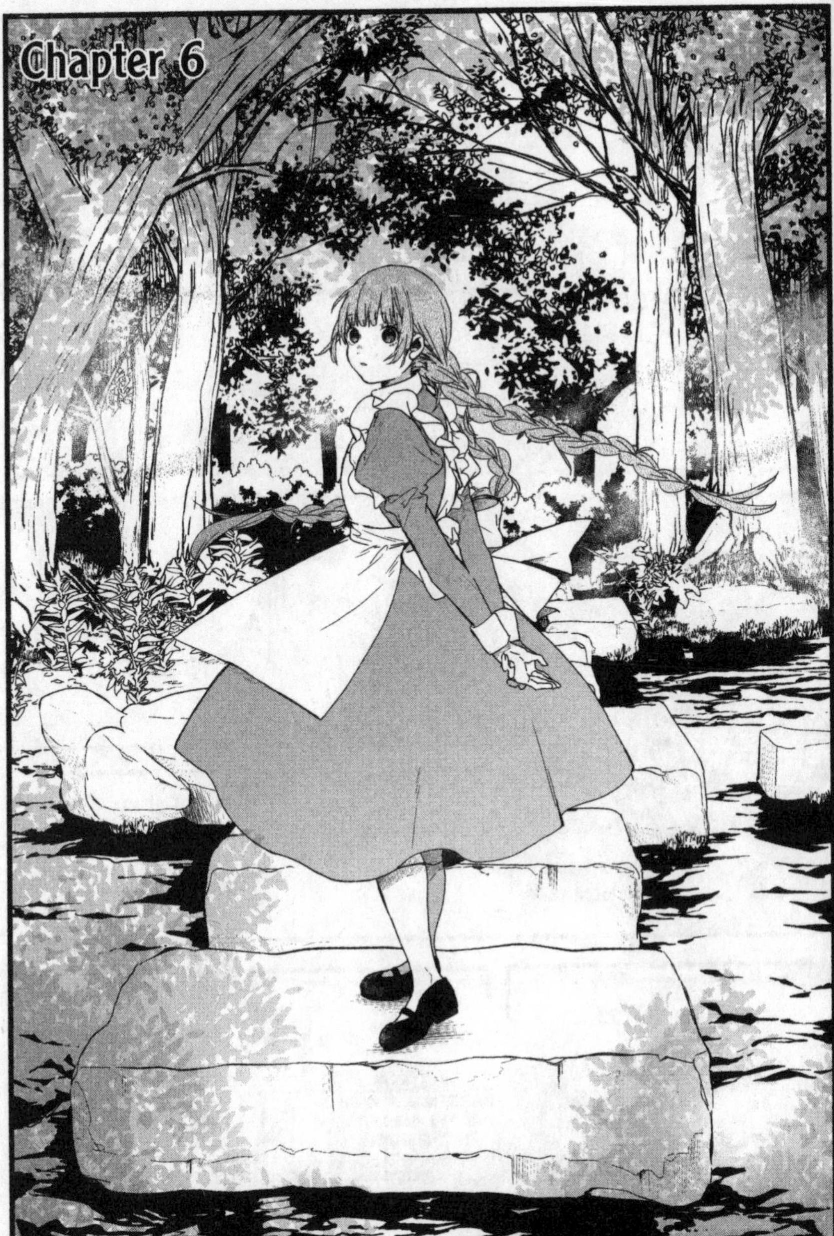
Chapter 6

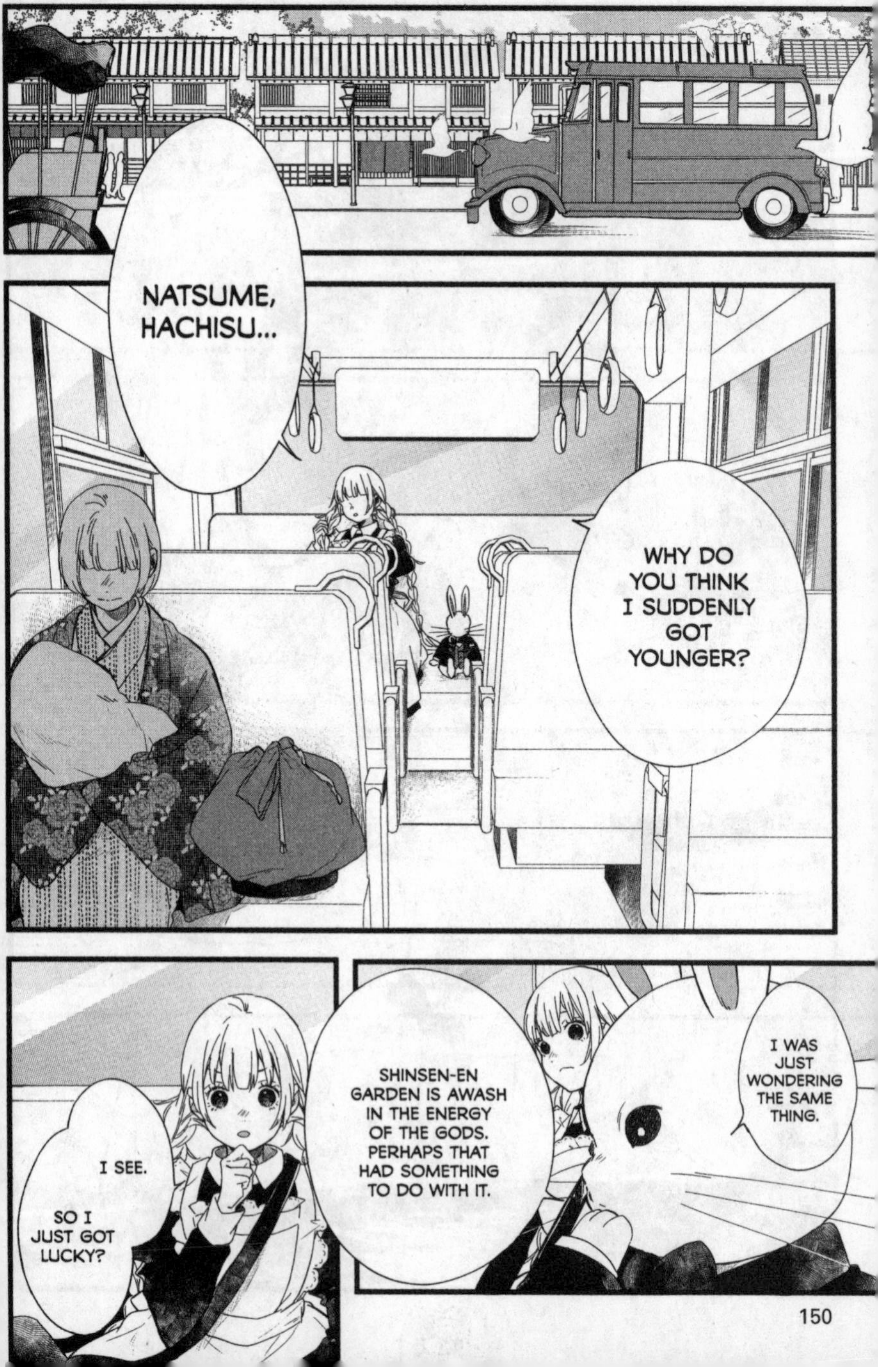
NATSUME, HACHISU...
WHY DO YOU THINK I SUDDENLY GOT YOUNGER?
I WAS JUST WONDERING THE SAME THING.
SHINSEN-EN GARDEN IS AWASH IN THE ENERGY OF THE GODS. PERHAPS THAT HAD SOMETHING TO DO WITH IT.
I SEE.
SO I JUST GOT LUCKY?

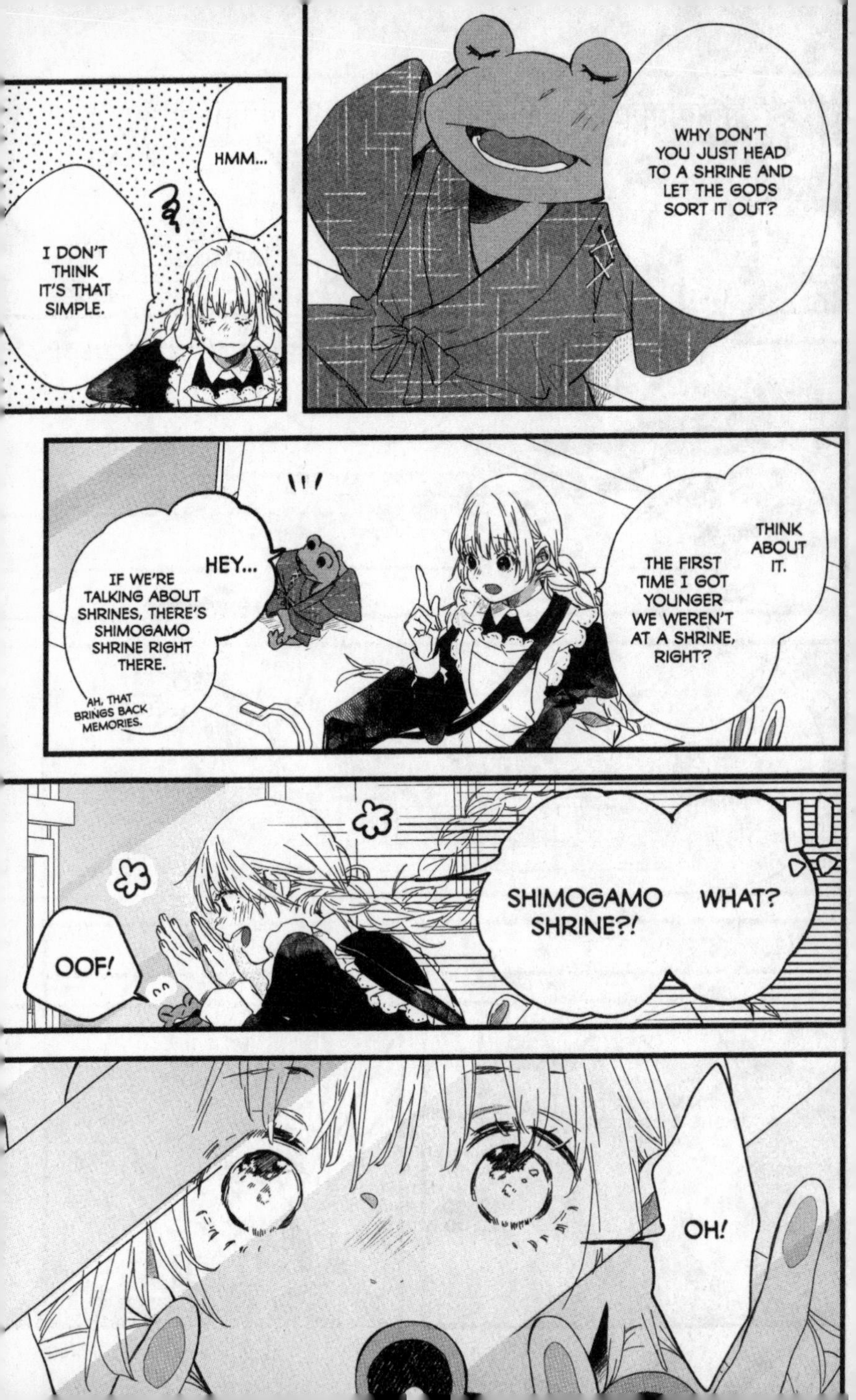
WHY DON'T YOU JUST HEAD TO A SHRINE AND LET THE GODS SORT IT OUT?
HMM...
I DON'T THINK IT'S THAT SIMPLE.
THINK ABOUT IT.
THE FIRST TIME I GOT YOUNGER WE WEREN'T AT A SHRINE, RIGHT?
HEY...
IF WE'RE TALKING ABOUT SHRINES, THERE'S SHIMOGAMO SHRINE RIGHT THERE.
AH, THAT BRINGS BACK MEMORIES.
WHAT?
SHIMOGAMO SHRINE?!
OOF!
OH!

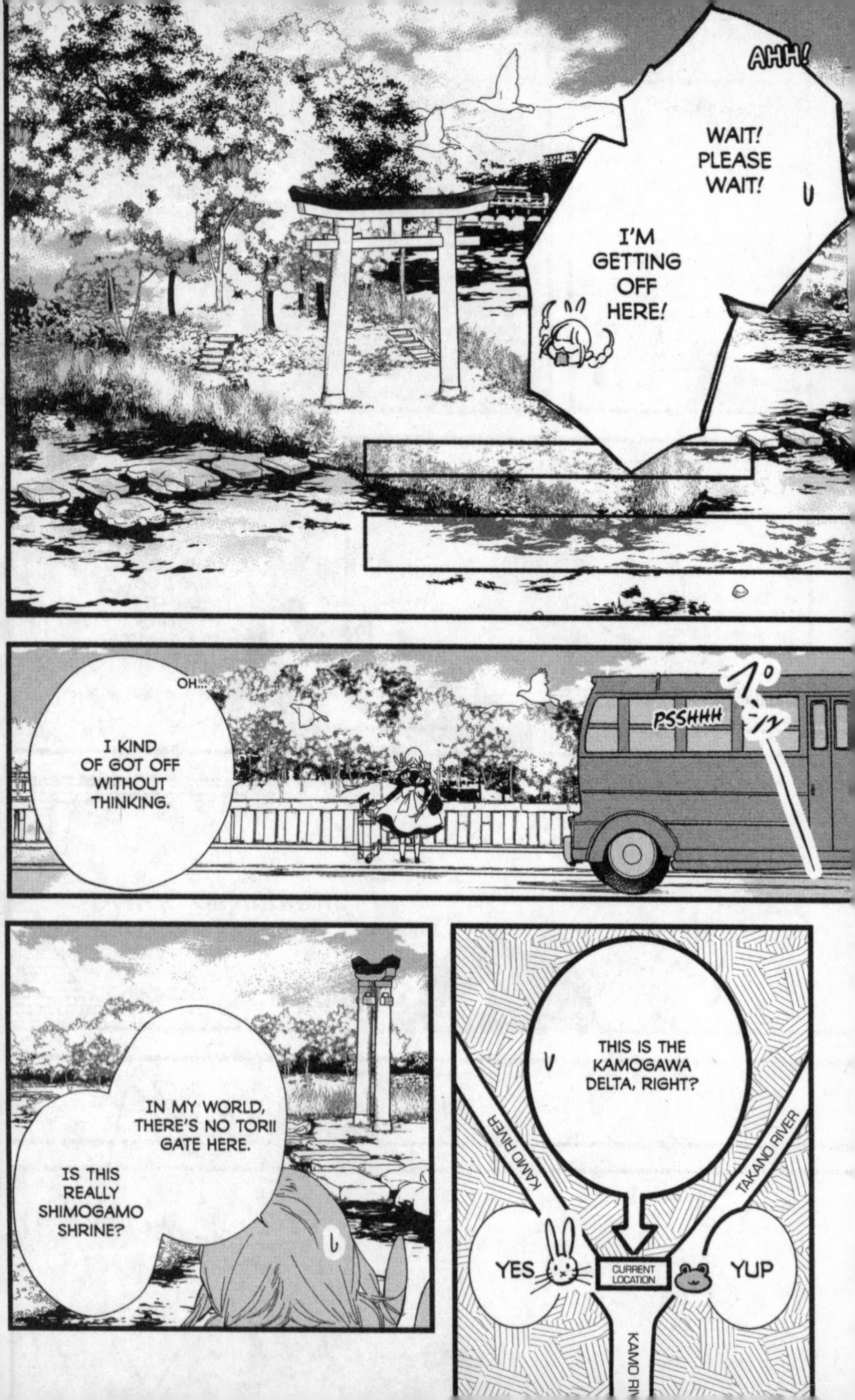
AHH!
WAIT! PLEASE WAIT!
I'M GETTING OFF HERE!
PSSHHH
OH...
I KIND OF GOT OFF WITHOUT THINKING.
THIS IS THE KAMOGAWA DELTA, RIGHT?
TAKANO RIVER
KAMO RIVER
YUP
CURRENT LOCATION
YES
IN MY WORLD, THERE'S NO TORII GATE HERE.
IS THIS REALLY SHIMOGAMO SHRINE?

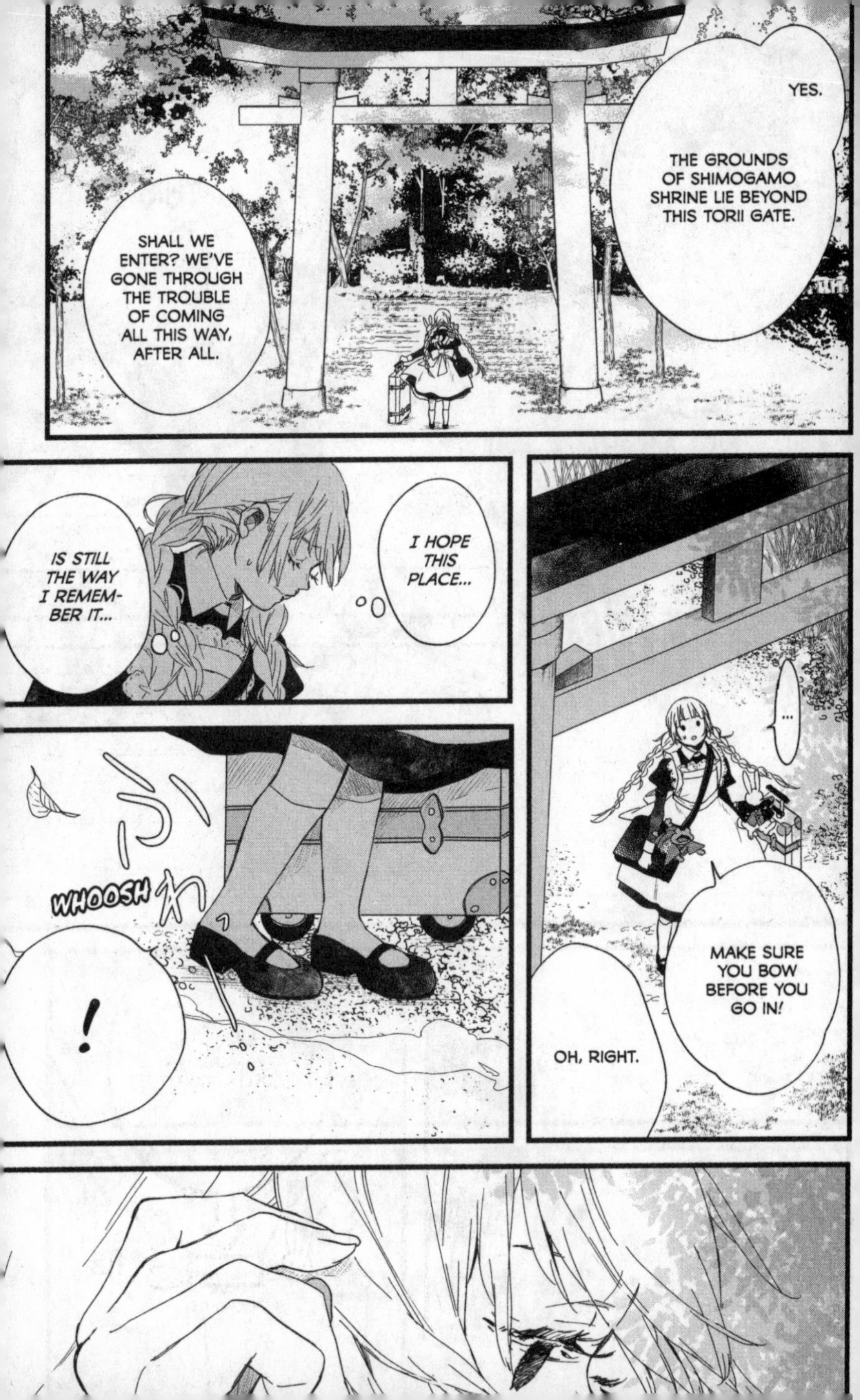
YES.
THE GROUNDS OF SHIMOGAMO SHRINE LIE BEYOND THIS TORII GATE.
SHALL WE ENTER? WE'VE GONE THROUGH THE TROUBLE OF COMING ALL THIS WAY, AFTER ALL.
...
MAKE SURE YOU BOW BEFORE YOU GO IN!
OH, RIGHT.
I HOPE THIS PLACE...
IS STILL THE WAY I REMEMBER IT...
WHOOSH
!

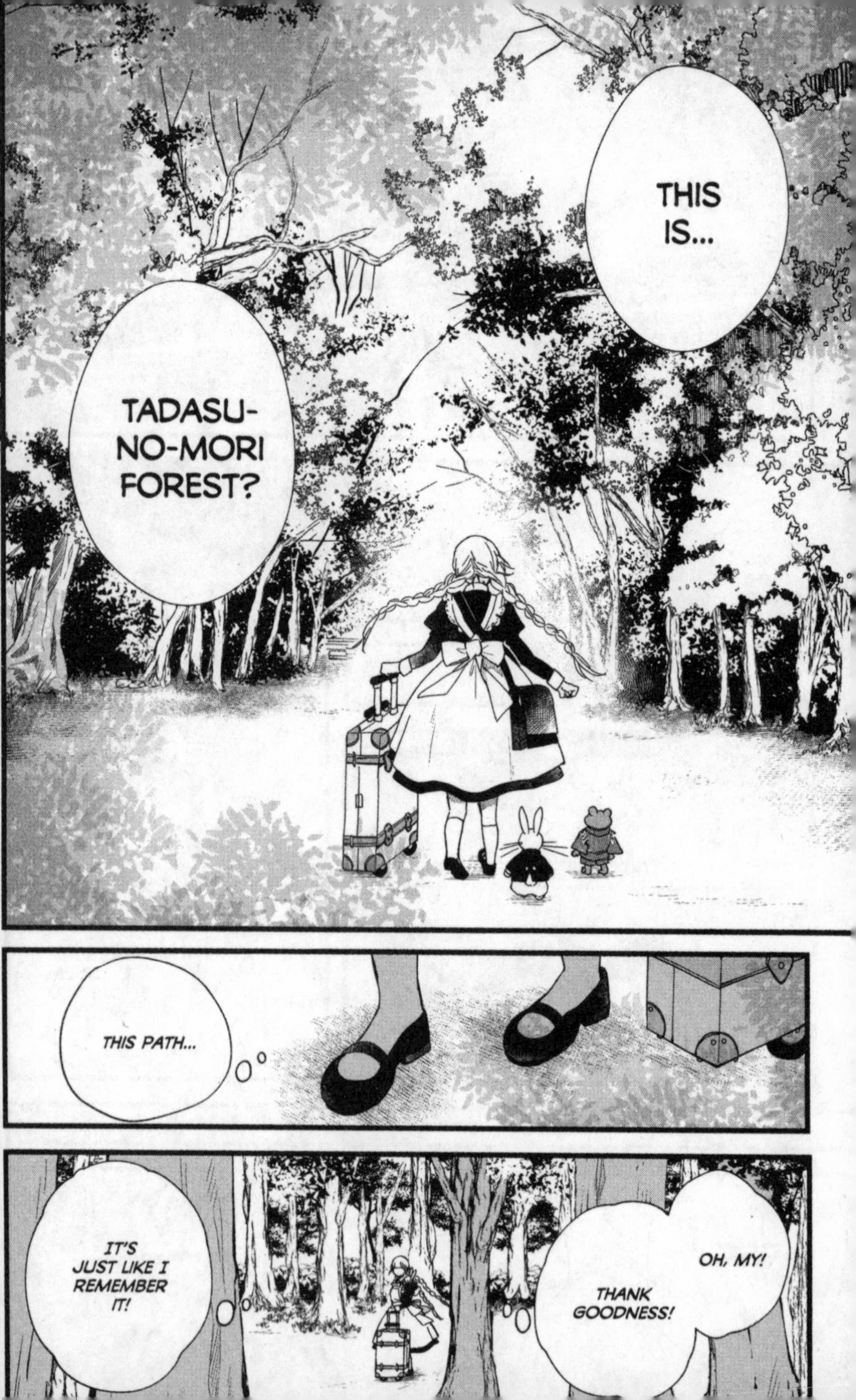
THIS IS...
TADASU-NO-MORI FOREST?
THIS PATH...
OH, MY!
THANK GOODNESS!
IT'S JUST LIKE I REMEMBER IT!

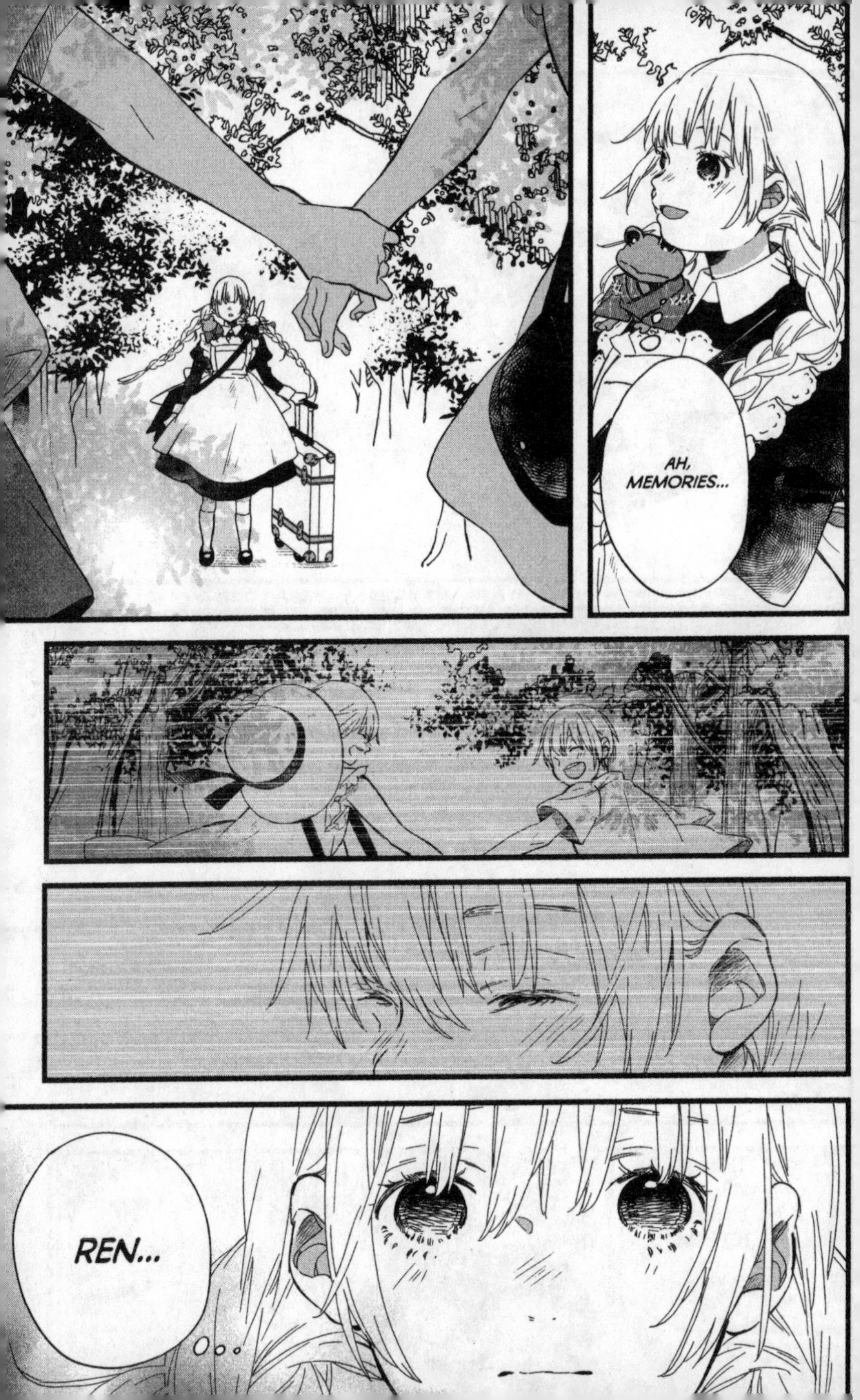
AH, MEMORIES...
REN...

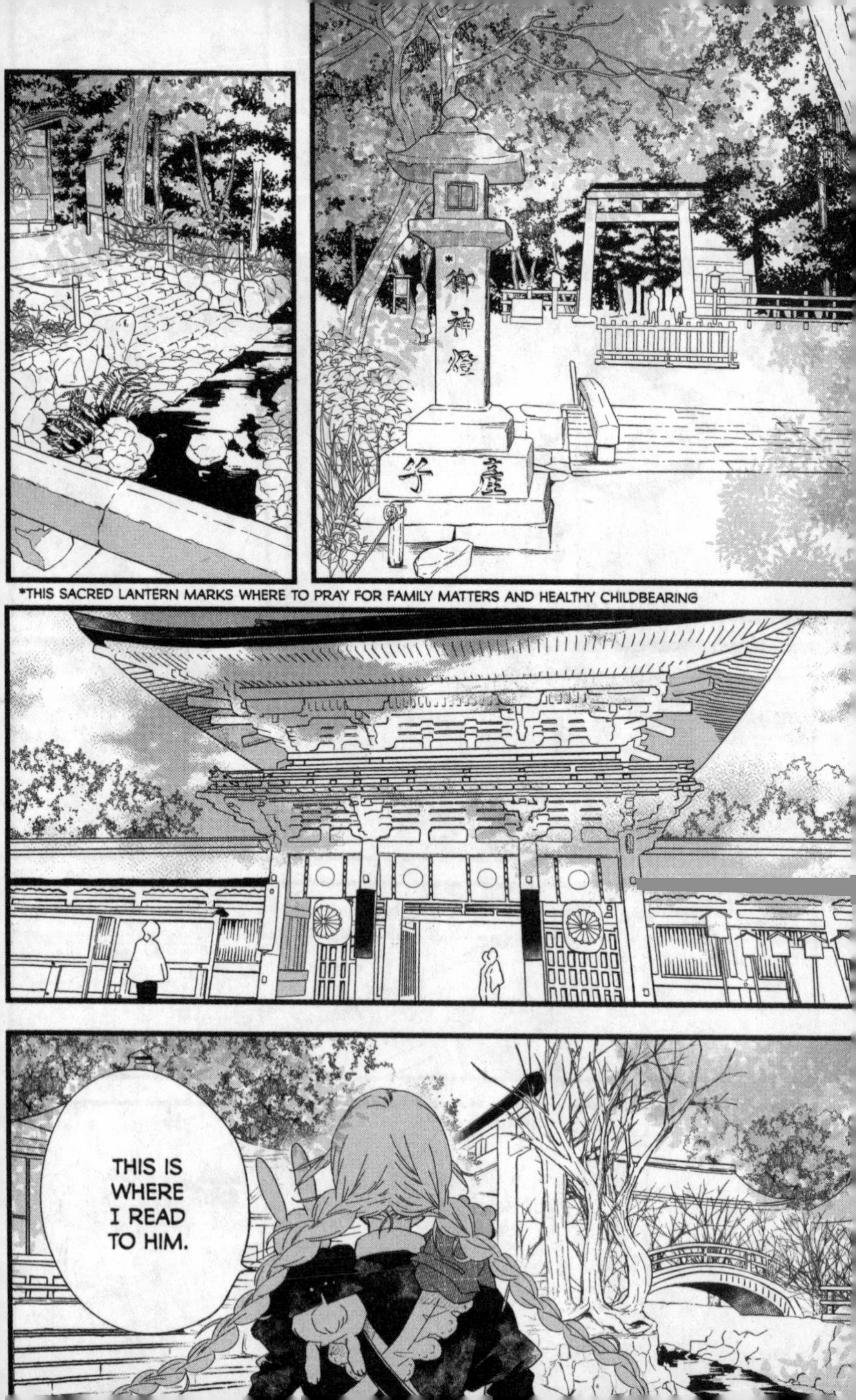
*御神燈
*THIS SACRED LANTERN MARKS WHERE TO PRAY FOR FAMILY MATTERS AND HEALTHY CHILDBEARING
THIS IS WHERE I READ TO HIM.

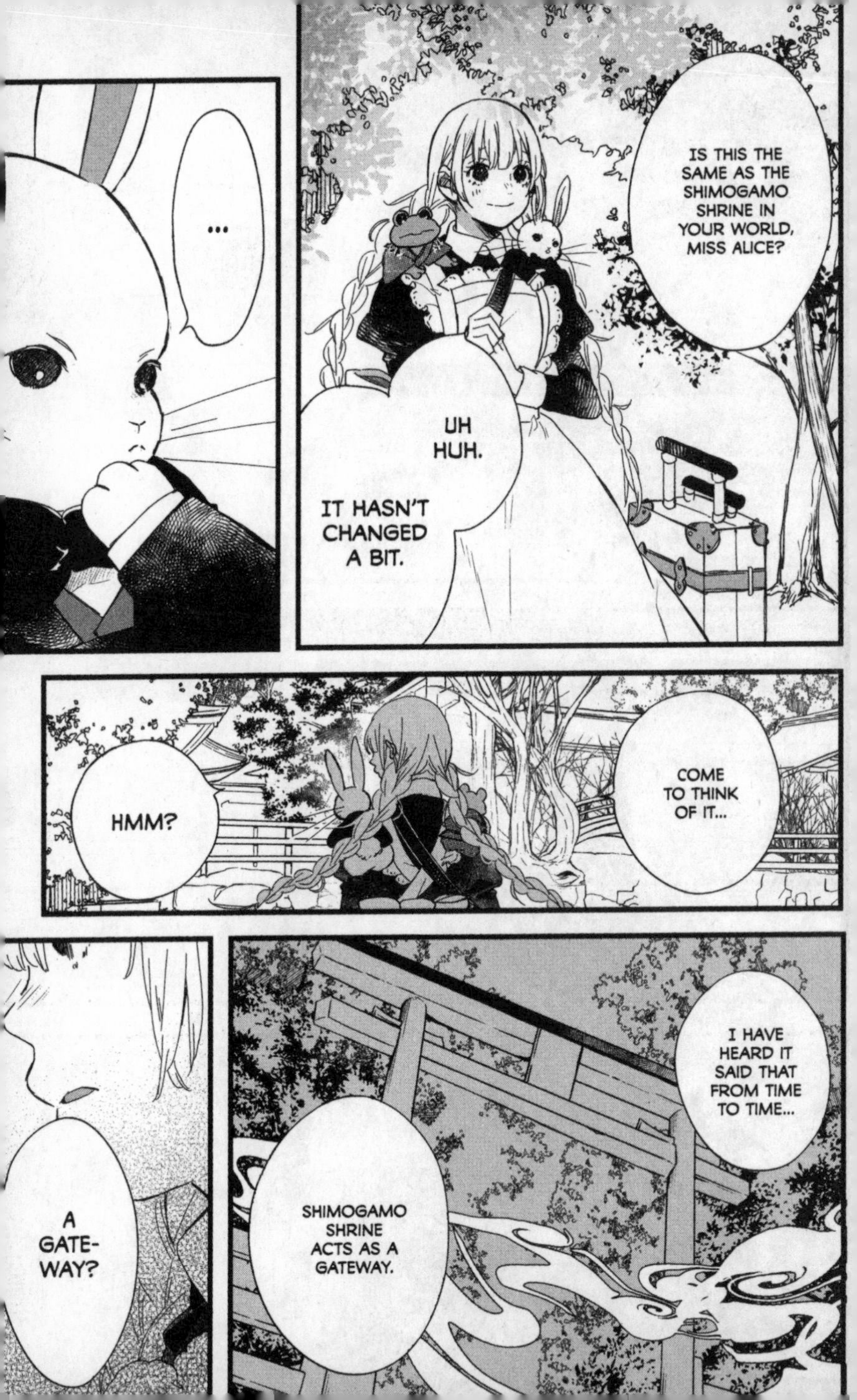
IS THIS THE SAME AS THE SHIMOGAMO SHRINE IN YOUR WORLD, MISS ALICE?
UH HUH.
IT HASN'T CHANGED A BIT.
...
COME TO THINK OF IT...
HMM?
I HAVE HEARD IT SAID THAT FROM TIME TO TIME...
SHIMOGAMO SHRINE ACTS AS A GATEWAY.
A GATE-WAY?

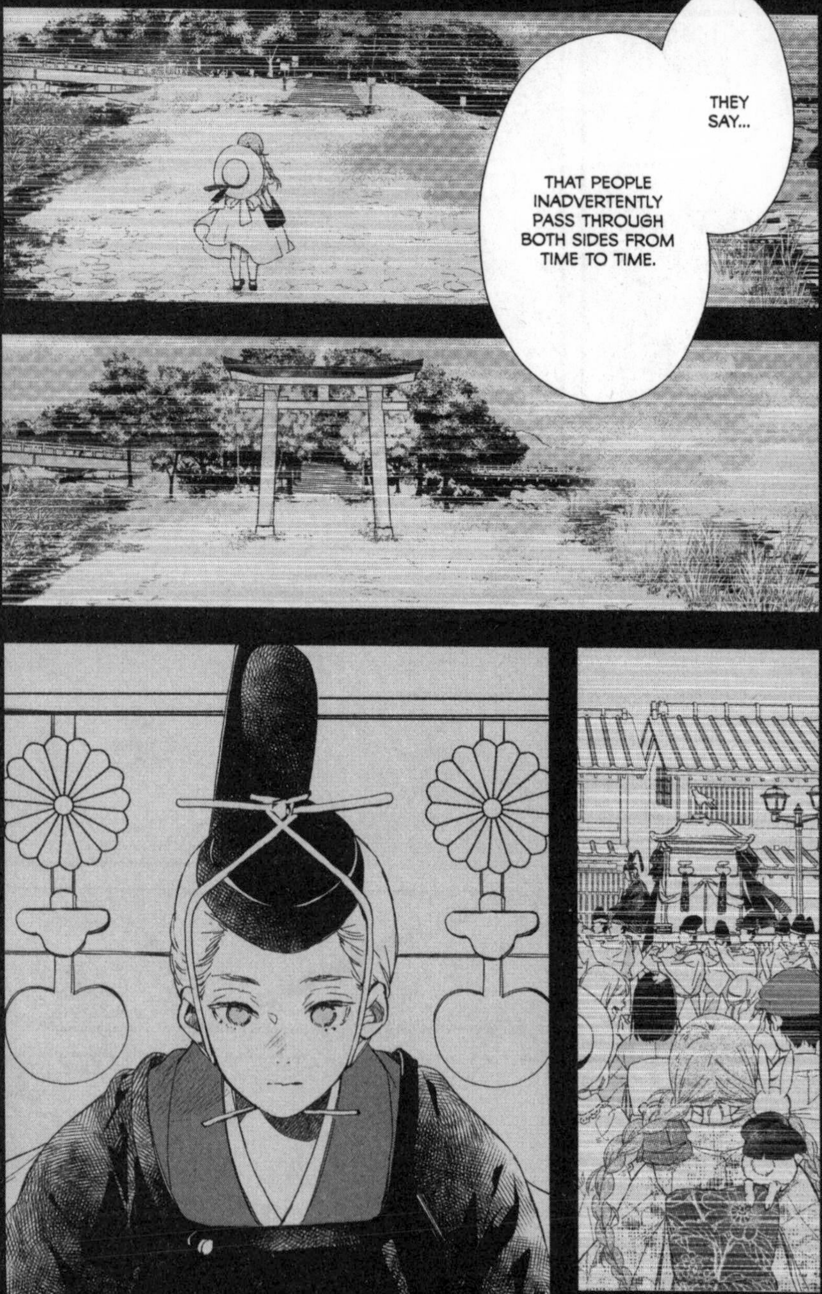
THEY SAY...
THAT PEOPLE INADVERTENTLY PASS THROUGH BOTH SIDES FROM TIME TO TIME.

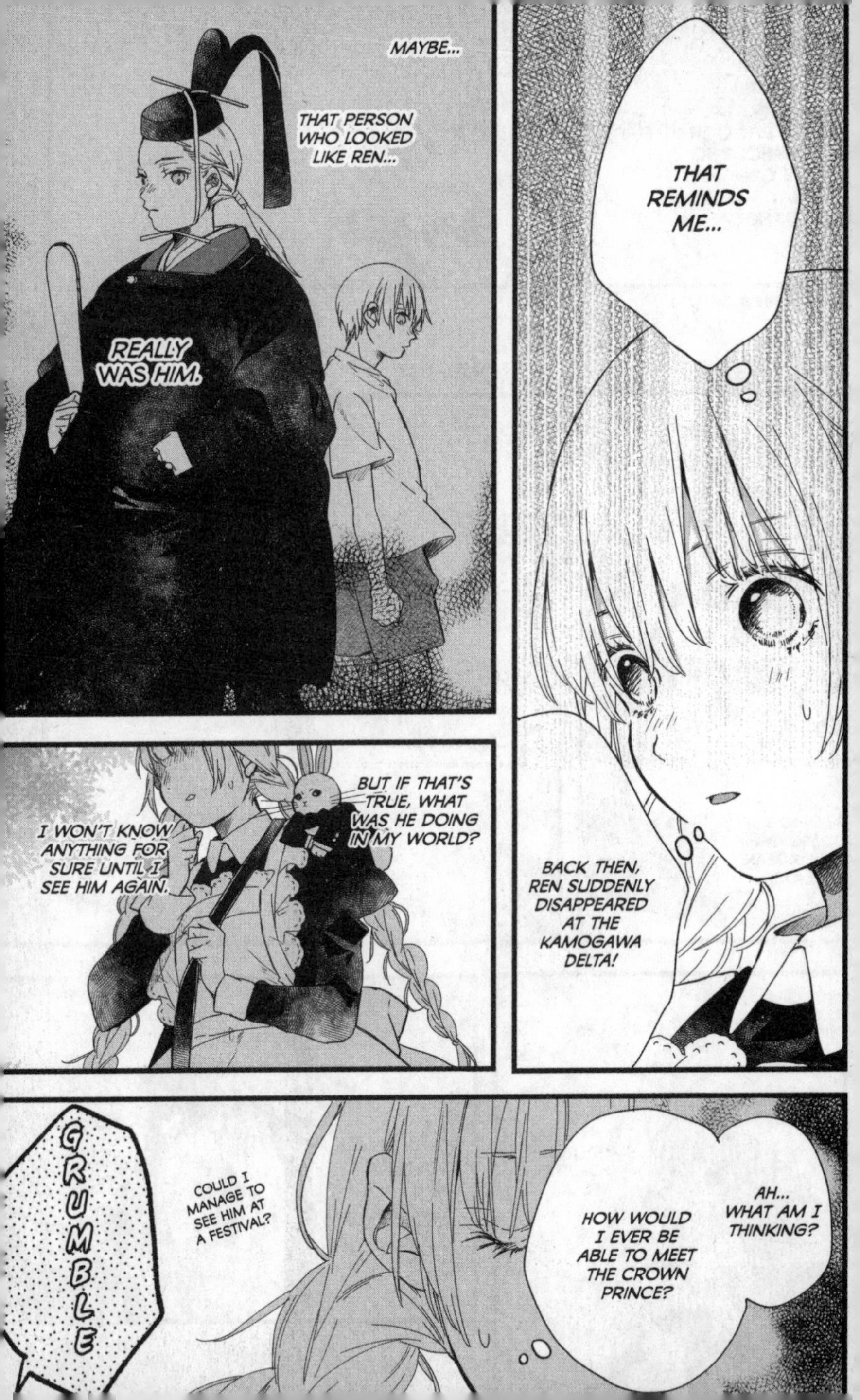
THAT REMINDS ME...
BACK THEN, REN SUDDENLY DISAPPEARED AT THE KAMOGAWA DELTA!
MAYBE...
THAT PERSON WHO LOOKED LIKE REN...
REALLY WAS HIM.
BUT IF THAT'S TRUE, WHAT WAS HE DOING IN MY WORLD?
I WON'T KNOW ANYTHING FOR SURE UNTIL I SEE HIM AGAIN.
AH... WHAT AM I THINKING?
HOW WOULD I EVER BE ABLE TO MEET THE CROWN PRINCE?
COULD I MANAGE TO SEE HIM AT A FESTIVAL?
GRUMBLE

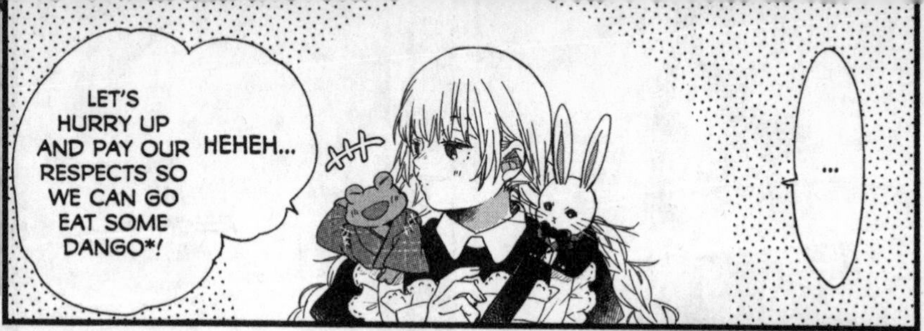
...
HEHEH...
LET'S HURRY UP AND PAY OUR RESPECTS SO WE CAN GO EAT SOME DANGO*!

* SWEET RICE DUMPLINGS

[redacted]

[redacted]

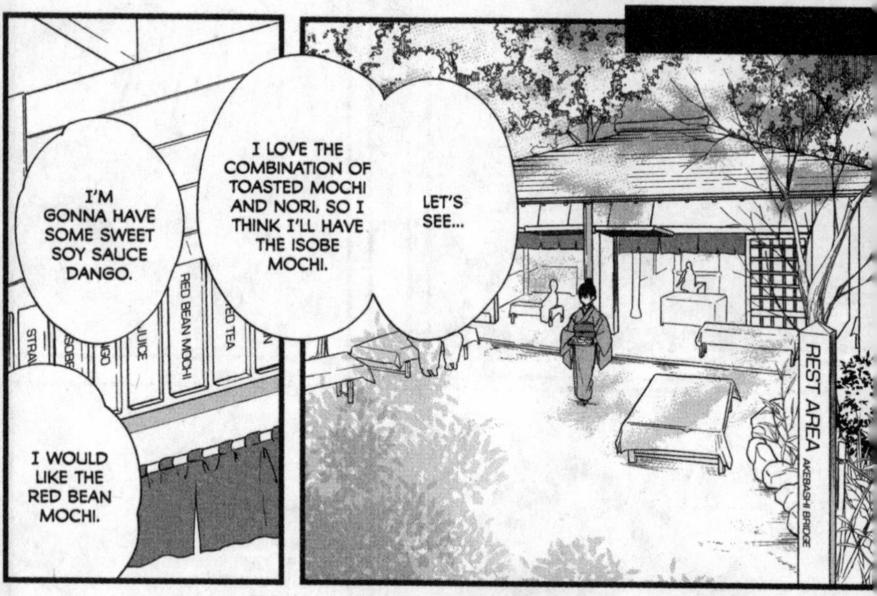
REST AREA
AKEBASHI BRIDGE
LET'S SEE...
I LOVE THE COMBINATION OF TOASTED MOCHI AND NORI, SO I THINK I'LL HAVE THE ISOBE MOCHI.
RED BEAN MOCHI
JUICE
I'M GONNA HAVE SOME SWEET SOY SAUCE DANGO.
I WOULD LIKE THE RED BEAN MOCHI.

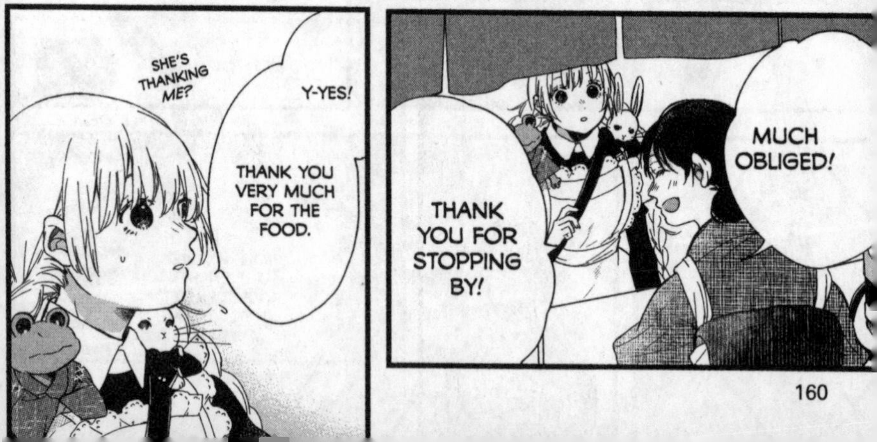
MUCH OBLIGED!
THANK YOU FOR STOPPING BY!
Y-YES!
THANK YOU VERY MUCH FOR THE FOOD.
SHE'S THANKING *ME*?

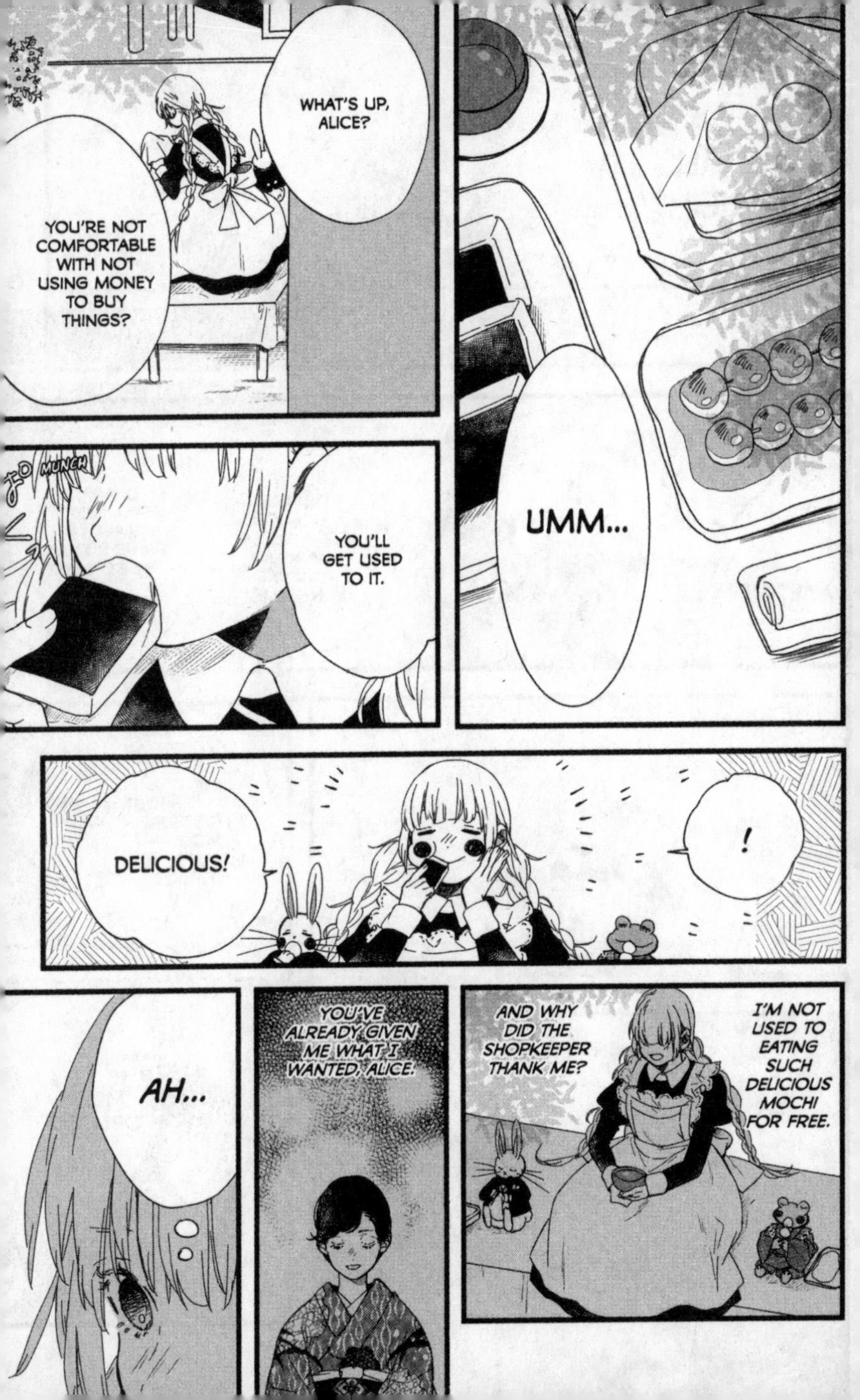
UMM...
WHAT'S UP, ALICE?
YOU'RE NOT COMFORTABLE WITH NOT USING MONEY TO BUY THINGS?
MUNCH
YOU'LL GET USED TO IT.
!
DELICIOUS!
I'M NOT USED TO EATING SUCH DELICIOUS MOCHI FOR FREE.
AND WHY DID THE SHOPKEEPER THANK ME?
YOU'VE ALREADY GIVEN ME WHAT I WANTED, ALICE.
AH...

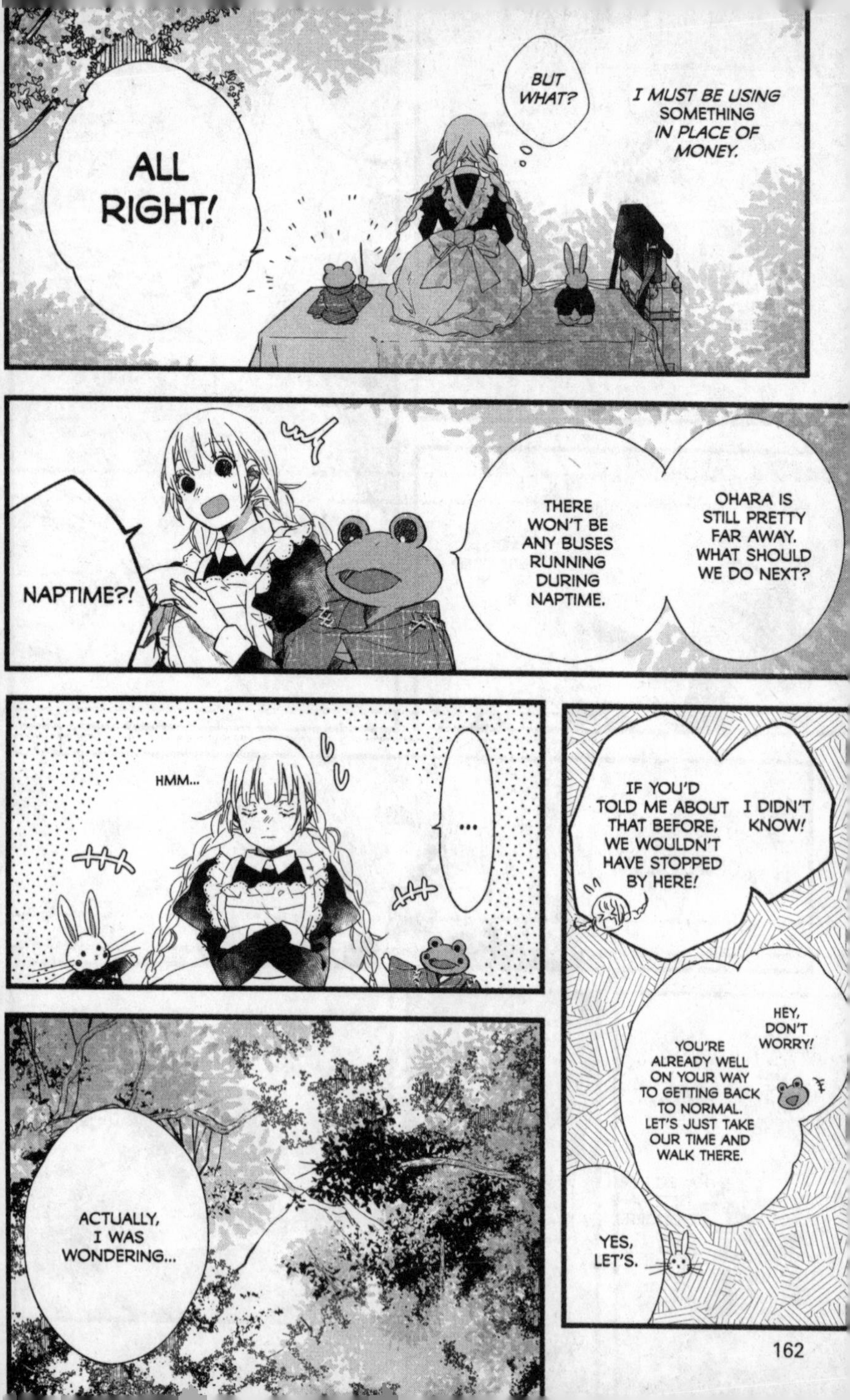
I MUST BE USING SOMETHING IN PLACE OF MONEY.
BUT WHAT?
ALL RIGHT!
OHARA IS STILL PRETTY FAR AWAY. WHAT SHOULD WE DO NEXT?
THERE WON'T BE ANY BUSES RUNNING DURING NAPTIME.
NAPTIME?!
I DIDN'T KNOW!
IF YOU'D TOLD ME ABOUT THAT BEFORE, WE WOULDN'T HAVE STOPPED BY HERE!
HEY, DON'T WORRY!
YOU'RE ALREADY WELL ON YOUR WAY TO GETTING BACK TO NORMAL. LET'S JUST TAKE OUR TIME AND WALK THERE.
YES, LET'S.
...
HMM...
ACTUALLY, I WAS WONDERING...

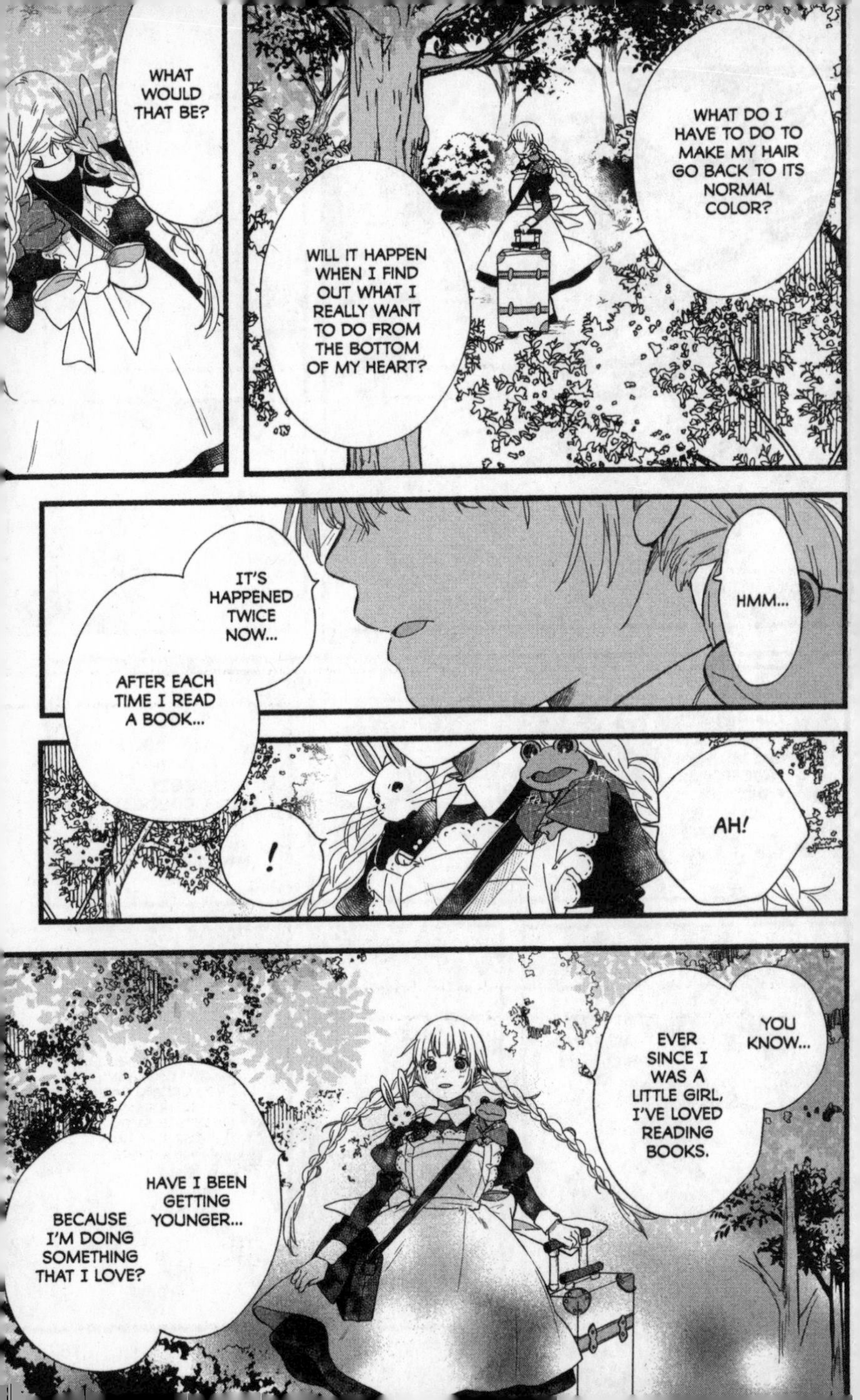
WHAT DO I HAVE TO DO TO MAKE MY HAIR GO BACK TO ITS NORMAL COLOR?
WILL IT HAPPEN WHEN I FIND OUT WHAT I REALLY WANT TO DO FROM THE BOTTOM OF MY HEART?
WHAT WOULD THAT BE?
HMM...
IT'S HAPPENED TWICE NOW...
AFTER EACH TIME I READ A BOOK...
AH!
!
YOU KNOW...
EVER SINCE I WAS A LITTLE GIRL, I'VE LOVED READING BOOKS.
HAVE I BEEN GETTING YOUNGER...
BECAUSE I'M DOING SOMETHING THAT I LOVE?

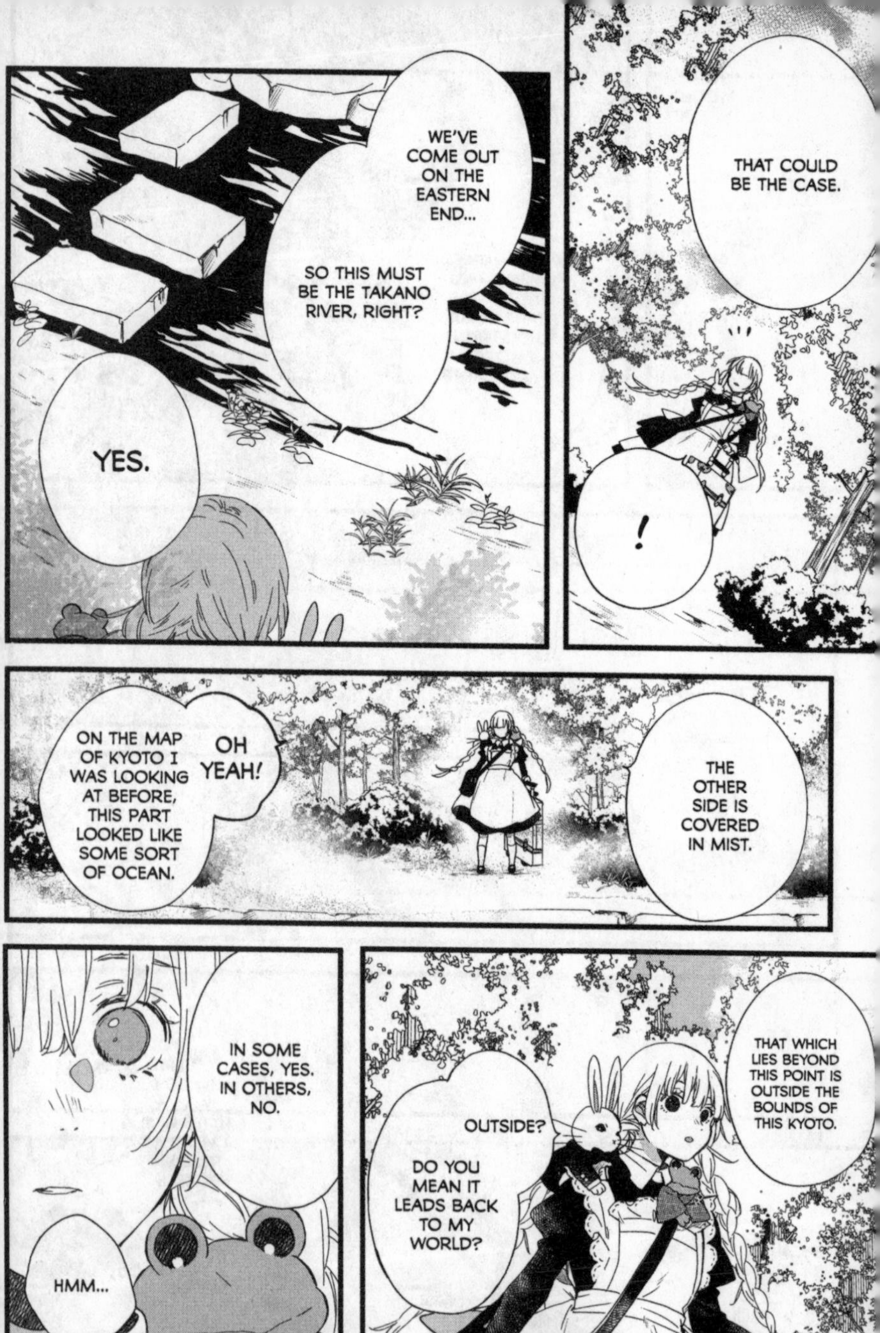

THAT COULD BE THE CASE.
!
WE'VE COME OUT ON THE EASTERN END...
SO THIS MUST BE THE TAKANO RIVER, RIGHT?
YES.
THE OTHER SIDE IS COVERED IN MIST.
OH YEAH!
ON THE MAP OF KYOTO I WAS LOOKING AT BEFORE, THIS PART LOOKED LIKE SOME SORT OF OCEAN.
THAT WHICH LIES BEYOND THIS POINT IS OUTSIDE THE BOUNDS OF THIS KYOTO.
OUTSIDE?
DO YOU MEAN IT LEADS BACK TO MY WORLD?
IN SOME CASES, YES. IN OTHERS, NO.
HMM...

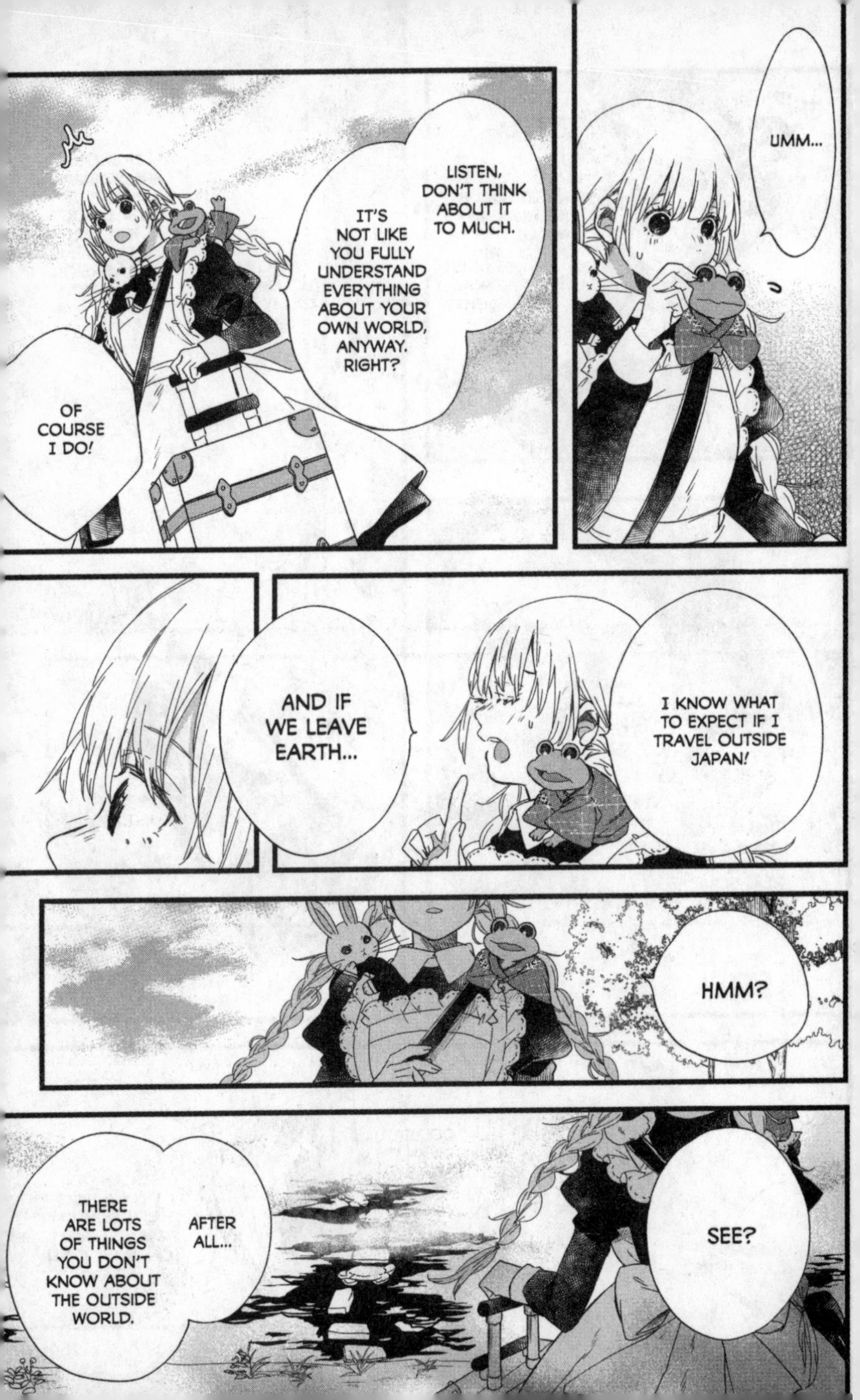
UMM...
LISTEN, DON'T THINK ABOUT IT TO MUCH.
IT'S NOT LIKE YOU FULLY UNDERSTAND EVERYTHING ABOUT YOUR OWN WORLD, ANYWAY. RIGHT?
OF COURSE I DO!
I KNOW WHAT TO EXPECT IF I TRAVEL OUTSIDE JAPAN!
AND IF WE LEAVE EARTH...
HMM?
SEE?
AFTER ALL...
THERE ARE LOTS OF THINGS YOU DON'T KNOW ABOUT THE OUTSIDE WORLD.

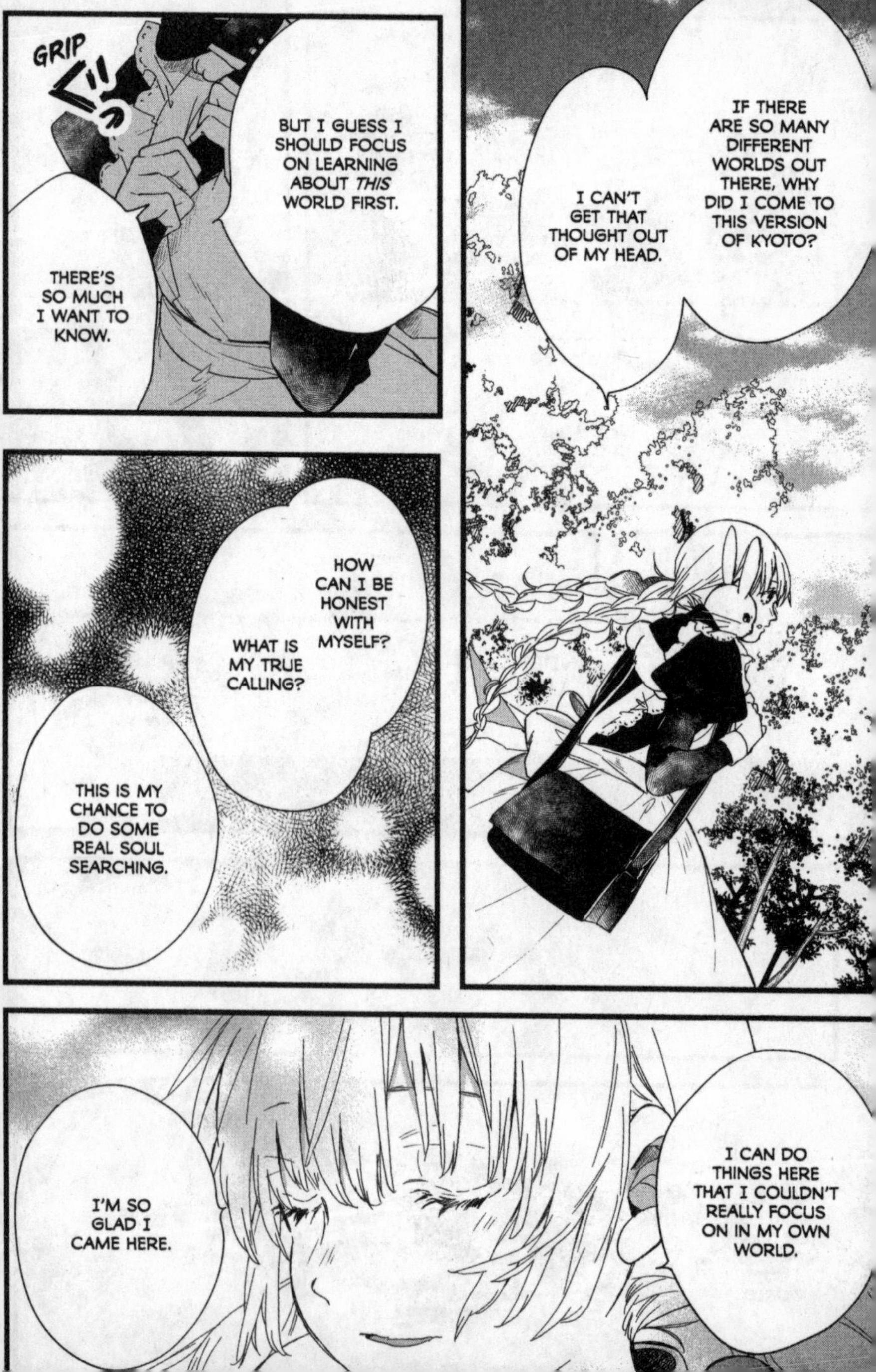
IF THERE ARE SO MANY DIFFERENT WORLDS OUT THERE, WHY DID I COME TO THIS VERSION OF KYOTO?
I CAN'T GET THAT THOUGHT OUT OF MY HEAD.
GRIP
BUT I GUESS I SHOULD FOCUS ON LEARNING ABOUT *THIS* WORLD FIRST.
THERE'S SO MUCH I WANT TO KNOW.
HOW CAN I BE HONEST WITH MYSELF?
WHAT IS MY TRUE CALLING?
THIS IS MY CHANCE TO DO SOME REAL SOUL SEARCHING.
I CAN DO THINGS HERE THAT I COULDN'T REALLY FOCUS ON IN MY OWN WORLD.
I'M SO GLAD I CAME HERE.

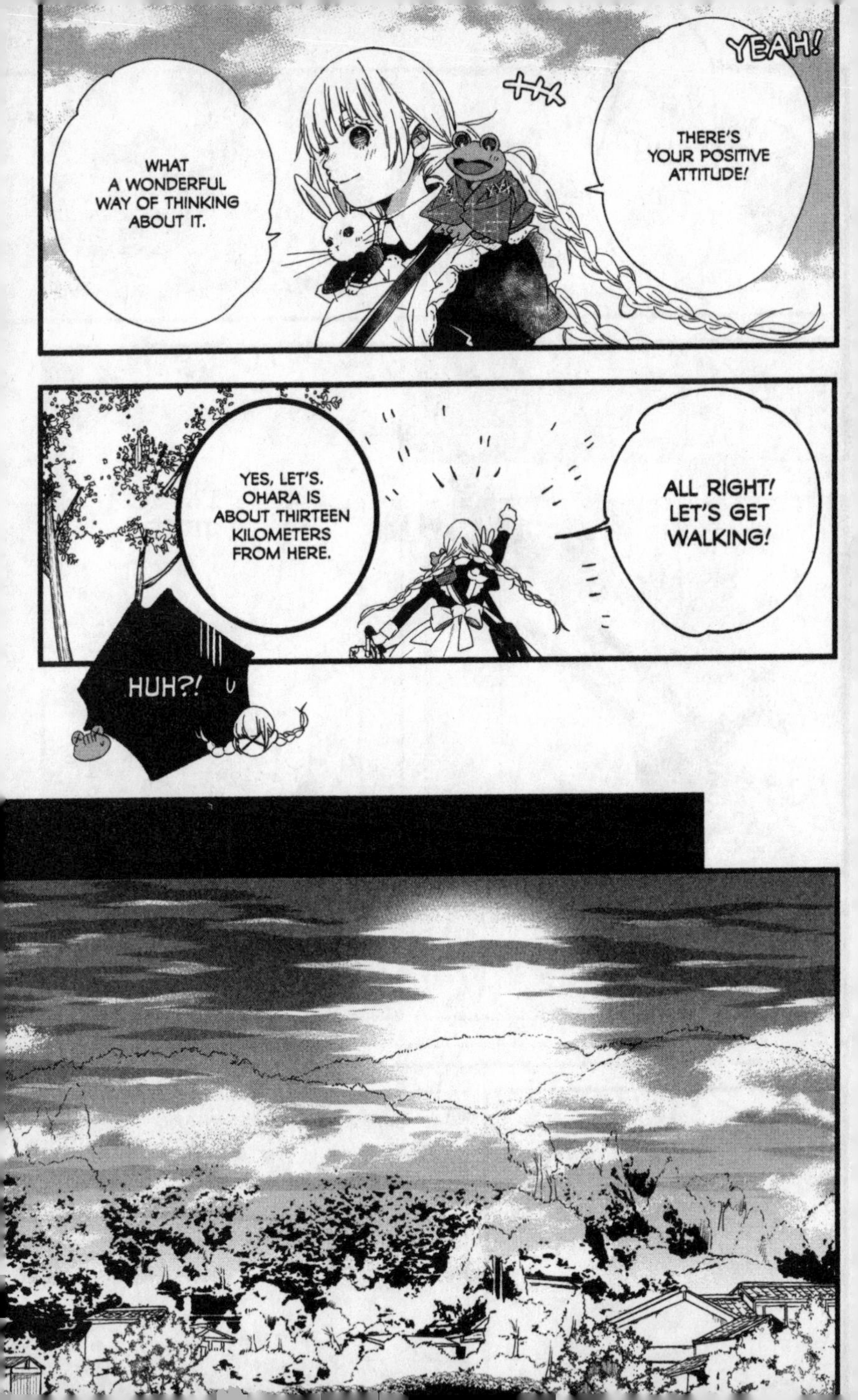
YEAH!
THERE'S YOUR POSITIVE ATTITUDE!
WHAT A WONDERFUL WAY OF THINKING ABOUT IT.
ALL RIGHT! LET'S GET WALKING!
YES, LET'S. OHARA IS ABOUT THIRTEEN KILOMETERS FROM HERE.
HUH?!

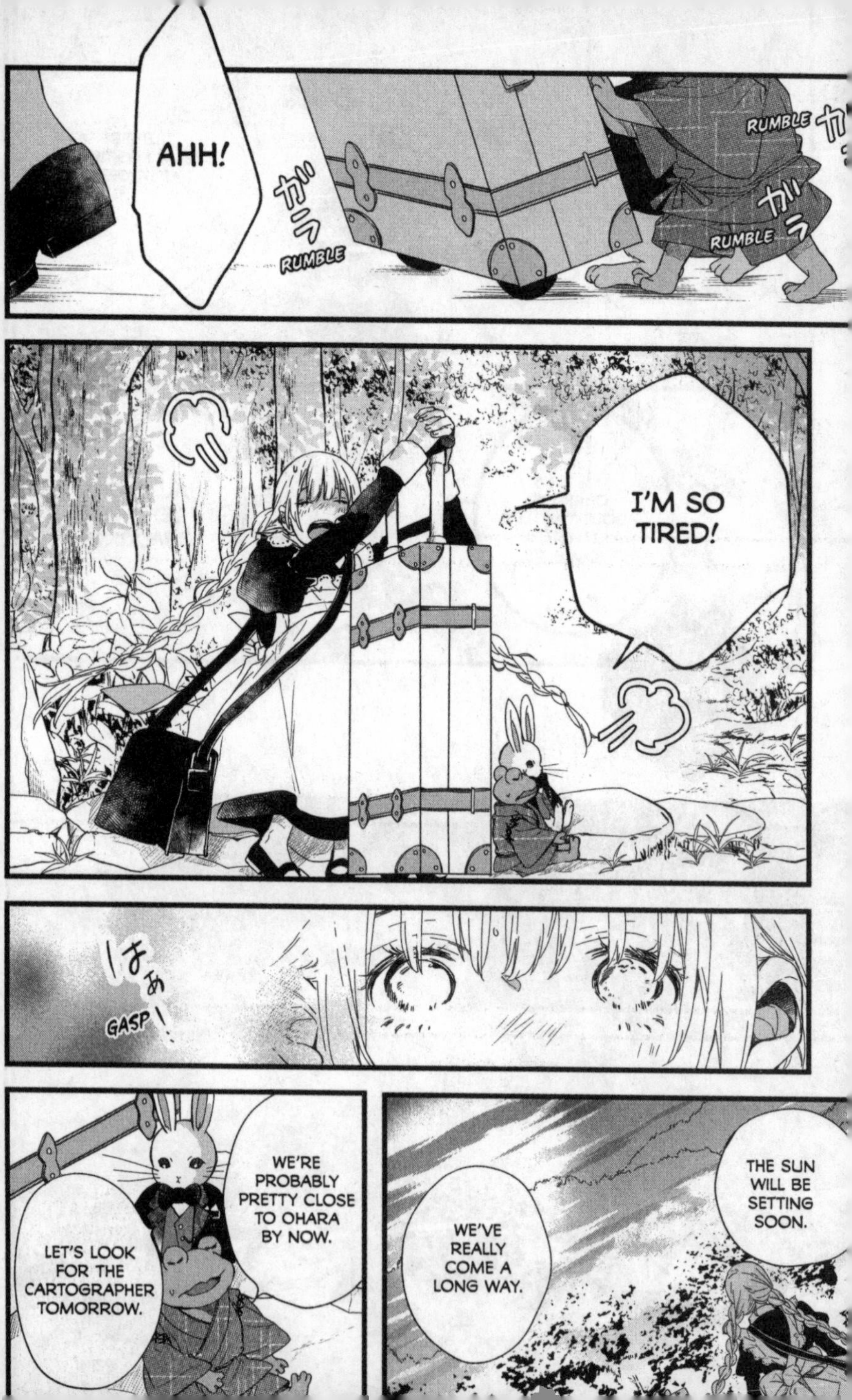
RUMBLE
ガラ
RUMBLE
ガラ
RUMBLE
AHH!
I'M SO TIRED!
はぁ!
GASP
THE SUN WILL BE SETTING SOON.
WE'VE REALLY COME A LONG WAY.
WE'RE PROBABLY PRETTY CLOSE TO OHARA BY NOW.
LET'S LOOK FOR THE CARTOGRAPHER TOMORROW.

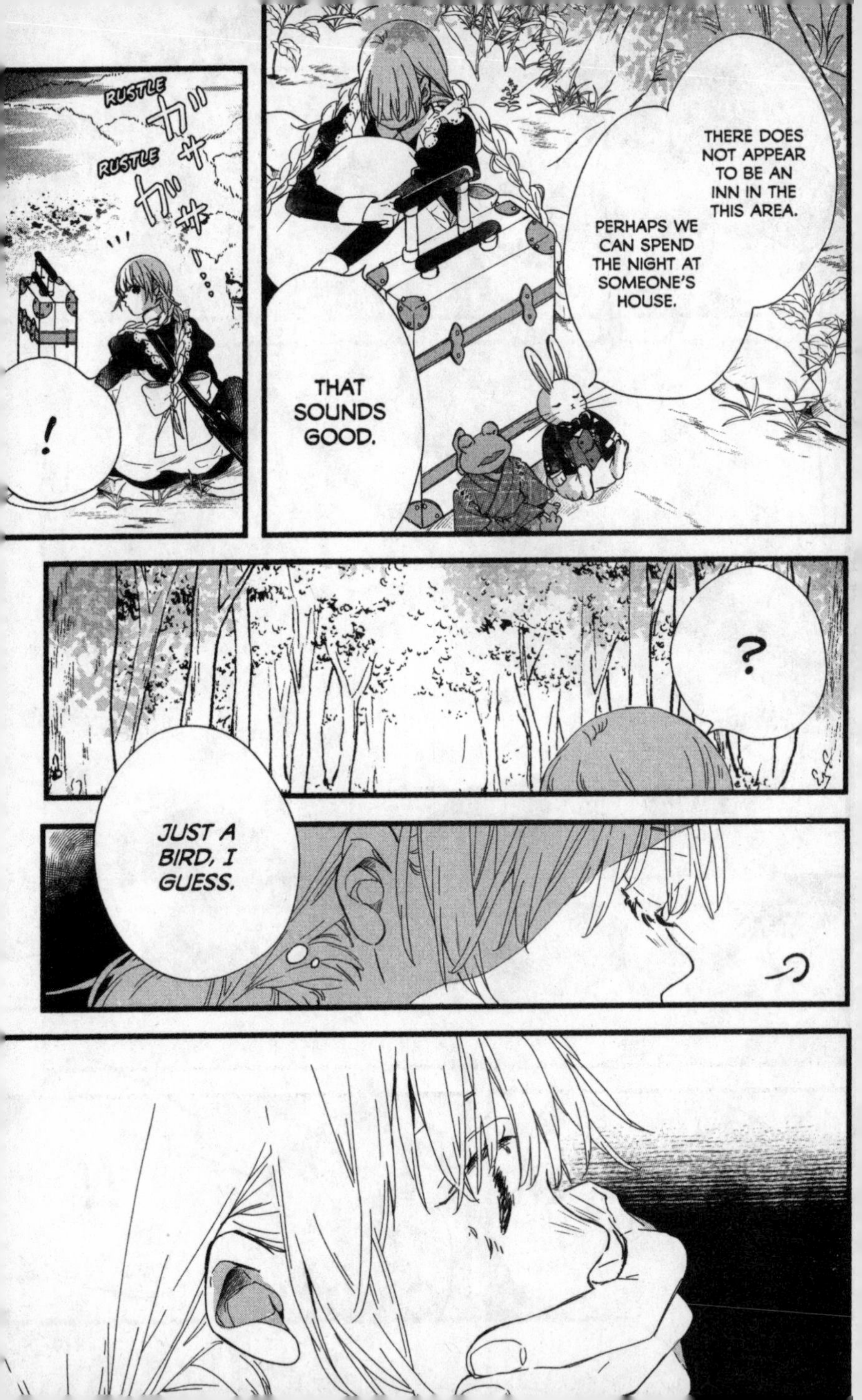
THERE DOES NOT APPEAR TO BE AN INN IN THE THIS AREA.
PERHAPS WE CAN SPEND THE NIGHT AT SOMEONE'S HOUSE.
THAT SOUNDS GOOD.
RUSTLE
ガサ
RUSTLE
ガサ
!
?
JUST A BIRD, I GUESS.

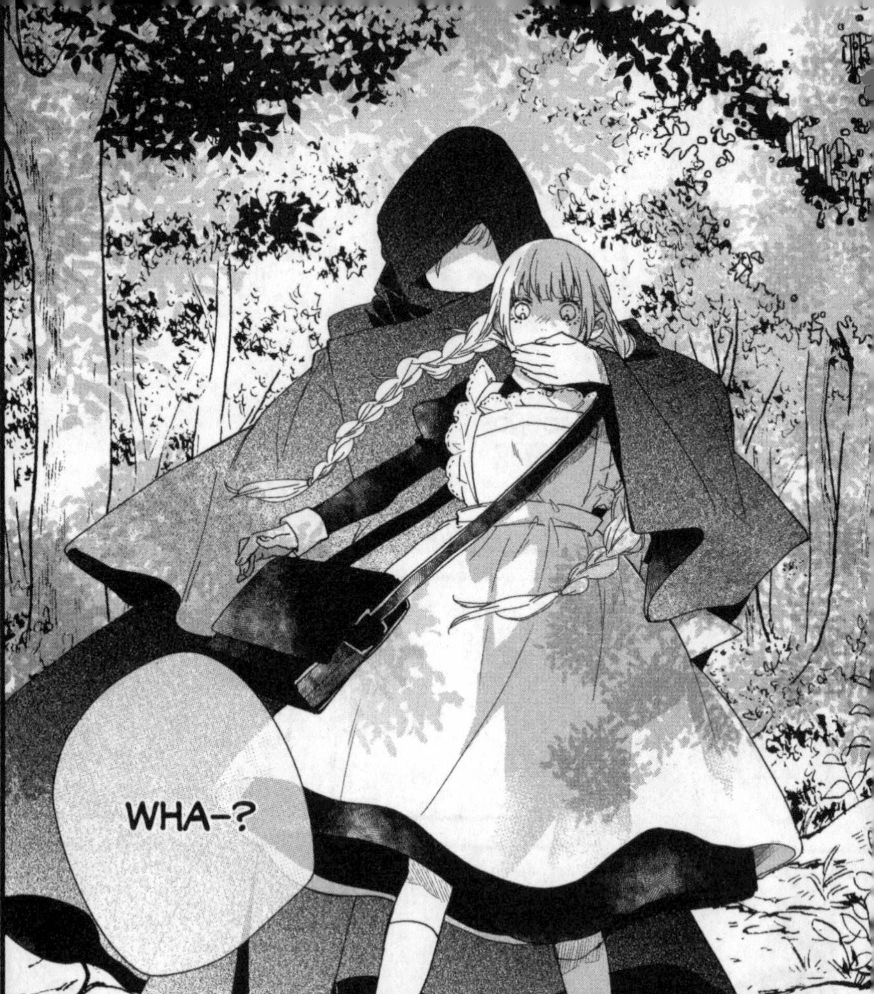
WHA-?

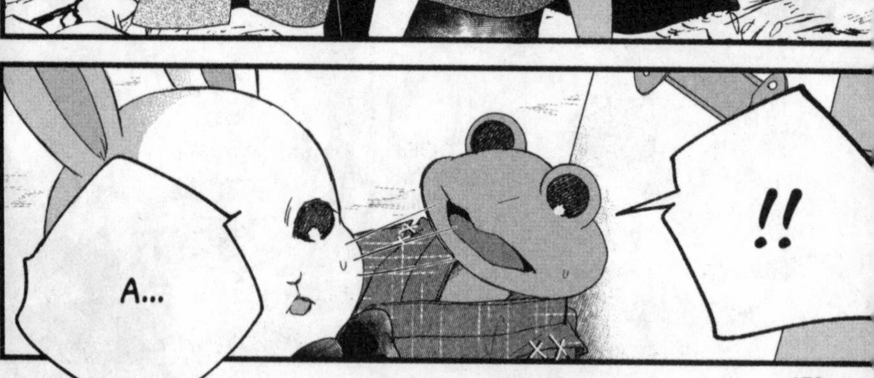
!!
A...

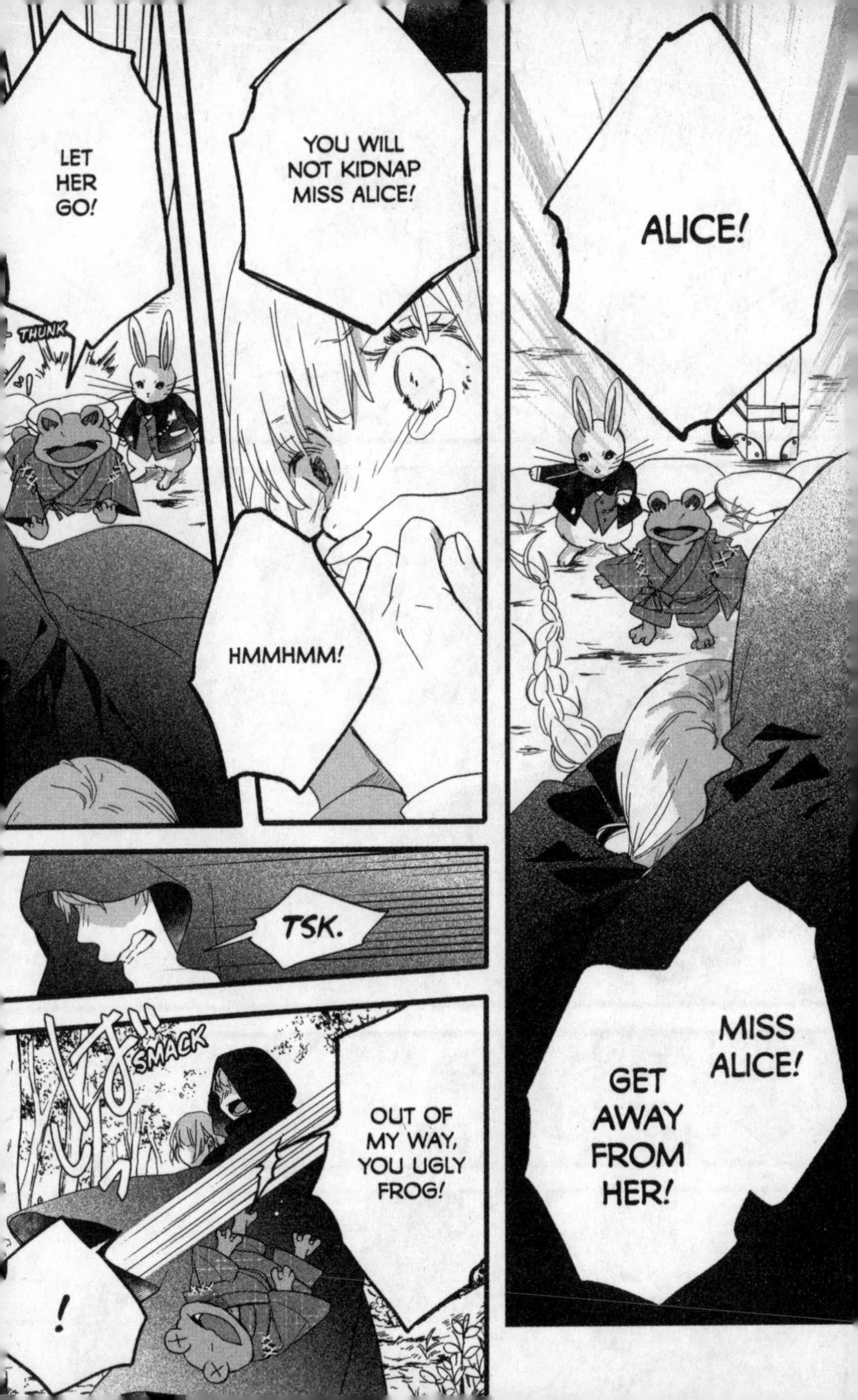
ALICE!
MISS ALICE!
GET AWAY FROM HER!
YOU WILL NOT KIDNAP MISS ALICE!
HMMHMM!
LET HER GO!
THUNK
TSK.
SMACK
OUT OF MY WAY, YOU UGLY FROG!
!

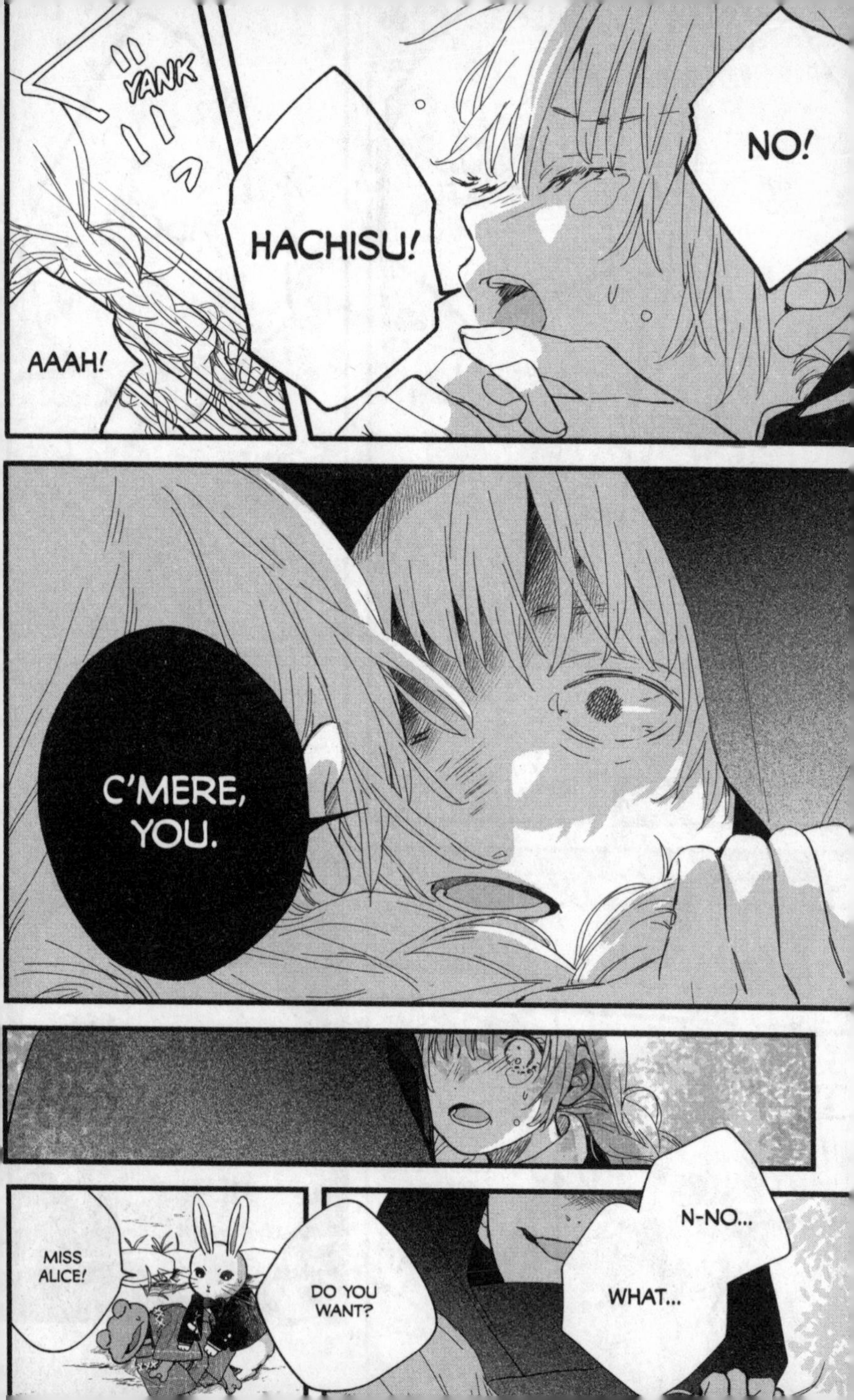
NO!
HACHISU!
YANK
AAAH!
C'MERE, YOU.
N-NO...
WHAT...
DO YOU WANT?
MISS ALICE!

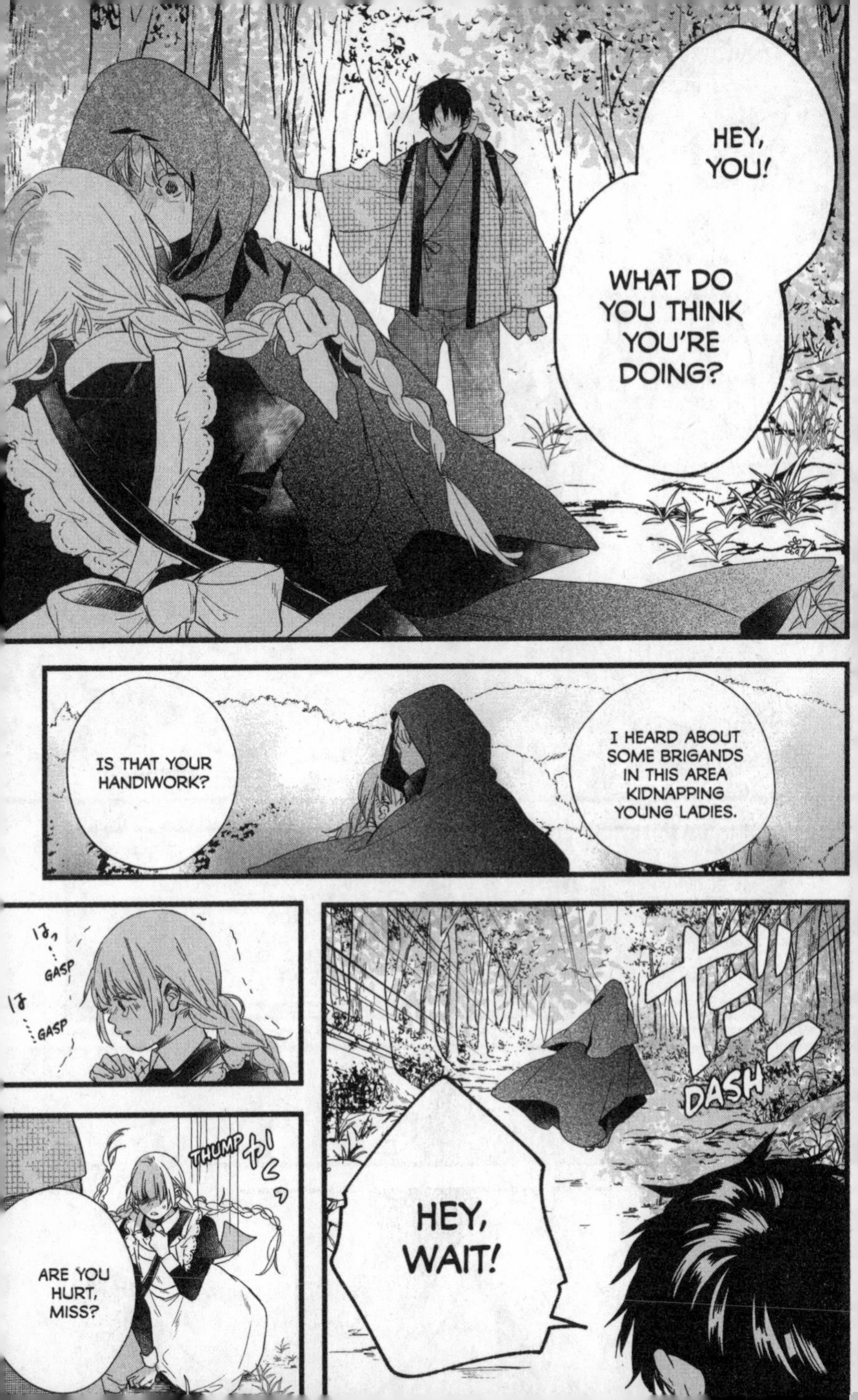
HEY, YOU!
WHAT DO YOU THINK YOU'RE DOING?
I HEARD ABOUT SOME BRIGANDS IN THIS AREA KIDNAPPING YOUNG LADIES.
IS THAT YOUR HANDIWORK?
ダッ
DASH
HEY, WAIT!
はっ
GASP
は
GASP
かくっ
THUMP
ARE YOU HURT, MISS?

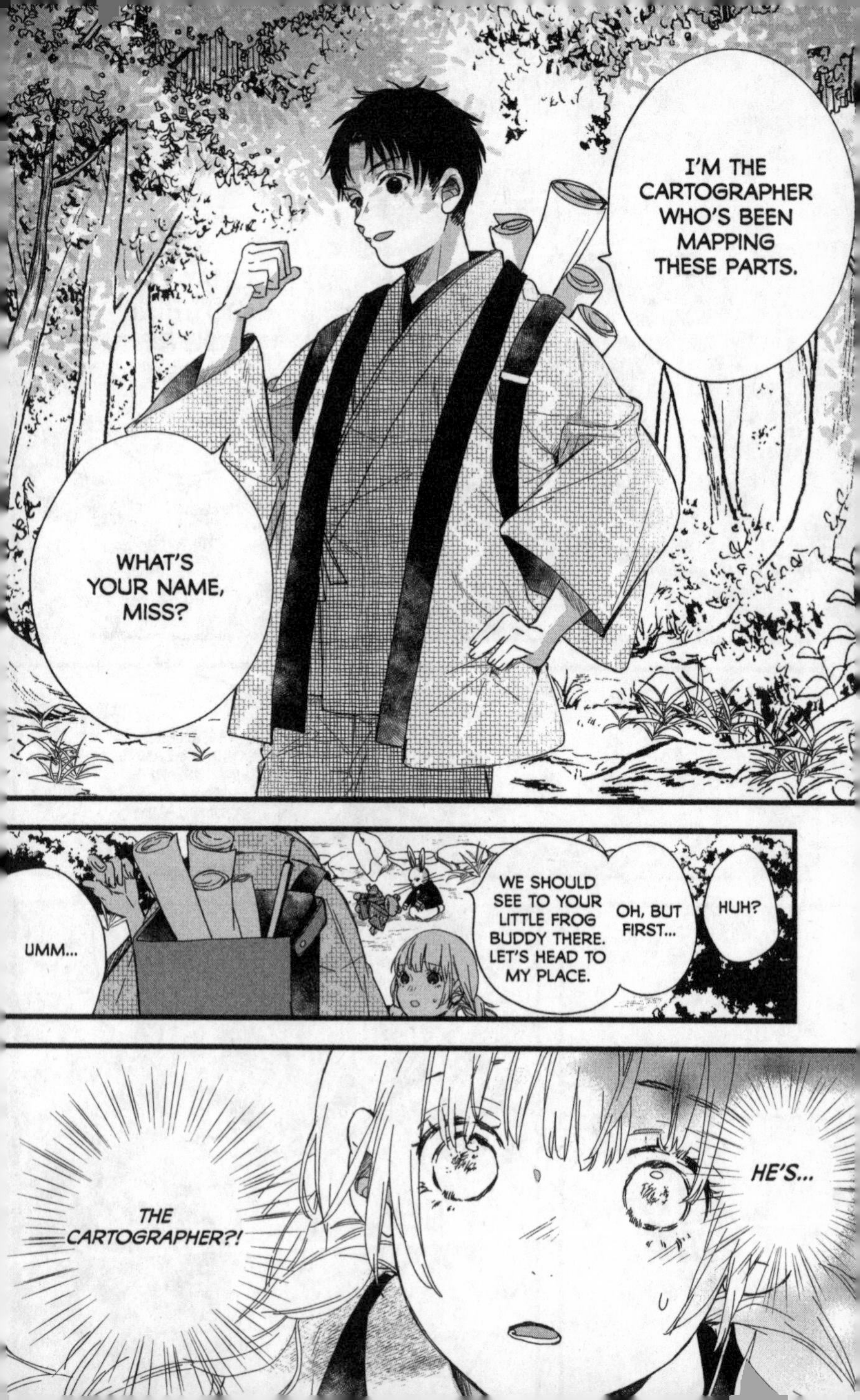
I'M THE CARTOGRAPHER WHO'S BEEN MAPPING THESE PARTS.
WHAT'S YOUR NAME, MISS?
HUH?
OH, BUT FIRST...
WE SHOULD SEE TO YOUR LITTLE FROG BUDDY THERE. LET'S HEAD TO MY PLACE.
UMM...
HE'S...
THE CARTOGRAPHER?!

Special thanks!

BIBI & MIYU, VOLUME 1

Hirara Natsume & Olivia Vieweg

Art by **Hirara Natsume**
Written by **Olivia Vieweg**

1

FANTASY

When a new student from Japan shows up at Bibi Blocksberg's school, she fits in immediately. But Bibi's suspicious; she knows Miyu's hiding something, and she's determined to find out what! Bibi's journey takes her all the way to Japan, and while learning about all the new rules and magic in this foreign land, she realizes that maybe she and Miyu can be friends after all!

THE FOX & LITTLE TANUKI, VOLUME 1

Mi Tagawa

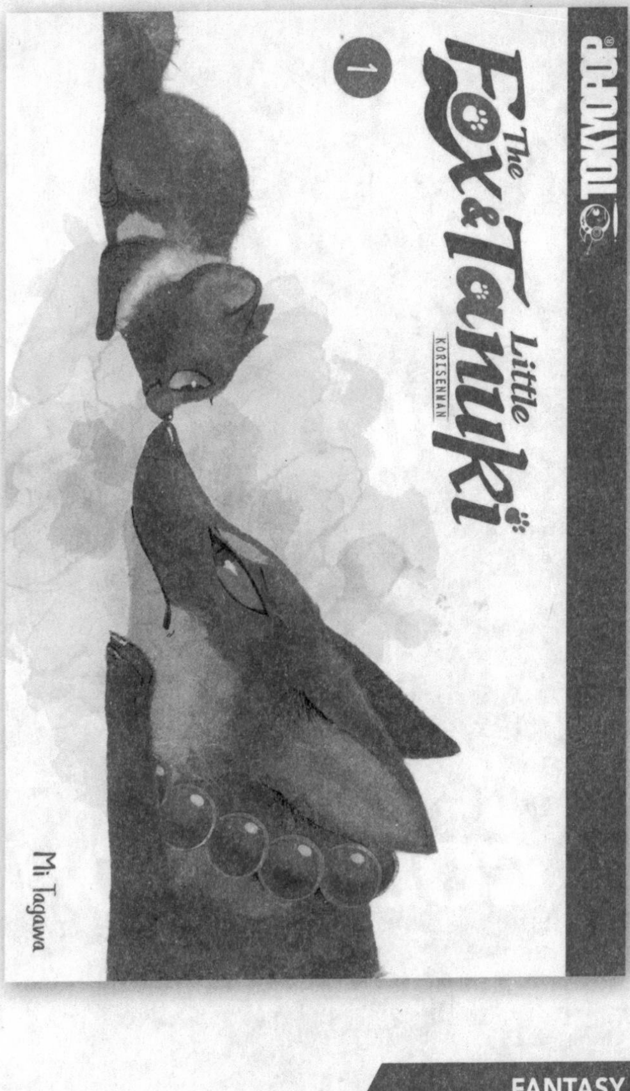
TOKYOPOP
The Fox & Little Tanuki
KORISENMAN
1
Mi Tagawa

FANTASY

It is said that there are some special animals occasionally born with great powers. Senzou the black fox is one of those... but instead of using his powers for good, he abused his strength until the Sun Goddess imprisoned him for his bad behavior. Three hundred years later, he's finally been released, but only on one condition — he can't have any of his abilities back until he successfully helps a tanuki cub named Manpachi become an assistant to the gods. Unfortunately for Senzou, there's no cheating when it comes to completing his task! The magic beads around his neck make sure he can't wander too far from his charge or ignore his duties, and so... Senzou the once-great Fox Spirit must figure out how to be an actually-great babysitter to an innocent little tanuki or risk being stuck without his powers forever!

TOKYOPOP

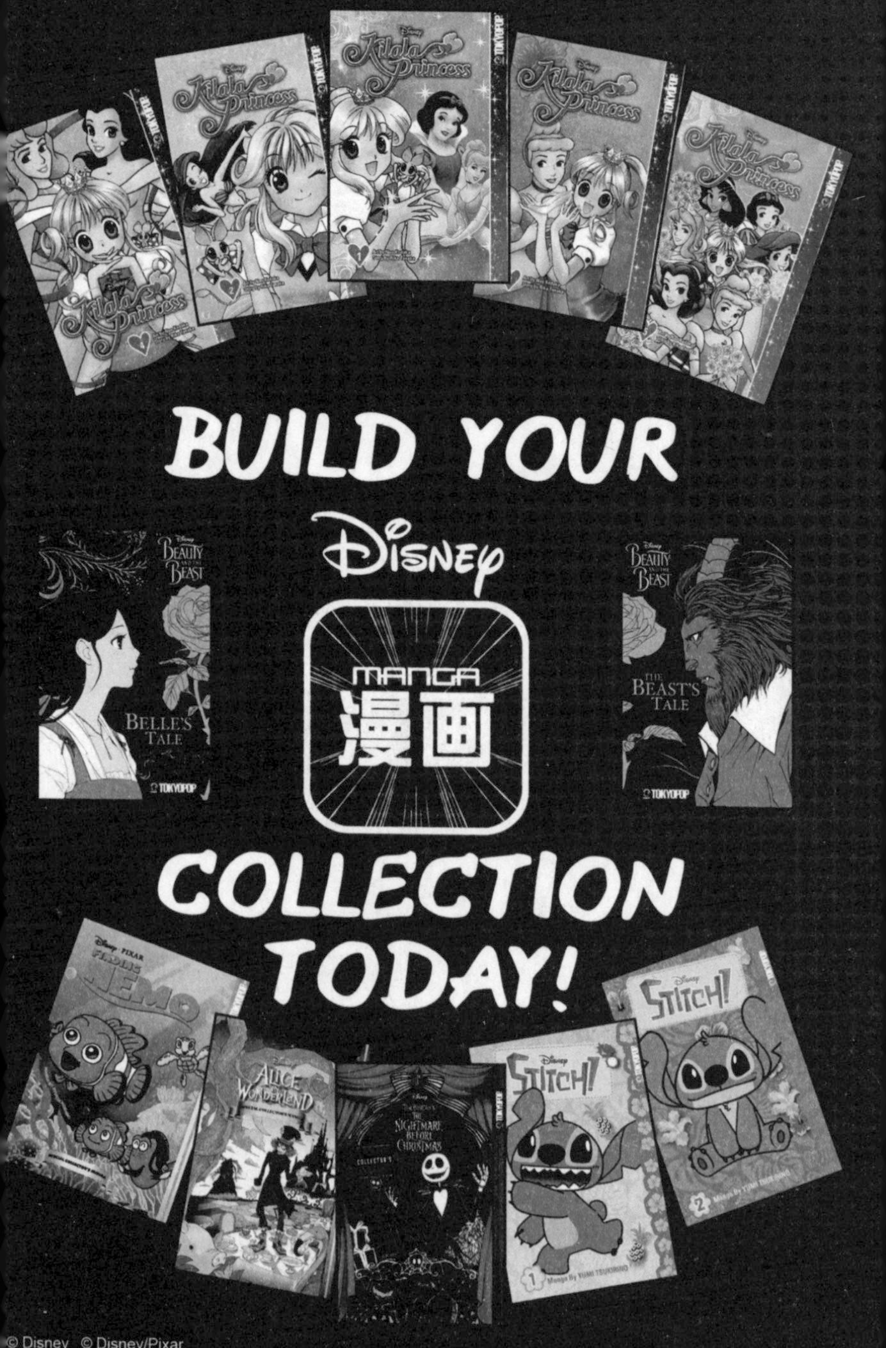
BUILD YOUR
DISNEY
MANGA
漫画
COLLECTION
TODAY!

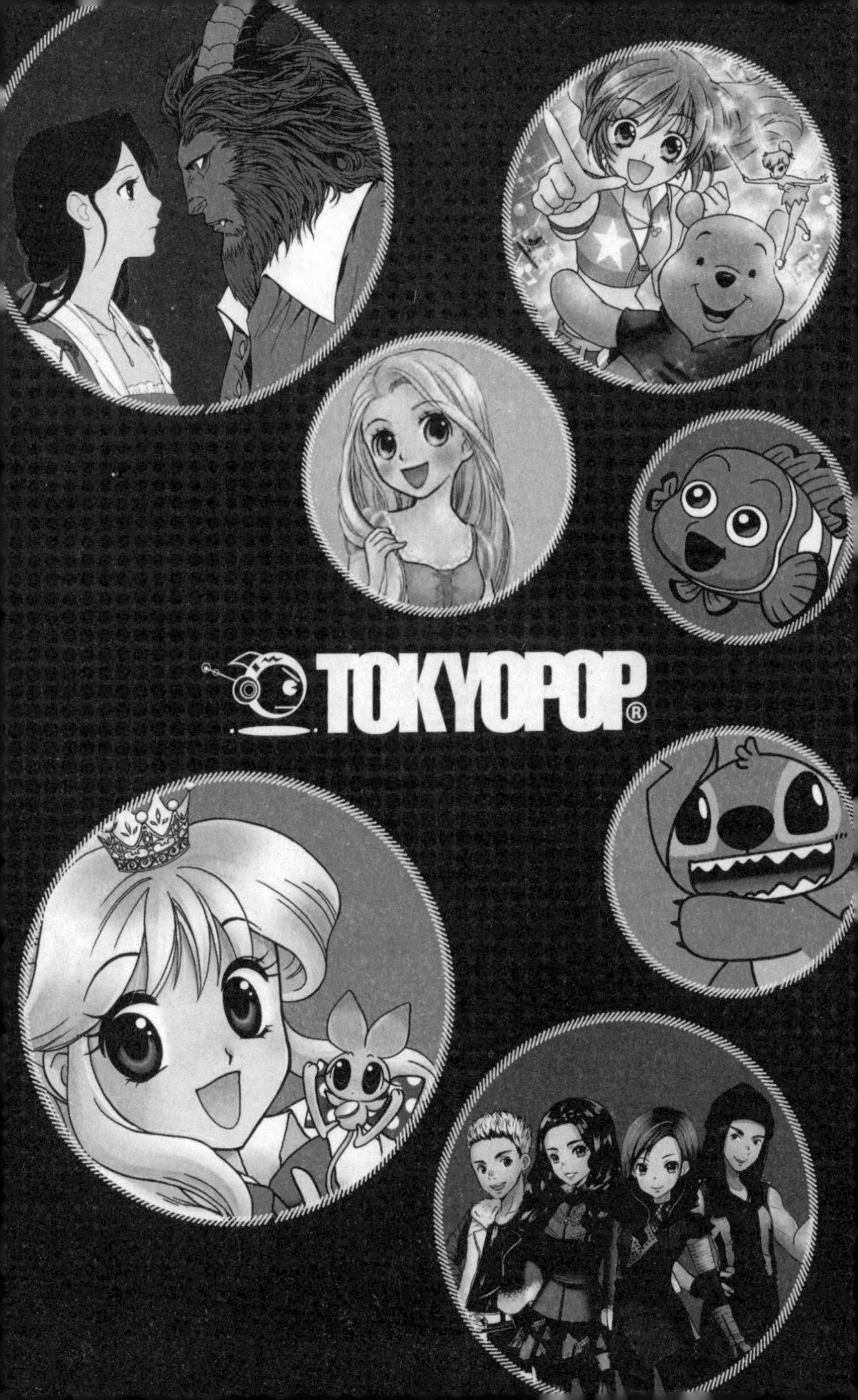
TOKYOPOP®

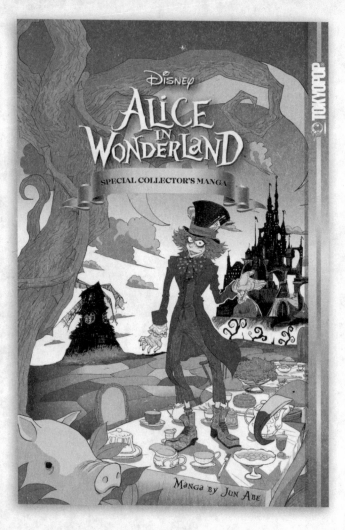

DISNEY MANGA: ALICE IN WONDERLAND

Jun Abe

DISNEY
ALICE IN WONDERLAND
SPECIAL COLLECTOR'S MANGA
TOKYOPOP
MANGA BY JUN ABE

DISNEY MANGA

Alice Kingsleigh was a young girl when she visited the magical world of Underland for the first time. Now a teenager, she spots a white rabbit at a garden party and tumbles down a hole after him where she is reunited with her old friends. Alice soon learns it is her destiny to end the Red Queen's reign of terror.

This special hardcover edition of Disney Tim Burton's *Alice in Wonderland* is a retelling of the film in manga style! Hardcover collectible with exclusive bonus features and illustrations from renowned artist Jun Abe.

TOKYOPOP

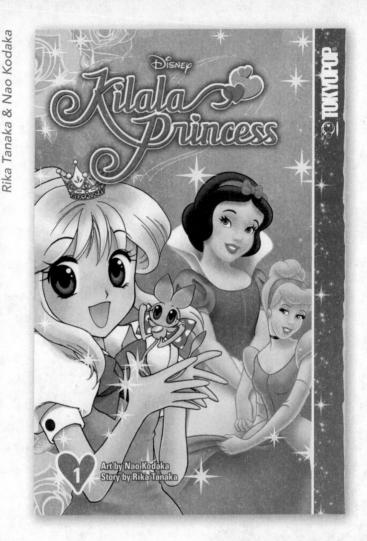

DISNEY MANGA: KILALA PRINCESS, VOLUME 1

Rika Tanaka & Nao Kodaka

DISNEY MANGA

When Kilala awakens a sleeping prince name Rei, she magically gains the power of the princesses! So when her friend Erica is kidnapped, Kilala decides she and Rei must set off on a quest to rescue her! Filled with the most popular Disney princesses Ariel, Cinderella, Jasmine, Snow White, Belle, Disney's *Kilala Princess* combines the magic of Disney with the fantasy of shoujo manga!

♀LOVE-x-LOVE♂

LOVE x LOVE

TOKYOPOP believes all types of romances deserve to be celebrated. *LOVE x LOVE* was born from that idea and our commitment to representing a variety of stories and voices as diverse as our fans.

TOKYOPOP

ALICE IN BISHOUNEN-LAND, VOLUME 1

Yushi Kawata & Yukito

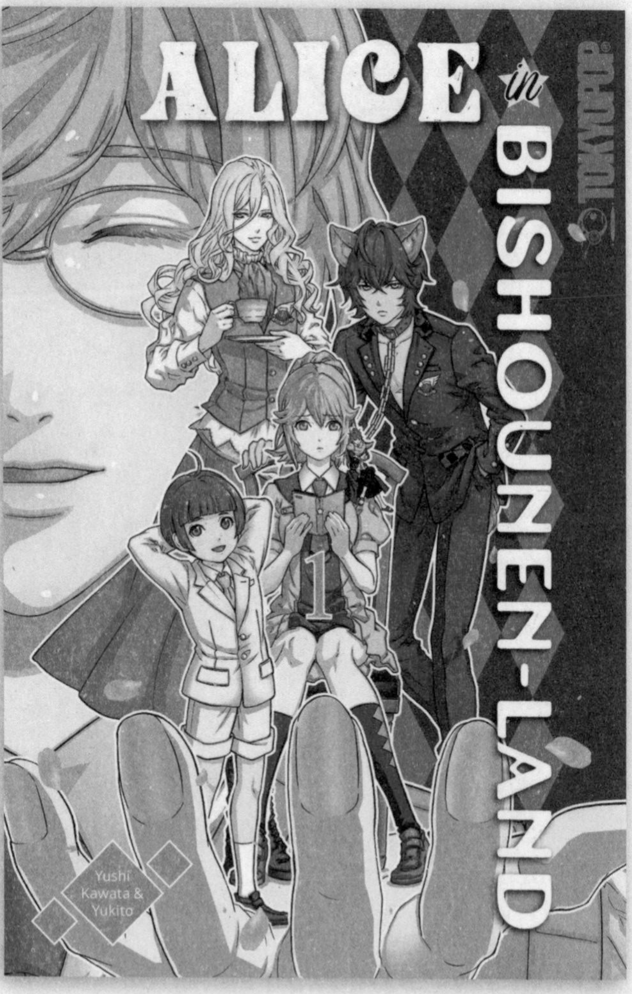

ALICE in BISHOUNEN-LAND
TOKYOPOP
1
Yushi Kawata & Yukito

COMEDY

Alice Kagami is an ordinary high school girl who doesn't really get her friend Tamami's obsession with idol games. There's more to life than handsome digital boys, dating sims, and mini-games, right? But then, Tamami is "chosen" as one of the top idol fangirls in the country and gets drawn into the game — and hapless Alice gets pulled in too! Between dealing with the mismatched members of her idol group to intense pressure to spend real money on gachas, how is a total idol game newbie supposed to take them to the top?

TOKYOPOP

SPRINGTIME BY THE WINDOW, VOLUME 1

Suzuyuki

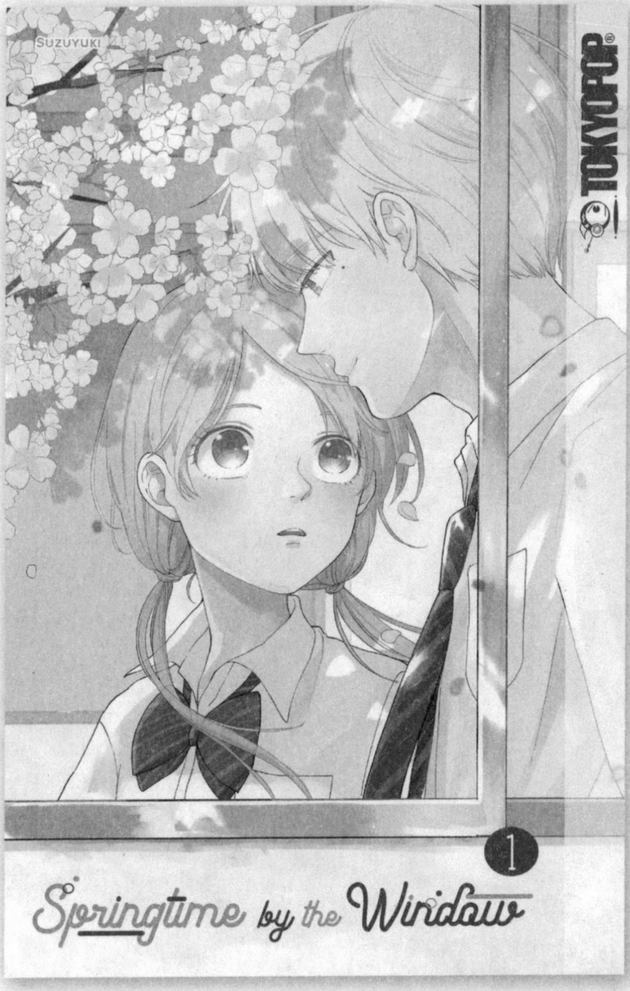

SUZUYUKI
TOKYOPOP
1
Springtime by the Window

LOVE-x-LOVE

Cool and collected second-year Yamada is in love with his childhood friend, Seno. His classmates Akama and Toda are also starting to think about romance, though neither of them realizes yet that they might actually feel the same way about each other...High school love in the spring of adolescence blooms with earnest, messy emotions.

TOKYOPOP

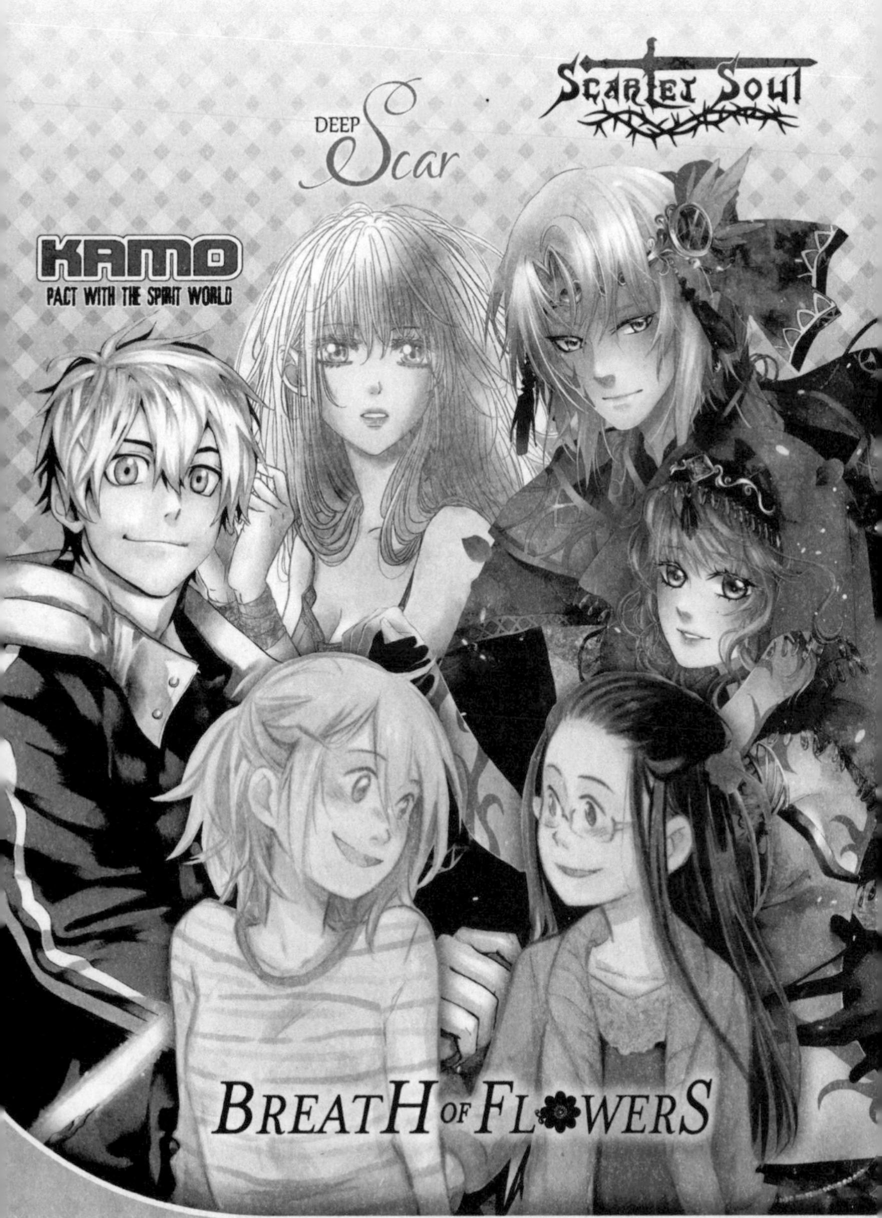
Scarlet Soul
DEEP Scar
KAMO
PACT WITH THE SPIRIT WORLD
BREATH OF FLOWERS

INTERNATIONAL WOMEN of MANGA

GOLDFISCH, VOLUME 1

Nana Yaa

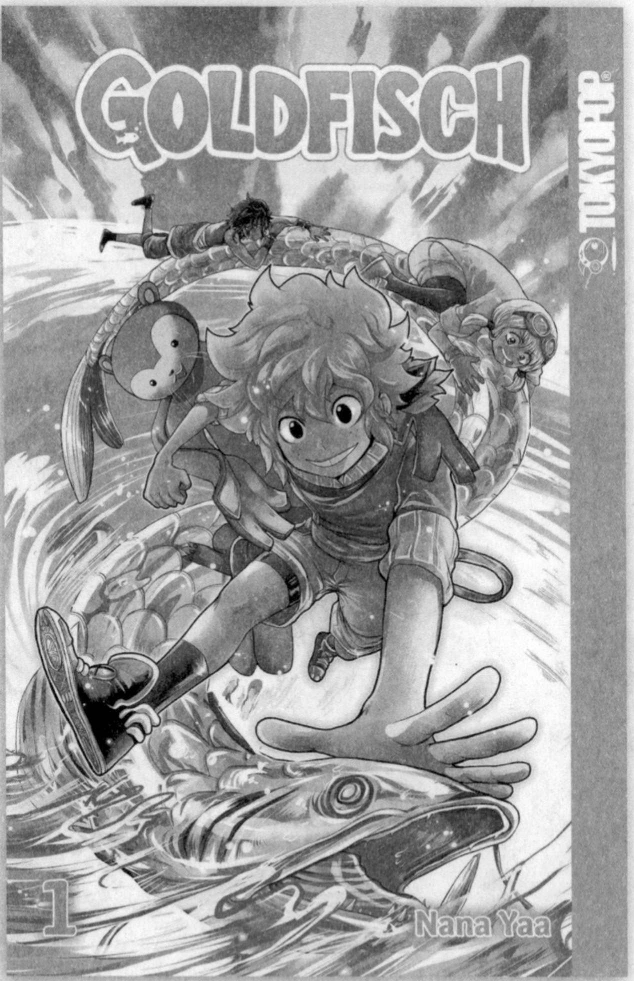
GOLDFISCH
TOKYOPOP
1
Nana Yaa

INTERNATIONAL
WOMEN of MANGA

Say hi to Morrey Gibbs! A fisher-boy in a flooded world overrun with dangerous mutated animals known as "anomals," he's got his own problems to worry about. Namely, how everything he touches turns to gold! Sure it sounds great, but gold underpants aren't exactly stylish — or comfortable! Together with his otter buddy and new inventor friend Shelly, Morrey's on a quest to rid himself of his blessing-turned-curse and undo the tragedy it caused. That is of course, if they can dodge the treasure-hungry bounty hunters...

TOKYOPOP